FURNITURE
Made In America
1875 ~ 1905

by Eileen and Richard Dubrow

77 Lower Valley Road, Atglen, PA 19310

Published by Schiffer Publishing, Ltd.
77 Lower Valley Road
Atglen, PA 19310
Please write for a free catalog.
This book may be purchased from the publisher.
Please include $2.95 postage.
Try your bookstore first.

We are interested in hearing from authors
with book ideas on related subjects.

Newly Revised.
Copyright © 1994 by Eileen and Richard Dubrow
Library of Congress Catalog Number: 82-50617

Printed in the United States of America.
ISBN: 0-88740-695-5

Dedication

Because he always asks, "Who made it?", "When?", "How was it made?", and because he made us aware of machinery, we gratefully dedicate this book to Grant Oakes.

The effect of machinery inventions was not so much the displacement of workers, but the lowering of the price of goods. For example, a 10 cent cigar could be had for 5 cents, a 50 cent telegram for 25 cents, and the homes of laboring men could be finished in a style and comfort for which their grandfathers could only long.

The examples in this book enable the reader to identify the makers of some of the machine-made furniture produced in America between 1875 and 1905. All of the illustrations are taken from the manufacturers' original catalogs, advertisments, or handbills. A list of the dated catalogs, and magazines from which the examples were taken is at the back of the book.

Introduction

Four generations have now lived with and taken for granted the furniture made between 1875 and 1905. While the furniture is still a few years short of being classified as "antique," it is being recognized by furniture historians because it reflects the improved mechanical technology of the times in which it was made; a technology that enabled a workman and his family to purchase furniture for their home that up to then they could only dream about.

Even before this furniture is 100 years old, reproductions are being made and sold to a receptive public. We must, therefore, attempt to identify the original manufacturers, the new forms and the design sources. As further identification is completed, this furniture will take its rightful place as part of the culture in which it was made and used.

During the 19th century, America emerged as a world power. Our ever-expanding economy caused business to change its form. The single entrepreneur had to join with others to form more efficient, consolidated businesses and even corporations. A strata of middle management people were needed between workmen and owners. This middle management formed the basis for a growing middle class who wanted all of the trappings that only the upper class formerly could afford. Improved machinery and mass production lowered the price of the items they wanted to a level they could afford.

These larger businesses developed away from home, in plants and factories where workers could convene. Increased production created a need for a larger commercial territories in which to market the goods, and improved transportation allowed the goods to be moved to these markets. The commercial office gave the furniture industry an opportunity to produce specialized forms for these more efficient work spaces. Roll top desks, revolving bookcases, filing shelves and cabinets were created. Folding beds, chairs and dressing cases made even the small home able to accommodate larger numbers of people.

This book shows the furniture that was sold in the local stores all across the country and circulated nationally by mail-order catalogues and handbills. Merchandising was becoming a refined science. Drummers (traveling salesmen) and catalogues took the new styles of merchandise to every state. A drummer often represented more than one manufacturer and many firms had branch offices in various cities. Large showy warerooms, and popular magazines kept the public aware of the new styles. Trade magazines kept the manufacturer aware of his competitors and of the new machinery being patented. Trade associations kept the factory owners aware of national legislation, tariffs and union growth.

Competition between manufacturers was keen. Trade magazines revealed and encouraged the exchange of ideas. Successes and new ideas were quickly publicized, and thereby encouraged modification and copying—in fact patent infringments were common.

Note: The first 100 years of American patents were completed on April 10, 1890. On that date patent #425,395 was issued. In the first 50 years only 12,421 patents were issued.

While new power machines were constantly being invented, foot power was in use until the 20th century. Magazines "for the trade" as late as the 1890's carry advertisements for foot powered machines.

The smaller cabinet shop or one not close to a power source had to use foot power. New large furniture centers did spring up in New England and the mid-west,[1] and towns grew up around these factories.[2] As these factories expanded and the industry grew, workers did not earn more. Rather, the price of the goods came down to a more affordable level and the "American Standard" of living rose quickly. This rise was the enviable "American Way" so sought after by people all over the world.

To further put this furniture in an affordable price range, it often could be purchased finished or unfinished, assembled or unassembled and with or without hardware. As the standards of living rose and the work day even decreased to 10 or 9 hours, leisure became an increasingly important part of life. More furniture was made that was upholstered, rocked or reclined. Relaxing at home became permissible.

It should be borne in mind that supportive industries grew up around the furniture industry. There were companies that made only wood ornaments to decorate chests and sideboards, hardware companies that supplied the trade, and veneer and inlay companies. Therefore, identification of furniture of this period cannot be made based on these details. In this book we have shown only those pieces of furniture that are labeled or in a manufacturer's catalogue. This book is intended as a guide through the maze of 1875—1905 furniture, and as a partial answer to the ongoing question, "Who made this piece?" We extend an invitation to readers to continue to expand our knowledge of this furniture.

Eileen and Richard Dubrow

---

[1] In Grand Rapids the first furniture factory was built by Robert Hilson and Sylvester Granger in 1836. Mr. Hilson also opened the first chair factory in 1837. By 1890 there were 38 factories in Grand Rapids because they had an unlimited supply of hard woods and the Grand Rapids and Indiana R.R. extended the entire length of the state through the hardwood territory.

[2] In 1850 the population of Grand Rapids was 3000 people; in 1870 — 16,000; in 1880, — 32,000; in 1884, — 42,000.

Table of Contents

FROM THE "SCIENTIFIC AMERICAN." ARTICLE UNDER AMERICAN INDUSTRIES NO. 57. THE MANUFACTURE OF PARLOR FURNITURE.

LOG BAND SAW

BAND SAWS

SCROLL SAW

FRIEZER OR CARVING MACHINE

TURNING

VARIETY MOLDER

PLANING MACHINE

BORING MACHINE

JOINTER

SAND PAPERING MACHINE

CARVING

UPHOLSTERING AND FINISHING

FACTORY OF M. & H. SCHRENKEISEN, NEW YORK CITY.

E. M. Tibbett's Illustrated Catalog of   & H. Schrenkeisen, New York City.
Parlour Furniture Manufactured by M.   March, 1885, page 3.

Machinery

The improvement of power sources in the nineteenth century enabled furniture-making tools to be driven easier, harder, and faster. Therefore, the tool designers and inventers could expect more from new machines. New designs and patents exploded in numbers, and the manufacture of finished products was faster and less expensive than at any time previously.

The aim of the nineteenth century furniture working machinery was not automation but output. Specialized machinery replaced specific hand processes. For the average cabinet maker the cost of the necessary power plant may have ruled out the installation of power machinery. Human powered machinery was the only option for shops without steam or water power. As late as 1870 an important proportion of America's furniture output was manufactured in relatively small shops without the aid of steam power. Machines were used, but people powered lathes, mortising and boring machines.

Saws have been discovered in Germany and Denmark that belong to the Bronze Age. The metal of which they are composed was cast into a thin shaft and serrated by breaking the edge.

Saws made of obsidian (a kind of glass produced by volcanoes) were used during the Stone Age in Mexico, and saws and knives of the same material have been found in alluvial deposits in New Jersey.

The early inhabitants of Europe are credited with having saws made of flint, and natives of the West Indies had saws of notched shells.

It is from such crude and inefficient implements as these that the modern saw developed.

According to "Knights" *"American Mechanical Dictionary"* the circular saw is well described in Miller's English patent #

1152 granted in 1777.[3] Power saws (especially band saws) were introduced quite slowly in the furniture industry. This was because the wide commercial use of the band saw required high grade steel to prevent the blade from snapping and a heavy iron frame to prevent vibration. Circular and band saws presupposed a steam or water source strong enough to drive them at optimum speeds. The circular saw was used widely by the 1840's and 50's, but was subject to strain and metal fatigue until the Bessemer steel process was discovered by William Kelly in 1851. The band saw was shown as a novelty in England in 1855 and by 1865 was widely used in America.

The lathe can be considered the parent of most machine tools. The lathe machined round parts. Leonardo da Vinci's records show a lathe with a pole drive apparently in use in the 1500's. John Wilkinson improved the lathe for boring purposes in 1776. In 1794, Henry Mandslay developed the first all metal lathe. Mandslay adapted a lead screw to his lathe in 1810 making possible the construction of lathes, planers, and milling machines. A milling machine produces plane or curved surfaces rather than holes.

After the lathe there was need for flat surfaces of greater accuracy than those produced by hand filing and this resulted in the development of planing machines. By 1830 these tools were well established. The mortising machine was developed in 1830.

The Jordan machine for carving was invented in England in 1847. It copied a form by means of a tracer and revolving cutters. With this machine the table moved rather than the cutters, and the pieces

[3] *Evolution of the saw,* **Rockford Furniture Journal,** February 15, 1889.

required hand finishing. American carving machines used templates, cut in the form of the design to be created. The work table moved but only vertically, to bring the work in contact with the cutter. With his hands, the workman moved the wood with the template on top of it, so that the cutter cut along the edges of the template.

All these machines lead to greatly increased production of furniture at lower prices, and enabled designs to be copied so that more ornate designs could be afforded in the average home. In its largest terms, this revolution meant releasing the production and transportation of goods from the limitations of human hands and strength. Production could be expanded indefinitely by the substitution of mechanical fingers and mechanical power. For the first time in the history of the human race the possibility of an abundant production loomed on the horizon of people capable of developing the goals set by the potentials of technology.

The Furniture Worker, May 25, 1887, page 21.

The Furniture Worker, May 25, 1887, page 20.

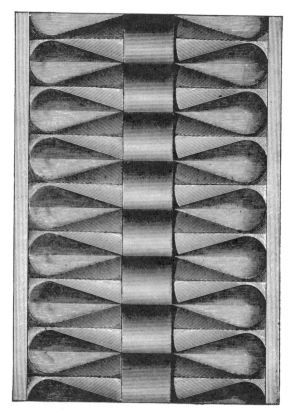

We guarantee this Carver to cut 25 per cent. more than any other Carver mad
for the same number of spindles.

The King Four-Spindle Carving Machine will carve four pieces one and one-half feet wide, five feet long; is simple and durable and perfect in operation.

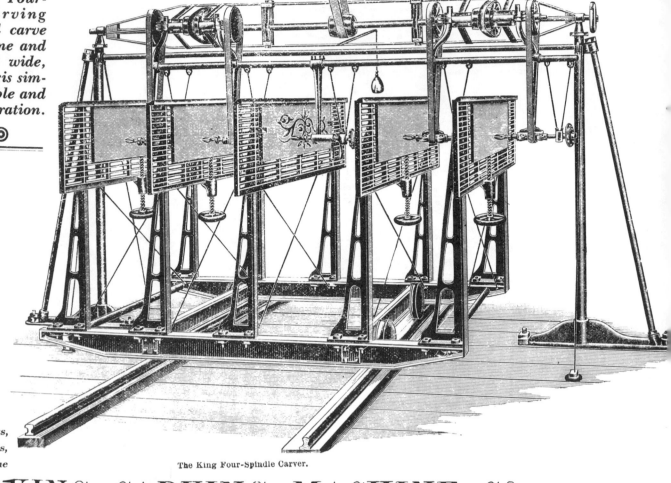

The King Four-Spindle Carver.

or Further Particulars, Price and Terms, Address the

KING CARVING MACHINE CO.,

57 South Front St.,
GRAND RAPIDS, MICH.

Michigan Artisan, February, 1891, page 41.

For the year ending June 1, 1860, the total value of machine and hand manufacture was placed at $1,900,000. This was twice the output of 1850 and four times the total national wealth of 1787. By 1860 America ceased to be a mere raw material country for the manufacturing nations of the old world. Though we were in the midst of what was termed an "Industrial Revolution", the transition from hand to machine work was a slow complex transition and human powered machinery was used all through the nineteenth century.

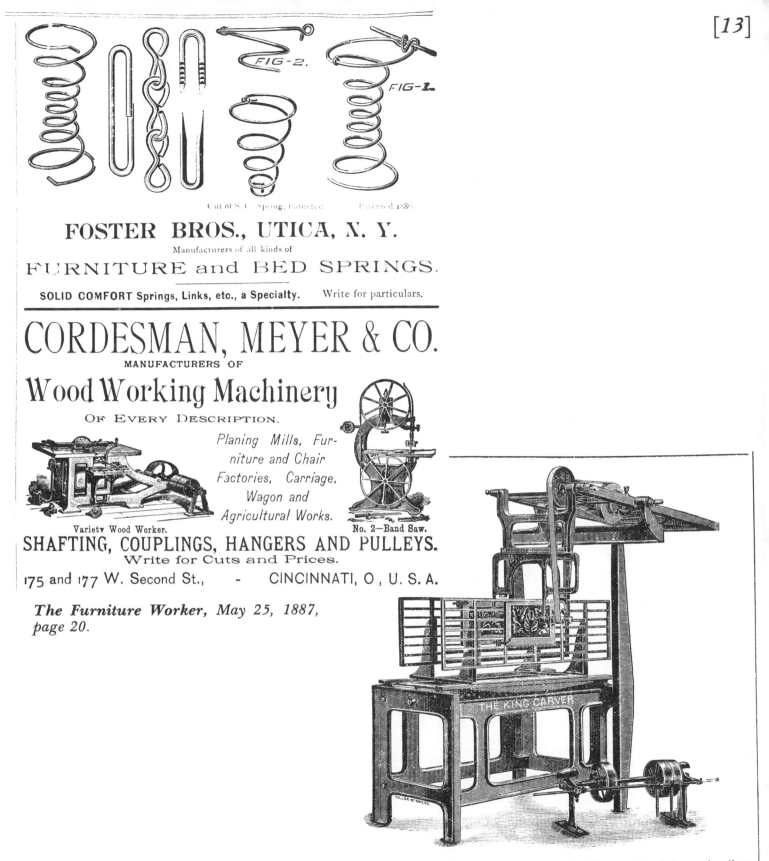

Cut of S. C. Spring, Patented   Patented 1886

FOSTER BROS., UTICA, N. Y.

Manufacturers of all kinds of

FURNITURE and BED SPRINGS.

SOLID COMFORT Springs, Links, etc., **a Specialty.**   Write for particulars.

CORDESMAN, MEYER & CO.

MANUFACTURERS OF

Wood Working Machinery

OF EVERY DESCRIPTION.

Planing Mills, Furniture and Chair Factories, Carriage, Wagon and Agricultural Works.

Variety Wood Worker.   **No. 2—Band Saw.**

SHAFTING, COUPLINGS, HANGERS AND PULLEYS.

Write for Cuts and Prices.

175 and 177 W. Second St.,   -   CINCINNATI, O, U. S. A.

The Furniture Worker, May 25, 1887, page 20.

Michigan Artisan, April, 1890, page 55.

This machine is all iron and self-contained. The counter balance is all on the over-hanging frame and the frame that holds the cutter and follower are free of any weights, thus allowing quick and easy action in every direction.

The sliding frames that hold the stock and pattern are iron and cannot warp out of line (wood frames will). Stock five feet long and fourteen inches wide can be cut without swinging the cutter out of natural position.

Beware of infringements, as a similar machine is offered, and we shall protect our rights.

KING CARVING MACHINE CO.

57 South Front St., Grand Rapids, Mich,

PENNINGTON MACHINE WORKS

Manufacturers of 300 Varieties of Fine Patent

Wood=Cutting Machines.

THE ONLY CONCERN IN THE UNITED STATES USING CUT GEARING ON ALL MACHINES.

FT. WAYNE, IND.

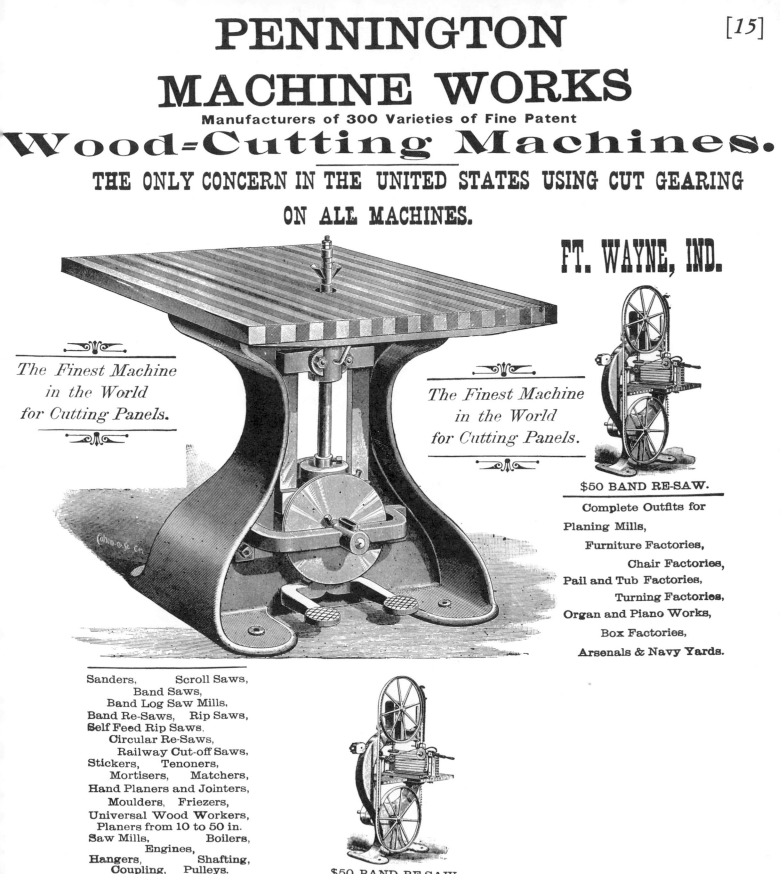

*The Finest Machine
in the World
for Cutting Panels.*

*The Finest Machine
in the World
for Cutting Panels.*

$50 BAND RE-SAW.

Complete Outfits for

Planing Mills,

Furniture Factories,

Chair Factories,

Pail and Tub Factories,

Turning Factories,

Organ and Piano Works,

Box Factories,

Arsenals & Navy Yards.

Sanders,   Scroll Saws,
Band Saws,
Band Log Saw Mills,
Band Re-Saws,   Rip Saws,
Self Feed Rip Saws,
Circular Re-Saws,
Railway Cut-off Saws,
Stickers,   Tenoners,
Mortisers,   Matchers,
Hand Planers and Jointers,
Moulders,   Friezers,
Universal Wood Workers,
Planers from 10 to 50 in.
Saw Mills,   Boilers,
Engines,
Hangers,   Shafting,
Coupling,   Pulleys.

$50 BAND RE-SAW.

*The Furniture Worker, September 25,
1887, page 37.*

JOHN A. WHITE,

CONCORD, N. H.

MANUFACTURER OF

WOOD-WORKING MACHINERY.

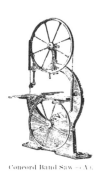

Post Band Saw and Re-Saw. Concord Band Saw—(A). Concord Band Saw—(B).

Tenoning Machine.

Paneling Machine.

3, 4 and 5 inch 4-side Moulder.

12 and 15 inch Buzz Planer.

20, 24 and 27 inch Concord Planer.

Medium Mortiser—(No.

20-inch Buzz Planer.

Gordon Planer, 16 and 24 inch. Patented.

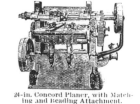

24-in. Concord Planer, with Matching and Beading Attachment.

Gordon Single Saw Bench.

Concord Double Saw Bench.

Planers, Band Saws, Saw Benches, Swing Saws, Band Saw Re-saws, Tenoning Machines, Mortising Machines, Paneling Machines, Moulding Machines, Buzz Planers.

IT LEADS THE WORLD!

The great contest between Sand Papering Machines, at the Robert Mitchell Furniture Company's factory, at Cincinnati, ended in a complete victory for the Egan Company. The contest assumed very large proportions, and was awaited as a standard test by many manufacturers. Both machines were 30-inch Double Drum Sand Papering Machines, and both were handled by experts. The Berlin Company had four experts, and exhausted all that science and energy could do to make their machine a success. The Egan Company, of Cincinnati, may well feel proud of the distinction they have gained, and the great progress they have made in building Improved Wood-Working Machinery, especially Sand Papering Machines.

—CABINET MAKER.

DOUBLE DRUM SAND-PAPERING MACHINE.
We make four sizes of this machine, 24, 30, 36 & 40 in.

DOUBLE CUT-OFF SAW.

MORE OF THE SAME KIND.
Sand Papering Machine received. We do more work with a *small boy* on your machine than we could with a first-class hand on the "Boss."
KNOXVILLE FURNITURE CO
Knoxville, Tenn.   A. J. Price, Supt.

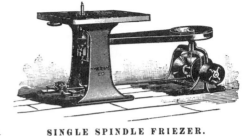

SINGLE SPINDLE FRIEZER.

A RIVAL MACHINE IDLE.
The 24-inch Sander you sent us proves a very valuable machine for clock case work, and is used almost constantly, while *a rival machine by its side stands idle.*
Yours respectfully,
[Signed]   SETH THOMAS CLOCK CO.
Thomaston, Conn.   A. Thomas, Prest.

No. 4½ BAND SCROLL AND RE-SAW.
Adjusted for Re-Sawing.

FAR AHEAD OF THE BOSS.
The 30-inch Double Drum Sand-Papering Machine is A No. 1, and no mistake. We have used the "Boss" Machine for several years, but your machine is far ahead of it in simplicity of construction and speed of doing its work. Yours truly,
[Signed]   FULLER & HUTSINPILLER CO.
Gallipolis, O.   W. G. Fuller, Sec'y and Treas.

WAVY MARKS AVOIDED.
We are well pleased with the Sander bought of you. The work is *done rapidly*, and the *wavy mark experienced with other machines avoided.*
Yours truly,
[Signed]   LOUISVILLE MFG. CO.
Louisville, Ky.   W. Bennett, Supt.

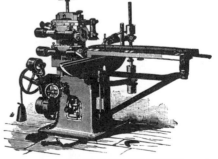

No. 2½ DOUBLE CYLINDER PLANER
Planes both sides, 26 in. wide and 6 in. thick.

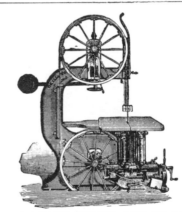

No. 4½ BAND SCROLL AND RE-SAW.
Adjusted for Scroll Sawing.

No. 1 TENONING MACHINE.
With or without Cut-off Attachment.

PERFECTION.
After giving your Double Drum Sander a thorough test, we feel that it is due you to give our opinion of it. Our dictionary don't contain a word that would express too highly the praise that your machine merits. We think *perfection* comes as nearly expressing it as any word we can think of.
Shelbyville, Ind.   CONREY, BIRELY & CO.

THE EGAN COMPANY,
—MANUFACTURERS OF—
IMPROVED WOOD-WORKING MACHINERY

THOS. P. EGAN, *Pres't.*
EDWIN RUTHVEN, *Sec'y.*
FREDERICK DANNER, *Supt.*

N. W. Cor. FRONT AND CENTRAL AVE., CINCINNATI, O., U. S. A.

The Furniture Worker, May 25, 1887, page 34.

The Robert Mitchell Furniture Co

Robert Mitchell Prest
Albert H Mitchell Treas
Richard H Mitchell Secy

Cincinnati Sept 20th 1886

The Egan Co
      Gentlemen?

          After a competitive trial between your Sandpaper Machine and that of the Berlin Excelsior machine where we used your 30" Double Drum machine and the Berlin 30" Drum Side by side we have decided to order your machine in preference to the Berlin machine because of its greater simplicity and consequent less liability to get out of order, its greater durability and for the fine quality of its work. Our tests shewing that your machine leaves less of its fibre or hair on the wood than the other machine We do not think the quality of the work done by your machine can be surpassed by any machine extant

          Very truly Yours
          The Robt Mitchell Furniture Co
          RW Mitchell Secy

The Furniture Worker, May 25, 1887, page 34.

The Egan Co. makers of machinery were located at 252 W. Front Street in Cincinnati, Ohio. In June of 1888, they brought suit against the J. A. Fay Co. for $20,000 in damages. They claimed a patent infringment by Fay on their shaping machine with patent friction reverse. J. A. Fay Co. was a leading wood working firm. **The Egan Co.** dovetailing machine cut any thinkness from $\frac{1}{4}$ to $1\frac{1}{2}$ inches and up to 13 inches in width. It dovetailed both the front and sides of a drawer at one time.

J.L. Perry and Co. of Berlin, Wisconsin were the manufacturers of the "Boss" wood polisher and sanding machine. In 1883 they came out with a new machine that combined a resurfacing planer and polisher in one machine. It was made in 24, 30 and 40 inch sizes.

Furniture, June, 1890, page 36.

Parlour and Library Furniture

FOREST·CITY·FURNITURE·COMPANY,

ROCKFORD
ILLINOIS

WHOLESALE
MANUFACTURERS
OF

CHAMBER
SUITS, ©

SIDE-
BOARDS

OFFICE
DESKS,

No. 461. Genuine Mahogany.   No. 463. Genuine Mahogany.   No. 460. Oak or Walnut.

BOOK CASES ∴ LIBRARY CASES ∴ LADIES' DESKS ∴ TABLE BEDS ∴ TABLE WASHSTANDS ∴ ETC

Furniture, June, 1890, page 3.

1890   **1890**

ILLUSTRATED CATALOGUE

OF

OTT LOUNGE COMPANY,

OTT & SCHOEN, PROPRIETORS.

MANUFACTURERS OF

SINGLE AND BED LOUNGES

AND

OTT'S PATENT SOFA BED,

Nos. 93, 95 and 97 Dayton Street,

CORNER WEED STREET,

TAKE CLYBOURN AVENUE CABLE.   CHICAGO, ILL.

MAX STERN & CO., PRINTERS, 84 & 86 FIFTH AVE., CHICAGO.

ILLUSTRATED CATALOGUE

ROCKFORD + UNION + FURNITURE + COMPANY,

LIBRARY CASES.
BOOKCASES.
SECRETARIES.
LADIES' CABINETS.
OFFICE DESKS.
CENTER TABLES.
EXTENSION TABLES.

THE ROCKFORD FURNITURE JOURNAL PRINT, ROCKFORD, ILL.

1890   WHOLESALE MANUFACTURERS.

ROCKFORD, ILLINOIS.

E. M. TEBBETT'S

ILLUSTRATED CATALOGUE

OF PARLOR FURNITURE

MANUFACTURED BY

M & H. SCHRENKEISEN

Nº 23 TO 29

Elizabeth Street,

NEW YORK.

COPYRIGHT, 1885, BY M. & H. SCHRENKEISEN.

The furniture catalogs display artwork and design concepts typical of their period and relevant to the furniture designs they display. Four examples are reproduced here.

⇛ ESTABLISHED 1866 ⇚

1884

COLIE & SON,

MANUFACTURERS OF

PARLOR FURNITURE

Patent Rocking Chairs, Center Tables,

LOUNGES, MATTRESSES, &c.

OFFICE AND WAREROOMS,	FACTORY,
112 to 122 Exchange Street,	284 to 290 Pearl Street,

BUFFALO, N. Y.

BAKER, JONES & CO., PRINTERS AND BINDERS, BUFFALO, N. Y.

No. 836. Tyler's Fancy Roll Curtain Library Desk. Walnut, Old Oak or Cherry.

Size, 24 inches wide, 36 inches long, 55½ inches high; Extension Writing Table; Zinc Bottoms; Elegantly Carved, and Finest Fancy Veneers; Covered with Billiard Cloth; also furnished in Ebony Finish at same price. Weight, 90 lbs. Price, F. O. B **$36 00**

No. 398. Tyler's Fancy Parlor Curtain Cabinet. Mahoganized Cherry, Walnut or Antique Oak.

Size, 35x22 inches. Elegantly Veneered and Carved; Bevel French Plate in Top 12 inches in diameter. Handsomest Cabinet in the market. Weight, 100 lbs. Price, F. O. B **$55 00**

No. 846. Tyler's Ladies' Desk. Walnut or Mahoganized Cherry.

Size, 24 inches wide and 36 inches long; Elegantly Carved; Very Handsome; Finest Fancy Veneers; Covered with Billiard Cloth; furnished in Ebony Finish at same price if desired. Weight, 90 lbs. Price, F. O. B **$25 00**

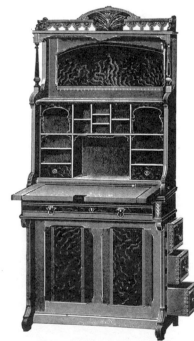

No. 395. Tyler's Parlor Cabinet Desk. Walnut, Antique Oak or Cherry Mahogany Finish.

Size, 30x18 inches. Writing Part Covered with Billiard Cloth; Portable. Price, F. O. B **$20 00**

No. 348. Tyler's Fancy Parlor Desk. Walnut, Antique Oak or Cherry.

Size, 34x23 inches. Sliding Table; Ornamental Shelf on Top; Billiard Cloth on Slide; Elegantly Veneered. Guaranteed to please any one. Weight, 100 lbs. Price, F. O. B **$30 00**

No. 396. Tyler's Parlor Cabinet Desk. Walnut, Antique Oak or Cherry Mahogany Finish.

Size, 30x18 inches. Writing Part Covered with Billiard Cloth. If desired, will put Mirror in Back, in place of Veneered Panels, at same price. Portable. Price, F. O. B **$25 00**

Secretaries of Antique and Modern Designs.—Tyler Desk Co., St. Louis, Mo.

[23]

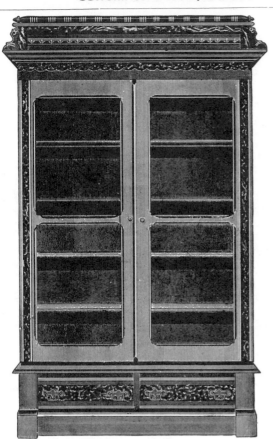

**No. I A.   Tyler's Walnut or Cherry Library Book Case.
Veneered Panels.**

Size, 4 ft. wide, 7 ft. 5 in. high.   Paneled Ends; Portable Top and Base;
Casters Complete. Portable Shelves. Weight, 150 lbs. Price, F. O. B **$28 00**

No. 2 B.   Lawyer's Book Case.   Walnut or Cherry Front.

Size, 3 ft. 10 in. wide, 7 ft. 2 in. high by 11 in. deep   Poplar Ends;
Easily handled; Movable Shelves. Casters Fitted.   Weight, 140
lbs.   Price, F. O. B.... ....$20 00

**No. 410. Tyler's Dwarf
Book Case. Walnut,
Antique Oak or Cherry.**

**No. 412. Tyler's Cabinet Book Case. Walnut, Antique
Oak or Cherry.**

CHITTENDEN & EASTMAN,

MANUFACTURERS OF

BOOK CASES AND ALL KINDS OF FURNITURE,

BURLINGTON, - - IOWA.

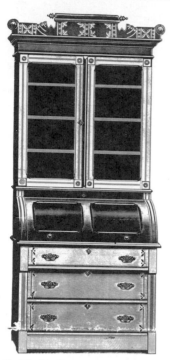

No. 612—Oak, Height 7 ft. 6 in.; Width 3 ft. 6 in.;
Polish Finish.

No. 603—All Walnut, Height 8 ft. 2 in.;
Width 3 ft. 6 in.

No. 604—All Walnut, Height 7 ft. 9 in.;
Width 3 ft. 6 in.

No. 605—All Walnut, Height 7 ft. 9 in;
Width 3 ft. 6 in.

No. 608—All Walnut, Height 7 ft. 10 in.;
Width 2 ft. 11 in.

No. 609—All Walnut, Height 7 ft. 10 in.;
Width 2 ft. 11 in.

No. 26—Walnut.

Height, 6 ft. 9 in.　Width, 4 ft. 2 in.

No. 26½—China Case.　Same as above, but 4 in. deeper.

BOOKCASES.

No. 25—Walnut and Oak.

Height, 6 ft. 6 in.　Width, 4 ft. 6 in.

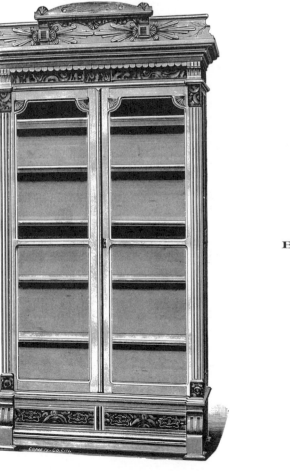

BOOKCASES.

No. 288 Library.

Oak, Antique, or XVIth Century Finish. Height, 5 ft. 8 in.; width, 3 ft. 10 in.
Glass, 18x38. French bevel plate mirror, 10x17.

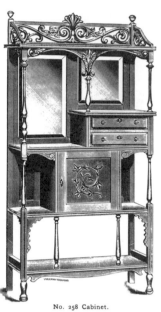

No. 258 Cabinet.

Antique Oak. 2 ft. 10 in. wide, 5 ft. 8 in. high.
French beveled plates—12x12 and 12x20.

No. 259 Parlor Cabinet.

Antique Oak. 3 ft. 2 in. wide, 5 ft. 8 in. high. French
beveled plates—two 8x20, one 12x18, one 9x9.

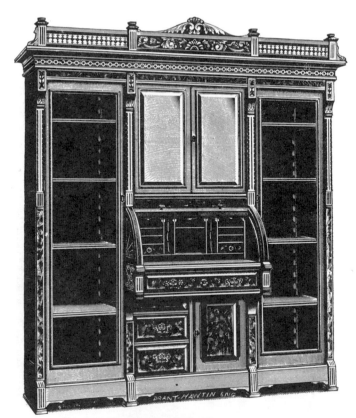

No. 278 CYLINDER LIBRARY SECRETARY.

Size, 5 feet 11 inches wide, 6 feet 9 inches high.

Bevel French mirror plates in cabinet above desk, 20x10 inches; double thick
French glass in doors 56x14 inches; adjustable shelves.

Price—In Walnut, Cherry or Oak, in white, $60.00; finished, $75.00.

277 CYLINDER LIBRARY SECRETARY.

Size, 5 feet 11 inches wide, 6 feet 6 inches high.

Cylinder Secretary 27 inches wide, bevel French plate in center, 12x24; Billiard
Cloth on slide; double thick French glass in doors, 12x50;
adjustable shelves.

Price—In Walnut, Cherry or Oak, in white, $58.00; finished, $71.00.

No. 207 CYLINDER DESK.

Size, 43x26 inches.

Walnut, Cherry or Oak, plain back ; Billiard Cloth on slide.

Price—In white, $32.00; finished, $38.00.

No. 205 CYLINDER DESK.

No. 208 CYLINDER DESK.

Size, 34x23 inches.

Walnut, Cherry or Oak, plain back ; Billiard Cloth on slide.

Price—In white, $22.00; finished, $25.00.

ROCKFORD UNION FURNITURE COMPANY, ROCKFORD, ILLINOIS.

No. 105 LIBRARY.

Antique Oak or XVI. century ; 4 ft. wide, 7 ft. high.

(Closed.)   **No. 512 LADIES' DESK.** Antique or XVI century ; 2 ft. 7 in. wide, 5 ft. high ; French bevel plate 12x16.   (Open.)

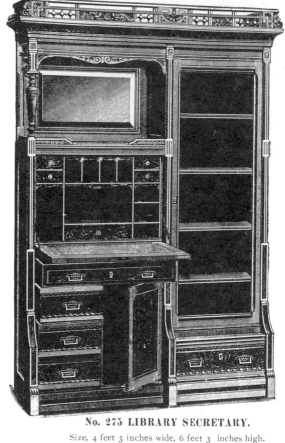

No. 275 LIBRARY SECRETARY.

Size, 4 feet 3 inches wide, 6 feet 3 inches high.

Bevel French plate above desk, size, 12x20; double thick French glass in door, 16x48 inches; adjustable shelves.

Price—In Walnut, Cherry or Oak, in white, $52.00; finished, $65.00.

In solid Mahogany, in white, $62.00; finished, $75.00.

No. 274 FALL LEAF LIBRARY SECRETARY.

Size, 3 feet 9 inches wide, 6 feet 2½ inches high.

Bevel French plate, mirror above desk 18x18 inches; double thick French glass in door 38x12 inches; adjustable shelves.

Price—In Walnut, Cherry or Oak, in white, $35.00; finished, $45.00.

No. 270 LIBRARY BOOK CASE.

Size, 6 feet wide, 6 feet 4 inches high.

Double thick French glass, 44x16 and 44x20; adjustable shelves.

Price—In Walnut, Cherry or Oak, in white, $50.00; finished, $60.00.

In solid Mahogany, in white, $60.00; finished, $70.00.

No. 273 LIBRARY BOOK CASE.

Size, 5 feet 3 inches wide, 7 feet 1 inch high.

Bevel French plate mirror in top of center door, 18x6 inches; double thick French glass in doors, 56x18 and 50x18 inches; adjustable shelves.

Price—In Walnut, Cherry or Oak, in white, $34.00; finished, $45.00.

No. 252 CYLINDER SECRETARY.

Size, 45x26 inches, 8 feet 6 inches high.

Two drawers and closet with shelf in base, double thick French glass, 16x34 inches, adjustable shelves; Billiard Cloth on slide.

Price—In Walnut, Cherry or Oak, in white, $38.00; finished, $46.00.

No. 216 PARLOR CURTAIN DESK.

Size, 35x22 inches.

Bevel French plate in top, size, 10x18 inches.

Price—In Walnut, Cherry or Oak, in white, $37.00; finished, $45.00.

In solid Mahogany, in white, $43.00; finished, $50.00.

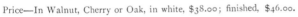
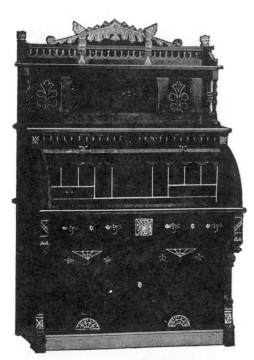

No. 206 CYLINDER DESK.

Size, 43x26 inches.

Walnut, Cherry or Oak, ornamental shelf on top; Billiard Cloth on slide.

Price—In white, $30.50; finished, $36.00.

No. 276 LIBRARY SECRETARY.

Size, 5 feet 9 inches wide, 6 feet 6 inches high.

Fall leaf Secretary, 25 inches wide; writing part covered with Billiard Cloth; double thick French glass in doors, 12x50 inches; adjustable shelves.
Bevel French plate mirror above desk, 20x12 inches.

Price—In Walnut, Cherry or Oak, in white, $58.00; finished, $71.00.

No. 3.
Dwarf Book Case.
65 in. high; 30 in. wide.

No. 9. Cylinder Secretary.
90 in. high; 36 in. wide.

No. 4. Dwarf Book Case.
67 in. high; 46 in. wide.
Handsomely ornamented with French Burl Pillars.

No. 16. Cylinder Secretary.
96 in. high; 42 in. wide.
Ornamented with Burl Pillars. A beautiful
piece of furniture.

No. 15. High Book Case.
87 in. high; 42 in. wide.

No. 18. High Book Case.
90 in. high; 46 in. wide.
Ornamented with French Burl Pillars. The most
elegant case in the market at a similar price.

No. 19. Cylinder Parlor Desk.
55 in. high; 34 in. wide.

No. 2. Desk.
48 in. long; 27 in. wide.
Has one centre and seven side drawers, one of them double usual depth for
books. Can be made with door at
same price.

No. 6. Desk.
48 in. long; 27 in. wide.
French veneers on rim and drawers.

No. 7. Office Table.
All lengths.

No. 5. Desk.
42 in. long; 26 in. wide.
French veneer on rim and drawers.

ORPIN BROS. & POND

No. 668. Book-Case, Golden Quartered Oak or Mahogany finish, 61 inches high, 36 inches long, 14 inches deep.
Price $11.00

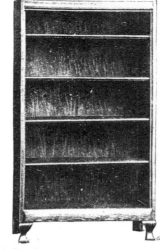

No. 656. Book-Case, Golden Oak or Mahogany finish, 57 inches high, 33 inches long, 13 inches deep.
Price . . . . $ 9.85
No. 655. Same, but 24 inches long . . . . Price 8.95
No. 654. Same, with one glass door, 33 inches long . . Price 13.25

No. 659. Book-Case, Golden Quartered Oak or Mahogany finish, two shaped drawers at the bottom, 56 inches high, 41 inches long, 14 inches deep, two glass doors.
Price $28.00

No. 985 1-2. Desk, Golden Oak, one drawer, shaped shelf, 26 inches wide.
Price $4.25
No. 986. Same, without shelf and drawer.
Price 4.00
No. 984 1-2. Same as 985½, with pattern French bevel plate on top.
Price 5.25

No. 996. Desk, Golden Oak, carved lid, shelf across the top, 32 inches wide.
Price $10.50
No. 997. Same, without the shelf across the top.
Price 9.75

No. 988. Desk, Golden Oak, 66 inches high, 30 inches wide, carved lid.
Price $6.95

No. 982. Desk, Golden Quartered Oak, piano polish, French legs, shaped drawers, 28 inches wide.
Price $7.75
No. 982 1-2. Same, but with French bevel mirror on top back, 4x14 inches.
Price $8.75

No. 893 1-2. Desk, Golden Quartered Oak, 30 inches wide, full serpentine front, French bevel mirror, 4x6 inches. French legs, piano polish, with three drawers . . . . . Price $16.50
No. 894 1-2. Same, two drawers, Price 15.75
No. 893. Same as 893½, but with moulded rail across the top in place of the mirror. With three drawers . . . . Price $16.25
No. 893. With two drawers . . . . . Price 14.00

No. 446. Desk, Solid Golden Oak, polish finish, full serpentine front and French legs, French bevel mirror, 10x12, 30 inches wide.
Price $12.50

No. 530. Desk, Golden Quartered Oak, piano polish, 44 inches high, 31 inches wide, 17 inches deep, shaped drawer, carved top.
Price $14.50
Same in Solid Mahogany . . . . Price 18.00

No. 527. Desk, Golden Quartered Oak, piano polish, French legs, claw feet, drawers across the top and shaped drawer under lid, 44 inches high, 32 inches wide, 18 inches deep.
Price $23.50
Same in Solid Mahogany . . . . Price 26.75

See Special Discount on Inside Cover

No. 394. Book-Case and Writing Desk Combined, 5 ft. 2 in. high, 37 in. wide, Solid Golden Oak. French bevel mirror 14x6.
Price.................................$11.90

No. 403. Book-Case and Writing Desk Combined, 5 ft. 6 in. high, 40 in. wide. French bevel mirror 18x12. Golden Quartered Oak.
Price.............................$17.90

No. 392. Book-Case and Writing Desk Combined, Golden Quartered Oak, 40 in. wide, 68 in. high, French bevel mirror 10x17, bent glass in door.
Price.............................$18.90

No. 400. Book-Case and Writing Desk Combined, Golden Quartered Oak, polish finish, 5 ft. 8 in. high, 40 in. wide, adjustable shelves, pattern French bevel mirror 12x16.
Price.........................$18.75

No. 684. Book-Case and Writing Desk Combined, Golden Quartered Oak, 36 in. wide, 7 feet high.
Price. $19.85

No. 393. Book-Case and Writing Desk Combined, Golden Quartered Oak, 40 in. wide, 68 in. high. French bevel mirror 10x17, bent glass door.
Price........................... $19.85

No. 391. Book-Case and Writing Desk Combined, 68 in. high, 42 in. wide, pattern French bevel mirror 16x12, Golden Quartered Oak
Price..........................$21.00

No. 396. Book-Case and Writing Desk Combined, Golden Quartered Oak, 44 in. wide, 70 in. high, French bevel mirror 14x16.
Price.......................... $24.50

No. 796. Book-Case and Writing Desk Combined, 6 ft. 3 in. high, 46 in. wide. Golden Quartered Oak, piano polish. Full serpentine front and glass door, pattern French bevel mirror 18x18.
Price................................$37.50

No. 928. Book-Case. Golden Oak, 40 in. wide, 62 in. high.
Price...........................$ 8.75
No. 926. Same, 36 in. wide. Price...........................7.25
No. 927. Same, with 2 glass doors, 40 in. wide, 62 in. high.
Price...........................11.90
No. 925. Same, 1 glass door, 36 in. wide. Price............9.90
No. 929. Same, 1 glass door, 30 in. wide. Price............8.50

No. 650. Book-Case. Golden Oak, 3 glass doors, 47 in. high, 55 in. long, 13 in. deep.
Price.........................$17.25

No. 651. Book-Case. Golden Oak, 2 glass doors, 47 in. high, 41 in. long, 13 in. deep.
Price...........................$12.50
No. 652. Same, with 1 glass door and 33 in. long. Price.... 9 75
No. 653. Same, without glass door, 33 in. wide. Price.... 6.25

See Special Discount on Inside of Cover

No. 204

Office or library table. Golden Quartered Oak. Piano polish.

No. 204, 4 feet (1 drawer) $12.00
No. 205, 5 feet (2 drawers) 15.00
No. 206, 6 feet (2 drawers) 17.75
No. 208, 8 feet (3 drawers) 21.50

(N. B.—This cut fails to show the table well. It is a strongly built table with very best select stock.)

No. 600

Library or office table. Size of top 28x48 inches. Elegantly carved rims. Fluted legs. Two drawers. Golden Quartered Oak or Mahogany finish.

Price..$16.00

No. 678

Library or office table. Size of top 28x45 inches. Shaped top. Golden Quartered Oak or Solid Mahogany. Piano polish.

Oak $23.00
Mahoghany...................................... 28.00

No. 602

Library or office table. Size of top 28x48 inches. Carved around the top. Shaped drawers and spiral turned legs. Claw feet. Piano polish. Golden Quartered Oak.

Price $19.50

No. 599

Library or office table. Size of top 30x48 inches. Shaped top and double serpentine rim all around. French legs. Claw feet. A large drawer in each end. Piano polish.

Golden Quartered Oak......................... $30.00
Solid Mahogany................................... 37.50

No. 535

Library, office or director's table. Very heavy and massive. Shaped rim, and heavy fluted legs. Piano polish. Size of top 36x72 inches.
Golden Quartered Oak.........................$39.00
Solid Mahogany..................... .... 49.00

No. 534

Same. Size of top, 42x96 inches (with center leg).
Golden Quartered Oak $48.50
Solid Mahogany................... ... 59.50
N. B.—This cut does not do justice to the table. It has a 5 inch leg and is very massive.

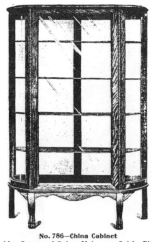

No. 783—China Cabinet
Oak or Mahogany finish. Piano polish, wood back. Bent glass ends, 64 in. high, 39 in. wide, 14 in. deep.
Each...............................$17.00

No. 784—China Cabinet
Golden Oak or Mahogany finish. Piano polish, wood back. Bent glass ends, oval French bevel mirror on the top, 66 in. high, 39 in. wide, 14 in. deep.
Each.......................$20.00

No. 786—China Cabinet
Golden Quartered Oak or Mahogany finish. Piano polish, wood back. Bent glass ends, 61 in. high, 42 in. wide, 15 in. deep.
Each..........................$23.25
Glass Backs and Glass Shelves for any of these Cabinets furnished on application.

No. 782—China Cabinet
Golden Quartered Oak or Mahogany finish. Piano polish, wood back. Bent glass ends, 64 in. high, 40 in. wide, 14 in. deep.
Each............. ....$29.00

No. 4562. Five Pieces. Golden Quartered Oak or Mahogany finish. Piano polish. Tufted backs, full spring edges, elegantly carved frame. Upholstered in fancy figured velours, plain corduroys, fine satin damask, imported tapestries or silk plush, 5 pieces...$49.50
Sofa is 51 inches long... 16.75

No. 4577. Five Pieces. Mahogany finish, piano polish. Tufted backs, full spring edges. Elegantly carved. In fancy figured velours, plain corduroys, fine satin damask, imported tapestries and silk plush, 5 pieces $64.00
Sofa is 53 inches long... 22.00

No. 4562. Arm Chair $10.75
Side Chair... 5.50

No. 4577. Rocker $16.50
Side Chair... 7.50

No. 4562. Rocker...$12.50
Side Chair... 5.50

No. 4577. Arm Chair. $15.00
Side Chair... 7.50

See Special Discount on Inside Cover

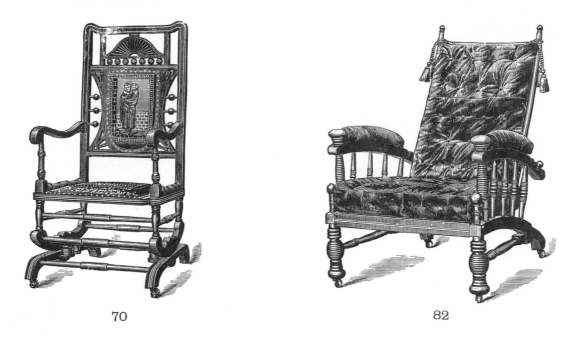

70   82

THE MOST PRACTICAL, COMFORTABLE, AND COMMON-SENSE CHAIR MADE.

THE CELEBRATED MORRIS CHAIR.

FOUR RECLINING POSITIONS.

WITH REVERSIBLE CUSHIONS.

TAPESTRY ON ONE SIDE.   PLUSH ON THE OTHER.

Made in Oak, Walnut, Ebony, or Mahogany.

Frames in wood, $9.00; Polished or Ebonized, $10.00; Mahogany, $2.50 extra; Nice Tapestry and Plush Upholstering, $35.00. All hair; 12 lbs. Gray Drawings in Cushions. Terms 5% Cash.

SUMMER FURNITURE

SUITABLE for verandas, cottages, dens, &c., &c. Made with rush seats, seats upholstered in Japanese matting or imitation leather. The wood is maple, finished light, green, or red, while Nos. 307, 305 and 306 are made in oak with golden quartered or weathered finish.

No. 352 Each.....................$4.00	**No. 351** Each.....................$4.00	**No. 353** Each.....................$7.35
No. 307 Each.....................$10.65	**No. 305** Each.....................$5.67	**No. 306** Each.....................$5.67

This Suit is also made in Golden or Weathered Oak.

No. 362 Each.....................$4.35	**No. 361** Each.....................$4.35	**No. 363** Each.....................$8.00

See Special Discount on Inside Cover

No. 4512. Five Pieces. Golden Quartered Oak or Mahogany finish. Piano polish. Spring seat.
Upholstered in fine grade of figured velour or tapestry...................................$34.00
Sofa...12.00

Five Pieces in Imported Tapestry or Satin Damask........................... .... 42.50
Sofa... .... 14.75

No. 4514. Five Pieces. Golden Quartered Oak or Mahogany finish. Piano polish. Upholstered in
fine figured velour or tapestry..$34.00
Sofa...12.00

Five Pieces in Imported Tapestry or Fine Satin Damask...................................... 42.50
Sofa... .... 14.75

No. 4512
In fine grade Velour or Tapestry.
Rocker.......................... ....$8.75   Side Chair............................ ......$3.75
In Imported Tapestry or Fine Satin Damask.
Rocker ....$10.75   Side Chair................................$4.75

No. 4514
Upholstered in Fine Figured Velour or Tapestry.
Rocker ... .$8.75   Side Chair............................. ....$3.75
In Upholstered Tapestry or Fine Satin Damask.
Rocker...................................$10.75   Side Chair................................$4.75

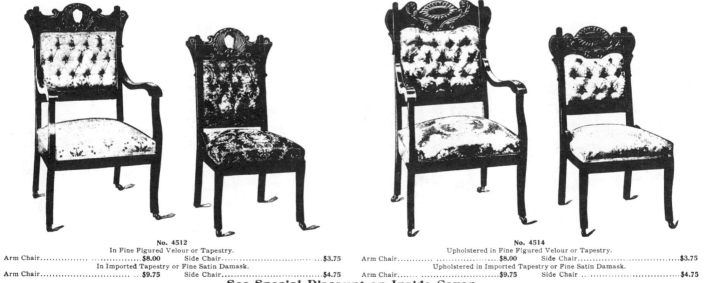

No. 4512
In Fine Figured Velour or Tapestry.
Arm Chair.............. ....$8.00   Side Chair................................$3.75
In Imported Tapestry or Fine Satin Damask.
Arm Chair..............................$9.75   Side Chair................................$4.75

No. 4514
Upholstered in Fine Figured Velour or Tapestry.
Arm Chair........... ....$8.00   Side Chair................................$3.75
Upholstered in Imported Tapestry or Fine Satin Damask.
Arm Chair...... ....$9.75   Side Chair $4.75

See Special Discount on Inside Cover

No. 832

No. 831

No. 525

No. 802

Each...$20.70   Each..$20.70

Colonial Chair and Rocker. Genuine Mahogany. Piano polish.

(Chair to match is No. 525½.)
Golden Quartered Oak or Genuine Mahogany.
Piano polish.
Oak.............$5.20 Mahogany.......$7.40

(Chair to match is No. 802½.)
Golden Quartered Oak or Genuine Mahogany.
Piano polish.
Oak.............$6.65 Mahogany....:$8.15

No. 586

(Chair to match is 587. With claw feet like 588.)
Oak.................$14.00 Mahogany.......$17.75

No. 588

Oak.....................................$10.35
Mahogany.............................13.35

No. 589

Oak...$29.60
Mahogany..35.55

Golden Quartered Oak or Genuine Mahogany.   Piano polish.   Elegantly carved.

No. 532—Fancy Rocker

Oak...............................$ 8.15
Mahogany.........................10.35

No. 660—Fancy Rocker

Oak.................................$14.00
Mahogany.............................17.00

No. 698—Hall or Reception Chair

Oak...............................$10.35
Mahogany...........................13.35

Nn. 815 1-2—Colonial Chair

Rocker to match is No. 815.
Genuine Mahogany only. Piano polish.
Price..................................$10.35

The above are all made in Golden Quartered Oak and Genuine Mahogany.   Piano polish.

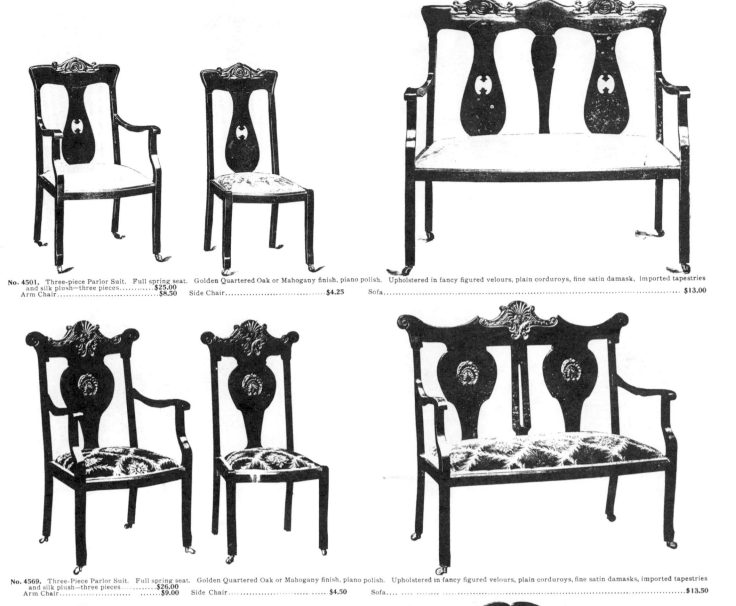

No. 4501. Three-piece Parlor Suit. Full spring seat. Golden Quartered Oak or Mahogany finish, piano polish. Upholstered in fancy figured velours, plain corduroys, fine satin damask, imported tapestries and silk plush—three pieces...........$25.00
Arm Chair.................................$8.50   Side Chair.................................$4.25   Sofa..$13.00

No. 4569. Three-Piece Parlor Suit. Full spring seat. Golden Quartered Oak or Mahogany finish, piano polish. Upholstered in fancy figured velours, plain corduroys, fine satin damasks, imported tapestries and silk plush—three pieces............$26.00
Arm Chair........................ ....$9.00   Side Chair......................... ......$4.50   Sofa...., ...$13.50

No. 4555. Three-Piece Parlor Suit. Full spring seat. Golden Quartered Oak or Mahogany finish, piano polish. Upholstered in fancy figured velours, plain corduroys, fine satin damask, imported tapestries and silk plush—three pieces............$31.00
Arm Chair............•.................$11.00   Side Chair.................................$5.25   Sofa...$16.00

See Special Discount on Inside Cover

No. 954. Morris Chair. Solid Golden Oak, upholstered in good quality fancy figured velour.
Each $5.40

No. 953. Morris Chair. Solid Golden Oak, elegantly carved, shaped front, upholstered in good quality fancy figured velour.
Each $6.11

No. 930. Morris Chair. Solid Golden Oak, shaped front, claw feet, upholstered in good quality of fancy figured velour.
Each $7.75

No. 894. Morris Chair. Solid Golden Oak, elegantly carved front, upholstered in good quality of fancy figured velour.
Each $8.85

The Backs on these Chairs Adjust to Any Angle Desired.

(Though the Cuts are Smaller Than the Large Ones the Chairs are Equally as Large.)

No. 7674. Morris Chair. Golden Quartered Oak, elegantly carved front and claw feet, piano polish, upholstered in best quality fancy figured velour.
Each $12.85
(This chair is as large as any of the following.)

No. 999. Morris Chair. Golden Quartered Oak or Mahogany finish, piano polish, upholstered in best quality of fancy figured velour.
Each $8.75

No. 971. Morris Chair. Golden Quartered Oak or Mahogany finish, piano polish, upholstered in best quality fancy figured velour.
Each $15.95

No. 970. Morris Chair. Golden Quartered Oak or genuine Mahogany, piano polish, upholstered in best quality fancy figured velour.
Oak $22.25
Mahogany 28.15

The Backs on These Chairs Adjust to Any Angle Desired.

No. 969. Morris Chair. Golden Quartered Oak or Mahogany finish, piano polish, upholstered in best quality fancy figured velour.
Each $10.35

No. 972. Morris Chair. Golden Quartered Oak or Mahogany finish, piano polish, upholstered in best quality fancy figured velour.
Each $12.60

No. 998. Morris Chair. Golden Quartered Oak or Mahogany finish, piano polish, upholstered in best quality fancy figured velour.
Each $13.30

No. 990. Morris Chair. Golden Quartered Oak or Genuine Mahogany, piano polish, upholstered in best quality fancy figured velour.
Oak ....$24.45   Mahogany.......$29.50

The Backs on These Chairs Adjust to Any Angle Desired.

See Special Discount on Inside of Cover

No. 4329. Arm Chair. Golden Quartered Oak or Mahogany finish, piano polish. Tufted seat and back. Upholstered in fancy figured velour, corduroy, imported tapestries or imitation leather.

Each...$11.95
Genuine Leather, each 14.00

No. 3758. Arm Chair or Rocker. Golden Quartered Oak or Mahogany finish, piano polish. Upholstered in fancy figured velour, corduroy, imported tapestries or imitation leather.

Each..$23.00
Genuine Leather, each 26.00

No. 4733. Arm Chair. Golden Quartered Oak or Mahogany finish, piano polish. Upholstered in fancy figured velour, plain corduroy, imported tapestries or imitation leather.

Each..$24.00
Genuine Leather, each 30.00

No. 2358. Full Turkish Rocker. Iron frame. Tufted back and arms. Very large and comfortable. Upholstered in fancy figured velour, plain corduroy, imported tapestries or imitation leather.

Each..................... .... $45.00
Genuine Leather, each.............................. ...... 51.50

No. 3341. Full Turkish Rocker. Tufted back and arms. Very large and luxurious. Upholstered in fancy figured velour, plain corduroy, imported tapestries or imitation leather.

Each..................................... ....$35.00
Genuine Leather, each..................................... 41.00

No. 4025. Turkish Rocker (chair to match). Golden Quartered Oak or Mahogany finish. Upholstered in fancy figured velour, plain corduroy, imported tapestries or imitation leather.

Each.................................... .... $33.00
Genuine Leather, each.,..................................... 40.00

No. 1767. Turkish Rocker (chair to match). Tufted back and arms. Very large and luxurious. Upholstered in fancy figured velour, plain corduroy, imported tapestries and imitation leather.

Each..$35.00
Genuine Leather, each..................................... 41.00

No. 4572. Turkish Rocker (chair to match). Golden Quartered Oak or Mahogany finish. Piano polish. Elegantly carved fronts.

Genuine Leather, each.....................................$32.50

No. 4075. Full Turkish Chair. Steel frame. Golden Quartered Oak or Mahogany finish. Piano polish. Claw feet. Upholstered in fancy figured velour, plain corduroy, imported tapestries and imitation leather.

Each................... ....$41.50
Genuine Leather, each 48.50

See Special Discount on Inside Cover

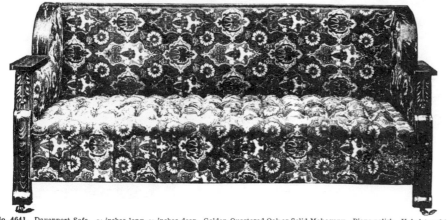

No. 4641. Davenport Sofa. 74 inches long, 30 inches deep. Golden Quartered Oak or Solid Mahogany. Piano polish. Upholstered in fine fancy figured velour or tapestry.
Oak....................................$38.50   Mahogany.................................$40.00
Same. Upholstered in imported tapestry, Roman silk velour, Bokhara velour or Verona velour.
Oak....................................$50.00   Mahogany................................$55.00

No. 4723. Rocker. Golden Quartered Oak or Mahogany finish. Piano polish. Full size Turkish chair with ruffled sides. Upholstered in genuine leather..........................$41.50

No. 4741. Rocker. Golden Quartered Oak or Mahogany finish. Piano polish. A large size Turkish rocker, 35 inches wide and 40 inches high. Upholstered in fine fancy figured velour or tapestry..$26.50
Same. In genuine leather............................$33.50

No. 4683. Davenport Sofa. 81 inches long, 31 inches deep. Golden Quartered Oak or Mahogany finish. Piano polish. Upholstered in fine fancy figured velour or tapestry..$50.00
Same. Upholstered in imported tapestry, Roman silk velour, Bokhara velour or Verona velour........................$55.00

No. 4288. Davenport Sofa. 79 inches long, 32 inches deep. Genuine Mahogany with Crotch Mahogany top. Upholstered in fine fancy figured velour or tapestry....................................$54.00
Same. Upholstered in imported tapestry, Roman silk velour, Bokhara velour or Verona velour................................$77.00

No. 3390. A large luxurious arm rocker. Upholstered in fine fancy figured velour or tapestry.
Each...$23.00
Same. Upholstered in genuine leather.
Each...$27.50

See Special Discount on Inside Cover

THE HARTLEY CHAIR.

Style No. 3.

Has all of the Reclining Positions, but no Foot Rest.

WE upholster it in two grades, the first, or No. 1 grade, having Springs in the Seat, Back and Pillow, with a Hair Top, and the Seat being a Spring Edge Front.

The second, or No. 2 grade, has Springs in the Seat only, the Back and Pillow being made without any. It has the appearance of the 1st grade apparently, but is not as comfortable or as durable.

	1st grade	2nd grade
Prices, Upholstered in Spun Silk, Wool Rep or Hair Cloth	$12.00	$10.00
" " trimmed with Plush Border	14.00	12.00
" " in any Shades of Plush or Leather	16.00	14.00

Style No. 5.

We have this Chair in either Walnut, Cherry, Mahogany or Ebony Finish at the same price. It has heavy Carving, Burl Panels, and is an elegant as well as a durable piece of Furniture.

Style No. 4.

Has all of the Reclining Positions and the Adjustable Foot Rest. It is an Upholstered Chair throughout, and is the best Reclining Chair in the market for Ease, Durability and Price.

This Chair we Upholster both in the First and Second Grade.

	1st grade	2nd grade
Prices, Upholstered in Spun Silk, Wool Rep or Hair Cloth	$14.00	$12.00
" " trimmed with Plush Border	16.00	14.00
" " in any Shade of Plush or Leather	18.00	16.00
" " " Imported	20.00	18.00

This Chair, like the No. 4, has all the Reclining positions and the Adjustable Foot Rest. We upholster it in the first grade, as explained with Chair No. 3 (see cut No. 5, at left), also in extra fine or Turkish style, which is with best steel springs and hair throughout, with spring edge in seat, back, pillow and arms.

See Cut No. 5, with fringe, at right.

	Turkish	First Grade
Prices, Upholstered in Wool Reps, Tapestry, or Hair cloth	$30.00	$20.00
" " any Shade of American Plushes	32.50	22.50
" " Imported Plushes	35.00	25.00

Upholstered in Extra fine goods with fringe will cost from $40.00 to $60.00 per chair.

THE HARTLEY LOUNGE.

Style No. I, Extra.

Showing the same Frame, only Upholstered in better goods, with Plush Border and Fringe.

All of our Lounges are the same on both sides, making them suitable for any part of the room.

PRICES VARY FROM $15.00 TO $50.00, ACCORDING TO THE PRICE OF MATERIAL USED.

By adding the following to the price given with No. 1 and 2 Lounge, you get the price of this style :
For 5 yards of Fringe to a Lounge at a cost of from 50 cents to $2.50 per yard, add from .... $2.50 to $12.00 to prices.
" Spring Edge all around, or Turkish Upholstery, with Best Steel Springs and Hair, add .... 10.00 "

Style No. I.

This cut shows it Upholstered in Spun Silk, or Wool Rep, and Trimmed with Plush Border.

MEASUREMENT OF FRAME.
Full length, 6 ft. 2 in.　　Length of Seat, 4 ft. 2 in.
Width, 21 in.
The back of our Lounges can be adjusted to any heighth desired.

UPHOLSTERED WITH SPRINGS THROUGHOUT THE SEAT, BACK AND PILLOW.

Price, Covered with either Spun Silk, Wool Rep or Hair Cloth	$10.00
" " and trimmed with Plush Border	12.50
" " any shade of American Plush, Moss top	15.00
" " Imported Plush, with Hair top	18.00

Style No. 4.

This Lounge is the same shape and size as Lounge No. 3, and like that is designed only for Brussels Carpet, Leather or Woven Rattan without Springs; the frame is entirely of wood and bolted together in such a manner as to withstand the heat of a Turkish Bath Room, or the weather if wanted for out door use.

IT HAS ALSO ALL THE DIFFERENT RECLINING POSITIONS.

Prices, Finished with Tapestry Brussels Carpet	$10.00
" " Body	12.00
" " Plain Leather, or Woven Rattan	14.00

No. 500. DOUBLE FACED COUCH.

c 6 feet by 26 inches. Spring Edge all around. Tufted. Filled with Hair and Moss.

No. 501.

Size 6 feet by 24 inches. No Hair or Moss.

Fitted with Fox Patent Casters.

No. 93. RECLINING CHAIR.

No. 10. DOUBLE FACED COUCH.

Walnut or Oak Frame. Size, 6 feet by 26 inches.
Fitted with Fox Patent Casters.

No. 506. DRAPERY SPRING EDGE COACH.

Size. 6 feet by 26 inches. Made in three grades of Drapery.

No. 505.

Size. 6 feet by 24 inches. Made in one grade of Drapery.

Fitted with Fox Patent Casters.

No. 98. ROLL HEAD SINGLE LOUNGE.

Walnut or Oak Frame. Spring Edge. Banded Front and Back. Full Size Lounge.
Fitted with Fox Patent Casters.

No. 8. DOUBLE FACED COUCH.

Walnut or Oak Frame. Spring Edge. Size, 6 feet by 24 inches, and 6 feet by 26 inches.
Fitted with Fox Patent Casters.

No. 16. SPRING EDGE SINGLE LOUNGE.

Pillow Back and Fringed Front.
Fitted with Fox Patent Casters.

No. 1. SINGLE LOUNGE.

Walnut Frame. Size, 5 feet 10 inches; width, 22 inches. Plain Front.

No. 3. SINGLE LOUNGE.

Walnut Frame. Size, 5 feet 10 inches by 22 inches. Banded Front and Back in Plush.
Fitted with Fox Patent Casters.

No. 207. BED LOUNGE.

Walnut or Oak Frame. Medium size Lounge. Spring Mattress or Full Spring and Cotton Top at extra charge.
6½ feet by 3½ feet.
Fitted with Fox Patent Casters.

No. 202. BED LOUNGE.

Walnut Frame. Small Size Lounge. Spring Mattress, 6 feet by 3½ feet.
Fitted with Fox Patent Casters.

No. 99. BED LOUNGE.

No. 208. BED LOUNGE.

[46]

No. 5. SINGLE LOUNGE.

Walnut or Oak Frame. Size, 5 feet 10 inches; width, 22 inches. Hard Edge, Plain Front, or Banded Front on extra charge.
Fitted with Fox Patent Casters.

No. 53. SINGLE LOUNGE.

Walnut or Oak Frame. Spring Edge. Banded Front and Back. Full Size Lounge.
Fitted with Fox Patent Casters.

No. 2. SINGLE LOUNGE.

Walnut Frame. Size, 6 feet by 22 inches. Banded Front and Back in Plush.
Fitted with Fox Patent Casters.

No. 4. SINGLE LOUNGE.

Walnut Frame. Size, 6 feet by 22 inches. Banded Front and Back in Plush.
Fitted with Fox Patent Casters.

No. 57. SINGLE LOUNGE.

Walnut Frame. Full size. Hard Edge, Banded Front. No. 56, all Plain. No. 58, Banded Front and Back.
Fitted with Fox Patent Casters.

No. 54. SINGLE LOUNGE.

Walnut or Oak Frame. Spring Edge. Banded Front and Back. Full Size Lounge.
Fitted with Fox Patent Casters.

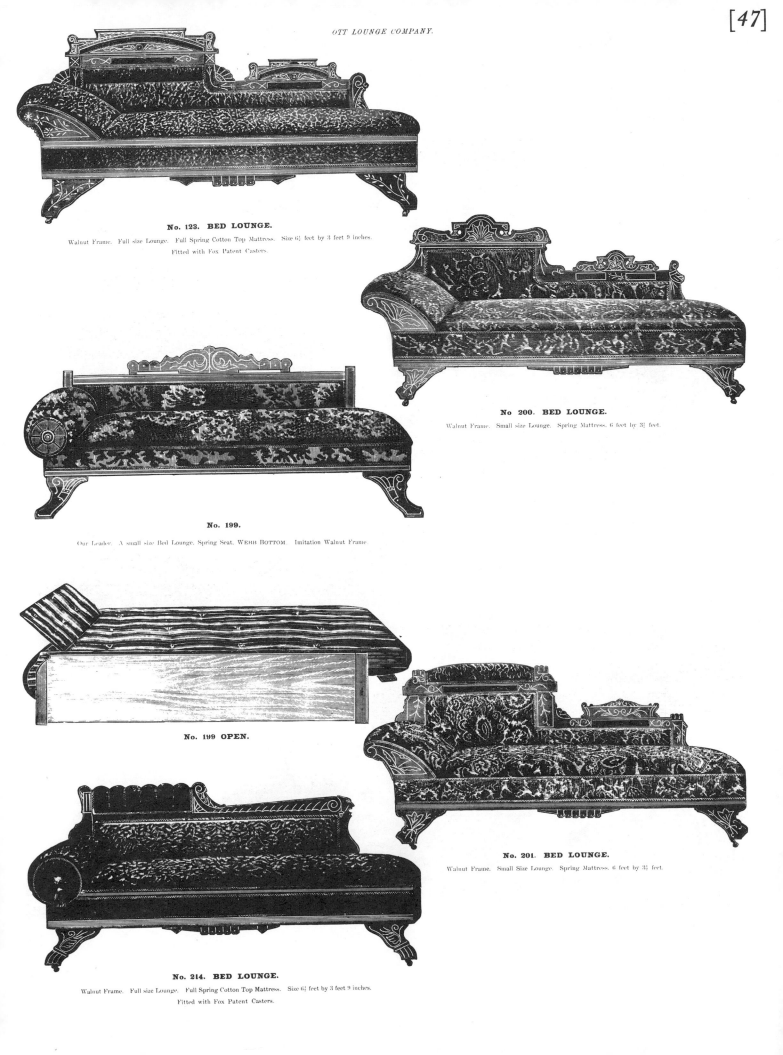

No. 123. BED LOUNGE.

Walnut Frame. Full size Lounge. Full Spring Cotton Top Mattress. Size 6½ feet by 3 feet 9 inches.
Fitted with Fox Patent Casters.

No 200. BED LOUNGE.

Walnut Frame. Small size Lounge. Spring Mattress. 6 feet by 3½ feet.

No. 199.

Our Leader. A small size Bed Lounge. Spring Seat, WEBB BOTTOM. Imitation Walnut Frame.

No. 199 OPEN.

No. 201. BED LOUNGE.

Walnut Frame. Small Size Lounge. Spring Mattress. 6 feet by 3½ feet.

No. 214. BED LOUNGE.

Walnut Frame. Full size Lounge. Full Spring Cotton Top Mattress. Size 6½ feet by 3 feet 9 inches.
Fitted with Fox Patent Casters.

LOUNGES.

No. **4,** Roll Arm Lounge, Seat 25 in.

Represented in Cretonne, with Plush Front.   A very comfortable Lounge.

Walnut.

No. **5,** Pillow Lounge, without Back, Seat 26 in.

Represented in Tapestry Cover and Puffing, with Plush Bands around Seat and Pillow.

Walnut only.

No. **24,** Cushion Head.

Width of Seat, 26 inches.   Represented in Crêpe Cloth, with Plush Border and Spring Edge.
(The head of this lounge is a soft spring cushion.)

Walnut.

No. **15,** Cushion Lounge.

Represented in Silk Brocade, with Puffing all around.   Makes up very handsome when Puffed with Plush.

Walnut.

MISCELLANEOUS.

No. **13,** Sleepy Hollow Chair.

Represented in Embossed Plush.   Pleated Seat and Back.
Walnut.

No. **37,** "Conversation" Chair.

Extreme length of frame, 4 ft. 2 in.   Represented in Embossed Plush.   A full sized, commodious chair.
Ebony or Imitation Mahogany.

The Howard "**B**" Easy Chair.

Represented in Jute Velour, with Plush Border and Sides and
Spring Front and Back.   A good Easy Chair.

Walnut, Imitation Mahogany, or Ebony.

THE "CUSHION" SUITE.

Represented in Embossed Mohair Plush, trimmed with Moss Edging.   The Backs and Arms form regular Cushions ; a very
comfortable, full-sized Suite, consisting of 1 Sofa, 2 Armchairs, and 4 Chairs.   (Sofa front, 5 ft. outside.)

Imitation Mahogany or Ebony.

Couches

Our Couches are all hand made. We use the best of materials, and tempered steel, Japanned springs. Our frames are well made and well put together. Samples of Upholstery Goods sent free on application.

Upholstery Goods

Grades of Upholstery Goods are as follows:

L. D.—Imitation figured denims (for box couches only).

F. D.—Satin duck, art ticking, plain or figured denims (for box couches only).

A.—Three and four-colored velours. All colors. Handsome patterns.

B.—Four and five-colored velour, self tones, plain Oxford and Holland corduroys.

D.—Eight and nine-colored velours or heavy plain corduroys.

F.—Good grades of tapestries in floral and Oriental effects. Also fine grades of plain Titian velours.

H.—Beautiful patterns of tapestries in Oriental and floral designs, both foreign and domestic.

K.—Very heavy embossed velours, veronas in beautiful colorings. Imported tapestries and Mohair plush.

M.—Figured silk plushes, plain silk plushes, Bokharas (imported goods of the texture of Turkish rugs).

Pantasote—Or imitation leather. You cannot tell it from leather by its looks, and it will wear as long.

Leather—Genuine leather of best grade. All colors.

No. 506. Turkish Couch. Button tufted, 27 inches wide, 74 inches long, spring edges all round. In the following grades:

A	$7.25	D	$9.50	H	$11.75
B	8.25	F	10.50	K	12.75

No. 888. Turkish Couch. Deep tufted, golden quartered oak frame, claw feet, spring edges all round, 29 inches wide, 76 inches long.

A	$14.00	F	$16.50	M	$23.25
B	14.50	H	17.95	Pantasote	21.50
D	15.50	K	20.50	Genuine leather	33.00

No. 746. Turkish Couch. (Not tufted), 26 inches wide, 75 inches long, claw feet. Handsome Rococo frame.

A	$9.25	D	$10.50	H	$12.50
B	9.75	F	11.25	K	13.25

No. 747. Turkish Couch. Deep tufted, golden quartered oak frame, full spring edges, 29 inches wide, 77 inches long. Frame elegantly carved.

A	$15.75	F	$18.00	M	$24.50
B	16.25	H	19.00	Pantasote	25.00
D	17.00	K	21.25	Genuine leather	37.00

No. 897. Turkish Couch. Deep tufted, oak or mahoganized frame, claw feet, spring edges all round, 28 inches wide, 75 inches long.

A	$12.00	F	$14.00	M	$19.50
B	12.50	H	15.25	Pantasote	20.50
D	13.25	K	17.00	Genuine leather	35.00

No. 794. Turkish Couch. Deep tufted, golden quartered oak or mahoganized frame, claw feet, Rococo pattern, full spring edges, 31 inches wide, 76 inches long.

A	$16.25	F	$18.50	M	$25.00
B	16.75	H	19.50	Pantasote	25.50
D	17.50	K	21.75	Genuine leather	37.50

See Special Discount on Inside Cover

OUR AUTOMATIC SOFA BEDS

Are the finest in the market. They open up to a full size luxurious bed. Work automatically. Only one motion required to open them. They do not need to be moved from the wall to open them. The raising of the seat brings the base forward and lowers the backs at the same time, thus making a full size bed. Made in Golden Quartered Oak or Mahogany finish. Piano polish.

No. 4885. Upholstered in fancy figured, velour or tapestry. Each.. ....$55.00
Same. Upholstered in Roman silk velour, mohair plush, Bokhara velour or Verona velour. Each............................. . 66.65
Size 78 inches long, 32 inches wide.

No. 4875. Upholstered in fancy figured velour or tapestry. Each...................................... ....$62.50
Same. Upholstered in Roman silk velour, mohair plush, Bokhara velour or Verona velour. Each................................... 75.00
Size 72 inches long, 32 inches wide.

No. 4874. Upholstered in fancy figured velour or tapestry. Each...$56.75
Same. Upholstered in Roman silk velour, mohair plush, Bokhara velour or Verona velour. Each................................ 66.75
Size 80 inches long, 32 inches wide.

No. 400 SUIT. SOFA 5 FEET. FOUR PIECES.

No. 190 Rocker, Mahogany
or Walnut Polish Finish.

No. 200 Rocker, Walnut or
Mahogany Polish Finish.

No. 109½ Rocker Antique Oak or
Mahogany Polish Finish.

No. 140 Rocker, 16th Century, Mahogany
or Walnut Polish Finish.

No. 128 Rocker, Walnut or
Mahogany Polish Finish.

No. 95 Suit.   Sofa 4 ft. 2 in.   5 Pieces, 16th Century or Mahogany Polish Finish.

PARLOR SUITES.

One Armchair.

One Divan.   Length of Front Rail, 34 inches.

One Side Chair.

One Fancy Chair.

No. 18, Turkish (iron frames) Suite.

Consisting of 1 Sofa, 1 Armchair, 1 Smoking Chair, and 4 Side Chairs, all full size and finely upholstered with spring backs, arms, and edges; fronts of frames carved in *bas-relief*. A luxurious and commodious suit. (Sofa front, 5 ft. 3 in.)

Walnut, Imitation Mahogany, or Ebony.

No. 14, Square Piano Stool, in Ebony or Walnut.

No. 17, Piano Stool, in Walnut or Ebony.

One Sofa.   Length of Front Rail, 4 ft. 9 in.

No. 167, Suite consisting of five pieces as shown.

TURKISH PATENT ROCKERS.

No. 11, Turkish Rocker. Full Size. Iron Frame. Walnut.

No. 13, Turkish Rocker. Full Size. Iron Frame. Walnut, Ebony, or Imitation Mahogany.

No. 21, Turkish Rocker. Full Size. Walnut. Iron Frame.

No. 23, Large Sized Turkish Rocker. Iron Frame.

LOUNGES.

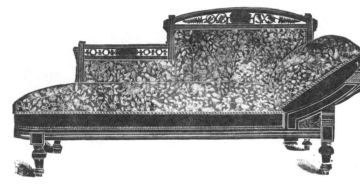

The "Lincoln" Lounge.   Width of Seat, 27 inches.

Represented in Figured Velveteen, Pleated Back and Arm, and Plush Border ; with Spring Edges and Arm (head).

A comfortable Lounge.

No. 10, Turkish (Iron Frame) Lounge.   Width of Seat, 28 inches.

Represented in Tapestry, with Plush Puffing, Spring Edge, Back, and Arm.   Soft and Comfortable.

NOTE.—This Lounge has been changed and much improved in the woodwork since this cut was made.

No. 21, Cushion Head Lounge.

Pleated Back, Plain Seat, and Soft Spring Cushion Head.

Walnut or Mahogany.

EASY CHAIRS.

No. 54, Odd Chair.

Represented in Plain Silk Plush.

Mahogany only.

No. 5, Large Turkish Armchair, Iron Frame.   Full Size.
Walnut, Ebony, or Imitation Mahogany.

No. 6, Turkish Armchair, Iron Frame, Full Size.
Walnut

No. 55, Easy Chair.

Represented in Figured Velveteen, Deep Spring Back and Seat.

Walnut or Imitation Mahogany.

No. 3, "Howard" Easy Chair.
Finely Upholstered, Soft Spring Back and Seat.

No. 29, Patent Rocker, Full Size.
Walnut or Imitation Mahogany.

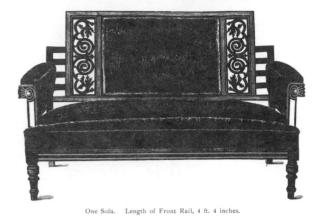

One Sofa.   Length of Front Rail, 4 ft. 4 inches.

No. **169,** Suite consisting of seven pieces.

One Sofa.   Length of Front Rail, 4 ft. 4 inches.

No. **102,** Suite consisting of six pieces.

One Armchair.

One Armchair.

One Corner Chair.

One Low-back Armchair.

Two Side Chairs.

One Fancy Chair.

Three Side Chairs.

One Fancy Chair.

Made in Imitation Mahogany, Cocobola, or Ebony.

Made in Imitation Mahogany, Cocobola, or Ebony.

No. **84,** Marble Top Table, 20 x 28.

Walnut only.

No. **56,** Full Size, Walnut, 24 x 42.

These Tables can be covered with Leather if desired.

No. **49,** Full Size, 24 x 42, in Walnut or Mahogany.

These Tables can be covered with Leather if desired.

CORNER AND WINDOW CHAIRS.

No. 66—Corner Chair.
Size of Seat, 25½ x 21½.

No. 68½—Window Chair.
Size of Seat, 25½ x 21½.

No. 63½—Window Chair.
Size of Seat, 25½ x 21½.

No. 67—Corner Chair.
Size of Seat, 25½ x 21½.

STUDENTS' CHAIRS.

No. 68—Corner Chair.
Size of Seat, 25½ x 21½.

No. 2.

No. 9.

No. 3.

KILBORN WHITMAN & CO.,
46 CANAL ST. BOSTON, U.S.A.
PARLOR FURNITURE MANUFACTURERS.

153   164   46   71

153

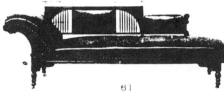

61

164

167

143

146.A

146

167

143

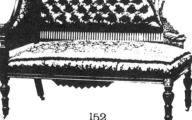

152

167

151

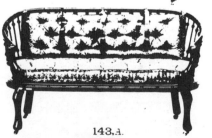

143.A

62   1.S   148

KILBORN WHITMAN & CO.,
PARLOR FURNITURE MANUFACTURERS,
34 Canal St., Boston. Mass.. U.S.A.

90

9

68

69

185

194

20

91

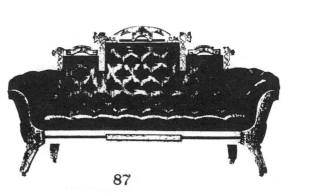

87

67

191

8

1

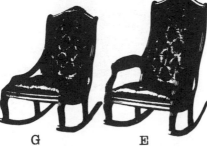

G

E

KILBORN WHITMAN & CO.,
PARLOR FURNITURE MANUFACTURERS,
34 Canal St., Boston, Mass., U.S.A.

45

44

42

38

34

T

46

K

33

1

89

15

38

81

84

87

88

I

6

3

4

ALBERTYPE FORBES CO.

4

3

1

2

9

O

R

M

5

8

7

81

1776

PARLOR SUITES.

No. 70½—Consists of 6 pieces: I Tete, I Arm Chair, I Window Chair, I Patent Rocker and 2 Chairs.
No. 70 —Consists of 7 pieces: I Tete, I Arm Chair, I Patent Rocker and 4 Chairs.

LOUNGES.

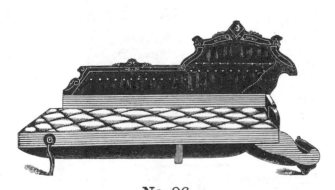

No. 96.
PATENT BED LOUNGE, CLOSED.
Walnut Frame, with French Walnut Panels.

No. 96.
PATENT BED LOUNGE, OPENED.
Showing Upholstered Spring Bed, 6 feet long by 3 feet 10 inches wide.

MARBLE TOP TABLES.

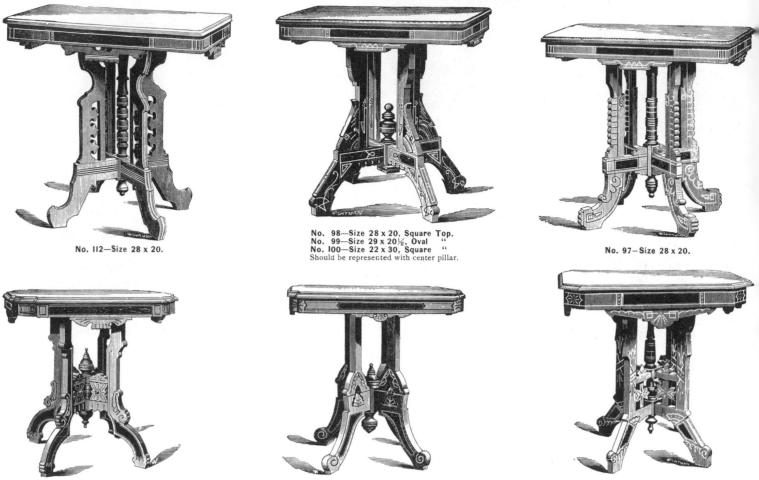

No. 112—Size 28 x 20.

No. 98—Size 28 x 20, Square Top.
No. 99—Size 29 x 20½, Oval "
No. 100—Size 22 x 30, Square "
Should be represented with center pillar.

No. 97—Size 28 x 20.

No. 75—Size 28 x 20.

No. 76—Size 28 x 20.

No. 78—Size 23½ x 17.
No. 80—Size 28 x 20.

THE SIZES QUOTED ARE THE ACTUAL SIZES OF THE MARBLE TOPS.

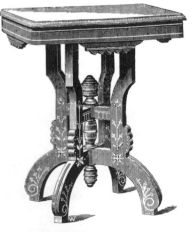

No. 114—Size 21 x 16, Square Top.
No. 116—Size 21 x 16, Oval "
No. 115—Size 23½ x 17, Square "
No. 117—Size 23½ x 17, Oval "

No. 96—Size 20 x 15.

LOUNGES.

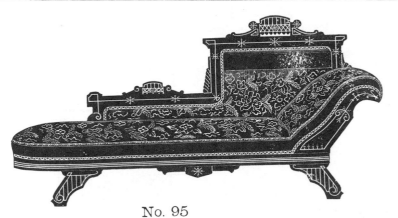

No. 95

Walnut Frame, with Board Bottom.

No. 78.

Walnut Frame, with French Walnut Panels and Web Bottom.

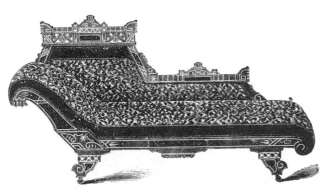

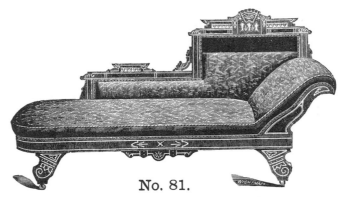

No. 81.

Walnut Frame, with French Walnut Panels and Board Bottom.

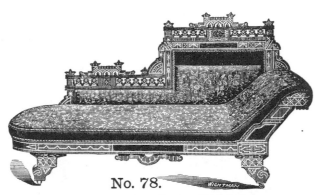

No. 90 —Imitation of Walnut, Ebonized and Gilt.
No. 90½—Walnut, with French Walnut Panels.

No. 79—Walnut Frame, with French Walnut Panels and Web Bottom.

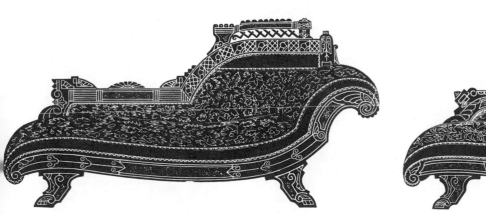

No. 93 —Imitation of Walnut, Ebonized and Gilt.
No. 93½—Walnut, with French Walnut Panels.

No. 94 —Imitation of Walnut, Ebonized and Gilt.
No. 94½—Walnut, with French Walnut Panels.

PARLOR SUITES.

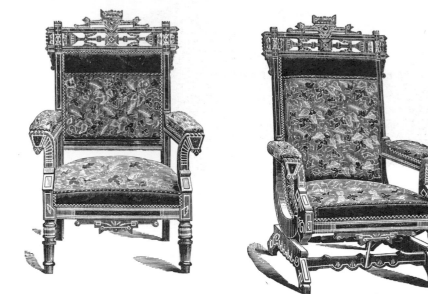

No. 67½—Consists of 6 pieces: 1 Tete, 1 Arm Chair, 1 Window Chair, 1 Patent Rocker and 2 Chairs.
No. 67 —Consists of 7 pieces: 1 Tete, 1 Arm Chair, 1 Patent Rocker and 4 Chairs.

Nos. 67 and 68 Corner Chairs and No. 68½ Window Chair match the above Suite.

No. 533. Tyler's Library Couch. Full Plain Leather.

Finished and Trimmed alike on both sides. Extra Width. Full Spring Edges. Weight, 100 lbs. Price, in Full Leather, F. O. B...... ..$40 00

No. 533 A. Same in Embossed Plush. Price, F. O. B.. 36 00

No. 49. Tyler's Mahoganized Cherry or Walnut. .$50 00

Extra Large; Covered and Bound with Leather; Hair Stuffed; Spring Edge and Bolster; Library Finish; Leather Fringe. Weight, 125 lbs. Price, F. O. B.

No. 49 A. Same in Embossed Plush. Worsted Fringe. Price, F. O. B.. 44 00

No. 218. Tyler's Fine Library or Bank Table. Mahogany Finish or Walnut.

Leather or Fine Cloth Cover, Gilt Drop Bar Handles, Gilt Keys, Carved and Veneered, size, 24 x 40 inches.

Price, F. O. B.... ....$28 00

No. 347½. Tyler's Fancy Parlor Cabinet Desk. Walnut, Antique Oak or Cherry Mahogany Finish.

Size, 43x26 inches, Ornamental Shelf on Top, Billiard Cloth Sliding Table, an Elegant Cylinder Cabinet Desk, Portable. Weight, 100 lbs.

Price, F. O. B.... ....$40 00

LOUNGES.

(WITH BOARD BOTTOMS.)

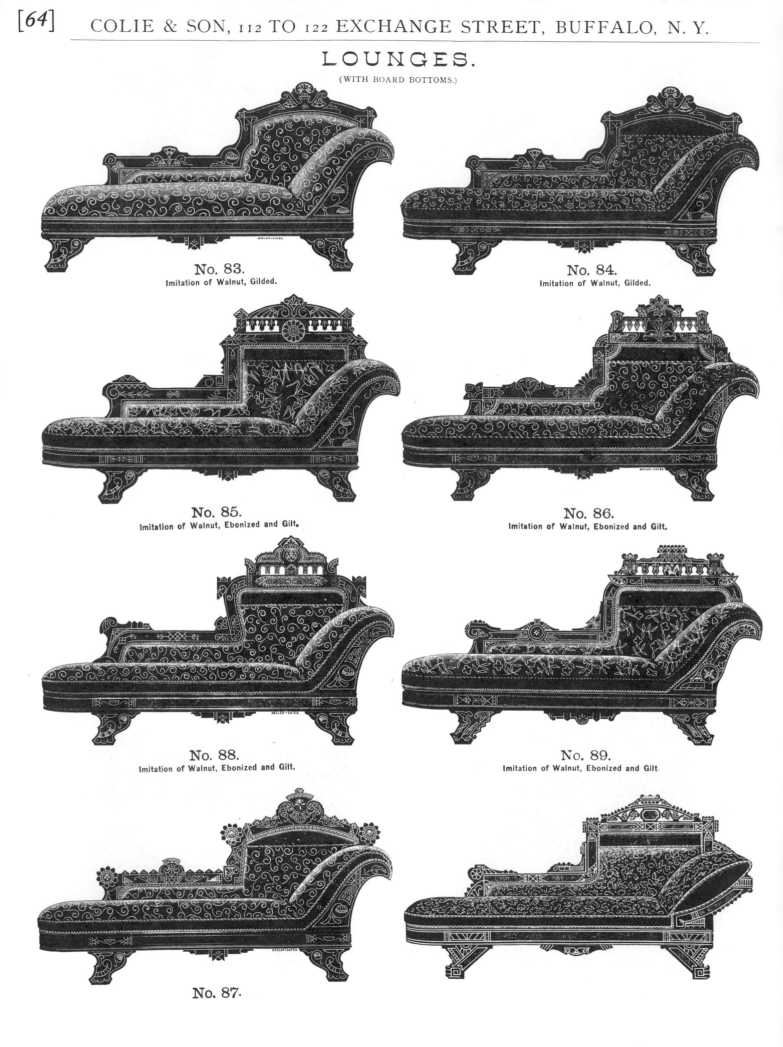

No. 83.
Imitation of Walnut, Gilded.

No. 84.
Imitation of Walnut, Gilded.

No. 85.
Imitation of Walnut, Ebonized and Gilt.

No. 86.
Imitation of Walnut, Ebonized and Gilt.

No. 88.
Imitation of Walnut, Ebonized and Gilt.

No. 89.
Imitation of Walnut, Ebonized and Gilt.

No. 87.

KILBORN WHITMAN & CO.,
46 CANAL ST., BOSTON, U.S.A.
PARLOR FURNITURE MANUFACTURERS.

51 86 4

50 55

57 47

39 23½ 62

59 64 25 51

1 2 3 46

KILBORN WHITMAN & CO.,
PARLOR FURNITURE MANUFACTURERS,
34 Canal St., Boston, Mass., U.S.A.

50½

26

47

95

80

106

42

52

91

48

No. 954. Morris Chair. Solid Golden Oak, upholstered in good quality fancy figured velour.
Each $5.40

No. 953. Morris Chair. Solid Golden Oak, elegantly carved, shaped front, upholstered in good quality fancy velour.
Each $6.11

No. 930. Morris Chair. Solid Golden Oak, shaped front, claw feet, upholstered in good quality of fancy figured velour.
Each $7.75

No. 894. Morris Chair. Solid Golden Oak, elegantly carved front, upholstered in good quality of fancy figured velour.
Each $8.85

The Backs on these Chairs Adjust to Any Angle Desired.

(Though the Cuts are Smaller Than the Large Ones the Chairs are Equally as Large.)

No. 7674. Morris Chair. Golden Quartered Oak, elegantly carved front and claw feet, piano polish, upholstered in best quality fancy figured velour.
Each $12.85
(This chair is as large as any of the following.)

No. 999. Morris Chair. Golden Quartered Oak or Mahogany finish, piano polish, upholstered in best quality of fancy figured velour.
Each $8.75

No. 971. Morris Chair. Golden Quartered Oak or Mahogany finish, piano polish, upholstered in best quality fancy figured velour.
Each $15.95

No. 970. Morris Chair. Golden Quartered Oak or genuine Mahogany, piano polish, upholstered in best quality fancy figured velour.
Oak $22.25
Mahogany 28.15

The Backs on These Chairs Adjust to Any Angle Desired.

No. 969. Morris Chair. Golden Quartered Oak or Mahogany finish, piano polish, upholstered in best quality fancy figured velour.
Each $10.35

No. 972. Morris Chair. Golden Quartered Oak or Mahogany finish, piano polish, upholstered in best quality fancy figured velour.
Each $12.60

No. 998. Morris Chair. Golden Quartered Oak or Mahogany finish, piano polish, upholstered in best quality fancy figured velour.
Each $13.30

No. 990. Morris Chair. Golden Quartered Oak or Genuine Mahogany, piano polish, upholstered in best quality fancy figured velour.
Oak .... $24.45　　Mahogany $29.50

The Backs on These Chairs Adjust to Any Angle Desired.

See Special Discount on Inside of Cover

For Explanation of Grades See Page 13

Desk, Reception or Bed Room Chairs

No. 887. Victoria. Both ends let down at any angle desired and independent of each other. Turkish tufted, spring edges, Golden Quartered Oak, claw feet, 28 inches deep, 75 inches long.

Grade A..........$18.45	Grade D..........$19.75	Grade H..........$22.00
Grade B..........19.00	Grade F..........20.75	Grade K..........24.50

No. 810. Victoria. Both ends let down at any angle desired and independent of each other. Turkish tufted, spring edges, Golden Quartered Oak, elegantly carved, 29 inches deep, 75 inches long.

Grade A..........$23.25	Grade D..........$25.00	Grade H..........$28.25
Grade B..........23.75	Grade F..........26.25	Grade K..........31.50

No. 831. Victoria. Both ends let down at any angle desired and independent of each other. Turkish tufted, spring edges, Golden Quartered Oak or Solid Mahogany frame, 28 inches deep, 74 inches long.

Grade A..........$25.00	Grade D..........$26.75	Grade H..........$29.50
Grade B..........25.50	Grade F..........27.50	Grade K..........31.50

No. 755. Victoria. Both ends let down at any angle desired and independent of each other. Turkish tufted, spring edges, Golden Quartered Oak frame, 28 inches deep, 77 inches long.

Grade A..........$27.50	Grade D..........$29.25	Grade H..........$32.50
Grade B..........28.00	Grade F..........30.50	Grade K..........35.75

No. 836
Price..................$3.25

No. 700
Price..................$3.25

No. 702
Price..................$3.70

Golden Quartered Oak or Mahogany finish. Piano polish.

No. 714
Price..............$4.45

No. 708
Price..............$4.85

No. 704
Price..................$5.20

Golden Quartered Oak, Mahogany finish, or Natural Maple. Rush seats, piano polish.

No. 706
Rush Seat. Price.....$5.55

No. 835
Saddle Seat. Price.....$4.10

No. 814 1-2
Saddle Seat. Price..........$7.40

Golden Quartered Oak, Mahogany finish or Natural Maple. Piano polish.

Genuine Mahogany only. Piano polish.

No. 117. DINING, OR PILLAR EXTENSION TABLE.

Length, 8, 10, 12, 14, or 16 feet; width, 4 feet.

Unique and elegant Design, with rich Carving.

Walnut, Quartered Oak, or Mahogany.

No. **147.** PEDESTAL.

Length 20 inches; width 14 inches; height 3 feet.

Elaborately carved Storks. Engraved Rim, Column, and Base.

MAHOGANY, OR EBONIZED.

No. **146.** PEDESTAL.

Length 14 inches; width 14 inches; height 38 inches.

Richly carved Capital, Column, and Base.

MAHOGANY, OR EBONIZED.

No. 48. ORNAMENTAL TABLE.

Length, 3 feet; width, 24 inches.

Italian Renaissance with elaborate Carving. Wood top.

Walnut, Imitation Mahogany, Quartered Oak, or Mahogany.

No. 62. ORNAMENTAL TABLE.

Length, 40 inches; width, 26 inches.

Renaissance style with rich and ornate Carving. Wood top.

Walnut, Imitation Mahogany, Quartered Oak, or Mahogany.

No. 143. ORNAMENTAL TABLE.

Length, 30 inches; width, 30 inches.

A finely carved Modern Antique, with massive proportions. Wood top.

Walnut, Quartered Oak, or Mahogany.

No. 114. DINING, OR PILLAR EXTENSION TABLE.

Length, 8, 10, 12, 14, 16, or 18 feet; width, 4 feet.

Heavy Base, rich with Carving.

The Top when closed is made either 4 feet or 5 feet long.

Walnut, Quartered Oak, or Mahogany.

No. 15. ORNAMENTAL TABLE.

Length, 32 inches; width, 22 inches.

Molded Rim. Fluted Base. Wood top.

Walnut, Imitation Mahogany, Quartered Oak, or Mahogany.

KENT FURNITURE MANUFACTURING CO., Grand Rapids, Mich.

LOOK AT THIS
ONLY $7.
FOR A
FINELY FINISHED TABLE.

E. M. Tebbetts
Dexter
Maine

CENTER TABLE.—TOP 22 x 32.
NO. 109. MAHOGANY FINISH.
NO. 110. WALNUT FINISH.
NO. 111. OAK.

TABLE. Top 24 x 34. Polished Top.
No. 116. Maple, Mahogany Finish.
No. 116. Maple, Walnut Finish.
No. 116. Ash, Natural Finish.
No. 116. Ash, Antique Finish.

CENTER TABLE. Top 27 x 27. Polish Finish.
No. 113. Birch, Mahogany Finish
No. 113. Birch, Walnut Finish

Top, 20 x 28.
No. 102. Maple, Walnut Finish.

CENTER TABLE. Top 20 x 24. Sh'pped K. D.
No. 119. Maple, Mahogany Finish.

Top, 17 x 24.
No. . Maple, Walnut Finish.

M. & H. SCHRENKEISEN,
23 TO 29 ELIZABETH STREET,
Corner Canal Street,
NEW YORK.

MARBLE TOP TABLES.

BARDWELL, ANDERSON & CO., BOSTON, MASS.   FOR THE TRADE ONLY.

No. 18. ORNAMENTAL TABLE.

Length, 30 inches; width, 30 inches.

Egyptian composite in new outline and rich Carving. Wood top.

Walnut, Imitation Mahogany, Quartered Oak, or Mahogany.

No. 9, in Walnut, 14 x 20.

No. 8, in Walnut, 18 x 24.

No. 5, in Walnut, 22 x 32.

No. 7, in Walnut, 21 x 30.

NOTE.—Sizes above are actual sizes of tops.   Marble measurement is 2 inches more each way.

No. **22½.** PLUSH-TOP TABLE.

Length 31 inches; width 21 inches.

Richly carved and engraved Rim.   Massive Columns and Base elaborately carved.

Plain, or Embossed Silk Plush top raised above the surrounding border.

WALNUT, CHERRY, OR EBONIZED.

No. **65.** CHAMBER-SET TABLE, OR BIBLE STAND.

Length 18 inches; width 14 inches.

Mitered and dovetailed Corners.   Fluted Rim and molded Base.   Marble, or Wood top.

WALNUT, OR ASH.

No. **56.** CENTER TABLE.

Length 32 inches; width 22 inches.

Nicely molded and carved Rim, with Drawer.   Heavy Base, fluted, veneered, and carved.   Marble, or Wood top.

WALNUT, OR CHERRY.

No. **144½.** ORNAMENTAL TABLE.

Length 26 inches; width 18 inches.

Richly engraved Base, shelf, and ornate Rim.

CHERRY, EBONIZED, WALNUT, OR MAHOGANY.

No. **42.** CHESS, OR CHECKER TABLE.

Length 18 inches; width 18 inches.

Real Marquetry top of Ebony and White Holly, inclosed by a heavy border of costly fancy woods.   Carved Base.

EBONIZED, OR WALNUT BASE.

No. **162.** CENTER TABLE.

Length, 30 inches; width, 20 inches.

Romanesque style, with burl on Rim and Base.   Marble, or Wood Top.

Walnut, Imitation Mahogany, or Quartered Oak.

No. **95½.** PLUSH-TOP TABLE.

Length 29 inches; width 19 inches.

Richly carved Rim.   Fluted and finely carved Columns and Base.   Plain, or Embossed Silk Plush top raised above the surrounding border.

CHERRY, OR EBONIZED.

No. **111.** ORNAMENTAL TABLE, OR MUSIC STAND.

Length, 22 inches; width, 22 inches.

Molded Rim and turned Base.   Two Shelves.   Wood top.

Walnut, Imitation Mahogany, Quartered Oak, or Mahogany.

BOUQUET, OR BIBLE STANDS.

No. 41.   No. 112.   No. 24.   No. 21.

No. 139. ORNAMENTAL TABLE.

Diameter 16 inches.

Engraved Base.   Wood top.

WALNUT.

Diameter 16 inches.

Engraved and fluted Base.   Wood top.

WALNUT.

Length 14 inches; width 12 inches.

Spiral carving on Base.   Wood top.

WALNUT, CHERRY, OR EBONIZED.

Diameter 15 inches.

Carved and fluted Base.   Wood top.

WALNUT.

Length, 27 inches; width, 27 inches.

Renaissance in full detail, with rich Carving.

Walnut, Imitation Mahogany, Quartered Oak, or Mahogany.

No. **172.** CENTER TABLE.   No. **25.** CENTER TABLE.   No. **144.** ORNAMENTAL TABLE.

Length 32 inches; width 22 inches.

Finely carved Rim and Base.   Marble, or Wood top.

WALNUT.

This Table is also made 34 inches long, 24 inches wide, and is numbered **173.**

Length 31 inches; width 21 inches.

Carved and molded Rim.   Richly carved Base.   Marble, or Wood top.

WALNUT.

Length 18 inches; width 18 inches.

Richly engraved Base, shelf, and ornate Rim.

CHERRY, EBONIZED, WALNUT, OR MAHOGANY.

No. **133.** LIBRARY TABLE.

No. 150. ORNAMENTAL TABLE.

Length 5 feet; width 30 inches.

Wood top, or Cloth top, with French burl veneer border.   Five Drawers, locks, and fancy plated key.   Rich and elaborate carving on Case.
Massive Columns and Base richly carved.

MAHOGANY, OR WALNUT.

Length, 40 inches; width, 29 inches.

Romanesque style, with massive and beautiful proportions.   Wood top.

Walnut, Quartered Oak, or Mahogany.

No. 26.   ORNAMENTAL TABLE.

Length, 24 inches; width, 24 inches.

Top engraved; molded Shelf. Spiral turning on Legs. Wood top.

Walnut, Imitation Mahogany, Quartered Oak, or Mahogany.

No. 85½.   DESK, or SECRETARY.   Open.

Length, 32 inches; width, 20 inches; height, 6¾ feet.

The Base of this Secretary is the same Desk as that described on pages 74 and 75.

Walnut, Imitation Mahogany, or Quartered Oak.

No. 166.   ORNAMENTAL TABLE.

Length, 35 inches; width, 24 inches.

Molded Rim, and Shelf. Turned and molded Legs, with carved Feet. Wood top.

Walnut, Imitation Mahogany, Quartered Oak, or Mahogany.

No. 39.   ORNAMENTAL TABLE.

Length, 3 feet; width, 24 inches.

A pleasing Design, in Ionic style. Carved Base and fluted Columns. Wood top.

Walnut, Imitation Mahogany, Quartered Oak, or Mahogany.

No. 30.   ORNAMENTAL TABLE.

No. 27.   ORNAMENTAL TABLE.

Length, 24 inches; width, 24 inches.

Engraved Rim and molded Shelf. Spiral turning on Legs. Wood top.

Walnut, Imitation Mahogany, Quartered Oak, or Mahogany.

No. 85½.   DESK, or SECRETARY.   Closed.

No. 91.   DESK.

Length, 32 inches; width, 18 inches; height, 4½ feet.

A beautiful Design in Colonial style. Richly carved Front. Paneled Ends. Five Drawers, locks, and keys.

Walnut, Imitation Mahogany, or Quartered Oak.

No. 86.   DESK.

Length, 4 feet; width, 18 inches; height, 7½ feet.

American adaptation of Renaissance style. Bevel French plate 24 x 22. Eight Drawers, and a secret Receptacle.

Walnut, or Quartered Oak.

No. 46.   ORNAMENTAL TABLE.

No. 142.   ORNAMENTAL TABLE.

No. 54.   ORNAMENTAL TABLE.

Length, 24 inches; width, 24 inches.

Molded Rim and Shelf. Fluted Columns. Wood top.

Walnut, Imitation Mahogany, Quartered Oak, or Mahogany.

Length, 28 inches; width, 28 inches.

Massive, Colonial Design, with carved Rim and Base. Fluted Columns   Wood top.

Walnut, Imitation Mahogany, Quartered Oak, or Mahogany.

No. 15.   ORNAMENTAL TABLE.

No. 75.   ORNAMENTAL TABLE.

No. 100.   ORNAMENTAL TABLE.

Length, 32 inches; width, 22 inches.

Molded Rim. Fluted Base. Wood top.

Walnut, Imitation Mahogany, Quartered Oak, or Mahogany.

Length, 26 inches; width, 26 inches.

Attractive design, in Romanesque Style. Carved Columns, and Feet. Wood top.

This Table is also made with heavy brass claw Feet, holding glass balls, and is numbered **101**.

Walnut, Imitation Mahogany, Quartered Oak, or Mahogany.

No. 140.   ORNAMENTAL TABLE.

No. 151.   ORNAMENTAL TABLE.

No. 14.   ORNAMENTAL TABLE.

Length, 24 inches; width, 24 inches.

Molded Rim. Spiral turning on Legs. Carved Feet. Wood top.

This Table is also made with a brass rail around the Shelf, and is numbered **141**.

Walnut, Imitation Mahogany, Quartered Oak, or Mahogany.

Length, 32 inches; width, 22 inches.

Richly carved Base, with Shelf. Wood top.

Walnut, Imitation Mahogany, Quartered Oak, or Mahogany.

No. 62. ORNAMENTAL TABLE.

Length, 40 inches; width, 26 inches.

Renaissance style with rich and ornate Carving. Wood top.

Walnut, Imitation Mahogany, Quartered Oak, or Mahogany.

No. 43. ORNAMENTAL TABLE.

Length 20 inches; width 16 inches.

Wood top, with molded edge richly carved.

WALNUT, MAHOGANY, CHERRY, OR EBONIZED.

No. 48. ORNAMENTAL TABLE.

Length, 3 feet; width, 24 inches.

Italian Renaissance with elaborate Carving. Wood top.

Walnut, Imitation Mahogany, Quartered Oak, or Mahogany.

No. 57. ORNAMENTAL TABLE.

Length, 28 inches; width, 28 inches.

Modern, antique Design with expression and thought in every line. Wood top.

Walnut, Imitation Mahogany, Quartered Oak, or Mahogany.

No. 139. ORNAMENTAL TABLE.

Length 30 inches; width 24 inches.

Molded Rim, and carved and molded Base. Wood top.

CHERRY, OR WALNUT.

No. 153. ORNAMENTAL TABLE.

Diameter of Top, when open, 3 feet; when closed, 13 inches.

Modern antique style, with new construction. Wood top.

Walnut, Imitation Mahogany, Quartered Oak, or Mahogany.

No. 59. ORNAMENTAL TABLE.

No. 28. ORNAMENTAL TABLE.

Length, 30 inches; width, 30 inches.

Engraved Rim and molded Shelf. Spiral turning on Legs. Wood top.

Walnut, Imitation Mahogany, Quartered Oak, or Mahogany.

No. 152. ORNAMENTAL TABLE.

Length, 24 inches; width, 24 inches.

Fluted Columns and carved Feet. Two Shelves. Wood top.

Walnut, Imitation Mahogany, Quartered Oak, or Mahogany.

Length, 26 inches; width, 26 inches.

Engraved Rim and Shelf. Spiral turning on Legs. Wood top.

Walnut, Imitation Mahogany, Quartered Oak, or Mahogany.

MARBLE TOP TABLES.

No. 102—Size 23½ x 17.
No. 103—Size 28 x 20.

No. 61—Size 29 x 20½.
No. 62—Size 33 x 24.

No. 70—Size 28 x 20.
A very strong table, and looks much better than
engraving represents.

No. 82—Size 28 x 20.
Has a solid bottom.

No. 33—Size 29 x 20½.

No. 31—Size 29 x 20½.
No. 51—Size 33 x 24.

THE SIZES QUOTED ARE THE ACTUAL SIZES OF THE MARBLE TOPS.

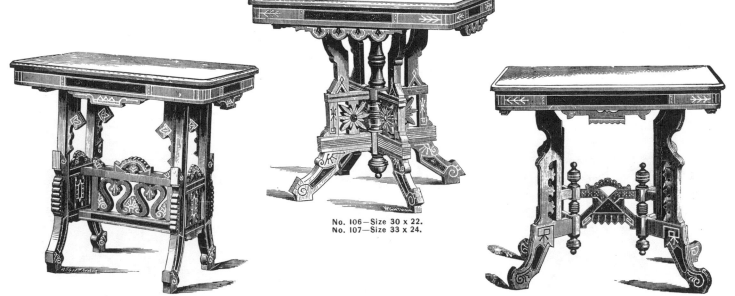

No. 101—Size 28 x 20.

No. 106—Size 30 x 22.
No. 107—Size 33 x 24.

No. 113—Size 30 x 22.

A PAGE FULL OF PARLOR TABLE BARGAINS

(While the cuts are small, the Tables are all regular table height.)

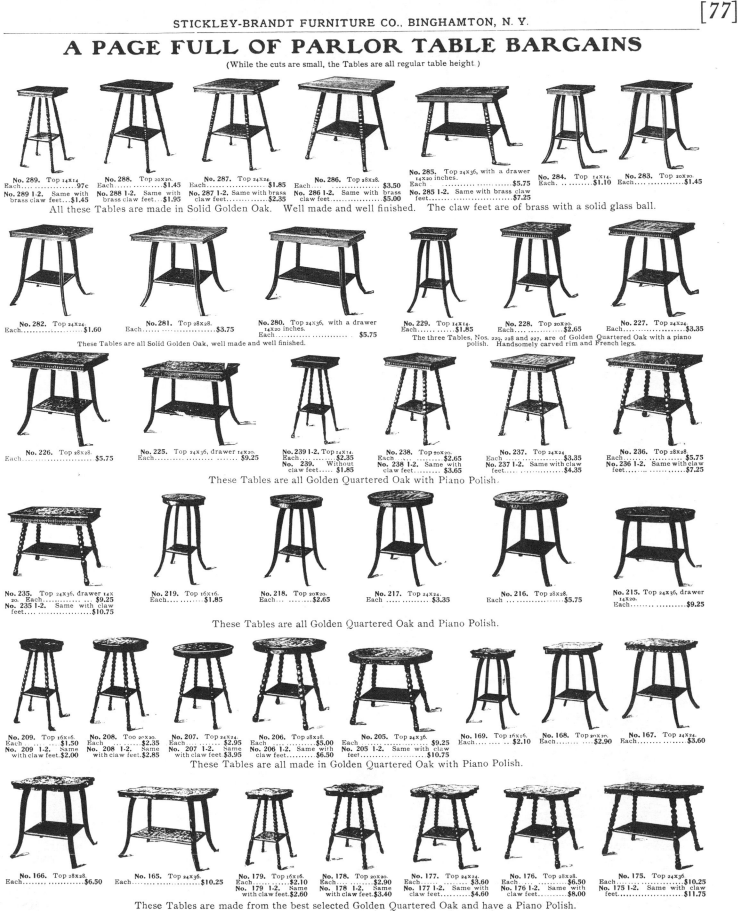

No. 289. Top 14x14.
Each...................97c
No. 289 1-2. Same with brass claw feet...$1.45

No. 288. Top 20x20.
Each................$1.45
No. 288 1-2. Same with brass claw feet...$1.95

No. 287. Top 24x24.
Each................$1.85
No. 287 1-2. Same with brass claw feet...........$2.35

No. 286. Top 28x28.
Each................$3.50
No. 286 1-2. Same with brass claw feet...........$5.00

No. 285. Top 24x36, with a drawer 14x20 inches.
Each...................$5.75
No. 285 1-2. Same with brass claw feet...................$7.25

No. 284. Top 14x14.
Each............$1.10

No. 283. Top 20x20.
Each................$1.45

All these Tables are made in Solid Golden Oak. Well made and well finished. The claw feet are of brass with a solid glass ball.

No. 282. Top 24x24.
Each...................$1.60

No. 281. Top 28x28.
Each................$3.75

No. 280. Top 24x36, with a drawer 14x20 inches.
Each................. $5.75

These Tables are all Solid Golden Oak, well made and well finished.

No. 229. Top 14x14.
Each...................$1.85

No. 228. Top 20x20.
Each................$2.65

No. 227. Top 24x24.
Each................$3.35

The three Tables, Nos. 229, 228 and 227, are of Golden Quartered Oak with a piano polish. Handsomely carved rim and French legs.

No. 226. Top 28x28.
Each................. $5.75

No. 225. Top 24x36, drawer 14x20.
Each................. $9.25

No. 239 1-2. Top 14x14.
Each...................$2.35
No. 239. Without claw feet..... $1.85

No. 238. Top 20x20.
Each................$2.65
No. 238 1-2. Same with claw feet............$3.65

No. 237. Top 24x24
Each................$3.35
No. 237 1-2. Same with claw feet................$4.35

No. 236. Top 28x28
Each................$5.75
No. 236 1-2. Same with claw feet..............$7.25

These Tables are all Golden Quartered Oak with Piano Polish.

No. 235. Top 24x36, drawer 14x20.
Each................. $9.25
No. 235 1-2. Same with claw feet................$10.75

No. 219. Top 16x16.
Each...................$1.85

No. 218. Top 20x20.
Each................$2.65

No. 217. Top 24x24.
Each............. $3.35

No. 216. Top 28x28.
Each................. $5.75

No. 215. Top 24x36, drawer 14x20.
Each................. $9.25

These Tables are all Golden Quartered Oak and Piano Polish.

No. 209. Top 16x16.
Each................. $1.50
No. 209 1-2. Same with claw feet.$2.00

No. 208. Too 20x20.
Each................$2.35
No. 208 1-2. Same with claw feet.$2.85

No. 207. Top 24x24.
Each................$2.95
No. 207 1-2. Same with claw feet.$3.95

No. 206. Top 28x28.
Each................$5.00
No. 206 1-2. Same with claw feet.........$6.50

No. 205. Top 24x36.
Each................. $9.25
No. 205 1-2. Same with claw feet...................$10.75

No. 169. Top 16x16.
Each......... $2.10

No. 168. Top 20x20.
Each......... $2.90

No. 167. Top 24x24.
Each................$3.60

These Tables are all made in Golden Quartered Oak with Piano Polish.

No. 166. Top 28x28.
Each................. $6.50

No. 165. Top 24x36.
Each................$10.25

No. 179. Top 16x16.
Each................$2.10
No. 179 1-2. Same with claw feet.$2.60

No. 178. Top 20x20.
Each................$2.90
No. 178 1-2. Same with claw feet.$3.40

No. 177. Top 24x24.
Each................$3.60
No. 177 1-2. Same with claw feet.........$4.60

No. 176. Top 28x28.
Each................$6.50
No. 176 1-2. Same with claw feet.........$8.00

No. 175. Top 24x36.
Each................$10.25
No. 175 1-2. Same with claw feet...................$11.75

These Tables are made from the best selected Golden Quartered Oak and have a Piano Polish.

See Special Discount on Inside Cover

MARBLE TOP TABLES.

No. 104—Size 30 x 22.
No. 105—Size 33 x 24.

No. 108 - Size 30 x 22.
No. 109—Size 33 x 24.

No. 110—Size 33 x 24.

No. 111—Size 33 x 24.

THE SIZES QUOTED ARE THE ACTUAL SIZES OF THE MARBLE TOPS.

PATENT ROCKERS AND ADJUSTABLE CHAIRS COMBINED.

No. 20.   No. 61.   No. 62.   No. 64.

102

104

113

114

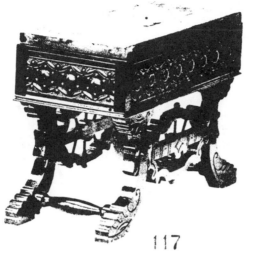

117

115

109

110

112

80

82

LIBRARY TABLES.

LIBRARY TABLES.

No. **55**, Medium Size, Walnut, 22 x 36.

No. **48**, Large Size, Walnut, 26 x 48, with 2 drawers.

One Armchair.

One Corner Chair.

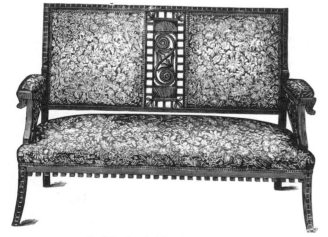

One Sofa.   Length of Front Rail, 4 ft. 6 inches.

No. **162**, Suite consisting of six pieces.

Two Side Chairs.

One Fancy Chair.

Made in Imitation Mahogany, Cocobola, or Ebony.

—OFFICE OF—
M. & H. SCHRENKEISEN,
23 TO 29 ELIZABETH STREET.
Corner Canal Street,
NEW YORK.

◁ SPRING OF 1885. ▷

To Our Customers :

Your attention is again directed to a New Catalogue herewith presented to the Trade, in which will be found a portion of our large and varied line.

When Photographs are wanted of goods not shown in this Catalogue, state which particular kind is desired.

Dealers are most cordially invited to call when in town, and inspect our complete stock.

We remain,

Yours very truly,

M. & H. SCHRENKEISEN.

Doing a Strictly Wholesale Business, we accept no Orders

from Private Parties, unless introduced by Dealers.

MARBLE TOP TABLES.

No. **9.** in Walnut, 14 x 20.

No. **8,** in Walnut, 18 x 24.

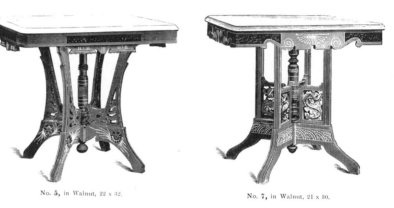

No. **5,** in Walnut, 22 x 32.

No. **7,** in Walnut, 21 x 30.

NOTE.—Sizes above are actual sizes of tops.   Marble measurement is 2 inches more each way.

No. **1,** Pedestal, 14 x 20.

No. **2,** Pedestal, 14 x 20.

Bedroom Furniture and Sets

New England Furniture Company,

GRAND RAPIDS, MICHIGAN,

MANUFACTURERS OF

SOAK ∴ CHAMBER ∴ UITES,

And BEDS, BUREAUS, TABLES and WASHSTANDS, in Antique and Imitation Cherry, Walnut and Mahogany.

SUITE No. 117½. OAK, FINISHED ANTIQUE OR 16TH CENTURY.
BED, 6 feet 6 inches by 4 feet 6 inches.
BUREAU, 22 x 48. French Plates, 28 x 34 and 16 x 26.
COMMODE, 20 x 36.

Furniture, June, 1890, page 3.

S. C. SMALL & CO.

MANUFACTURERS OF THE

BOND PATENT SANITARY WASHSTAND

Most Useful Invention of the Age.   Running Water without Sewer Connection.

7I and 73 Portland Street, Boston, Mass.

No. 1.   Hotel Washstand.

Without Cover,	. . .	$ 23.00
With Cover,	. . .	25.00

Size 20 in. wide, 3 ft. 6 in. high.

No. 2.   WASHSTAND.

Size 20 in. wide, 3 ft. 6 in. high, $ 30.00

Decorated Bowl, $2.00 extra.

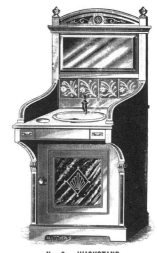

No. 3.   WASHSTAND.

Size 24 in. wide, 5 ft. high,	.	$ 40.00
With Tiles,	. . .	43.00

Decorated Bowl, $2.00 extra.

No. 1 Hotel Washstand in Sections, showing Construction.

The Mechanism is very simple and not liable to get out of order.

Duplicate parts can be furnished.

No. 4.   COMMODE, $45.00.

This includes Set of Crockery worth $10.00. We have Sets from $10.00 to $20.00 according to Decoration.

For altering commodes and furnishing four pieces of Crockery and Pail, $20.00.

WASHSTANDS.

Nos. 54, 55, 60—Top, 32 x 18.

No. 64—Top, 37 x 18.

Nos. 54, 55, 60—Top, 32 x 18. Glass, 16 x 24.

No. 64—Top, 37 x 18. Glass, 16 x 28.

Nos. 67, 68—Top, 39 x 19.

CRON, KILLS & CO., PIQUA, OHIO.

CRON, KILLS & CO., PIQUA, OHIO.

NO. 73. CHIFFONIER.

Antique. Oil Finish.

French Bevel Glass 8x8.

Width, 2 feet 8 in.

Depth, 4 foot 4 in.

Height, 4 feet 4 in.

NO. 74. CHIFFONIER.

French Bevel Glass 10x12.

Antique Finish.

Width 3 feet 2 in.

Depth, 1 foot 4 in.

Height, 4 feet 4 in.

WASHSTANDS.

No. 58—Top, 30 x 17. Glass, 20 x 24.

No. 50—Top, 32 x 18. Glass, 20 x 24.

No. 59—Top, 32 x 18. Glass, 22 x 24.

WASHSTANDS.

No. 66—Top, 32 x 18. Glass, 22 x 24.

No. 53—Top, 32 x 18. Glass, 22 x 24.

No. 52—Top, 32 x 18. Glass, 22 x 24.

Sample and Salesroom of the Princess Dressing Case Co.,
COR. CANAL AND BRIDGE STS., GRAND RAPIDS, MICH.

NO. 104, Closed and Open. Top, 24 x 48. Reversible Mirror, 20 x 30. Marble, 22½ x 22½. Height of Wardrobe, 45 in.; Width, 21 in.; Depth, 17 in.
PRICE, with Panel in Wardrobe Door, $45.00. With Bevel Plate Mirror 17 x 30, $48.50.

An elegant piece, especially adapted to boarding and apartment houses, rooms in hotels used by regular boarders or liable to be needed as sitting rooms or parlors in the day-time. Also adapted to Sanitarium and boarding school use. Three pieces in one. Note the wonderful saving in space.

Room 10 feet square, furnished with **No. 16 Princess Dressing Case** and folding bed—both open for bedroom use.

A handsome Center Table—much better than the cut
represents.   Worthy to go into the finest residences
and stand beside the finest furniture.

NO. 11. Closed and Open. Top, 24 x 36. Marble, 16 x 18.
PRICE $24 00

Room 10 feet square, furnished with **No. 16 Princess Dressing Case** and ordinary Folding bed—both pieces closed-

NO. 14. Closed and Open. Top, 20 x 40. Reversible Mirror, 20 x 34. Marble, 19 x 19.

PRICE, $38 00.

A standard, serviceable piece. Good almost anywhere. All drawers can be used except small one under marble. Note places for brushes, combs, soap, towels, etc., at side of Mirror .

No. 7. Closed and Open. Top 22 x 27. Marble, 19 x 19. PRICE, $16 00

With Bevel Plate Mirror 18 x 20 in underside of top, PRICE, $19 00

This little piece is without equal where merely a concealed wash-stand is desired. It costs little if any more than a good marble top wash-stand. It contains an ample supply of water, and no washbowl, pitcher or slop jar need be purchased to accompany it. The cheapest and best thing of the kind in the world.

NO. 17.   Marble Top, 18½ x 22½.
PRICE,   -   - $18 00

No. 102.   Top, 24 x 48.   Wardrobe, 45 in. high, 23 in wide
and 22 in. deep.
Marble, 22½ x 22½.   Mirror in Door, 17 x 30.
PRICE,   -   -   - $43 00

The concealed feature is omitted in these pieces.   They are suitable for transient rooms in hotels, summer and winter resorts, private houses, etc.   They have all the elegance and convenience of stationary wash-stands, with no possibility of sewer gas.   No. 102 contains three pieces in one.   Note the saving of space and cost.   No crockery to break.   No injury to carpets from slopping of water when poured into slop jar.

NO. 9.   Closed and Open.   Top, 24 x 36.   Marble, 16 x 18.
PRICE, $20 00

An excellent Table for general use.   Good in a bedroom where one already has a dressing case, and very desirable in the hall or elsewhere on the ground floor where the bedrooms are all above.   Suitable for offices and stores.   Note the Splasher which protects articles on the table.

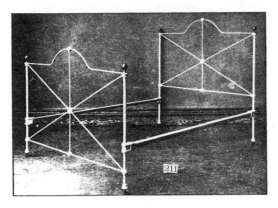

No. 211

White Enamel Iron Bed. 3 feet 6 inches, 4 foot, and 4 foot 6 inches wide. Lacquered brass knobs. 55 inches high.

Each..$3.50

No. 460. Chiffonier. White enamel or Golden Ash. Shaped top, 33x18 inches.
Each.................................$5.50
No. 455. Same, with swell top drawer.
Each.................................$6.00
No. 445. Same, with two swell top drawers.
Each.................................$6.50
No. 450. Full serpentine front..Each 8.90
For hat box in each like 447½ add..... .85

No. 499 1-2

Dresser. White Enamel or Golden ash Shaped top, 38x18 inches. French plate mirror 24x14 inches.
Each.................................$9.50

No. 499. Same, with glass running lengthwise instead of up and down
Each.................................$9.50

No. 496

Dresser. White Enamel or Golden Ash. Shaped top, 38x20. Swell top drawer. French bevel mirror 24x18.
Each.................................$11.50

No. 493. Same, with full serpentine front like 487½.
Each.................................$13.25

No. 459

Chiffonier. White Enamel and Golden Ash. Shaped top, 33x18 inches. French bevel mirror 20x12 inches.
Each...............................$8.50

No. 454. Same, with swell top drawer.
Each...............................$9.25
Hat box 85c extra.

No. 487 1-2

Dresser. White Enamel. Shaped top, 40x20 inches. Oval French bevel mirror 24x20 inches. Serpentine front.

Each...............................$15.25

No. 447 1-2. Chiffonier. White Enamel or Golden Ash. Full serpentine front and top, 33x20 inches. Oval French bevel mirror 20x16 inches. With hat box.
Each.................................$15.00
No. 447. Same. No hat box.... 14.00
No. 457. Same as 447. Straight front............................ 10.90
No. 457 1-2. Same as 447½. Straight front......................... 9.90

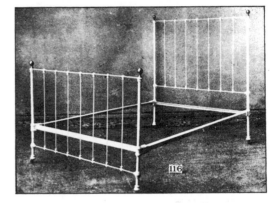

No. 116

White Enamel Iron Bed. 3 feet 6 inches, 4 foot, and 4 foot 6 inches wide. Lacquered brass knobs. 58 inches high.

Each..$3.95

No. 24

White Enamel Iron Bed. 3 feet 6 inches, 4 foot, and 4 foot 6 inches wide. Lacquered brass ornaments. 66 inches high.

Each..$5.80

No. 489. Dresser. White Enamel or Golden Ash. Full serpentine front and top, 38x20 inches. Oval French bevel mirror 24x20 inches.
Each.................................$15.00

No. 494. Same, with swell top drawer only............... 13.25

No. 492. Same, with two swell top drawers............... 13.75

No. 486

Dresser. White Enamel. Full serpentine front and top, 38x20 inches. Pattern French Bevel mirror 24x 20 inches.

Each.................................$15.50

No. 446 1-2

Chiffonier. White Enamel or Golden Ash. Full serpentine front and top, 33x20 inches. Pattern French bevel mirror 20x16 inches. With hat box.
Each.................................$14.50

No. 446. Same, no hat box...... 13.75

N. B.—Wash stands to match as follows: **No. 499.**   Straight front, 27x16 inches, **$4.50.**   **No. 494.**   Serpentine top drawer, 27x18 inches, **$5.00**
No. 483.   Full serpentine front, 31x19 inches, **$7.00.**

No. 999

Chiffonier. Base 33 x 18½. Five drawers. Solid Golden Oak.

Each..... .... $4.94

No. 998

Same, with hat box (like 996).

Each...................... .$5.50

No. 996

Chiffonier. Solid Golden Oak. Base 33x 18½ with hat box French bevel mirror 20x12.

Each.......... ....$8.50

No. 997

Same, without the hat box (like 999).

Each........ ....$8.25

No. 968

Chiffonier. Base is 32x18½ and has hat box. Pattern French bevel mirror 20x16. Made in Golden Quartered Oak, Bird's-eye Maple and Mahogany. Piano polish.

Oak...........................$14.50
Bird's-eye Maple or Mahogany.. 16.50

No. 970

Same, without hat box.

Oak...........................$13.95
Bird's-eye Maple or Mahogany.. 15.50

No. 967

Same, with double serpentine front. Base 33x19½. Mirror 22x16.

Oak...........................$19.50
Bird's-eye Maple or Mahogany.. 22.75

No. 980

Chiffonier. Base is 25x18. Full swell front with hat box. Pattern French bevel plate 18x14. Piano polish.

Golden Quartered Oak..........$14.50
Bird's-eye Maple or Mahogany.. 16.50

No. 977

Same, with straight front and top drawer divided into two serpentine shaped drawers.

Oak...........................$13.95
Bird's-eye Maple or Mahogany.. 15.50

No. 969

Chiffonier. Base is 3½x19½ inches. Pattern French bevel mirror 20x16 inches. Full serpentine front. Golden Quartered Oak, Bird's-eye Maple or Mahogany.

Oak. $16.50

Bird's-eye Maple or Mahogany. 19.00

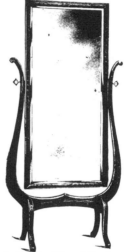

No. 972

Chiffonier. Base is 33x19 inches. Full serpentine front. With hat box. Pattern French bevel mirror 20x16 inches. Golden Quartered Oak, Bird's-eye Maple or Mahogany.

Oak...........................$17.25
Bird's-eye Maple or Mahogany.. 20.00

No. 983

Same, with straight front and two swell top drawers.

Oak...........................$16.00
Bird's-eye Maple or Mahogany.. 18.75

No. 964

Chiffonier. Base is 33x19½ inches. Full serpentine front. With hat box. Pattern French bevel mirror 20x16 inches. Golden Quartered Oak or Bird's-eye Maple or Mahogany.

Oak...........................$20.00
Bird's-eye Maple or Mahogany.. 23.25

No. 963

Same, without hat box.

Oak...........................$19.00
Bird's-eye Maple or Mahogany.. 20.75

No. 973

Chiffonier. Base is 36 x 19½ inches. Double serpentine front, Hat box in centre. Pattern French bevel mirror 24x16 Golden Quartered Oak, Bird's-eye Maple or Mahogany.

Oak.... .... $30.00

Bird's-eye Maple or Mahogany.. 32.75

No. 197. Cheval Glass. Golden Quartered Oak or Genuine Mahogany. Piano polish. French bevel plate mirror 50x22 in., 68 in. high, 34 in. wide.

Oak.....$25.75   Mahogany..$30.00

No. 196. Cheval Glass. Golden Quartered Oak or Genuine Mahogany. Piano polish. Pattern French bevel mirror 50x22, 70 in. high, 31 in. wide.

Oak,.........................$34.00
Mahogany.................... 38.00

KENT FURNITURE MANUFACTURING CO., GRAND RAPIDS, MICH.   **KENT FURNITURE MANUFACTURING CO., GRAND RAPIDS, MICH.**

BEDSTEAD 6 ft. 2 in. high, 4 ft. 6 in wide. Beveled Mirror, 24 x 30. Polished.
No. 236. Ash, Antique Finish.
No. 236. Ash, Natural Finish.
No. 236 Maple, Mahogany Finish.

BEDSTEAD, 5 ft. 6 in. high, 4 ft. 2 in. wide. Plain Mirror 15 x 26. Varnish Finish.
No. 255. Maple, Mahogany Finish.
No. 255. Maple, Walnut Finish.
No. 235. Ash.

Kent Furniture Manufacturing Co., Grand Rapids, Mich.

FOR THESE SUITES,

$19.00 for No. 238. $20.00 for No. 238½.

BEDSTEAD, 5 ft. 9 in. high, 4 ft. 2 in. wide. Beveled Mirror, 22x26.
Full Oil Rubbed Finish.

No. **238.** Mahogany Finish on Maple.
No. **238.** Walnut Finish on Maple.
No. **238.** Ash.

BEDSTEAD, 5 ft. 9 in. high, 4 ft. 6 in. wide. Beveled Mirror, 24x30.
Polish Finish.

No. **238½.** Mahogany Finish on Maple.
No. **238½.** Walnut Finish on Maple.
No. **238½.** Ash.

KENT FURNITURE MANUFACTURING CO., GRAND RAPIDS, MICH.

KENT FURNITURE MANUFACTURING CO., GRAND RAPIDS, MICH.

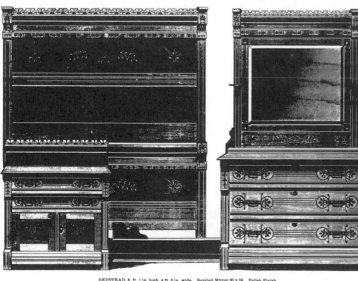

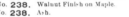

BEDSTEAD, 6 ft. 1 in. high, 4 ft. 6 in. wide. Beveled Mirror 30 x 24. Polish Finish

No. **248.** Maple, Mahogany Finish.
No. **248.** Maple, Walnut Finish.
No. **248.** Ash, Natural Finish.
No. **248.** Antique Finish on Ash.

WARDROBE, 6 ft. 10 in. high, 3 ft. 6 in. wide. Polish Finish.

No. **165.** Maple, Mahogany Finish.
No. **165.** Ash.   "
No. **165.** Antique

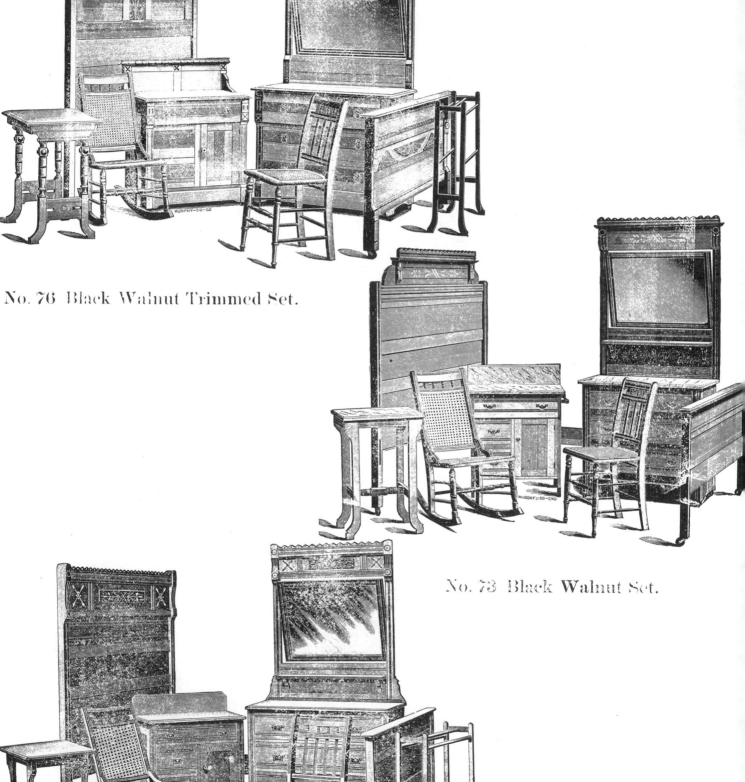

No. 76 Black Walnut Trimmed Set.

No. 78 Black Walnut Set.

No. 69 Cherry Set.

RING, MERRILL & TILLOTSON,
SAGINAW, MICH.

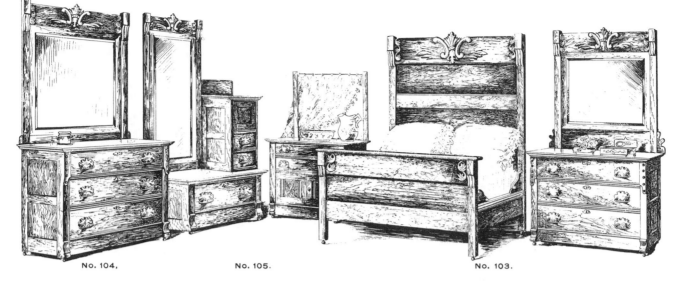

NO. 104,   No. 105.   No. 103.

KLINGMAN & LIMBERT, Selling Agents,
GRAND RAPIDS, MICH.

(OVER)

CRON, KILLS & CO., PIQUA, OHIO.   CRON, KILLS & CO., PIQUA, OHIO.

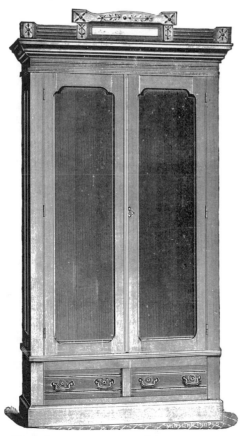

No. 45. Wardrobe,   -   -   Ash.
No. 46. Wardrobe,   -   -   Ash, Antique.
No. 47. Wardrobe,   -   -   Maple, Imitation Mahogany.
Portable. Oil Finish.
Height, 7 feet 6 in.   Width, 3 feet 9 in.   Depth 1 foot 6 in.

No. 50. Wardrobe,   -   -   -   Walnut.
No. 51. Wardrobe.   -   -   -   Oak, Antique.
Portable. Oil Finish.
Height, 7 feet 6 in.   Width, 3 feet 9 in.   Depth, 1 foot 6 in.

NO. 73. CHIFFONIER.

Antique. Oil Finish.

French Bevel Glass 8x8.

Height, 4 feet 4 in.   Width, 2 feet 8 in.   Depth, 4 foot 4 in.

No. 30. Wardrobe, - - - Imitation Walnut.

Portable. Oil Finish.

Height. 6 feet 3 in.   Width, 3 feet 3 in.   Depth, 1 foot 4 in.

NO. 70. CHIFFONIER.

Antique. Oil Finish.

Height, 4 feet 4 in.   Width, 2 feet 8 in.   Depth, 1 foot 4 in.

NO. 74. CHIFFONIER.

French Bevel Glass 10x12.

Antique Finish.

Height, 4 feet 4 in.   Width 3 feet 2 in.   Depth, 1 foot 4 in.

This cut represents my No. 42 1-2 Black Walnut Chamber Suit, 3 pieces, Marble tops, which I will ship to your address on receipt of order enclosing check for $30.00 NO CHARGES FOR PACKING. I will also refund $1.50 for mats and box when returned free. Or I will complete the suit to ten pieces, 5 chairs, table and towel rack, all walnut, for $39.00 and refund the same am't. for mats and box when returned free of expense.

Well made, and fine finish, stock thoroughly seasoned in my own kiln under personal supervision.

Bed and Dresser 6ft. 3in. high. Large Bureau and Commode. Double Hook on all Bed Rails.

S.E.BROWN

Chas. P. Whittle,
35 FULTON ST., - - - - - BOSTON.

N. B. The above will be forwarded to regular customers on usual terms.

(OVER.)

CRON, KILLS & CO., PIQUA, OHIO.

NO. 72. CHIFFONIER.

BROOKS BRO'S. MANUFACTURERS.
ROCHESTER, N. Y.

NUMBER 122 SUIT.

KENT FURNITURE MANUFACTURING CO., GRAND RAPIDS, MICH.

WARDROBE, 6 ft. 3 in. high, 3 ft. 6 in. wide. Polish Finish.
No. 164. Maple, Mahogany Finish.
No. 164. Maple, Walnut Finish.
No. 164. Ash, Natural Finish.
No. 164. Ash, Antique Finish.

No. 932   **Bed 932 and 900**   **No. 900**

Solid Golden Oak Chamber Suit. Bed is 5 ft. 10 in. length, 4 ft. 6 in. wide. Mirror is 12x20 in. Size of Dresser case is 40x18. Handsomely carved Bed and Dresser.

Three pieces	$11.00
Dresser	5.85
Bed	2.95
Wash Stand	3.50
Remember the Suit nets you only	9.90

Solid Golden Oak Chamber Suit. Bed is 5 ft. 10 in. high, 4 ft. 6 in. wide. Dresser has French bevel plate mirror 18x20 in. Size of Dresser base is 40x18 in. Handsomely carved Bed and Dresser.

Three pieces	$13.85
Dresser	8.10
Bed	4.25
Wash Stand	3.50

No. 899. Solid Golden Oak Suit. 3 pieces, bed, dresser and wash stand. Bed is 6 ft. 2 in. high, 4 ft. 6 in. wide. Dresser has French bevel plate mirror 24x20 inches. Base is 18x40 inches. Handsomely carved.

Three pieces	$16.75
Dresser	9.75
Bed	4.50
Wash Stand	3.50

No. 898. Solid Golden Oak Chamber Suit. 3 pieces. Bed, dresser and wash stand. Elegantly carved. Bed is 6 ft. 2 in. high, 4 ft. 6 in. wide. Dresser has serpentine shaped top. Base is 42x20. French bevel plate mirror 30x24.

Three pieces	$18.50
Dresser	10.50
Bed	4.50
Wash Stand	4.50

No. 898 1-2. Solid Golden Oak Chamber Suit. 3 pieces. Bed, dresser and wash stand. Elegantly carved. Bed is 6 ft. 2 in. high, 4 ft. 6 in. wide. Cheval dresser has French bevel plate mirror 36x18 inches. Base is 42x20 in., two long drawers, one small drawer and large roomy cupboard. Mirror tilts so that a lady can see full length.

Three pieces	$19.25
Dresser	11.25
Bed	4.50
Wash Stand	4.50

No. 897. Solid Golden Oak Chamber Suit. 3 pieces. Bed, dresser and wash stand. Elegantly carved. Bed is 6 ft. 4 in. high, 4 ft. 6 in. wide. Dresser base is 42x20 in. and has serpentine shaped top. French bevel plate mirror 30x24 in. Two top drawers.

Three pieces	$21.75
Dresser	12.50
Bed	5.00
Wash Stand	5.00

No. 376. Chamber Suit. Solid Golden Oak. Bed is 80 in. high, 4 ft. 6 in. wide. Dresser has full serpentine front and top with French legs. Base is 44x21 in. Glass frame has French bevel mirror 30x24 in.

Three pieces	$35.00
Dresser	23.50
Bed	7.50
Wash Stand	6.00

WARDROBE.

C. & A. KREIMER CO.

WASHSTANDS.

No. 56—Top, 39 x 19. Glass, 16 x 28.   No. 61—Top, 39 x 19. Glass, 22 x 26.   No. 63—Top, 39 x 19. Glass, 22 x 26.

BED,

Height, 10 ft. 10 in.   Slats, 4 ft. 9 in.

No. 52½ VICTORIA SUITE.

Walnut.

DRESSER.

Top, 48 x 22.   Glass, 30 x 34.

BED,

Height, 10 ft. 10 in.   Slats, 4 ft. 9 in.

No. 53½ VICTORIA SUITE.

Walnut.

DRESSER.

Top, 48 x 22.   Glass, 30 x 34.

BED,

Height, 10 ft. 7½ in.   Slats, 5 ft.

DRESSER,

Top, 52 x 24.   Glass, 34 x 40.

No. 56½
VICTORIA SUITE.
Walnut.

DRESSER,
Top, 48 x 22.   Glass, 30 x 34.

BED,
Height, 7 ft.   Slats, 4 ft. 8 in.

No. 66 SUITE.
Walnut or Natural Cherry.

DRESSER,
Top, 44 x 20.   Glass, 28 x 34.

No. 59 SUITE.
Walnut or Natural Cherry.

BED,
Height, 7 ft. 2 in.   Slats, 4 ft. 6 in.

. . . C. & A. KREIMER CO. . . .

BED,

Height 6 ft. 8 in.   Slats, 4 ft. 8 in.

No. 67 SUITE.
Antique Oak or Sixteenth Century.

DRESSER,

Top, 52 x 24 in.   Glass, 30 x 40 in.

BED,

Height, 6 ft. 8 in.   Slats, 4 ft. 8 in.

No. 68 SUITE.
Antique Oak or Sixteenth Century.

DRESSER,

Top, 52 x 24 in.   Glass, 30 x 40 in.

No. 550

Bed to match each of the following suits, Nos. 550, 549 and 547. Made in Golden Quartered Oak of best selected material. Elegantly carved. 6 feet 5 inches high, 4 feet 6 inches wide.

Price............................$7.50

No. 550

3 pieces. Bed, dresser and wash stand. All Golden Quartered Oak of best selected material. Elegantly carved. Dresser has two serpentine top drawers and serpentine shaped top. Base is 42x20 inches. Bevel plate mirror 20x24.

3 pieces.........................$25.00
Dresser...........................13.50
Bed..............................7.50
Wash stand.......................6.25

No. 549

3 pieces. Bed, dresser and wash stand. All Golden Quartered Oak of best selected material. Elegantly carved. Dresser has two serpentine top drawers and serpentine shaped top. Base is 42x20 inches. Bevel plate mirror 22x28 inches.

3 pieces.........................$27.00
Dresser...........................15.00
Bed (No. 550)....................7.50
Wash stand (No. 550).............6.25

No. 547

3 pieces. Bed, dresser and wash stand, All Golden Quartered Oak of best selected material. Elegantly carved. Dresser has two serpentine top drawers and serpentine shaped top. Base is 42x20 inches. Bevel plate mirror 24x30 inches.

3 pieces.........................$28.50
Dresser...........................16.50
Bed (No. 550)....................7.50
Wash stand (No. 550).............6.25

No. 550

Wash stand to match the previous suits Nos. 550, 549, 547. Golden Quartered Oak of best selected material. Base is 33x18 inches. Serpentine top and top drawer.

Price............................$6.25

No. 520

Bed to match each of the following suits, Nos. 520, 519 and 546. Made in Golden Quartered Oak of best selected material. Elegantly carved. 6 feet 6 inches high, 4 feet 6 inches wide.

Price............................$8.75

No. 520

3 pieces. Bed, dresser and wash stand. All Golden Quartered Oak of best selected material. Elegantly carved. Dresser has two serpentine top drawers and serpentine shaped top. Base is 44x22 inches. Bevel plate mirror 30x24 inches.

3 pieces.........................$32.00
Dresser...........................17.00
Bed..............................8.75
Wash stand.......................7.75

No. 519

3 pieces. Bed, dresser and wash stand. All Golden Quartered Oak of best selected material. Elegantly carved. Dresser has two serpentine top drawers and serpentine shaped top. Base is 44x22 inches. Bevel pattern plate mirror 30x24.

3 pieces.........................$33.00
Dresser...........................18.00
Bed (No. 520)....................8.75
Wash stand (520).................7.75

No. 546

3 pieces. Bed, dresser and wash stand. All Golden Quartered Oak of best selected material. Elegantly carved. Dresser has two serpentine top drawers and serpentine shaped top Base is 44x22. Oval French bevel plate mirror 30x24 inches.

3 pieces.........................$36.50
Dresser...........................21.00
Bed (No. 520)....................8.75
Wash stand (No. 520).............7.75

No. 520

Wash stand to match the previous suits Nos. 520, 519 and 546. Base is 34x18. Serpentine top and top drawers. Golden Quartered Oak of best selected material.

Price............................$7.75

No. 545

Three pieces. Bed, dresser and wash stand. All Golden Quartered Oak of best selected material. Elegantly carved. Dresser has two serpentine top drawers and serpentine shaped top. Base is 44x22 inches. Pattern French bevel plate mirror 30x24 inches.

Bed is massive and elegantly carved. Is 6 feet 8 inches high and 4 feet 6 inches wide. Best selected Golden Quartered Oak.

Three pieces......................$38.75
Dresser...........................22.00
Bed..............................9.75
Wash stand (No. 500)..............8.00

No. 500

Three pieces. Bed, dresser and wash stand. All Golden Quartered Oak of best selected material. Elegantly carved. Dresser has two shaped top drawers and full serpentine front, elegantly carved. Base is 46x22 inches. Pattern French bevel plate mirror 30x24.

Bed is elegantly carved. Has heavy shaped roll on head and foot. Is 6 feet 8 inches high and 4 feet 6 inches wide.

Three pieces......................$45.00
Dresser...........................26.00
Bed..............................12.00
Wash stand.......................8.00

No. 500

Wash stand to match these suits, Nos. 545 and 500. Base is 36x19. Shaped top drawer. Serpentine top. Golden Quartered Oak of best selected material.

Price............................$8.00

No. 815

Folding Bed. Golden Elm, (Quartered Oak panels) or Mahogany finish. Bed is 6 feet long, 4 feet wide, inside measurement.
Price.........................$15.00

No. 831

Same as 815 in ¾ size; 6 feet long and 3 feet 2 inches wide.
Price.........................$15.00

No. 822

Folding Bed. Golden Oak. Imitation quartered. Mirror 12x18. Size of bed 6 feet long, 4 feet wide inside measurement. Has two roomy cupboards on top which are not disturbed by the opening of the bed.
Price................$26.00

No. 714

Folding Bed. Quartered Golden Oak or Mahogany finish (Mahogany finish has Curly Birch panels.) French bevel mirror 40x18. Size of bed 6 feet, 2 inches by 4 feet, 2 inches, inside measurement. Piano polish.
Price................$32.25

No. 86

Combination Folding Bed. Has Wardrobe and writing desk combined. Golden Quartered Oak. French bevel mirror 20x18. Size of bed 6 feet, 3 inches x 4 feet, inside measurement.
Price................$35.50

The Freight on these Beds Would Cost You from $4.00 to $4.50. We Prepay Your Freight
ON APPLICATION WE WILL MAIL YOU OUR SPECIAL FOLDING BED CATALOG

Our Dressers are the Best. The Quality and Finish is fine. They will Match any Bed in this Catalog.

For Wash Stands see page 2.

No. 788

Dresser. Base has serpentine top drawer and is 38x20 inches. Pattern French bevel mirror 24x20 inches. Best selected Golden Quartered Oak, Bird's-eye Maple and Mahogany. Piano polish.
Oak..................$15.85
Bird's-eye Maple or Mahogany..........16.85

No. 789 1-2

Dresser. Base has full serpentine front and is 38x20 inches. Oval French bevel mirror 24x20 inches. Best selected Golden Quartered Oak, Bird's-eye Maple or Mahogany. Piano polish.
Oak..........$18.25
Bird's-eye Maple or Mahogany..........19.25

No. 794

Dresser. Base has two double serpentine top drawers and serpentine top and is 42x22 inches. Pattern French bevel mirror 30x24. Best selected Golden Quartered Oak, Bird's-eye Maple or Mahogany. Piano polish.
Oak..................$20.00
Bird's-eye Maple or Mahogany..........21.75

No. 794 1-2

Dresser. Base has two serpentine drawers and serpentine top and is 42x22 inches. Oval French bevel mirror 30x24. Best selected Golden Quartered Oak, Bird's-eye Maple or Mahogany.
Oak..................$20.00
Bird's-eye Maple or Mahogany..........21.75

No. 700

Dresser. Has two jewel drawers on top. One shaped top drawer and is 44x21 inches. Oval French bevel mirror 30x24. Made in Golden Quartered Oak of the best selected material.
Each..................$23.25

No. 800

Dresser. Base has full serpentine front and is 44x21 inches. Oval French plate mirror 30x24. Golden Quartered Oak of the best selected material.
Each..................$23.75

No. 793

Dresser. Base has full serpentine front and top and is 42x22 inches. Pattern French bevel mirror 30x24. Best selected Golden Quartered Oak, Bird's-eye Maple or Mahogany. Piano polish.
Oak..................$24.25
Bird's-eye Maple or Mahogany..............26.00

No. 793 1-2

Dresser. Base has full serpentine front and top and is 42x22 inches. Oval French Bevel mirror 30x24 inches. Best selected Golden Quartered Oak, Bird's-eye Maple or Mahogany. Piano polish.
Oak..................$24.25
Bird's-eye Maple or Mahogany..............26.00

No. 791 1-2

Dresser. Base has concave front and swell ends and is 44x22 inches. Oval French bevel mirror 30x24 inches. Best selected Golden Oak, Bird's-eye Maple or Mahogany. Piano polish.
Oak..................$26.50
Bird's-eye Maple or Mahogany..............28.50

No. 49. CHAMBER-SET TABLE, OR STAND.

Length, 20 inches; width, 16 inches.

Fluted Rim with mitered and dovetailed corners.   Molded Base.

Spiral turning on Columns.   One Shelf.   Marble, or Wood Top.

Walnut, Imitation Mahogany, Quartered Oak, or Mahogany.

No. **38.** CHAMBER-SET TABLE, OR BIBLE STAND.

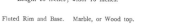

Length 20 inches; width 16 inches.

Fluted Rim and Base.   Marble, or Wood top.

WALNUT, CHERRY, OR ASH.

No. **65.** CHAMBER-SET TABLE, OR STAND.

Length, 18 inches; width, 14 inches.

Mitered and dovetailed corners on Rim.

Molded Base, with Shelf.   Marble, or Wood top.

Walnut, Imitation Mahogany, or Quartered Oak.

No. **65.** CHAMBER-SET TABLE, OR BIBLE STAND.

Length 18 inches; width 14 inches.

Mitered and dovetailed Corners.   Fluted Rim and molded Base.   Marble, or Wood top.

WALNUT, OR ASH.

No. **37.** CHAMBER-SET TABLE, OR BIBLE STAND.

Length 20 inches; width 16 inches.

French veneer on molded Rim, with mitered and dovetailed Corners.   Carved Base.   Marble, or Wood top.

WALNUT.

No. **65.** CHAMBER-SET TABLE, OR STAND.

Length, 18 inches; width, 14 inches.

Mitered and dovetailed corners on Rim.

Molded Base, with Shelf.   Marble, or Wood top.

Walnut, Imitation Mahogany, or Quartered Oak.

No. **84.** CHAMBER-SET TABLE, OR BIBLE STAND.

Length 20 inches; width 16 inches.

Mitered and dovetailed Corners.   Fluted Rim and molded Base.   Marble, or Wood top.

WALNUT, CHERRY, OR ASH.

Bureau No. 31.

PHŒNIX FURNITURE CO.
GRAND-RAPIDS MICH

PHŒNIX.
FOLDING BED
No. 3.

SQUIRES

SQUIRES
SOFA & CABINET BEDS

The Michigan Artisan, October, 1888, page 43.

Brass, Iron and Folding Beds

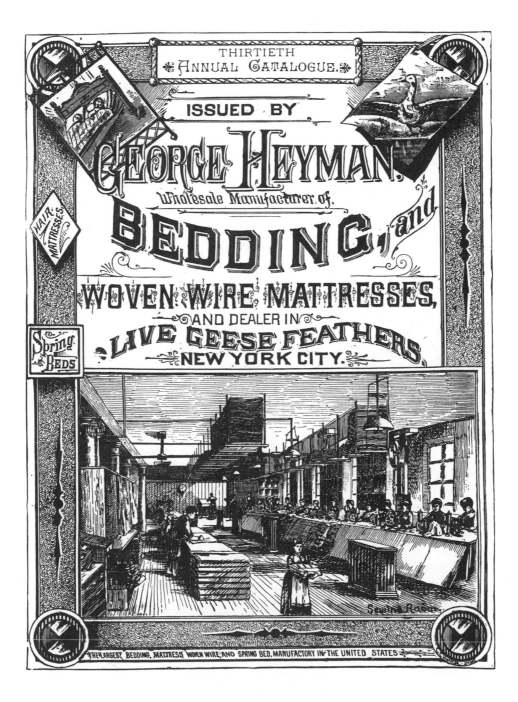

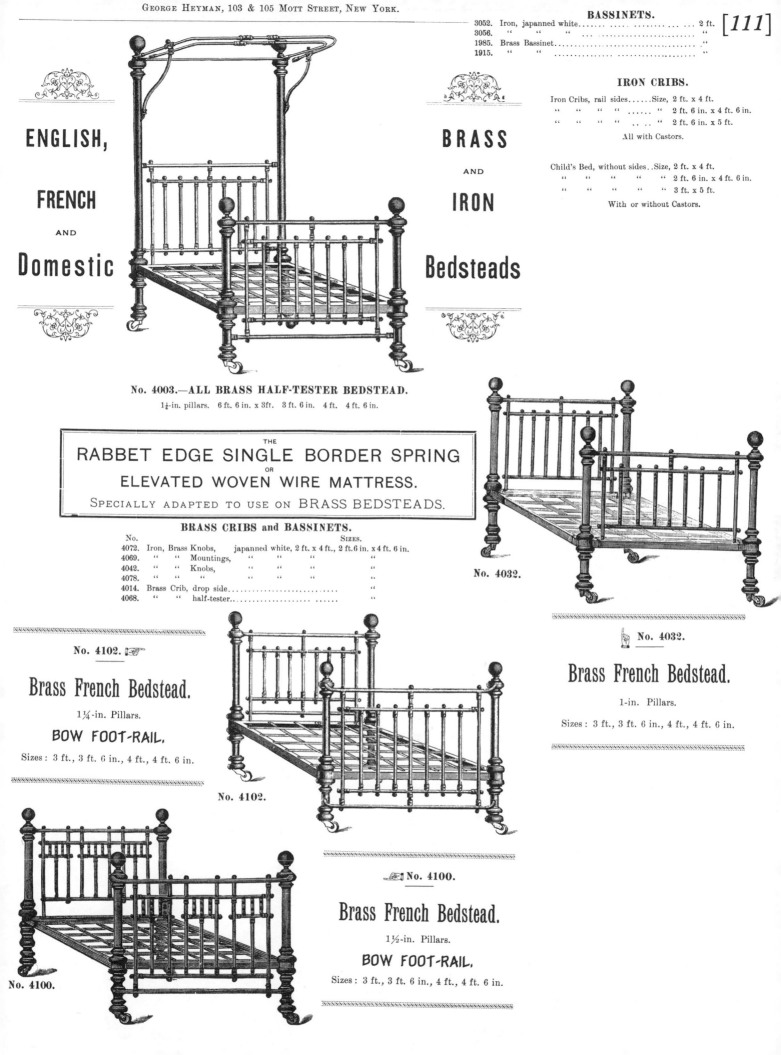

ENGLISH,

FRENCH

AND

Domestic

BASSINETS.

3052.	Iron, japanned white......	2 ft.
3056.	" " "	"
1985.	Brass Bassinet...........	"
1915.	" "	"

IRON CRIBS.

Iron Cribs, rail sides......Size, 2 ft. x 4 ft.

"   "   "   "   ...... " 2 ft. 6 in. x 4 ft. 6 in.

"   "   "   "   ... " 2 ft. 6 in. x 5 ft.

All with Castors.

Child's Bed, without sides..Size, 2 ft. x 4 ft.

"   "   "   "   " 2 ft. 6 in. x 4 ft. 6 in.

"   "   "   "   " 3 ft. x 5 ft.

With or without Castors.

BRASS

AND

IRON

Bedsteads

No. 4003.—ALL BRASS HALF-TESTER BEDSTEAD.

1¼-in. pillars. 6 ft. 6 in. x 3 ft. 3 ft. 6 in. 4 ft. 4 ft. 6 in.

THE

RABBET EDGE SINGLE BORDER SPRING
OR
ELEVATED WOVEN WIRE MATTRESS.

SPECIALLY ADAPTED TO USE ON BRASS BEDSTEADS.

BRASS CRIBS and BASSINETS.

No.			SIZES.
4072.	Iron, Brass Knobs,	japanned white, 2 ft. x 4 ft., 2 ft. 6 in. x 4 ft. 6 in.	
4069.	" " Mountings,	" " "	"
4042.	" " Knobs,	" " "	"
4078.	" "	" " "	"
4014.	Brass Crib, drop side.........................		"
4068.	" half-tester.....................		"

No. 4032.

No. 4032.

Brass French Bedstead.

1-in. Pillars.

Sizes : 3 ft., 3 ft. 6 in., 4 ft., 4 ft. 6 in.

No. 4102.

Brass French Bedstead.

1¼-in. Pillars.

BOW FOOT-RAIL,

Sizes : 3 ft., 3 ft. 6 in., 4 ft., 4 ft. 6 in.

No. 4102.

No. 4100.

Brass French Bedstead.

1½-in. Pillars.

BOW FOOT-RAIL,

Sizes : 3 ft., 3 ft. 6 in., 4 ft., 4 ft. 6 in.

No. 4100.

BRASS BEDSTEADS.

No. 4054.

No. 4054.

French Bedstead.

⅞ in. continuation tube.   Size, 3ft. x 6ft. 6 in.

JAPANNED MARONE or BLACK.

If Japanned White, Extra.

No. 4038.

No. 4066.

French Bedstead.

1-in. Pillars.

BRASS TOPS.

Size, 3 ft. x 6 ft. 6 in.

JAPANNED MARONE or BLACK.

If Japanned White, Extra.

No. 4066.

No. 4038.

FRENCH BEDSTEAD.

1¼-in. Pillars.

BRASS MOUNTED.

Japanned Black.

Sizes : 3 ft., 3 ft. 6 in., 4 ft., 4 ft. 6 in.

If Japanned White, Extra.

No. 4064.

No. 4064.

French Bedstead.

1-in. Pillars.

BRASS TOPS.

Size, 3 ft. x 6 ft. 6 in.

JAPANNED MARONE or BLACK.

If Japanned White, Extra.

No. 4034.

No. 4114.

FRENCH BEDSTEAD.

1-in. Pillars.   Bow Foot-rail.

BRASS TOP RODS.

Japanned Black.

Sizes : 3 ft., 3 ft. 6 in., 4 ft., 4 ft. 6 in.

If Japanned White, Extra.

No. 4114.

No. 4034.

FRENCH BEDSTEAD.

1-in. Pillars.

BRASS TOP RODS.

Japanned Black.

Sizes : 3 ft., 3 ft. 6 in., 4 ft., 4 ft. 6 in.

If Japanned White, Extra.

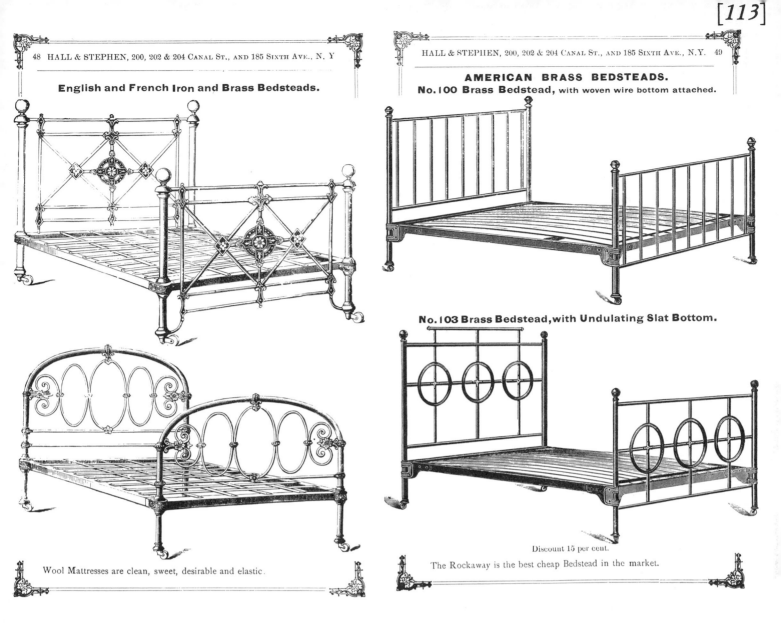

English and French Iron and Brass Bedsteads.

AMERICAN BRASS BEDSTEADS.
No. 100 Brass Bedstead, with woven wire bottom attached.

No. 103 Brass Bedstead, with Undulating Slat Bottom.

Discount 15 per cent.

The Rockaway is the best cheap Bedstead in the market.

Wool Mattresses are clean, sweet, desirable and elastic.

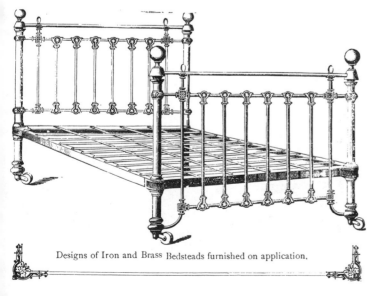

Designs of Iron and Brass Bedsteads furnished on application.

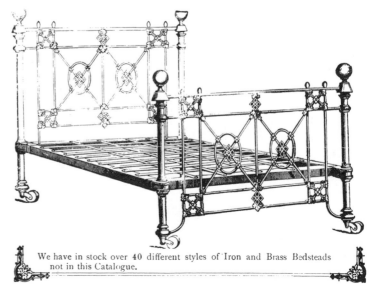

We have in stock over 40 different styles of Iron and Brass Bedsteads not in this Catalogue.

[114]

46 HALL & STEPHEN, 200, 202 & 204 Canal St., and 185 Sixth Ave., N. Y.

English and French Iron and Brass Bedsteads.

HALL & STEPHEN, 200, 202 & 204 Canal St., and 185 Sixth Ave., N. Y. 47

English and French Iron and Brass Bedsteads.

NATIONAL WIRE MATTRESS COMPANY. 19

NATIONAL WIRE MATTRESS COMPANY.

No. 100.

BRASS FRENCH BEDSTEAD.

2 INCH PILLARS, WITH ENGRAVED PANEL, EXTENSION FOOT
RAIL, EXTRA HEAVY MOUNTED.

METAL CASTERS, NICKEL PLATED.

With National Wire Mattress.

Weight of Bed complete. 350 lbs.

3 feet x 6 feet 6 inches	
3 feet 6 inches x 6 feet 6 inches	
4 feet x 6 feet 6 inches	Prices given on application.
4 feet 6 inches x 6 feet 6 inches	
5 feet x 6 feet 6 inches	

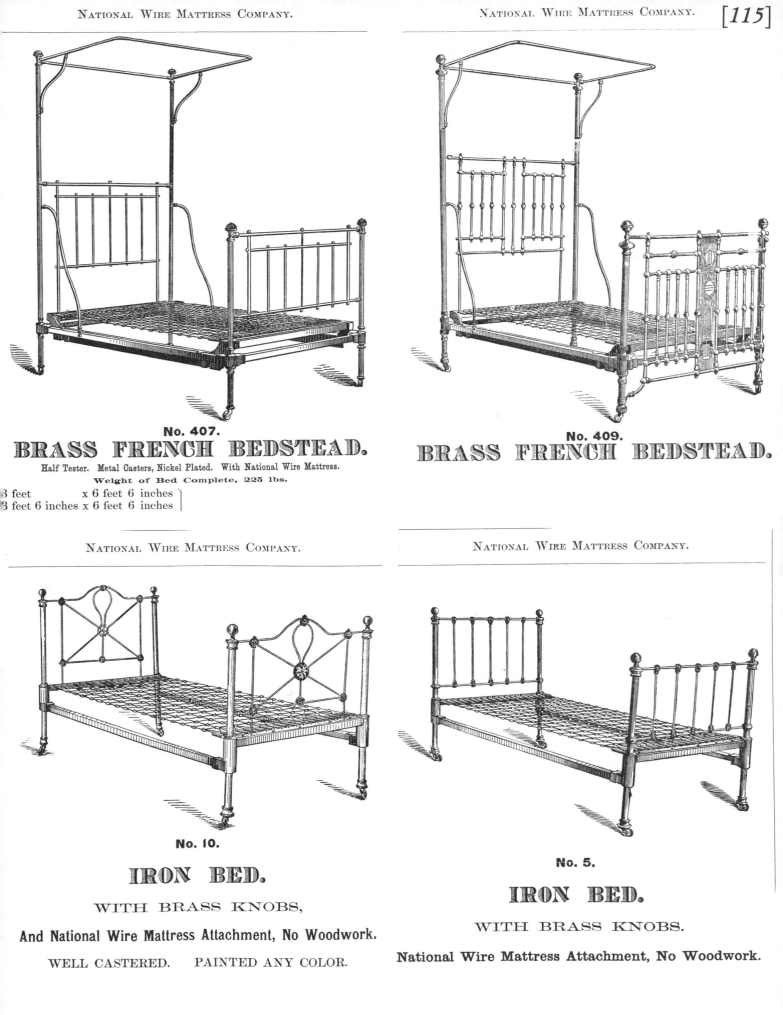

No. 407.
BRASS FRENCH BEDSTEAD.

Half Tester. Metal Casters, Nickel Plated. With National Wire Mattress.

Weight of Bed Complete, 225 lbs.

3 feet   x 6 feet 6 inches
3 feet 6 inches x 6 feet 6 inches

No. 409.
BRASS FRENCH BEDSTEAD.

No. 10.

IRON BED.

WITH BRASS KNOBS,

And National Wire Mattress Attachment, No Woodwork.

WELL CASTERED.   PAINTED ANY COLOR.

No. 5.

IRON BED.

WITH BRASS KNOBS.

National Wire Mattress Attachment, No Woodwork.

IRON BEDSTEADS.

No. 62 FOLDED.

No. 62. GOTHIC BEDSTEAD.

Sizes : 2 ft. 6 in., 3 ft., 3 ft. 6 in., 4 ft., 4 ft. 6 in.   Weight of 2 ft. 6 in. size, 77 lbs.

No. 63 CLOSED.

No. 63. FANCY BEDSTEAD.

Sizes : 2 ft. 6 in., 3 ft., 3 ft. 6 in., 4 ft., 4 ft. 6 in.   Weight of 2 ft. 6 in. size, 58 lbs.

26   NATIONAL WIRE MATTRESS COMPANY.

NATIONAL WIRE MATTRESS COMPANY.

No. 14.
IRON BED.

Half Tester, With Brass Knobs. National Wire Mattress Attachment, No Woodwork.

WELL CASTERED.   PAINTED ANY COLOR.

3 feet	x 6 feet 6 inches	-	-	-	-	$28.00
3 feet 6 inches x 6 feet 6 inches		-	-	-	-	29.00
4 feet	x 6 feet 6 inches	-	-	-	-	30.00
4 feet 6 inches x 6 feet 6 inches		-	-	-	-	33.00
5 feet	x 6 feet 6 inches	-	-	-	-	37.00

No. 15.
COMMON IRON BED.
WITH BRASS KNOBS,
And Iron Sacking.

WELL CASTERED.   PAINTED ANY COLOR.

3 feet	x 6 feet 6 inches	-	-	-	-	$12.0
3 feet 6 inches x 6 feet 6 inches		-	-	-	-	13.5
4 feet	x 6 feet 6 iuches	-	-	-	-	14.0
4 feet 6 inches x 6 feet 6 inches		-	-	-	-	14.0
5 feet	x 6 feet 6 inches	-	-	-	-	16.0

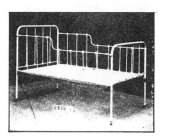

No. A

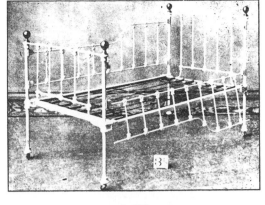

No. 3 1-2

Iron Crib A

White Enamel. With woven wire spring. (Wooden side rails.) 2 feet 6 inches wide, 4 feet 8 inches long.

Each........ ....$3.90

Iron Crib No. 3 1-2

White Enamel. (All iron.) With helical springs. Lacquered brass knobs. Drop sides. 2 feet 6 inches wide, 4 feet 8 inches long.

Each........ ....$4.90

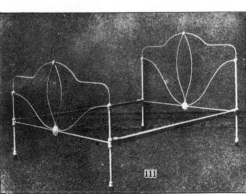

No. 2

Iron Crib No. 2

White Enamel. (All iron.) With woven wire spring (or helical as shown in cut). Lacquered brass knobs. Drop sides. 2 feet 6 inches wide, 4 feet 8 incees long.

Each...... ....$6.25

Iron Crib C

White Enamel. (All iron.) Woven wire spring. Sides drop by sliding on a lacquered brass rod. Lacquered brass knobs. 2 feet 6 inches wide, 4 feet 8 inches long.

Each........ ... .$7.75

No. C

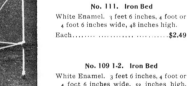

No. 111

No. 111. Iron Bed

White Enamel. 3 feet 6 inches, 4 foot or 4 foot 6 inches wide, 48 inches high.

Each........ ....$2.49

No. 109 1-2. Iron Bed

White Enamel. 3 feet 6 inches, 4 foot or 4 foot 6 inches wide, 52 inches high. Lacquered brass rods and knobs.

Each........ ....$4.35

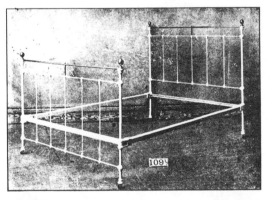

No. 109 1-2

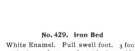

No. 429

No. 429. Iron Bed

White Enamel. Full swell foot. 3 foot 6 inches, 4 foot or 4 foot 6 inches wide. Lacquered brass rods and knobs. 58 inches high.

Each.... ....$6.25

No. 427. Same, with straight foot.

Each...... ....$5.50

No. 123. Iron Bed

White Enamel. 3 feet 6 inches, 4 foot or 4 foot 6 inches wide. Lacquered brass top rods and knobs. 58 inches high.

Each...... ....$6.75

No. 123

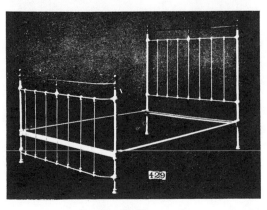

No. 217. White Enamel Iron Bed. 3 ft. 6 in., 4 foot and 4 ft. 6 in. wide, lacquered brass knobs, ornaments, and top rods, 58 inches high.
Each.. .. .. $5.97

No. 253. Dresser. White Enamel or Golden Ash, shaped top and serpentine top drawer 38x20 in., oval French bevel mirror 24x20.
(Without Decorations).$14.75
(With Decorations).... 16.50

No. 121. White Enamel Iron Bed. 3 ft. 6 in., 4 foot and 4 ft. 6 in. wide, lacquered brass top rods and ornaments, 59 in. high.
Each.. $8.75

No. 58. White Enamel Iron Bed. 3 ft. 6 in., 4 foot and 4 ft. 6 in. wide, lacquered brass knobs, ornaments and rods, full swell foot, 72 in. high.
Each $11.75

No. 481. Dresser. White Enamel or Golden Ash, full serpentine front and top, 41x22 wide, two top drawers, oval French bevel mirror 30x24.
Each.. .... $18.50
With Decorations (like 253), each.......... 20.25

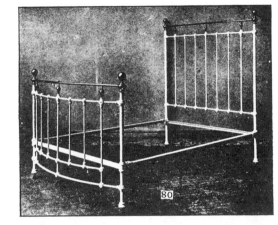

No. 80. White Enamel Iron Bed. 3 ft. 6 in., 4 foot and 4 ft. 6 in. wide, lacquered brass knobs, ornaments and rods, full swell foot, 66 in. high.
Each $12.50

No. 143. White Enamel Iron Bed. 3 ft. o in., 4 foot and 4 ft. 6 in. wide. lacquered brass knobs, ornaments and rods. full swell foot, 70 in. high.
Each... $14.75

No. 483. Dresser. White Enamel or Golden Ash, full serpentine front and top, 41x22 in., French bevel mirror 30x24 two top drawers.
Each.. .... $16.75
Decorated (like 253), each 18.50

No. 71. White Enamel Iron Bed. 3 ft. 6 in., 4 foot and 4 ft. 6 in. wide, lacquered brass rods and ornaments, 63 in. high.
Each...$16.50

THE "CHAMPION" AUTOMATIC FOLDING BEDSTEAD.

STYLE No. 18.

Solid Walnut Double Bedstead, Plain.

Inside measure, ... 76 in. x 52 in.
Outside measure, when closed, . . . 88 in. x 59 in.

Made also in Single size.

Inside measure, ... 76 in. x 36 in.
Outside measure, when closed, . . . 88 in. x 42 in.

The Double size can be fitted with Mirror if desired.

Accompanying price-list gives separate price for each article, as Bedstead, Spring, Mattress, Mirror; also the charge for packing for shipment.

In ordering Bedsteads please designate the Style and Size.

$65.00

No. 18. DOUBLE, PLAIN.—CLOSED.   **No. 18. DOUBLE, PLAIN.—OPEN.**

BRANCH STORES, NEW YORK AND BOSTON. SPECIAL AGENTS IN CHICAGO, ST. LOUIS, CLEVELAND, PITTSBURGH, BALTIMORE, BROOKLYN AND ALBANY.

THE "CHAMPION" AUTOMATIC FOLDING BEDSTEAD.

STYLE No. 23.

Solid Walnut Double Bedstead, Veneered.

Inside measure, ... 76 in. x 52 in.
Outside measure, when closed, . . . 88 in. x 58 in.

Made also in Single Size, Veneered.

Inside measure, ... 76 in. x 36 in.
Outside measure, when closed, . . . 88 in. x 42 in.

The Double Size can be fitted with Mirror if desired.

Accompanying price-list gives separate price for each article, as Bedstead, Spring, Mattress, Mirror; also for packing Bedstead for shipping.

$75.00

No. 23. DOUBLE, VENEERED.—CLOSED.   **No. 23. DOUBLE, VENEERED.—OPEN.**

THE "CHAMPION" AUTOMATIC FOLDING BEDSTEAD.

STYLE No. 24.

Solid Walnut, (made in two sizes,) Three-Quarter and Single, Plain and Veneered.

THREE-QUARTER SIZE.

Inside measure, ... 48 in. x 72 in.
Outside measure, when closed, . 53 in. x 85½ in.

SINGLE SIZE.

Inside measure, ... 36 in. x 72 in.
Outside measure, when closed, . 41 in. x 84½ in.

This pattern, as shown in the cuts, is nicely veneered and well finished, and considering style, work and finish is a very cheap Bedstead.

For prices see accompanying price-list.

In ordering please designate number, size and finish.

$50.00

No. 24. 4 FT., VENEERED.—OPEN.   **No. 24. 4 FT., VENEERED.—CLOSED.**

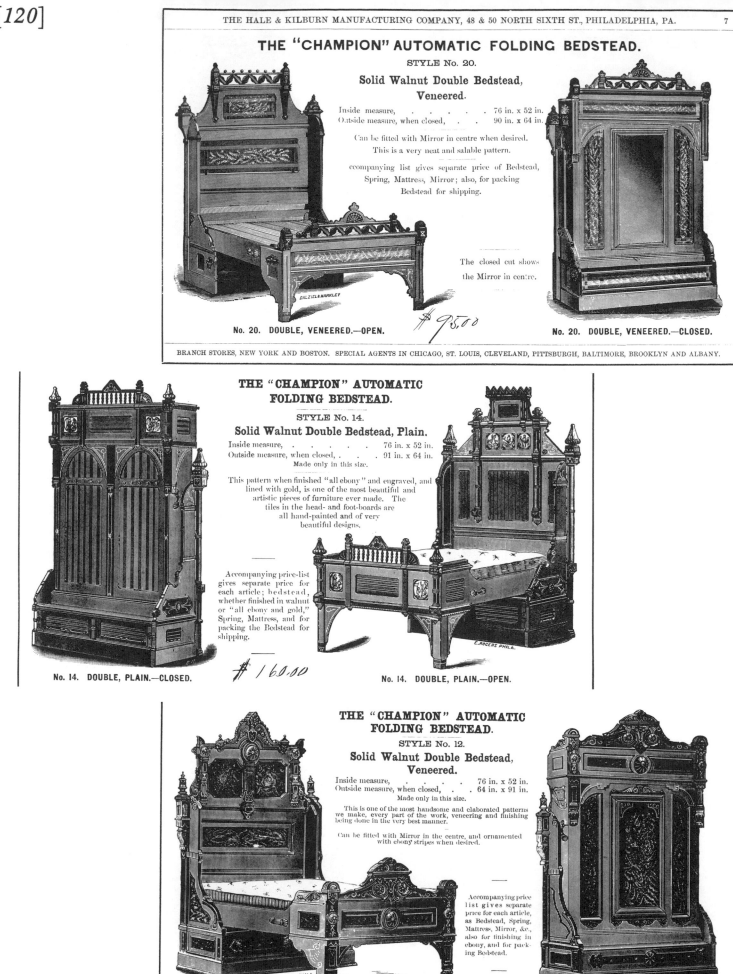

THE "CHAMPION" AUTOMATIC FOLDING BEDSTEAD.

STYLE No. 20.

Solid Walnut Double Bedstead, Veneered.

Inside measure, ... 76 in. x 52 in.
Outside measure, when closed, . . 90 in. x 64 in.

Can be fitted with Mirror in centre when desired.
This is a very neat and salable pattern.

ccompanying list gives separate price of Bedstead,
Spring, Mattress, Mirror; also, for packing
Bedstead for shipping.

The closed cut shows
the Mirror in centre.

No. 20. DOUBLE, VENEERED.—OPEN. $95.00   No. 20. DOUBLE, VENEERED.—CLOSED.

BRANCH STORES, NEW YORK AND BOSTON. SPECIAL AGENTS IN CHICAGO, ST. LOUIS, CLEVELAND, PITTSBURGH, BALTIMORE, BROOKLYN AND ALBANY.

THE "CHAMPION" AUTOMATIC FOLDING BEDSTEAD.

STYLE No. 14.

Solid Walnut Double Bedstead, Plain.

Inside measure, ... 76 in. x 52 in.
Outside measure, when closed, . . . 91 in. x 64 in.
Made only in this size.

This pattern when finished "all ebony" and engraved, and
lined with gold, is one of the most beautiful and
artistic pieces of furniture ever made. The
tiles in the head- and foot-boards are
all hand-painted and of very
beautiful designs.

Accompanying price-list
gives separate price for
each article; bedstead,
whether finished in walnut
or "all ebony and gold,"
Spring, Mattress, and for
packing the Bedstead for
shipping.

No. 14. DOUBLE, PLAIN.—CLOSED. $160.00   No. 14. DOUBLE, PLAIN.—OPEN.

THE "CHAMPION" AUTOMATIC FOLDING BEDSTEAD.

STYLE No. 12.

Solid Walnut Double Bedstead, Veneered.

Inside measure, ... 76 in. x 52 in.
Outside measure, when closed, . . . 64 in. x 91 in.
Made only in this size.

This is one of the most handsome and elaborated patterns
we make, every part of the work, veneering and finishing
being done in the very best manner.

Can be fitted with Mirror in the centre, and ornamented
with ebony stripes when desired.

Accompanying price
list gives separate
price for each article,
as Bedstead, Spring,
Mattress, Mirror, &c.,
also for finishing in
ebony, and for pack-
ing Bedstead.

No. 12. DOUBLE, VENEERED.—OPEN. $170.00   No. 12. DOUBLE, VENEERED.—CLOSED.

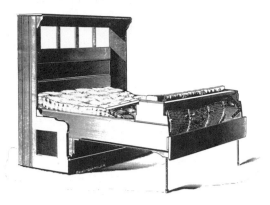

THE ANDREWS RUGBY BED.

No. 6. Partly Open.

It will be noticed by the cut that the mattress DOES NOT FOLD, but is simply turned up at the foot for closing, which allows ample ventilation of both sides of the mattress, even when the bed is closed. The silk curtains on the front of the bed are selected to harmonize in color with the finish of the wood. They are so mounted on brass rods that they may be easily removed when it is desirable to replace them with colors that match other furnishings of the apartment.

There is a convenient box, with lid, in the base of each bed.

A. H. ANDREWS & CO., CHICAGO.

THE ANDREWS RUGBY BED.

No. 7.

Widths : 4 feet ; 4 feet 6 inches

Woods : Birch—Natural Mahogany Finish.

Oak—Antique Finish ; 16th Century Finish ; Old English Finish

Walnut.

A. H. ANDREWS & CO., 215–221 WABASH AVENUE, CHICAGO.

SQUIRES' UPRIGHT FOLDING BEDS.

No. 15.

Antique Ash, Imitation Walnut or Mahogany.
18x40 German Bevel Mirror.

No. 25.

Walnut, 18x40 German Bevel Mirror.

No. 26.

Oak and Walnut, 24x50 French Bevel Mirror.

No. 20.

Ash.—Imitation Walnut Finish.
Imitation Mahogany Finish.

No. 30.

Ash.—Imitation Walnut Finish.
Imitation Mahogany Finish.

No. 13.

Antique Ash, Imitation Walnut or Mahogany.
18x40 German Bevel Mirror.

"COLUMBIA A."

In Imitation Walnut, Mahogany, Oak and Solid Ash.

Sizes—3 ft., 3 ft. 6 and 4 ft.   Special Sizes Extra.   Weights, $2.50 to $3.50.

Pole and Brass Trimmings Included.

"COLUMBIA B."

CLOSED.   OPEN.

CLOSED.   OPEN.

"MANTEL BED."

Imitation Walnut, Mahogany, Oak and Solid Ash.

Sizes—3 ft., 3 ft. 6 and 4 ft.   Special Sizes Extra.

CLOSED.   OPEN.

"CHILDREN'S FOLDING BEDS."

Hardwood—In Imitation Walnut, Cherry and Solid Ash.

Sizes—3x5 ft , 2 ft 6 x 4 ft 6.

CLOSED.   OPEN.

"THE FULTON."

In Imitation Walnut, Mahogany and Oak.

Sizes—3 ft., 3 ft. 6 and 4 ft.

CLOSED.   OPEN.

"MANHATTAN."

Hardwood—In Imitation Walnut, Mahogany, Oak and Solid As

Sizes—3 ft., 3 ft. 6 and 4 ft.

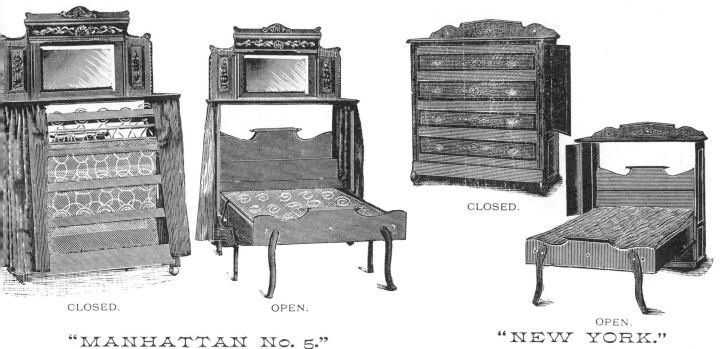

CLOSED.   OPEN.

"MANHATTAN No. 5."

Hardwood—In Imitation Walnut and Mahogany.

Size—4 feet only.

With 15 x 26 German Beveled Plate Glass.

With 15 x 26 French Beveled Plate Glass, $1.00 extra.

OPEN.

"NEW YORK."

Hardwood—In Imitation Walnut, Mahogany and Solid Ash.

Sizes— 3 ft., 3 ft. 6 and 4 ft.

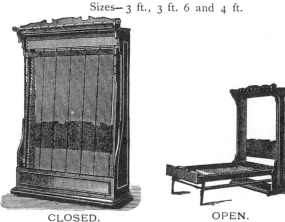

CLOSED.   OPEN.

"PORTIER."

Imitation Walnut, Mahogany, Oak and Solid Ash.

Sizes—3 ft., 3 ft. 6 and 4 ft. Special Sizes Extra.

Weights, $2.50 to $3.50.   Pole and Brass Trimmings included.

CLOSED.   OPEN.

"NEW YORK No. 2."

Hardwood—In Imitation Walnut and Mahogany.

Size—4 feet only.

With 15 x 26 German Beveled Plate Glass.

With 15 x 26 French Beveled Plate Glass, $1.00 extra.

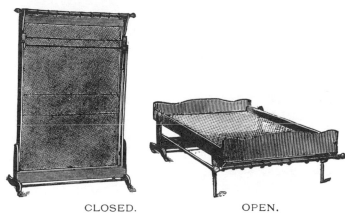

CLOSED.   OPEN.

"EXCELSIOR."

Imitation Walnut, Mahogany and Oak.

Sizes—3 ft., 3 ft. 6 and 4 ft.   Special Sizes Extra.

Pole and Brass Trimmings included.

MILLVILLE WORKS.

PRICE LIST.

CASE'S

PATENT

Folding Bed and Settee

COMBINED.

AS A BED

AS A SETTEE   FOLDED UP

					Spindle Back
No. 1 Imitation Walnut,	2 feet 6 in. wide				$12 00
" 1 "	3 " 6 "				15 00
" 3 "	2 " 10 "				14 00
" 4 "	4 "				19 00
" 5 Maple Varnish,	2 " 6 "				12 00
" 5 "	3 " 6 "				15 00
					Cane Back.
" 2 Imitation Walnut,	2 " 6 "				13 00
" 2 "	3 " 6 "				16 00
" 3 "	2 " 10 "				15 00
" 4 "	4 "				20 00
" 6 Maple Varnish,	2 " 6 "				13 00
" 6 "	2 " 10 "				15 00
" 6 "	3 " 6 "				16 00
" 8 Black Walnut,	2 " 6 "				15 00
" 8 "	3 " 6 "				18 00

Additional, with Gardner Patent Seat, { 2 feet 6 in. wide, $2 00
{ 3 " 6 " " 2 50

Discount, 33⅓ per cent.

We are the Sole Agents in the United States for the Millville Works. All Settees are made with cane seat. Agents wanted in large cities.

Self Adjustable Canopy.
WITH STANDARD FIXTURE.

Common Square Canopy.

PRICE LIST, WITHOUT ATTACHMENT.

	White.	Pink.
No. 120 Gauze 100 in. 10 Yard Skirt	$3 05	$3 35
Netting with Fringe, 108 in. 11 Yard Skirt	3 55	3 85
No. 156 Gauze, 100 in. 11 Yard Skirt	3 60	3 95
Netting with Fringe, 108 in. 11 Yard Skirt	3 95	4 30
Lace Netting, 96 in. 11 Yard Skirt	8 75	9 50
" " 108 " 11 "	8 75	9 50

COMMON SQUARE CANOPY.

MADE OF CORDS, BARRED OR PLAIN GAUZE NETTING WITH TAPE ON THE CORNERS.

	Per Doz.
Single Bed Nets, 40x72	$8 75
Double Bed Nets, 50x72	9 50
Extra Double Bed Nets, 60x72	10 26

PRICES FOR CANOPY FRAMES.

Turnover, White Ash Ribs, Crib or Full Size	$ 60
Flexible Hoop, centre piece, Crib or Full Size	60
Self-Adjustable, White Ash Ribs	85

PRICES FOR ATTACHMENTS.

Coiling Attachment, consisting of Pulley, Cord and Tassel	$ 25
Bedstead, Full Size	2 10
" Crib Size	1 50
Standard, Full Size	3 50
" Crib Size	2 75

Discount, 20 per cent.

COTS, at Manufacturers Prices.
WIRE COT, with Canopy.

JOHNSON SC.
Price, $5.75.

XX CANVAS COT, with Canopy.

Price, $3.25.

Flexible Hoop Canopy.
Patented Feb. 2d, 1875.

Turn Over Canopy.
CEILING FIXTURE.

FULL SIZE.

PRICE LIST WITHOUT ATTACHMENT.

	White.	Pink.
Striped and Plain Gauze, Assorted, with Fringe, 90 in. 9 Yard Skirt	$2 50	$2 70
No. 120 Gauze, 100 in. 10 Yard Skirt	2 80	$3 10
Netting with Fringe, 108 in. 11 Yard Skirt	3 30	3 60
No. 156 Gauze, 100 in. 11 Yard Skirt	2 80	3 10
Netting with Fringe, 108 in. 11 Yards Skirt	4 40	3 75
Lace Netting, 96 in. 11 Yard Skirt	8 50	9 25
" " 108 " 11 "	9 25	10 00

CRIB SIZES.

Gauze Netting, 70 in. 8 Yard Skirt	1 80	2 00
Lace " 80 " 8 " Skirt	5 00	5 70

FOR ATTACHMENTS, SEE LIST.

SOMETHING NEW.—SERVANTS' COMFORT.
The ROCKAWAY

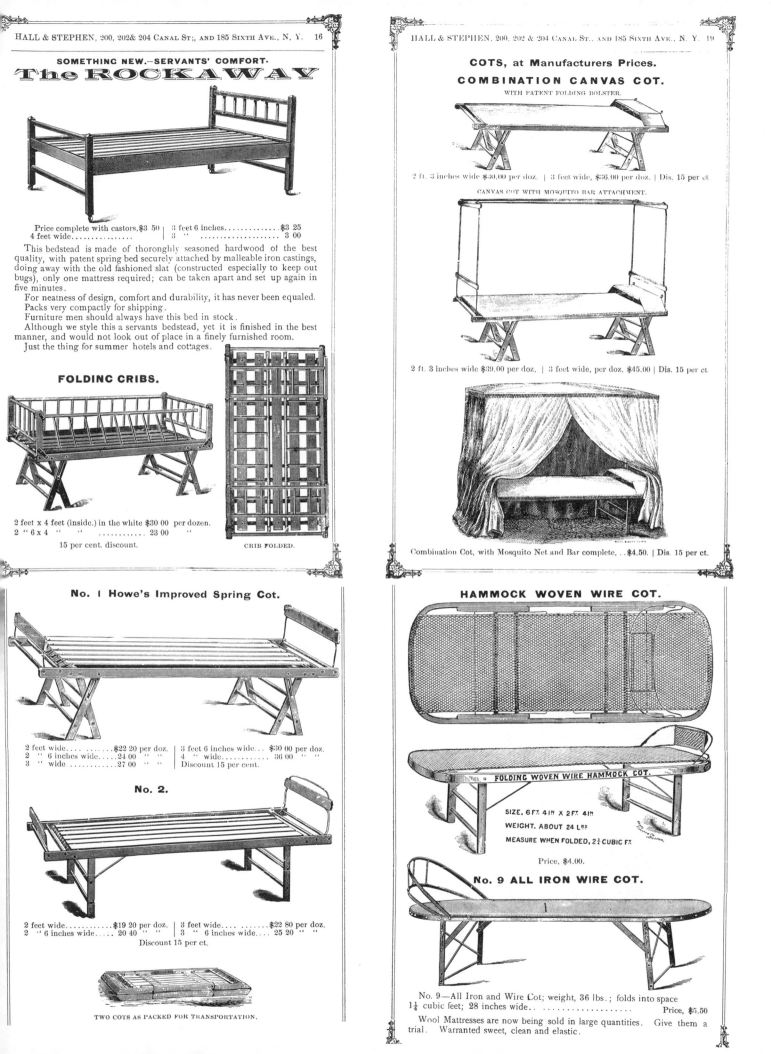

Price complete with castors, $3 50 | 3 feet 6 inches.............$3 25
4 feet wide............... | 3 " 3 00

This bedstead is made of thoroughly seasoned hardwood of the best quality, with patent spring bed securely attached by malleable iron castings, doing away with the old fashioned slat (constructed especially to keep out bugs), only one mattress required; can be taken apart and set up again in five minutes.

For neatness of design, comfort and durability, it has never been equaled. Packs very compactly for shipping.

Furniture men should always have this bed in stock.

Although we style this a servants bedstead, yet it is finished in the best manner, and would not look out of place in a finely furnished room.

Just the thing for summer hotels and cottages.

FOLDING CRIBS.

2 feet x 4 feet (inside.) in the white $30 00 per dozen.
2 " 6 x 4 " .... 23 00 " "

15 per cent. discount.

CRIB FOLDED.

COTS, at Manufacturers Prices.
COMBINATION CANVAS COT.
WITH PATENT FOLDING BOLSTER.

2 ft. 3 inches wide $30.00 per doz.. | 3 feet wide, $36.00 per doz. | Dis. 15 per ct

CANVAS COT WITH MOSQUITO BAR ATTACHMENT.

2 ft. 3 inches wide $39.00 per doz., | 3 feet wide, per doz., $45.00 | Dis. 15 per ct

Combination Cot, with Mosquito Net and Bar complete, .. $4.50. | Dis. 15 per ct.

No. 1 Howe's Improved Spring Cot.

2 feet wide. .... $22 20 per doz. | 3 feet 6 inches wide... . $30 00 per doz.
2 " 6 inches wide....24 00 " " | 4 " wide........... 36 00 " "
3 " wide...........27 00 " " | Discount 15 per cent.

No. 2.

2 feet wide...........$19 20 per doz. | 3 feet wide.... ......$22 80 per doz.
2 " 6 inches wide..... 20 40 " " | 3 " 6 inches wide.... 25 20 " "
Discount 15 per ct.

TWO COTS AS PACKED FOR TRANSPORTATION.

HAMMOCK WOVEN WIRE COT.

FOLDING WOVEN WIRE HAMMOCK COT.

SIZE, 6 FT. 4 IN. X 2 FT. 4 IN.

WEIGHT, ABOUT 24 LBS.

MEASURE WHEN FOLDED, 2½ CUBIC FT.

Price, $4.00.

No. 9 ALL IRON WIRE COT.

No. 9—All Iron and Wire Cot; weight, 36 lbs.; folds into space 1¼ cubic feet; 28 inches wide.. .... Price, $5.50.

Wool Mattresses are now being sold in large quantities. Give them a trial. Warranted sweet, clean and elastic.

COTS, at Manufacturers Prices.
LADD AUTOMATIC FOLDING COT.

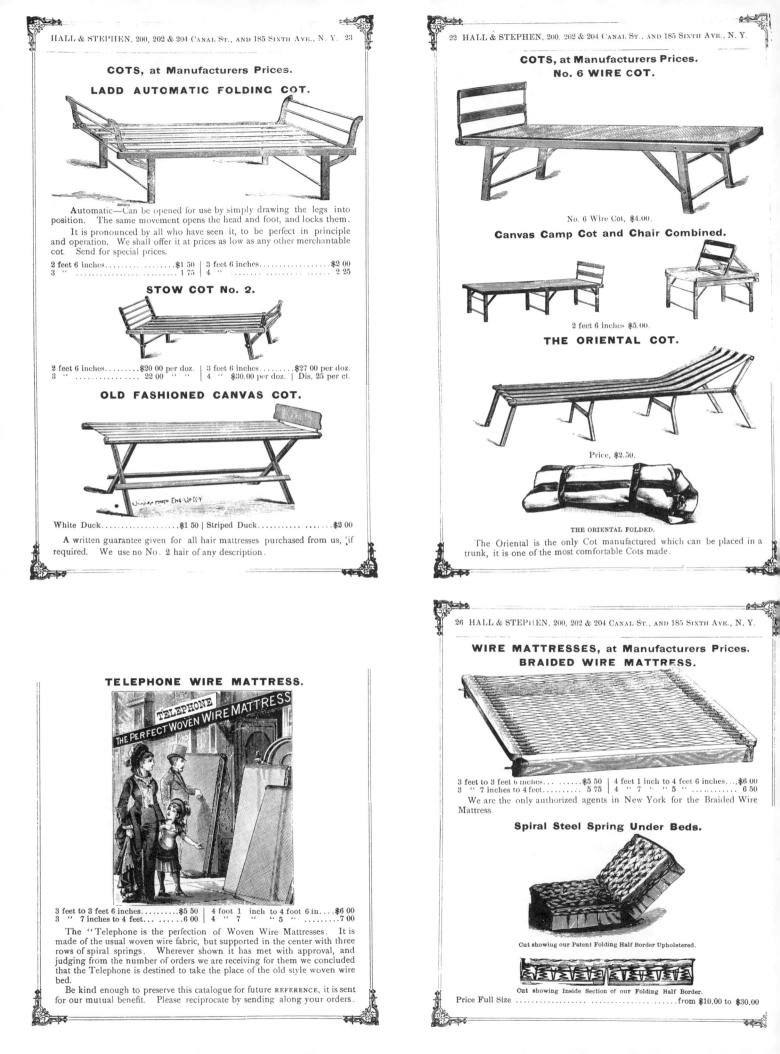

Automatic—Can be opened for use by simply drawing the legs into position. The same movement opens the head and foot, and locks them.

It is pronounced by all who have seen it, to be perfect in principle and operation. We shall offer it at prices as low as any other merchantable cot. Send for special prices.

2 feet 6 inches	$1 50	3 feet 6 inches	$2 00
3 "	1 75	4 "	2 25

STOW COT No. 2.

2 feet 6 inches	$20 00 per doz.	3 feet 6 inches	$27 00 per doz.
3 "	22 00 " "	4 " $30.00 per doz.	Dis. 25 per ct.

OLD FASHIONED CANVAS COT.

White Duck	$1 50	Striped Duck	$2 00

A written guarantee given for all hair mattresses purchased from us, if required. We use no No. 2 hair of any description.

COTS, at Manufacturers Prices.
No. 6 WIRE COT.

No. 6 Wire Cot, $4.00.

Canvas Camp Cot and Chair Combined.

2 feet 6 inches $5.00.

THE ORIENTAL COT.

Price, $2.50.

THE ORIENTAL FOLDED.

The Oriental is the only Cot manufactured which can be placed in a trunk, it is one of the most comfortable Cots made.

TELEPHONE WIRE MATTRESS.

3 feet to 3 feet 6 inches	$5 50	4 foot 1 inch to 4 foot 6 in	$6 00
3 " 7 inches to 4 feet	6 00	4 " 7 " 5 "	7 00

The "Telephone is the perfection of Woven Wire Mattresses. It is made of the usual woven wire fabric, but supported in the center with three rows of spiral springs. Wherever shown it has met with approval, and judging from the number of orders we are receiving for them we concluded that the Telephone is destined to take the place of the old style woven wire bed.

Be kind enough to preserve this catalogue for future REFERENCE, it is sent for our mutual benefit. Please reciprocate by sending along your orders.

WIRE MATTRESSES, at Manufacturers Prices.
BRAIDED WIRE MATTRESS.

3 feet to 3 feet 6 inches	$5 50	4 feet 1 inch to 4 feet 6 inches	$6 00
3 " 7 inches to 4 feet	5 75	4 " 7 " 5 "	6 50

We are the only authorized agents in New York for the Braided Wire Mattress.

Spiral Steel Spring Under Beds.

Cut showing our Patent Folding Half Border Upholstered.

Cut showing Inside Section of our Folding Half Border.

Price Full Size .... from $10.00 to $30.00

WOVEN WIRE COTS.

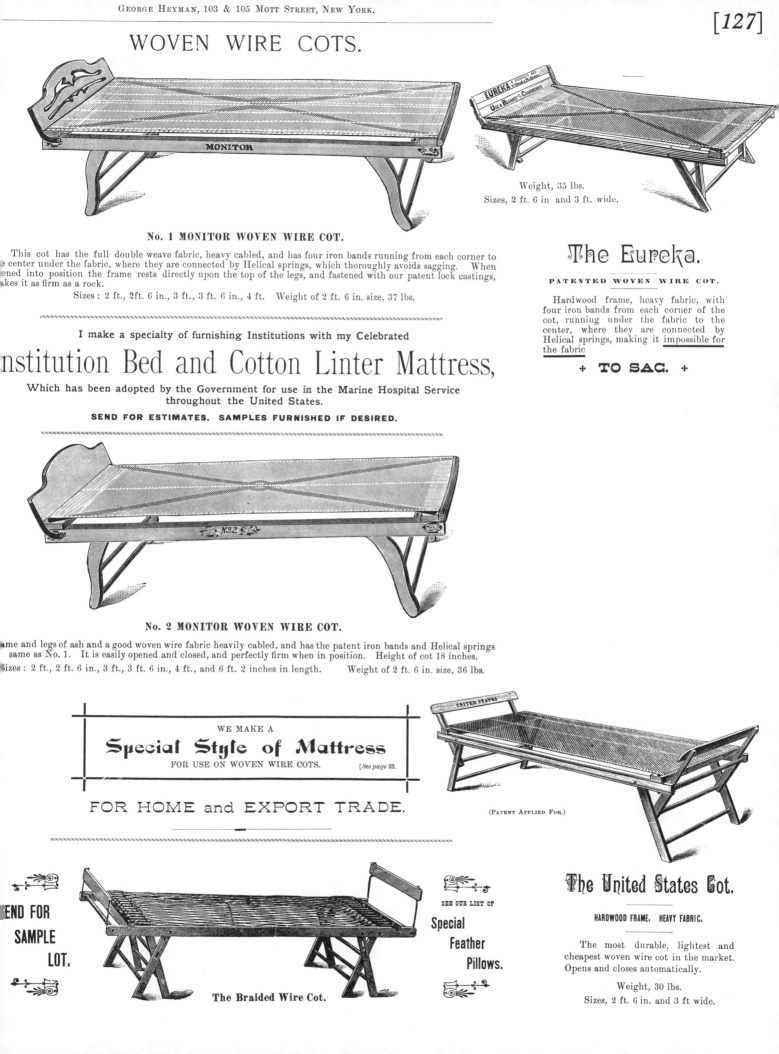

No. 1 MONITOR WOVEN WIRE COT.

This cot has the full double weave fabric, heavy cabled, and has four iron bands running from each corner to the center under the fabric, where they are connected by Helical springs, which thoroughly avoids sagging. When opened into position the frame rests directly upon the top of the legs, and fastened with our patent lock castings, makes it as firm as a rock.

Sizes : 2 ft., 2ft. 6 in., 3 ft., 3 ft. 6 in., 4 ft.   Weight of 2 ft. 6 in. size, 37 lbs.

I make a specialty of furnishing Institutions with my Celebrated

Institution Bed and Cotton Linter Mattress,

Which has been adopted by the Government for use in the Marine Hospital Service throughout the United States.

SEND FOR ESTIMATES. SAMPLES FURNISHED IF DESIRED.

No. 2 MONITOR WOVEN WIRE COT.

Frame and legs of ash and a good woven wire fabric heavily cabled, and has the patent iron bands and Helical springs same as No. 1. It is easily opened and closed, and perfectly firm when in position. Height of cot 18 inches.

Sizes: 2 ft., 2 ft. 6 in., 3 ft., 3 ft. 6 in., 4 ft., and 6 ft. 2 inches in length.   Weight of 2 ft. 6 in. size, 36 lbs.

WE MAKE A

Special Style of Mattress

FOR USE ON WOVEN WIRE COTS.   [See page 23.

FOR HOME and EXPORT TRADE.

SEND FOR SAMPLE LOT.

The Braided Wire Cot.

SEE OUR LIST OF

Special Feather Pillows.

The Eureka.

PATENTED WOVEN WIRE COT.

Hardwood frame, heavy fabric, with four iron bands from each corner of the cot, running under the fabric to the center, where they are connected by Helical springs, making it impossible for the fabric

✦ TO SAG. ✦

Weight, 35 lbs.
Sizes, 2 ft. 6 in and 3 ft. wide.

(Patent Applied For.)

The United States Cot.

HARDWOOD FRAME.   HEAVY FABRIC.

The most durable, lightest and cheapest woven wire cot in the market. Opens and closes automatically.

Weight, 30 lbs.
Sizes, 2 ft. 6 in. and 3 ft wide.

MOSQUITO CANOPIES.

UMBRELLA and TURN-OVER FRAME.

THE RIVAL.

No. 1. 72 in. x 8 yds., with ceiling attachment, turn-over frame.
" 2. 90 in. x 9 yds., " " " " "
" 3. 100 in. x 10 yds., " " " " "
" 4. 108 in. x 11 yds., " " " " "

THE LIVINGSTON.

No. 1. 72 in. x 8 yds., with ceiling attachment, turn-over frame.
" 2. 90 in. x 9 yds., " " " " "
" 3. 100 in. x 10 yds., " " " " "
" 4. 108 in. x 11 yds., " " " " "

THE BIJOU.

No. 1. 90 in. x 9 yds., with ceiling attachment, turn-over frame.
" 2. 100 in. x 10 yds., " " " " "
" 3. 108 in. x 11 yds., " " " " "

THE LARCHMONT.

No. 1. Umbrella Canopy, Ceiling Fixtures complete, single size.
" 2. " " " " " double "
" 3. " " " " " extra "

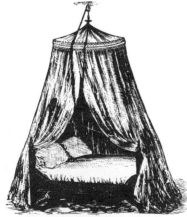

FLEXIBLE HOOP CANOPY.

LACE.—White Only.

A—Lace Canopies, turn-over frame, ceiling attachments.
B " " " " "
C " " " " "
D " " " " "
E " " " " "
F " " " " "

SPECIALS.

R—Special, Umbrella frame, ceiling attachments.
Florida, or Sand Fly Net frame " "

L or CRIB SIZE.

Plain Gauze, 72 in. x 8 yds., turn-over frame.
Lace Netting, 80 in. x 8 yds., " "

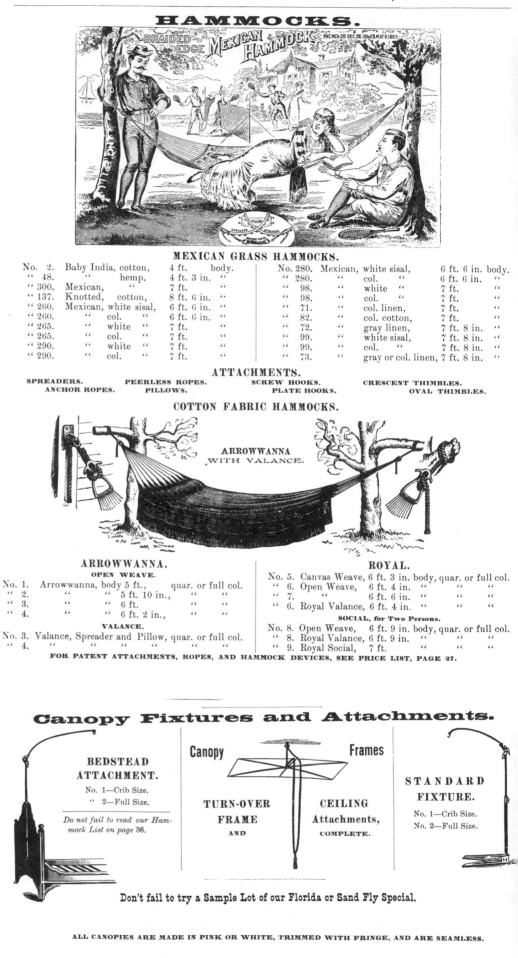

HAMMOCKS.

MEXICAN GRASS HAMMOCKS.

No. 2.	Baby India, cotton,	4 ft. body.		No. 280.	Mexican, white sisal,	6 ft. 6 in. body.
" 48.	" hemp,	4 ft. 3 in. "		" 280.	" col. "	6 ft. 6 in. "
" 300.	Mexican,	7 ft. "		" 98.	" white "	7 ft. "
" 137.	Knotted, cotton,	8 ft. 6 in. "		" 98.	" col. "	7 ft. "
" 260.	Mexican, white sisal,	6 ft. 6 in. "		" 71.	" col. linen,	7 ft. "
" 260.	" col. "	6 ft. 6 in. "		" 82.	" col. cotton,	7 ft. "
" 265.	" white "	7 ft. "		" 72.	" gray linen,	7 ft. 8 in. "
" 265.	" col. "	7 ft. "		" 99.	" white sisal,	7 ft. 8 in. "
" 290.	" white "	7 ft. "		" 99.	" col. "	7 ft. 8 in. "
" 290.	" col. "	7 ft. "		" 73.	" gray or col. linen,	7 ft. 8 in. "

ATTACHMENTS.

SPREADERS. PEERLESS ROPES. SCREW HOOKS. CRESCENT THIMBLES.
ANCHOR ROPES. PILLOWS. PLATE HOOKS. OVAL THIMBLES.

COTTON FABRIC HAMMOCKS.

ARROWWANNA.
OPEN WEAVE.

No. 1. Arrowwanna, body 5 ft., quar. or full col.
" 2. " " 5 ft. 10 in., " "
" 3. " " 6 ft. " "
" 4. " " 6 ft. 2 in., " "

VALANCE.

No. 3. Valance, Spreader and Pillow, quar. or full col.
" 4. " " " " "

ROYAL.

No. 5. Canvas Weave, 6 ft. 3 in. body, quar. or full col.
" 6. Open Weave, 6 ft. 4 in. " " "
" 7. " 6 ft. 6 in. " " "
" 6. Royal Valance, 6 ft. 4 in. " " "
SOCIAL, for Two Persons.
No. 8. Open Weave, 6 ft. 9 in. body, quar. or full col.
" 8. Royal Valance, 6 ft. 9 in. " " "
" 9. Royal Social, 7 ft. " " "

FOR PATENT ATTACHMENTS, ROPES, AND HAMMOCK DEVICES, SEE PRICE LIST, PAGE 27.

Canopy Fixtures and Attachments.

BEDSTEAD ATTACHMENT.

No. 1—Crib Size.
" 2—Full Size.

Do not fail to read our Hammock List on page 36.

Canopy Frames

TURN-OVER FRAME
AND

CEILING Attachments,
COMPLETE.

STANDARD FIXTURE.

No. 1—Crib Size.
No. 2—Full Size.

Don't fail to try a Sample Lot of our Florida or Sand Fly Special.

ALL CANOPIES ARE MADE IN PINK OR WHITE, TRIMMED WITH FRINGE, AND ARE SEAMLESS.

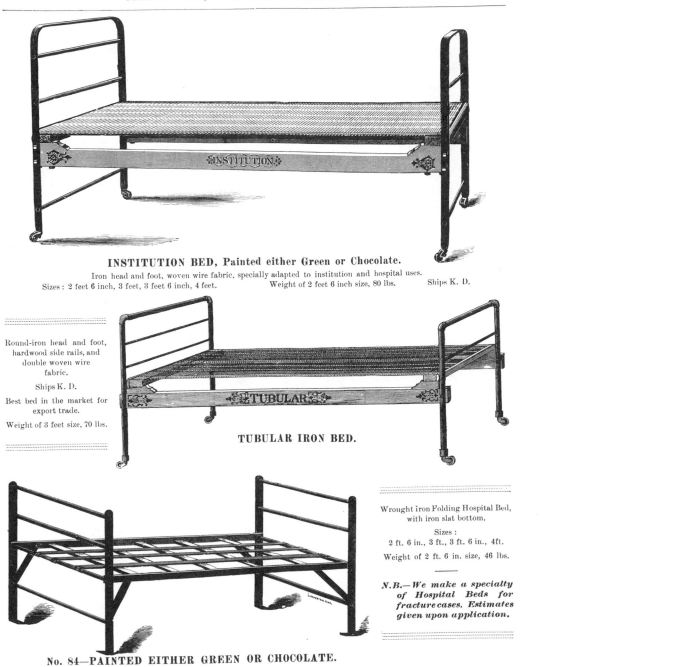

INSTITUTION BED, Painted either Green or Chocolate.

Iron head and foot, woven wire fabric, specially adapted to institution and hospital uses.

Sizes : 2 feet 6 inch, 3 feet, 3 feet 6 inch, 4 feet.   Weight of 2 feet 6 inch size, 80 lbs.   Ships K. D.

Round-iron head and foot, hardwood side rails, and double woven wire fabric.

Ships K. D.

Best bed in the market for export trade.

Weight of 3 feet size, 70 lbs.

TUBULAR IRON BED.

Wrought iron Folding Hospital Bed, with iron slat bottom.

Sizes :

2 ft. 6 in., 3 ft., 3 ft. 6 in., 4ft.

Weight of 2 ft. 6 in. size, 46 lbs.

N.B.—We make a specialty of Hospital Beds for fracture cases. Estimates given upon application.

No. 84—PAINTED EITHER GREEN OR CHOCOLATE.

M. SAMUELS & CO , 164 Mott Street, N. Y

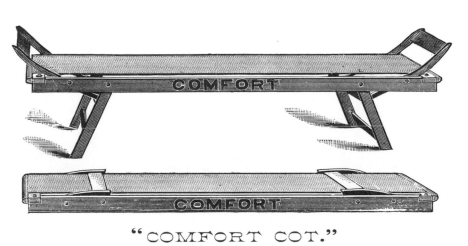

"COMFORT COT."

Sizes—2 ft. 6 and 3 ft.

No. 304 TABLE.   **No. 311 SIDEBOARD.**

The Rockford Furniture Journal, April
15, 1890, page 25.

Diningroom Furniture

It will Pay you to Correspond with Us before Ordering Goods elsewhere.

No. 51 Chiffonier.   No. 49 Sideboard.

The Rockford Furniture Journal, April
15, 1890, page 23.

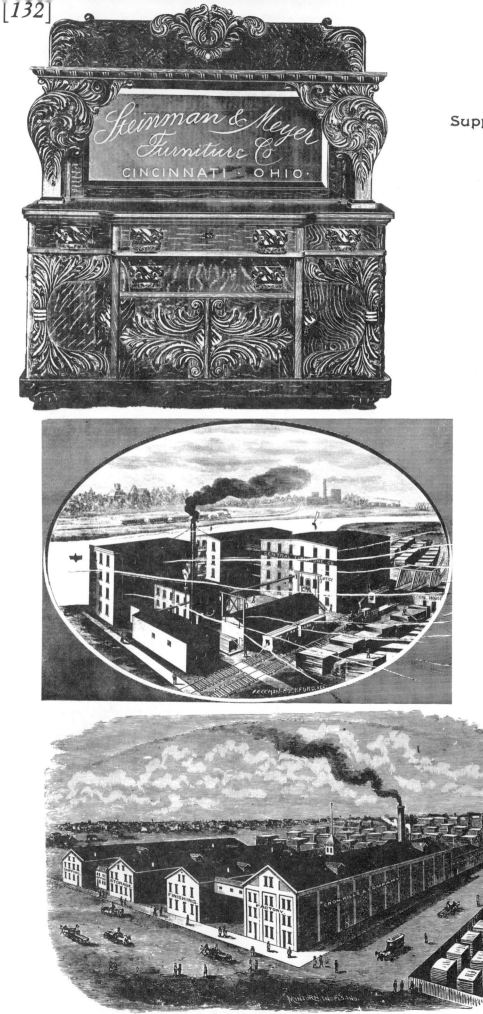

PRICE LIST

OF THE

Kent Furniture Manufacturing Co.

MANUFACTURERS OF

Medium and Low Priced Chamber Suites,

Chiffoniers Side Boards

BOOK CASES, WARDROBES, LIBRARY & CENTER TABLES.

JANUARY, 1, 1887.

GRAND RAPIDS, MICHIGAN.

No. 174.   SIDEBOARD.

Length, 5½ feet; width, 24 inches; height, 7¾ feet.
French beveled plate, 52 x 24 inches.   Rich and ornate Carving.   Eight Drawers with tumbler locks,
each requiring a different key.   The best bronze Handles.   Silver Drawer lined with Velvet.

Quartered Oak, or Mahogany.

No. 170.   SIDEBOARD.

Length, 4 feet; width, 20 inches; height, 6½ feet.
French beveled plate, 36 x 22 inches.   Rich and elaborate Carving on Front.   Deeply paneled Sides.
Heavy brass handles on Drawers.   Silver Drawer lined with Velvet.   Long Drawer for Linen.   Two Closets.

Walnut, Quartered Oak, or Mahogany.

No. 175.   SIDEBOARD.

Length, 5½ feet; width, 24 inches; height, 6½ feet.
Twelve French beveled plates 12 x 8 inches.   Richly carved Front and Sides.   Eight Drawers with locks,
and heavy brass handles.   Silver Drawer lined with Velvet.   Two Closets.

Walnut, Quartered Oak, or Mahogany.

KENT FURNITURE MANUFACTURING CO. GRAND RAPIDS, MICH.

No. 160.—German Bevel Glass.   18x36 inches.   4 feet wide.
French   "   "   6x6 inches.   6 feet 8 inches high.
One Drawer Lined.   Eight-day first-class New Haven Clock.
18x36 French Bevel $2.00 extra.   Oak and Walnut.

SIDEBOARD.   5 ft. 11 in. high.   Top 18 x 41.   Beveled Mirror 32 x 18.   Polished.
No. 187. Maple. Mahogany finish.
No. 187. Ash.
No. 187. Antique Finish on Ash.

BOOK CASE.   Height, 5 ft. 9 in.   Width, 2 ft. 8 in.   Polished.
No. 141. Maple Mahogany Finish.

No. 12—Oak.

Height, 7 ft. 5 in. Top, 60 x 24. Glasses, 20 x 36 and 6 x 14.

No. 4—Oak and Walnut.

Height, 7 ft. Top, 60 x 24. Glass, 20 x 48.

No. 3½—Oak and Walnut

Height, 6 ft. 11 in. Top, 54 x 24. Glasses, 20 x 42 and 10 x 20.

SIDEBOARDS.

No. 11—Oak.

Height, 7 ft. 2 in. Top, 60 x 24. Glass, 20 x 48.

No. 14—Oak.

SIDEBOARDS.

No. 9—Oak.

Height, 6 ft. 7 in.   Top, 48 x 24.   Glasses, 18 x 36 and 10 x 36.

Height, 7 ft.   Top, 54 x 24.   Glass, 20 x 42.

No. 7—Oak and Walnut.

No. 13—Oak.

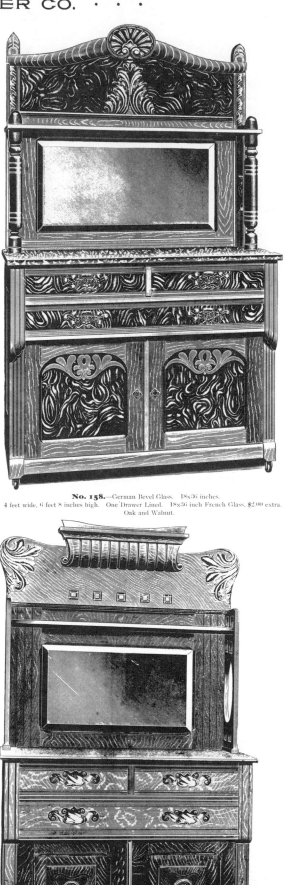

NO. 162.—French Bevel Glass. 18x40 and 8x8 inches.
4 feet 4 inches wide, 6 feet 8 inches high. One Drawer Lined.
Finished Inside. Oak.

NO. 158.—German Bevel Glass. 18x36 inches.
4 feet wide, 6 feet 8 inches high. One Drawer Lined. 18x36 inch French Glass, $2.00 extra.
Oak and Walnut.

NO. 161.—French Bevel Glass. 16x40 inches.
4 feet 6 inches wide, 6 feet 10 inches high. One Drawer Lined. Finished Inside.
Oak and Walnut.

NO. 157.—German Bevel Glass. 17x30 inches.
4 feet 9 inches wide, 6 feet 8 inches high. One Drawer Lined. Oak.

No. 1—Oak, 16th Century and Walnut.

Height, 6 ft. 6 in.　Top, 45 x 20.　Glass, 18 x 30.

No. 6—Oak and 16th Century.

Height, 6 ft. 6 in.　Top, 45 x 20.　Glass, 18 x 30.

SIDEBOARDS.

No. 12—Oak. **SIDEBOARDS.** No. 4—Oak and Walnut.

Height, 7 ft. 5 in. Top, 60 x 24. Glasses, 20 x 36 and 6 x 14.   Height, 7 ft. Top, 60 x 24. Glass, 20 x 48.

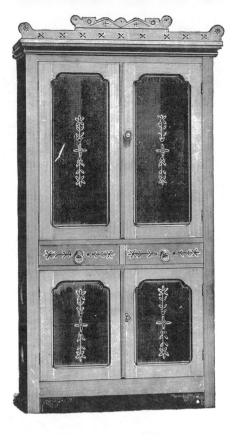

NO. 10. CUPBOARD SAFE.

Finished Light, Dark, or Antique. Varnish Finish.

Height, 6 feet 1 in.   Width, 3 feet 3 in.   Depth, 1 foot 4 in.

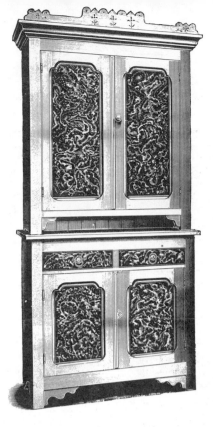

NO. 12. DOUBLE CUPBOARD.

Finished Light or Dark. Varnish Finish.

Height, 7 feet 3 in.   Width, 3 feet 3 in.   Depth, 1 foot 4 in.

NO. 23. SIDEBOARD.

Oil Finish. Antique.

Height, 6 feet.   Width, 3 feet 8 inches.   Depth, 1 foot 8 inches.

NO. 25. SIDEBOARD.

Antique Oak. Oil Finish.

French Bevel Glass 8x8 and 14x30.

Height, 6 feet 2 in.   Width, 3 feet 8 in.   Depth, 1 foot 8 in.

No. 345

Sideboard. Solid Golden Oak, elegantly carved top and base, base is 44x22 inches, has one lined drawer, two serpentine shaped top drawers, top has pattern French bevel plate mirror 32x18 inches, one large linen drawer across the bottom.

Price.................. $24.50

No. 597

Sideboard. Golden Quartered Oak, elegantly carved top and base, base has two shaped top drawers and swell doors, base is 48x24 inches, top has German bevel plate mirror 30x18 inches, one drawer lined, height of board 6 feet 10 inches.

Price.............. $25.00

No. 600

Sideboard. Golden Quartered Oak, elegantly carved top and base, three full swell top drawers, and one top drawer lined, base is 48x24 inches, top has German bevel plate mirror 30x18, height of board 6 feet 11 inches.

Price.................. $26.75

No. 326

Sideboard. Golden Quartered Oak, elegantly carved top and base, base has two shaped top drawers, one is lined, base is 48x24 inches, top has French bevel plate mirror 28x16.

Price................... $28.50

No. 599

Sideboard. Golden Quartered Oak, elegantly carved top and base, the three top drawers are full swell and one top drawer is lined, base is 48x24 inches, top has French bevel plate mirror 30x24 inches, height of board 6 feet 12 inches.

Price.................. $29.25

No. 323

Sideboard. Golden Quartered Oak, elegantly carved top and base, two shaped top drawers, one lined, base 48x24 inches, top has 36x18 French bevel plate mirror.

Price.................... $30.00

No. 318

Sideboard. Golden Quartered Oak, elegantly carved top and base, base is 48x23 inches, two swell drawers and swell doors one top drawer lined, large linen drawer across the bottom, top has pattern French bevel plate mirror 30x24 inches.

Price.................... $35.00

No. 325

Sideboard. Golden Quartered Oak, elegantly carved top and base, base is 48x23 inches, has two serpentine top drawers, one lined, deep wine drawer in center between the two doors, large linen drawer across the bottom, top has 28x16 French bevel plate mirror.

Price.................. $36.00

No. 296

Buffet or Side Table. Golden Quartered Oak, three small drawers underneath the top shelf, base is 42x21 inches.

Price............................ $17.95

No. 295

Buffet or Side Table. Golden Quartered Oak, full swell front and ends, shelf across the top, base is 42x22 inches.

Price.............................$20.00

No. 989

Buffet Sideboard. Golden Quartered Oak, base is 44x20 inches, one drawer lined, Buffet is 54 inches high, French bevel plate mirror 34x12 inches with shelves at each side.

Price..........................$25.75

No. 992

Buffet Sideboard. Golden Quartered Oak, base is 44x20 inches, one drawer lined, Buffet is 55 inches high, top has French bevel plate mirror 38x10 inches with a shelf above it.

Price..........................$27.50

No. 843

Sideboard. Solid Golden Oak, top and base handsomely carved, base is 42x20 inches, French bevel plate mirror 24x14 inches, height of board 6 feet, 5 inches. Top drawer lined.

Price **$11.50**

No. 840

Sideboard. Solid Golden Oak, top and base elegantly carved, shaped top drawers, base is 45x21 inches, French bevel plate mirror 24x14 inches, height of board 6 feet, 5 inches. Top drawer lined.

Price **$12.95**

No. 830

Sideboard. Solid Golden Oak, top and base elegantly carved, two serpentine top drawers, one top drawer lined, base is 45x21 inches, French bevel plate mirror 28x16 inches, height of board 6 feet, 7 inches.

Price **$15.95**

No. 833

Sideboard. Solid Golden Oak, top and base elegantly carved, two shaped top drawers, one top drawer lined, base is 45x21 inches, pattern French bevel plate mirror 28x16 inches, height of board 6 feet, 7 inches.

Price **$16.75**

No. 832

Sideboard. Solid Golden Oak, top and base elegantly carved, two shaped top drawers, one top drawer lined, base is 45x21 inches, pattern French bevel plate mirror 28x16 inches, oval French bevel plate in top piece, height of board 6 feet, 7 inches.

Price **$17.50**

No. 829

Sideboard. Solid Golden Oak, elegantly carved top and base, base has full serpentine front and top and is 45x21 inches, top drawer lined, pattern French bevel plate mirror 28x16 inches, height of board 6 feet, 7 inches.

Price **$19.50**

No. 846

Sideboard. Solid Golden Oak, elegantly carved top and base, two shaped top drawers, one drawer lined, base is 48x22 inches, pattern French bevel plate mirror 40x18 inches, height of board 6 feet, 7 inches.

Price **$20.50**

No. 835

Sideboard. Solid Golden Oak, elegantly carved top and base, base has two shaped top drawers and one full swell drawer and is 48x22 inches, top has pattern French bevel plate mirror 32x18 inches, one top drawer lined, height of board 6 feet, 7 inches.

Price **$20.75**

No. 850

Sideboard. Solid Golden Oak, elegantly carved top and base, base has two shaped top drawers, one drawer lined, base is 48x22 inches, French bevel plate mirror 24x14 and two pattern French bevel plate mirrors on sides, height of board 6 feet, 7 inches.

Price **$21.00**

No. 827

Sideboard. Solid Golden Oak, elegantly carved top and base, base has two shaped top drawers, one drawer lined, base is 48x22 inches, top has pattern French bevel plate mirror 32x18 inches height of board 6 feet, 7 inches.

Price **$21.00**

No. 822

Sideboard. Solid Golden Oak, elegantly carved top and base, base has two swell top drawers, one drawer lined, base is 48x22 inches, top has pattern French bevel plate mirror 32x18 inches, height of board 6 feet, 7 inches.

Price **$21.50**

No. 598

Sideboard. Golden Quartered Oak, elegantly carved top and base, base has two shaped top drawers and two swell doors, one drawer lined, base is 48x24 inches, German bevel plate mirror 30x18 inches, height of board 6 feet, 9 inches.

Price **$22.00**

No. 837

Sideboard. Solid Golden Oak, elegantly carved top and base, base has two shaped top drawers and one large full swell drawer, one top drawer lined, base is 48x22 inches, top has pattern French bevel plate mirror 36x18 inches, height of board 6 feet, 7 inches.

Price **$23.25**

No. 347

Sideboard. Solid Golden Oak with Quartered Oak top, elegantly carved top and base, two serpentine top drawers, one drawer lined, base is 44x22, top has French bevel plate mirror 28x16, long deep linen drawer at bottom.

Price **$23.25**

No. 828

Sideboard. Solid Golden Oak, elegantly carved top and base, base is full serpentine front and top and is 48x22 inches, one drawer lined, top has a pattern French bevel plate mirror 36x18 inches, height of board 6 feet, 7 inches.

Price **$24.50**

No. 128½. DINING, OR PILLAR EXTENSION TABLE.

Length 10, 12, 14, 16, or 18 feet; width 4½ feet.

Molded and carved Rim. Elegantly carved and engraved Base. Two middle Legs connected by a richly ornamented stretcher running lengthwise of the table when extended.

WALNUT, OAK, OR MAHOGANY.

No. 34. DINING, OR PILLAR EXTENSION TABLE.

Length 10, 12, 14, 16, or 18 feet; width 4 feet.

Carved Rim and veneered Base, with rich and unique carving.

MAHOGANY, OR WALNUT.

107. DINING, OR PILLAR EXTENSION TABLE.

Length 8, 10, 12, or 14 feet; width 3 feet 9 inches.

Molded Rim and Base, with two connected center Legs.

WALNUT, CHERRY, ASH, OR MAHOGANY.

No. 125. DINING, OR PILLAR EXTENSION TABLE.

Length 8, 10, 12, or 14 feet; width 3 feet 9 inches.

Fluted Rim and Base.

WALNUT, OR CHERRY.

No. 131. DINING, OR PILLAR EXTENSION TABLE.

Length 8, 10, 12, or 14 feet; width 3 feet 9 inches.

Round top, if so ordered.

WALNUT, CHERRY, OR ASH.

No. 36. DINING, OR PILLAR EXTENSION TABLE.

Length, 8, 10, 12, or 14 feet; width, 3 feet, 9 inches.

Molded and engraved Rim and Base.

Combines Strength, Solidity, and Beauty.

Walnut, Imitation Mahogany, or Quartered Oak.

No. 124. DINING, OR PILLAR EXTENSION TABLE.

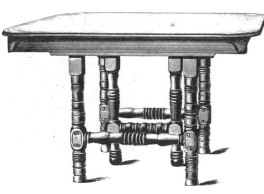

Length, 8, 10, or 12 feet; width, 3 feet, 9 inches.

Molded Rim, and turned Base.

Walnut, Imitation Mahogany, or Quartered Oak.

No. 109. DINING, OR PILLAR EXTENSION TABLE.

Length, 8, 10, or 12 feet; width, 3 feet, 6 inches.

Plain Oak, Imitation Walnut, or Imitation Mahogany.

No. 16. ENGLISH BREAKFAST TABLE. Closed.

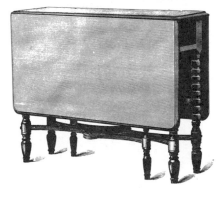

Length, 4 feet; width, 3 feet.

Four feet long when the leaves are extended. See illustration on preceding page. One long Drawer.

Walnut, Imitation Mahogany, Quartered Oak, or Mahogany.

ROCKFORD UNION FURNITURE COMPANY.

No. 201 EXTENSION TABLE.
Antique Oak or XVI. century; top 3 ft. 8 in.

No. 200 EXTENSION TABLE.
Antique Oak or XVI. century; top 4 ft.

No. 202 PILLAR EXTENSION TABLE.

Top 4 ft., Quarter-sawed, Antique Oak or XVI. century; 10 to 16 ft.
Heavy Brass trimmings on base and top. Very stylish table.

No. 203 PILLAR EXTENSION TABLE.

Top 4 ft., Quarter sawed Oak, Antique or XVI. century; 10 to 16 ft.
Heavily Carved base and Brass trimmings on corners.

BARDWELL, ANDERSON & CO., BOSTON, MASS.   FOR THE TRADE ONLY.

No. 7. DINING, OR PILLAR EXTENSION TABLE.

Length, 8, 10, 12, or 14 feet; width, 3 feet, 9 inches.

Molded Rim. Double spiral turning on Columns, with carved Feet.

Walnut, Imitation Mahogany, or Quartered Oak.

No. 105. DINING, OR PILLAR EXTENSION TABLE.

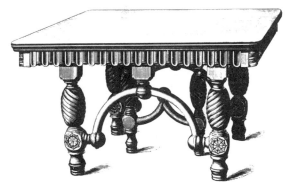

Length, 8, 10, 12, 14, or 16 feet; width, 4 feet.

Carved Rim and Base, with heavy spiral turned Columns.

Walnut, Imitation Mahogany, or Quartered Oak.

No. 157. ENGLISH BREAKFAST TABLE. Open.

Length, 3 feet; width, 3 feet.

Thirteen inches across the Top when the leaves are folded. See next illustration.

Walnut, Imitation Mahogany, or Quartered Oak.

No. 70. DINING, OR PILLAR EXTENSION TABLE.

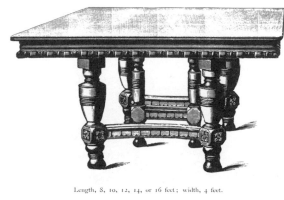

Length, 8, 10, 12, 14, or 16 feet; width, 4 feet.

Heavy molding on Rim, with massive Base.

The Top when closed is made either 4 feet or 5 feet long.

Walnut, Imitation Mahogany, Quartered Oak, or Mahogany.

No. 117. DINING, OR PILLAR EXTENSION TABLE.

Length, 8, 10, 12, 14, or 16 feet; width, 4 feet.

Unique and elegant Design, with rich Carving.

Walnut, Quartered Oak, or Mahogany.

No. 114. DINING, OR PILLAR EXTENSION TABLE.

Length, 8, 10, 12, 14, 16, or 18 feet; width, 4 feet.

Heavy Base, rich with Carving.

The Top when closed is made either 4 feet or 5 feet long.

Walnut, Quartered Oak, or Mahogany.

No. 134. DINING, OR PILLAR EXTENSION TABLE.

Length, 8, 10, 12, 14, or 16 feet; width, 4 feet.

Romanesque style.   Rich carving on Base.

Walnut, Quartered Oak, or Mahogany.

No. 102. DINING, OR PILLAR EXTENSION TABLE.

Length, 8, 10, 12, 14, or 16 feet; width, 4 feet.

Unique Carving on Rim and Base.

The Top when closed is made either 4 feet or 5 feet long.

Walnut, Imitation Mahogany, Quartered Oak, or Mahogany.

No. 113. DINING, OR PILLAR EXTENSION TABLE.

Length, 10, 12, 14, 16, or 18 feet; width, 4 feet.

Massive Rim and Base richly Carved.

Walnut, Quartered Oak, or Mahogany.

No. 135. DINING, OR PILLAR EXTENSION TABLE.

Length, 10, 12, 14, 16, or 18 feet; width, 4 feet.

Elegant and attractive Design, with richly carved Base.

Walnut, Quartered Oak, or Mahogany.

All These Extension Tables Have Our Patent Hercules Frame

No. 993—Extension Table

No. 980. (Without the stretchers underneath.) Top 42x42 inches, Solid Golden Oak.
6-foot.............$4.97   8 foot..........$6.50   10-foot..........$8.00
No. 993. (Like cut.) Top 42x42 inches, Solid Golden Oak.
6-foot............$6.85   8-foot,...........$8.35   10-foot...........$9.85

No. 985—Extension Table

No. 985. Solid Golden Oak. Top 42x42 inches, leg is 5 inches in diameter.
6-foot.....   ...$8.25   8-foot.........$9.75   10-foot..... . $11.25
No. 999. Same with 44x44 inch top:
8 foot.....   .... $10.75   10-foot.....................$12.25
No. 984. Same as 985, with the leaves inside the table:
6-foot............$9.25   8 foot.......$10.75   10-foot $12.25
For Golden Quartered Oak, add $2.50 list to the above prices.

No. 977—Extension Table

No. 977. Solid Golden Oak. Top is 42x42 inches, leg is 5 inches in diameter.
6-foot...........$8.50   8-foot..........$10.00   10-foot........$11.50
No. 997. Same with 44x44 inch top:
8-foot..........................$11.75   10-foot.........................•$13.25
These Tables are made with the leaves shutting up in the top for $1.00 list extra. For Golden Quartered Oak add $2.50 list to the above prices.

No. 975—Extension Table

No. 975. Solid Golden Oak, claw feet; top is 42x42 inches, leg is 5 inches in diameter.
6-foot............$9.50   8-foot...........$11.00   10-foot...... ..$12.50
No. 998. Same with 44x44 inch top:
8-foot............... ....$11.60   10-foot..... ....$13.10

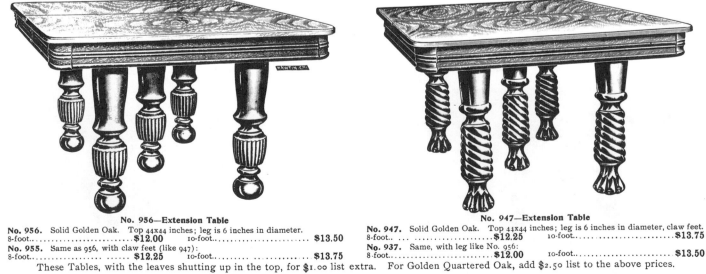

No. 956—Extension Table

No. 956. Solid Golden Oak. Top 44x44 inches; leg is 6 inches in diameter.
8-foot.........................$12.00   10-foot......................... $13.50
No. 955. Same as 956, with claw feet (like 947):
8-foot........... ....$12.25   10-foot........ .... $13.75
These Tables, with the leaves shutting up in the top, for $1.00 list extra.

No. 947—Extension Table

No. 947. Solid Golden Oak. Top 44x44 inches; leg is 6 inches in diameter, claw feet.
8-foot.. ....$12.25   10-foot.....................$13.75
No. 937. Same, with leg like No. 956:
8-foot..........................$12.00   10-foot.......................$13.50
For Golden Quartered Oak, add $2.50 list to the above prices.

See Special Discount on Inside Cover

No. 677. Golden Quartered Oak. Piano polish, fluted legs, shaped rims, size of top when closed 42 inches square. Lengths as follows:

6-foot	$11.25	12-foot	$15.75
8-foot	12.75	14-foot	17.25
10-foot	14.25		

No. 665. Golden Quartered Oak. Piano polish, fluted legs, shaped rim, size of top when closed 42 inches square. Lengths as follows:

6-foot	$10.00	12-foot	$14.50
8-foot	11.50	14-foot	16.00
10-foot	13.00		

No. 672. Golden Oak. Piano polish, fluted legs, shaped rims, size of top when closed 44 inches square. Lengths as follows:

6-foot	$12.50	12-foot	$20.00
8-foot	15.00	14-foot	22.50
10-foot	17.50		

No. 672 1-4. Same in Golden Quartered Oak, piano polish:

6-foot	$16.00	12-foot	$23.50
8-foot	18.50	14-foot	26.00
10-foot	21.00		

No. 699 1-2. Golden Quartered Oak. Piano polish, spiral turned legs, top when closed 44 inches in diameter. Lengths as follows:

6-foot	$14.00	12-foot	$21.50
8-foot	16.50	14-foot	24.00
10-foot	19.00		

No. 721. Golden Quartered Oak. Piano polish, French legs, size of top when closed 42 inches square. Lengths as follows:

6-foot	$14.25	12-foot	$19.50
8-foot	16.00	14-foot	21.25
10-foot	17.75		

No. 721 1-2. Golden Quartered Oak. Piano polish, French legs, top when closed 44 inches in diameter. Lengths as follows:

6-foot	$16.50	12-foot	$24.00
8-foot	19.00	14-foot	26.50
10-foot	21.50		

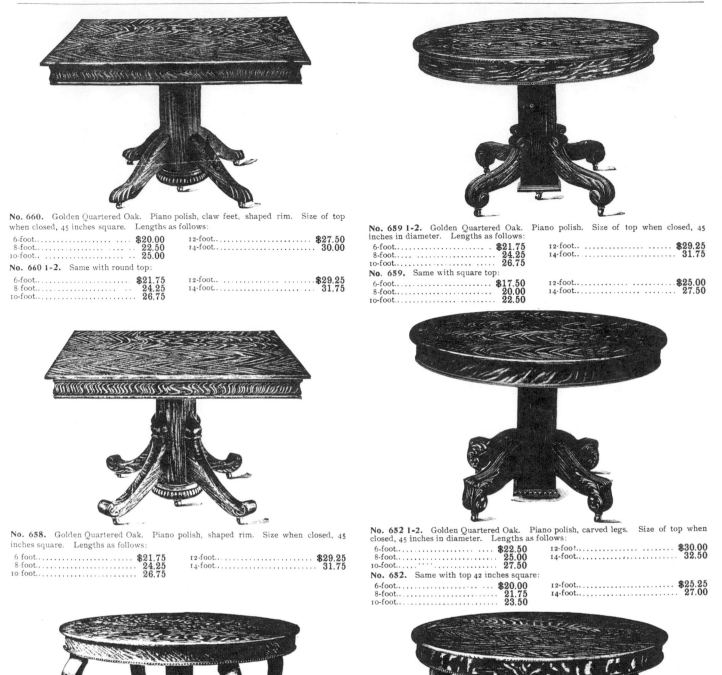

No. 660. Golden Quartered Oak. Piano polish, claw feet, shaped rim. Size of top when closed, 45 inches square. Lengths as follows:

6-foot	$20.00	12-foot	$27.50
8-foot	22.50	14-foot	30.00
10-foot	25.00		

No. 660 1-2. Same with round top:

6-foot	$21.75	12-foot	$29.25
8-foot	24.25	14-foot	31.75
10-foot	26.75		

No. 659 1-2. Golden Quartered Oak. Piano polish. Size of top when closed, 45 inches in diameter. Lengths as follows:

6-foot	$21.75	12-foot	$29.25
8-foot	24.25	14-foot	31.75
10-foot	26.75		

No. 659. Same with square top:

6-foot	$17.50	12-foot	$25.00
8-foot	20.00	14-foot	27.50
10-foot	22.50		

No. 658. Golden Quartered Oak. Piano polish, shaped rim. Size when closed, 45 inches square. Lengths as follows:

6-foot	$21.75	12-foot	$29.25
8-foot	24.25	14-foot	31.75
10-foot	26.75		

No. 652 1-2. Golden Quartered Oak. Piano polish, carved legs. Size of top when closed, 45 inches in diameter. Lengths as follows:

6-foot	$22.50	12-foot	$30.00
8-foot	25.00	14-foot	32.50
10-foot	27.50		

No. 652. Same with top 42 inches square:

6-foot	$20.00	12-foot	$25.25
8-foot	21.75	14-foot	27.00
10-foot	23.50		

No. 730 1-2. Golden Quartered Oak. Piano polish, French legs with claw feet. Size of top when closed, 48 inches in diameter. Lengths as follows:

8-foot	$23.25	14-foot	$33.00
10-foot	26.50	16-foot	36.25
12-foot	29.75		

No. 730. Same with top 48 inches square:

8-foot	$21.75	14-foot	$31.50
10-foot	25.00	16-foot	34.75
12-foot	28.25		

No. 655 1-2. Golden Quartered Oak. Piano polish, fluted legs. Size of top when closed, 48 inches in diameter. Lengths as follows:

8-foot	$25.00	14-foot	$34.75
10-foot	28.25	16-foot	38.00
12-foot	31.50		

No. 655. Same with top 48 inches square:

8-foot	$23.25	14-foot	$33.00
10-foot	26.50	16-foot	36.25
12 foot	29.75		

No. 9½

Five Spindle.
Perforated Seat.

No. 4

Bent Pillar.
Chestnut.   Spline Seat.

No. 4½

Washburn Dining.
Chestnut.

No. 1

Common Wood.

No. 8

Three Spindle.
Chestnut.

No. 9

Five Spindle.
Chestnut.

F. E. STUART.

No. 167

Dining.

No. 152

Grant Dining.

No. 166

Stuart Dining.

No. 159

Puritan Dining.

No. 165

Harrison Dining.

No. 153

Casino Dining.

No. 124.
QUEEN ANNE DINING B.

No. 125.
QUEEN ANNE DINING B.
(Cane Back.)

No. 128

Acme Dining.

No. 99

Queen Anne Dining.

No. 16.

FLORENCE DINING.

No. 32.

BENT DINING.

(Perforated Seat.)

No. 42.

QUAKER DINING.

(Chestnut Seat.)

No. 57.

LADIES' DINING.

No. 65.

FIVE SPINDLE.

(Chestnut Seat.)

No. 66.

WASHBURN DINING.

No. 112.

QUEEN ANNE COTTAGE A.

No. 123.

QUEEN ANNE COTTAGE B.

No. 162.

SPINDLE GRECIAN.

No. 164.

DAVIS GRECIAN.

THOMPSON, PERLEY & WAITE

No. 2L.
Star Dining.

No. 23
Rosette Dining.

No. 22.
Star Dining, Extra High or Tea..

No. 59.
Rosette Banister Dining,
veneered.

F. E. STUART.

No. 233. Dining Chair.

Walnut or Mahoganized Cherry. Price,
Cane Seat and Back............$3 50

No. 191.
Boston Wood Seat, Two Slat Dining.

No. 189.
Boston Wood Seat Dining.

No. 275. Dining Chair.

Walnut or Mahoganized Cherry.
Price, in Cane.............$4 00

—Tyler Desk Co., St. Louis, Mo.

Cortland ∗ Furniture ∗ Company,
Cortland, N. Y.

No. 7.
CONANT DINING.

No. 71.
EASTLAKE DINING.

E. F. PEIRCE, 162 NORTH ST. BOSTON.

No. 889
Dining Chair. Solid Golden Oak elegantly carved top and back slat cane seat, posts, spindles and front rounds fancy turned.
Each.................$1.08

No. 994
Dining Chair. Solid Golden Oak elegantly carved top and back slat, posts spindles and front rounds fancy turned cane seat.
Each.................$1.33

No. 992
Dining Chair. Solid Golden Oak elegantly carved top and back slat, posts, spindles and front rounds fancy turned cane seat.
Each.................$1.45

No. 990
Dining Chair. Solid Golden Oak cane seat, elegantly carved top and back slat, posts, spindles and front rounds fancy turned fan shaped spindles.
Each.................$1.56

No. 987
Dining Chair. Golden Quartered Oak cane seat, posts, spindles and front rounds fancy turned back spindles are shaped to fit your back, top and back slat are curved.
Each.................$1.60

No. 981
Dining Chair. Golden Quartered Oak elegantly carved top and back slat, round cane seat and round seat frame, banister back.
Each.................$1.70

No. 915
Dining Chair. Golden Quartered Oak elegantly carved top and back slat, posts and front rounds fancy turned banister back cane seat.
Each.................$1.70

No. 978
Dining Chair. Golden Quartered Oak cane seat top and back slat carved fancy turned top fancy turned posts spindles and front rounds.
Each.................$1.75

No. 977
Dining Chair. Golden Quartered Oak elegantly carved top and back slat fancy turned posts spindles and front rounds. Cane seat.
Each.................$1.75

No. 903
Box Seat Dining Chair. Golden Quartered Oak cane seat. French legs shaped seat.
Cane Seat, each...........$2.00
Genuine Leather, each.....3.00

No. 976
Box Seat Dining Chair. Golden Quartered Oak, cane seat, French legs, spiral turned spindles, shaped seat.
Cane Seat, each...........$2.00
Genuine Leather, each.....3.00

No. 7546
Box Seat Dining Chair. Golden Quartered Oak, piano polish, French legs.
Cane Seat, each...........$2.75
Genuine Leather, each.....3.75

Arm Chairs to Match 903 and 976 Furnished on Application.

No. 983
Box Seat Dining Chair. Golden Quartered Oak. French legs piano polish, banister back.
Cane Seat, each.........$3.00
Genuine Leather, each....4.00

No. 877
Box Seat Dining Chair. Golden Quartered Oak. French legs piano polish, banister back.
Cane Seat, each.........$3.20
Genuine Leather, each....4.20

No. 7635
Box Seat Dining Chair. Golden Quartered Oak, elegantly carved oval slat French legs and claw feet piano polish.
Cane Seat, each..........$3.80
Genuine Leather, each....4.80

No. 7637
Box Seat Dining Chair. Golden Quartered Oak, piano polish, elegantly carved top and back slat, French legs, claw feet.
Cane Seat, each........$4.00
Genuine Leather, each....5.00

No. 7599
Box Seat Dining Chair. Golden Quartered Oak, piano polish, banister back, shaped rim, French legs and claw feet.
Cane Seat, each.........$4.85
Genuine Leather, each....5.85

No. 7530
Dining Chair. Golden Quartered Oak, piano polish, elegantly carved, genuine leather seat and back, box seat.
Each.................$4.85

Arm Chairs to Match Each of the Above Dining Chairs Furnished on Application.

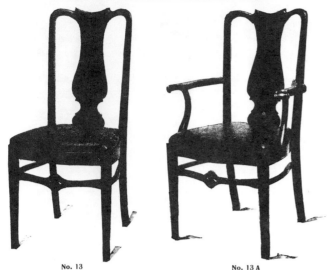

No. 13   **No. 13 A**

Dining Chairs. Golden Quartered Oak and Genuine Solid Mahogany, all of the best selected material. Piano polish. Rush seats or genuine leather seats.

Oak, each...............$5.50	Oak, each.......................$ 7.75
Mahogany, each..........7.75	Mahogany, each.................10.75

No. 15   **No. 15 A**

Dining Chairs. Golden Quartered Oak of the very best selected material. Piano polish. Rush seat or genuine leather seat.

Each..........................$5.95	Each.........................$8.15

No. 17   **No. 17 A**

Dining Chairs. Golden Quartered Oak of very best selected material. Rush seat or genuine leather seat. Piano polish.

Each..........................$7.00	Each.........................$ 9.15

No. 18   **No. 18 A**

Dining Chairs. Chippendale Pattern. Golden Quartered Oak or Genuine Solid Mahogany. All of the best selected material. Piano polish. Genuine leather seat.

Oak, each............$11.10	Oak, each.............$14.00
Mahogany, each.........14.00	Mahogany, each........17.75

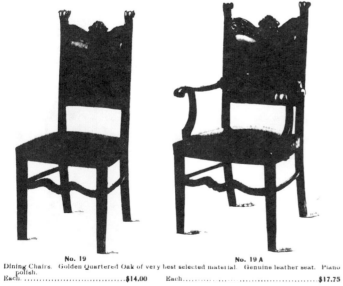

No. 19   **No. 19 A**

Dining Chairs. Golden Quartered Oak of very best selected material. Genuine leather seat. Piano polish.

Each..........................$14.00	Each........................$17.75

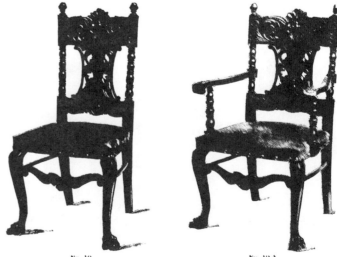

No. 10   **No. 10 A**

Dining Chairs. Golden Quartered Oak of very best selected material. Genuine leather seat. Piano polish.

Each..........................$17.75	Each........................$23.50

Desks and Office Furniture

THE ROCKFORD FURNITURE JOURNAL.

CHICAGO DESK
MANF'G COMP'Y

Michigan Artisan, April, 1890, page 42.

A. PETERSEN & CO.

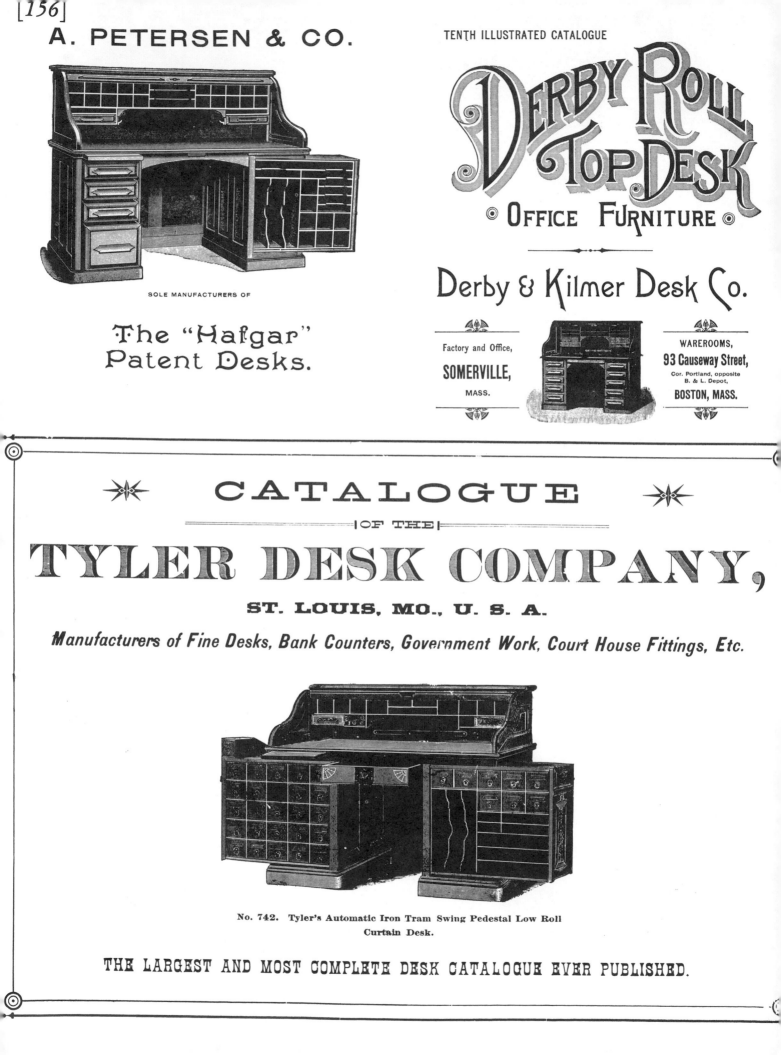

SOLE MANUFACTURERS OF

The "Hafgar" Patent Desks.

DERBY ROLL TOP DESK

◎ OFFICE FURNITURE ◎

Derby & Kilmer Desk Co.

Factory and Office,

SOMERVILLE,

MASS.

WAREROOMS,

93 Causeway Street,

Cor. Portland, opposite
B. & L. Depot,

BOSTON, MASS.

✳ CATALOGUE ✳

|OF THE|

TYLER DESK COMPANY,

ST. LOUIS, MO., U. S. A.

Manufacturers of Fine Desks, Bank Counters, Government Work, Court House Fittings, Etc.

No. 742. Tyler's Automatic Iron Tram Swing Pedestal Low Roll
Curtain Desk.

THE LARGEST AND MOST COMPLETE DESK CATALOGUE EVER PUBLISHED.

BURLINGTON, IOWA, U. S. A.

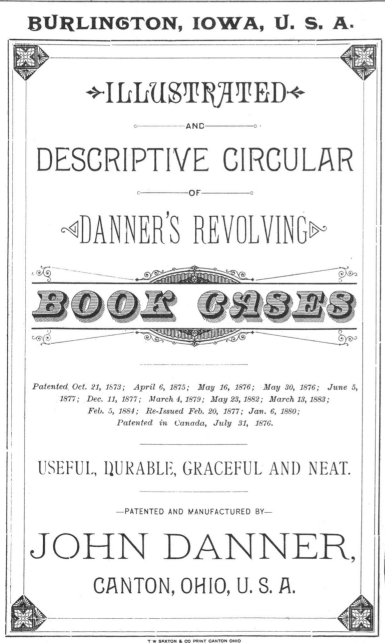

✦ILLUSTRATED✦

— AND —

DESCRIPTIVE CIRCULAR

— OF —

◄DANNER'S REVOLVING►

BOOK CASES

Patented Oct. 21, 1873; April 6, 1875; May 16, 1876; May 30, 1876; June 5, 1877; Dec. 11, 1877; March 4, 1879; May 23, 1882; March 13, 1883; Feb. 5, 1884; Re-Issued Feb. 20, 1877; Jan. 6, 1880; Patented in Canada, July 31, 1876.

USEFUL, DURABLE, GRACEFUL AND NEAT.

—PATENTED AND MANUFACTURED BY—

JOHN DANNER,

CANTON, OHIO, U. S. A.

T W SAXTON & CO PRINT CANTON OHIO

Central Manufacturing Co.

MANUFACTURERS OF

OFFICE · AND · LIBRARY

FURNITURE,

37, 39 & 41 Armour St.,

◄CHICAGO.►

GEO. B. BARLOW & CO., PRINTERS, 285 CLARK ST., CHICAGO.

TYLER DESK CO.

BUILDERS OF

Bank Counters, Office and Court House Fittings,

Salesrooms, 500 & 502 North Fourth Street, St. Louis, Mo., U. S. A.

No. 2251. Very Handsome Counter.

Made of any Hard Wood, and Mounted with Brass, Ground or Plain Glass, Finished in Finest Hand Polish.

No. 2245. Walnut, Antique Oak, Mahogany or Cherry.

Twisted Flat Brass; Plate, or Ground Glass; Names, on Brass, or Engraved; Plate-Glass Paywindow Sills; Woodwork all Hard Polish, Hand Finish. Portable. Shipped K. D., Boxed. Easily set up.

No. 2241. Made of any Hard Wood.

Plain or Twisted Brass; Ground, Opaque, or Plain Glass. All Counters Modeled to suit Customers. Portable. Shipped, K. D., Boxed.

No. 2205. Tyler's Money Table, 24 x 48 Inches.
No. 2206. Tyler's Money Table, 24 x 56 Inches.
Made of any Hard Wood; with two Drawers, both with Best Flat Key Locks; One Drawer with Coin Tray, and one for Bills.

No. 2207. Tyler's Check Desk.

Made of any Hard Wood; Portable. Fastens to Wall. Size, 24 by 40 inches, or 24 by 52 inches. Height, 43 inches; Legs resting on floor.

No. 1008. Tyler's Court House or Record Case.

Roller Bins in Base for Heavy Books. These Cases are made to order only, and made of any Size or Wood wanted.

The File Cases are of Heavy Cardboard and of any size desired.

ROSTRUM A.

Tyler's New Design for Judge and Clerk. Details made to order.
Made in Oak, Walnut or Cherry.

Bank, Court House and Office work, Imperial Finish.—Tyler Desk Co., St. Louis, Mo.

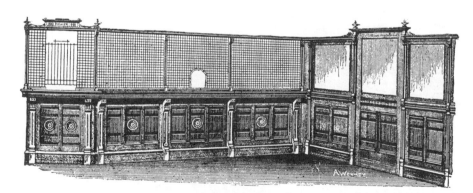

No. 2244.

Counter, with Glass, Brass or Bronze Wire; a very neat Design. Made in any Wood desired and Modeled in any Shape.

No. 2242.

Bank, Brokers, Real Estate or Commercial Office, with or without Railing, to which a finer or cheaper Rail can be adapted. Made in any Wood wanted and with Glass, Wire or Brass Screens.

70 OPEN.   79 CLOSED.

No. 70. Tyler's New King. Solid Walnut or Cherry.

OF SPECIAL INTEREST TO COUNTY CLERKS, INSURANCE AND REAL ESTATE OFFICES.

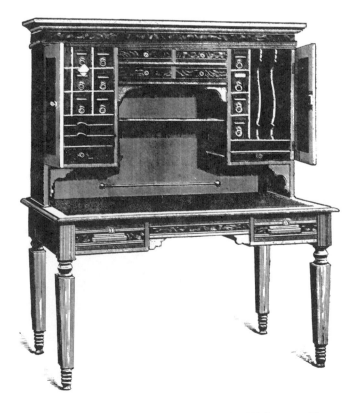

**No. 83. Tyler's New Style Wall Desk. Walnut or Cherry.
Handsomely Veneered.**

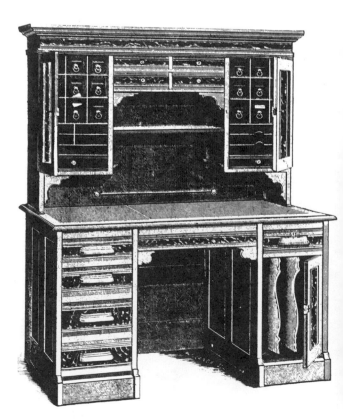

**No 8l. Tyler's New Style Wall Desk. Walnut or Cherry.
Veneered in French Walnut or Mahogany.**

852 CLOSED.

852 OPEN.

No. 852. Tyler's Gem Cylinder Desk—Walnut, Antique Oak or Cherry.

Size, 26 inches wide, 48 inches long, extreme height 55 inches. Finished all around; Fine Fancy Veneer on Drawer Fronts and Cylinder Panels; Fancy Carved Ornament; Sliding Table (extends 11 inches); Handsomest Business Cylinder Desk ever made for the money. Fitted complete. Weight, 125 lbs. Price, F. O. B.................................$40 00

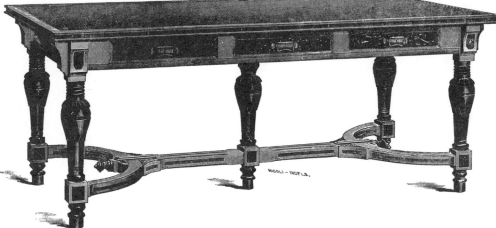

No. 4446. TYLER'S IMPERIAL DIRECTORY TABLE.

Old Oak, Walnut or Cherry. Weight, 125 Pounds.

This Table with our Solid Cast Brass Corners makes the Handsomest and Cheapest Table ever made. Covered with Billiard Cloth or Best Rubber Duck.

No. 4446A. Size, 6 feet long by 34 inches wide. Price, F. O. B...................$34 00   No. 4446B. Size, 7 feet long by 34 inches wide. Price, F. O. B.........$38 00

No. 4446C. Size, 8 feet long by 36 inches wide. Price, F. O. B.......................$42 00

872 OPEN.

872 CLOSED.

No. 872. Double Roll Curtain Desk—Walnut, Antique Oak or Cherry.

, 36 inches wide, 60 inches long, 59 inches high; our Patented Curtain; finished all around; Extension Slide over Drawers; Billiard Cloth or Veneered Writing Table; Extra Fine Fancy Veneer; all pigeon holes filled with 39 Cardboard Filing Boxes. Brass Card Rail.

Elegantly Veneered Front and Ends, Combination Lock; strictly first-class in every particular. Weight, 350 lbs. Price, F. O. B...................$116 00

All Tyler Desks have Best Secret Plate Casters Fitted. See page 4.

870 OPEN.

870 CLOSED.

No. 870. Tyler's Low Roll Curtain Desk—Walnut, Antique Oak or Cherry.

Size, 30 inches wide, 42 inches long, 43 inches high. Our Patented Curtain; our Built-up and Veneered Writing Table; Highly Polished; Finished Back; Panele
Ends and Back; Automatic Lock; one Key unlocks the entire Desk. Brass Rods; Files and Casters complete. Weight, 125 lbs. Price, F. O. B. **$36 0**

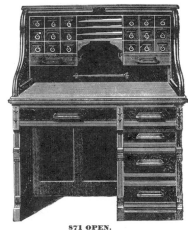

871 CLOSED.

871 OPEN.

No. 871. Tyler's High Roll Curtain Desk. Walnut, Antique Oak or Cherry.

Size, 30 inches wide, 42 inches long, 51 inches high. Our Patented Curtain; Finished Back; Five Fancy Veneered Panels; Extra Finish; Zinc Bottom; Cover
with Billiard Cloth; Arm Slide. Files; Brass Rod and Casters complete. Weight 125 lbs. Price, F. O. B....................**$48 0**

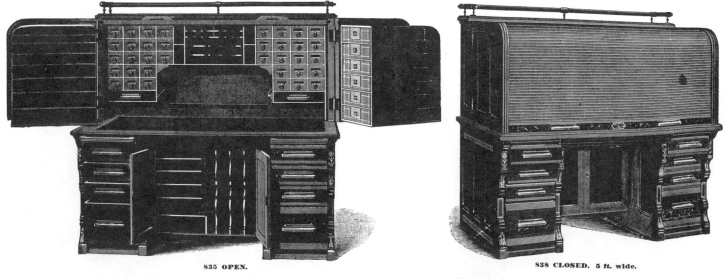

835 OPEN.

838 CLOSED. 5 ft. wide.

No. 835. Tyler's New Governor Madison—Patented.

Made of Best Antique Oak, Walnut or Cherry.

Size, when closed, 5 feet long, 36 inches wide, and 57 inches high, by 7 feet 6 inches wide when fully open as above. One of the finest, and most complete Desk
made. Fifty Filing Boxes; Best Billiard Cloth; Zinc Bottoms; Shelves from 7 inches to 19 inches long; will accommodate any size of Legal or Insurance Blanks; Swinging Cupboard underneath Writing Table, which can be pushed back out of the way, or drawn forward as desired; Eight Book Spaces
Drawers 27 inches long inside; Extension Slides under Writing Table; Six of our Patented Letter Files in the Swing, with Indexes and Patente
Trimmings complete—this feature alone would cost twenty-five dollars; entire Desk closed with one lock; Finished all around and none but the be
material used; Portable. Shipped K. D. Weight, 350 lbs. Price, F. O. B....................**$165 0**

No Man Living Makes Finer Desks Than These—Tyler Desk Co., St. Louis, Mo.

[163]

No. 734. Tyler's Automatic, Iron Tram, Swing Pedestal, Flat Top Desk. Walnut, Antique Oak or Cherry. (Government Standard.)

Size, 4 feet 6 inches by 2 feet 8 inches wide. Heavy Raised Panels; Finished all round; Solid Paneled Back; Billiard Cloth Top, and Arm Slide; Solid and Durable; Mice and Dust Proof; Files and Casters complete. Weight, 150 lbs. Price, F. O. B.. $50 00

No. 737. Tyler's Double, Automatic, Iron Tram, Swing Pedestal, Flat Top Desk. Walnut, Antique Oak or Cherry. (Government Standard.)

Size, 4 feet 6 inches by 4 feet 4 inches. Both Sides Alike; Heavy Raised Panels; Billiard Cloth Top and Arm Slide; Mice and Dust Proof; Files and Casters complete. Weighs, 250 lbs. Price, F. O. B................................. $70 00

No. 735. Tyler's Automatic, Iron Tram, Double, Swing Pedestal, Flat Top Desk. Walnut, Antique Oak or Cherry. (Government Standard.)

Size, 4 feet 6 inches long, by 2 feet 8 inches wide. Heavy Raised Paneled Ends and Back; Finished all round; Billiard Cloth Top; Files and Casters complete; Mice and Dust Proof. Weight, 175 lbs. Price, F. O. B................ $58 00

No. 99. Flat Top. Tyler's Little Maid. Walnut, Old Oak or Cherry.

32 inches wide, 52 inches long; Veneered Drawer Fronts; Finished all around; Paneled Ends and Sides; Covered with Rubber Drill or Felt Cloth; Front Cupboard filled with 15 Filing Boxes; End Cupboard partitioned for Books; Automatic Lock on Drawers; Full 5-ply Top; Casters Fitted. Weight, 125 lbs. Price, F. O. B. $28 00

No. 40. Flat Top. Tyler's Little Hero. Walnut, Oak or Cherry.

30 inches wide, and 48 inches long; Finished all around; Paneled Ends and Sides; Covered with Rubber Cloth; Cupboard in Ends; Casters Fitted. Weight, 100 lbs. Price, F. O. B.. $20 00

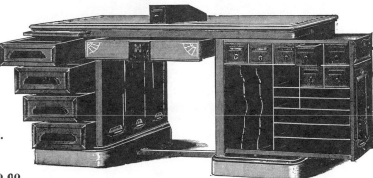

No. 738. Tyler's Extra Automatic, Iron Tram, Flat Top Desk. Walnut, Antique Oak or Cherry. (Government Standard.)

Size, 5 feet long by 3 feet wide. Heavy Raised Panels; Finished all round; Billiard Cloth Top; Mice and Dust Proof; Arm Slide; Files and Casters complete; Combination Lock. Weight, 200 lbs. Price, F. B. B...................... $58 00

No. 730. Tyler's Automatic Iron Tram, Government Standard, Swing Pedestal Flat Top Desk—Walnut, Antique Oak or Cherry.

Size, 3 ft. 8 in. long, 2 ft. 8 in. deep. Handsome Veneered Front; Top covered with Billiard Cloth; Best Tumbler Locks on Drawer and Revolving Case; Files and Casters complete. Mice and Dust Proof. Weight, 100 lbs. Price, F. O. B....**$38 00**

No. 731. Tyler's Automatic Iron Tram, Government Standard, Swing Pedestal Bevel Top Desk—Walnut, Antique Oak or Cherry.

Size, 3 ft. 8 in. long, 2 ft. 8 in. wide. Extra Heavy Frame; Full-raised Panels; Double Moulded Base. Very Handsome. Opens same as No. 730. Files and Casters complete. Weight, 100 lbs. Price, F. O. B...............................**$38 00**

No. 733. Tyler's Automatic Iron Tram, Government Standard, Double Swing Pedestal Flat Top Desk—Walnut, Antique Oak or Cherry.

Size, 4 ft. 6 in. long, 2 ft. 8 in. wide. No finer Desk made. Raised Panels; Finished all around; Billiard Cloth Top and Arm Slide; Mice and Dust Proof; Files and Casters complete. Weight, 175 lbs. Price, F. O. B.........................**$56 00**

861 OPEN.

No. 861. Tyler's Low Roll Curtain Desk. Walnut, Antique Oak or Cherry.

Size, 34 inches wide, 52 inches long, 45 inches high. Our Latest Patented Curtain; Felt Cloth on Writing Table and Slides; Finished all around; Automatic Lock; Files; Brass Rod and Casters complete. Weight 175 lbs. Price, F. O. B.......**$54 00**

818 OPEN.

No. 818. Tyler's Low Roll Curtain Desk. Walnut, Antique Oak or Cherry.

Size, 30 inches wide, 43 inches long, 43 inches high. Our Patented Curtain; Finished Back; Fine Finish; Zinc Bottom; Covered with Felt Cloth; Files; Brass Rod and Casters complete. Weight, 100 lbs. Price, F. O. B.

No. 732. Tyler's Automatic Iron Tram, Government Standard, Swing Pedestal Flat Top Desk—Walnut, Antique Oak or Cherry.

Size, 4 ft. 6 in. long, 2 ft. 8 in. wide. Combination Lock; Absolutely Perfect; Heavy Raised Panels; Finished all around; Arm Slide; Billiard Cloth Top; Mice and Dust Proof; Files and Casters complete. Weight, 150 lbs. Price, F. O. B....**$48 00**

IN THIS STYLE YOU HAVE SPACE, ELEGANCE AND COMFORT.

OVER 900 OF THESE SOLD WITHOUT A COMPLAINT.

No. 834. Tyler's High Roll Curtain Desk. Cherry, Antique Oak or Walnut Veneered.

FANCY BRASS CARD RAIL AND 26 FILE CASES.

Size, 36 in. wide, 5 ft. long, 52 in. high. Our Patented Brass Lined Curtains; Zinc Bottom; Paneled and Finished all around; Extra Fine Fancy Veneer Front and Ends; Elegantly Carved Post; Extension Arm Slides in table; Covered with Billiard Cloth; Built-up Panels and Tops; Combination Lock; Large Plate Casters. MICE AND DUST PROOF. Portable Upper Section; Weight 300 lbs. Price, F. O. B.................... **$90 00**

No. 834 A.

Same. 4 ft. 8 in. long. Price, F. O. B......................... **85 00**

No. 606 A. Tyler's New High Roll Curtain Desk. Walnut, Antique Oak or Cherry.

Size, 4 ft. 4 in. long, 34 in. wide, 50 in. high. 17 Filing Cases; Book Rack in each end of Pigeon Hole Case; Brass Card Rail; Veneered Front and Ends; Built-up Polished Wood Writing Table or Cloth; Arm Slides; Zinc Bottoms; Pencil Drawers, Pen Holders and Caster complete; Portable Top. Weight, 250 lbs. Price, F. O. B....... **$67 00**

No. 606 B.

Same. 5 ft. long. Price, F. O. B............................. **75 00**

All Tyler Desks have Best Secret Plate Casters Fitted. See page 4.

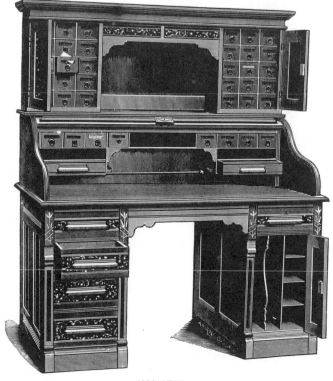

600A OPEN.

600A CLOSED.

No. 600A. Tyler's New Roll Top Mansard Desk—Walnut, Antique Oak or Cherry.

WE MAKE BUT ONE QUALITY OF WORK,

"THE BEST."

Our lowest priced Desks contain best material and workmanship and are as reliable in every respect as our highest priced Desks. No Desks of equal value have ever been offered at prices we quote.

No. 4.

27 in. deep, 46 in. high.

No. 4. Four feet wide, ... $37.50.

Made in Walnut, Cherry, or Antique Oak. High polish finish unless otherwise ordered. All drawers are locked automatically by the roll which is flexible and operates beautifully, also best quality Cabinet Cloth on desk surface and slides. We cannot say too much in favor of the above desk. Our price of a 4-foot desk of this description is liable to make a person suspicious, but we only ask you to look at the desk. Examine it thoroughly, look at any other desk of equal price, and we are willing every time to abide by the result. Our guarantee applies to this desk as well as to all others. All our desks finished polish finish unless otherwise ordered.

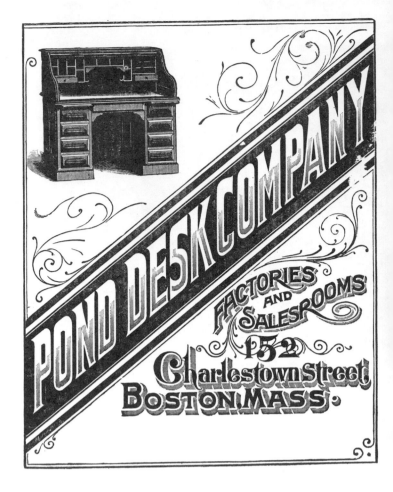

Perfect Light Assured.   No Shadows on Writing Bed.

NO LIGHT HID WHEN USING.

THE IDEAL ROLL TOP.

IMPROVED SWING ARM.

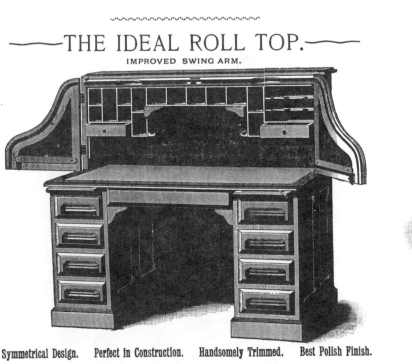

Symmetrical Design.   Perfect in Construction.   Handsomely Trimmed.   Best Polish Finish.

Having the best of facilities, and manufacturing in large quantity, we are enabled to offer these HIGH CLASS DESKS at very low prices. We invite careful inspection, and GUARANTEE satisfaction.

THE IDEAL ROLL TOP.

Every purchaser of our No. 1 or No 2 and No. 2½ Desk will get more and better value for his money than can be realized in the purchase of any other Desk made.

Nos. 1, 2, and 2½.

31 in. deep, 48 in. high.

No. 1. Four feet wide. Price,	. .	$45.00.
No. 2. Four feet six inches wide. Price,	.	47.50.
No. 2½. Five feet wide. Price,	. .	50.00.

In Black Walnut, Cherry or Antique Oak. A high grade desk at moderate price. All modern improvements, viz.: — Full Round Corners, Panels and Writing Bed of three-ply stock, preventing shrinking, swelling and warping. The best Double-Acting Spring Lock that can be produced, one motion securely locking the entire desk; moveable partitions in drawers. Letter Drop, Secret Drawers, Deep Drawers for books, and all possible conveniences. Furnished either with best quality Cabinet Cloth or Polished Wood Writing Bed. The best polish finish throughout entire desk.

No. 124 DESK.
Size, 52x31 inches.
Walnut, Cherry or Oak, bevel top, four drawers, plain back; top covered with Felt or Enameled Cloth. Price—In white, $10.50; finished, $12.50.

No. 128 DESK.
Size, 42x31 inches.
Walnut, Cherry or Oak, bevel top, plain back, four drawers, book-rack in lower drawer; top covered with Felt or Enameled Cloth. Price—In white, $11.50; finished, $13.50.

No. 125 DESK.
Size, 52x31 inches.
Walnut, Cherry or Oak, bevel top plain back, five drawers and book closet; top covered with Felt or Enameled Cloth. Price—In white, $14.00; finished $17.00.

No. 126 DESK.
Same as 125, with finished back. Price—In white, $17.00; Finished, $20.00.

No. 127 DESK.
Size, 52x31 inches.
Walnut, Cherry or Oak, bevel top, finished back; six drawers and book closet, also closet in end; top covered with Billiard Cloth. Price—In white, $21.00; finished, $24.00.

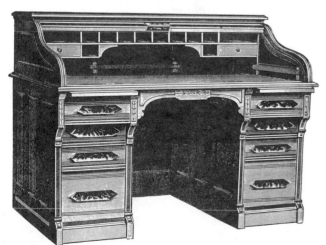

No. 221 CURTAIN DESK.

Size, 56x34 inches, 43 inches high.

Walnut, Cherry or Oak, finished back; Billiard Cloth or Polished Wood on writing part, combination lock on drawers, book-rack in lower right hand drawer.

Price—In white, $48.00; finished, $56.00.

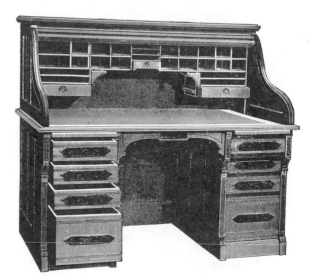

No. 222 CURTAIN DESK.

Size, 56x36 inches; 52 inches high.

Walnut, Cherry or Oak, finished back; Billiard Cloth or polished five-ply wood writing part, combination lock on drawers, book-rack in lower right hand drawer; slides above drawers.

Price—In white, $55.00; finished, $65.00.

No. 154 DOUBLE DESK.

Size, 52x50 inches.

Walnut, Cherry or Oak, bevel top, five drawers, and book-closet on each side, pigeon holes
in decks; top covered with Felt or Enameled Cloth. Price-In white, $30.00; finished, $35.00.

No. 217 LADIES' DESK.

Size, 22x22 inches.   Walnut, Cherry or Oak, top covered with Billiard Cloth.
Price—In white, $8.50; finished, $10.00.

No. 201 CYLINDER OFFICE DESK.

Size, 56x30 inches.

Walnut, Cherry or Oak, finished back, combination lock on drawers ; Billiard
Cloth on slide.

Price—In white; $43.00; finished, $52.00.

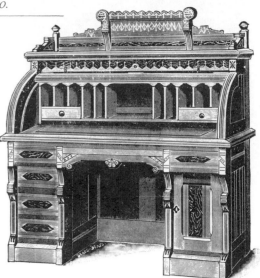

No. 198 CYLINDER OFFICE DESK.

Size, 52x26 inches.

Walnut, Cherry or Oak, finished back, combination lock on drawers; five
drawers and book-closet; Billiard Cloth on slide.

Price—In white, $38.00; finished, $44.00.

No. 200.

Size, 52x26 inches.

Plain back, Walnut, Cherry or Oak, combination lock on drawers.

Price—In white, $35.00; finished, $39.00.

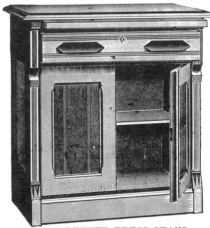

No. 218 LETTER PRESS STAND.

Size, 18x28 inches.   Walnut, Cherry or Oak, closet with shelf, one drawer and slide.
Price—In white, $8.50; finished, $10.00.

No. 142 DESK.

Size, 52x31 inches.

Walnut, Cherry or Oak, flat top, finished back, five drawers and book closet,
also closet in back ; top covered with Felt or Enameled Cloth.

48 in. long, 32 in. deep, 45 in. high.   Made only in Antique Finished Oak. Has solid panels and solid quartered Oak Polished Bed.   Three partitioned drawers.

CENTRAL MANUFACTURING CO.

No. 226 CURTAIN DESK.

Size, 44x30 inches.

Walnut, Cherry or Oak, finished back; book-rack in lower drawer; Billiard Cloth or polished five-ply wood writing part.

Price—In white, $28.00; finished, $32.50.

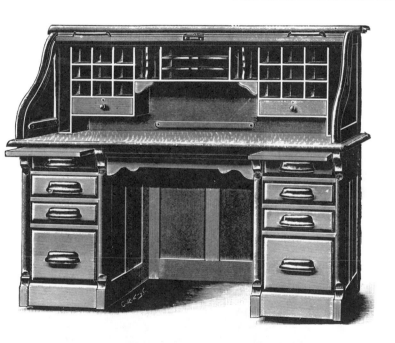

No. 155 Double Desk.

Same as No. 154 without Decks.   Price—In white, $26.00; finished, $30.00,

No. 225 CURTAIN DESK.

Size, 48x30 inches.

Walnut, Cherry or Oak, finished back, slide above drawers on left hand side; book-rack in lower right hand drawer; Billiard Cloth or polished five-ply wood writing part.

Price—In white, $34.00; finished, $38.00.

No. 156 Double Desk.
Size, 52x36 inches.

Walnut, Cherry or Oak, flat top, four drawers on each side; top covered with Felt or Enameled Cloth.   Price—In white, $15.00; finished, $17.00.

No. 158 Double Desk.

No. 194
CYLINDER DESK.

Size, 34x23 inches.

Walnut, Cherry or Oak, plain back ; Billiard Cloth on slide.

Price—In white, $16.00
Finished, $20.00

No. 121 TABLE DESK.

Size, 52x31 inches.
Walnut, Cherry or Oak, flat top, two drawers, finished back ; top covered with Felt or Enameled Cloth.
Price—In white, $7.50 ; finished, $9.50.

No. 120 TABLE DESK.

Walnut, Cherry or Oak, flat top, two drawers, finished back ; top covered with Felt or Enameled Cloth.
Price—In white, $6.50 ; finished, $8.00.

No. 123 TABLE DESK.

Size, 52x31 inches.
Walnut, Cherry or Oak, bevel top, two drawers, plain back ; top covered with Felt or Enameled Cloth.
Price—In white, $7.50 ; finished, $9.50.

No. 122 TABLE DESK.

Size, 42x30.
Walnut, Cherry or Oak, bevel top, two drawers, finished back ; top covered with Felt or Enameled Cloth.
Price—In White, $6.50 ; finished, $8.50.

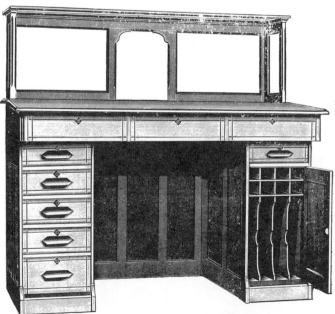

No. 192 CASHIER'S DESK.

Walnut, Cherry or Oak, finished back, solid wood top.

Price—6 foot Desk, in white, $48.00 ; finished, $56.00.

Figured or plain Glass in top, as desired, when ordered finished. Cash drawers with Yale lock, $1.50 extra. Extra sizes, $6.00 per foot additional.

No. 175 DESK.

Size, 52x31 inches, 60 inches high.

Walnut, Cherry or Oak, bevel top, plain back, two drawers in table ; four drawers in deck ; top covered with Felt or Enameled Cloth.

Price—In white, $17.50 ; finished, $21.00.

No. 162 Double Desk.
Size, 54x42 inches.
Walnut, Cherry or Oak, flat top, five drawers and book-closet on each side ; top covered with Billiard Cloth.
Price—In white, $30.00 ; finished, $36.00.

No. 164 Double Desk.
Size, 54x42 inches.
Walnut, Cherry or Oak, flat top, six drawers and book-closet on each side ; extra heavy, solid and substantial ; top covered with Billiard Cloth.
Price—In white, $42.00 ; finished, $48.00.

No. 168 DESK.

Size, 36x24 inches.

Walnut, Cherry or Oak, fall leaf, one drawer in table, plain back ; writing part covered with Felt or Enameled Cloth.

Price—In white, $10.00 ; finished, $13.00.

No. 196

CYLINDER DESK.

Size, 43x26 inches.

Walnut, Cherry or Oak finished back, five drawers, with combination lock on four right-hand drawers ; Billiard Cloth on slide.

Price–In white, $28.00
Finished, $32.00

No. 197.

CYLINDER DESK.

Size, 43x26 inches.

Walnut, Cherry or Oak finished back, five drawers, with combination lock on four right-hand drawers ; Billiard Cloth on slide.

Price–In white, $30.00
Finished, $35.00

No. 170 DESK.

Size, 42x31 inches.

Walnut, Cherry or Oak, bevel top, plain back, five drawers in base, pigeon-holes and one drawer in deck; top covered with Felt or Enameled Cloth.

Price—In white, $13.50; finished, $16.50.

No. 172 DESK.

Size, 42x31 inches.

Bevel top, book-rack and pigeon holes in deck; top covered with Felt or Enameled Cloth.

Price—In Walnut, Cherry or Oak, in white, $17.50; finished, $22.00·

No. 176 DESK.

Size, 52x31 inches, 60 inches high.

Walnut, Cherry or Oak, bevel top, plain back, four drawers in desk; top covered with Felt or Enameled Cloth. Deck same as on No. 175 when open.

Price—In white, $20.00; finished, $24.00.

No. 178 DESK.

Size, 51x32 inches.

Walnut, Cherry or Oak, bevel top, plain back, five drawers and book-closet in base; Felt or Enameled Cloth on top. Deck same as on No. 175 when open.

Price—In white, $24.50; finished, $28.00.

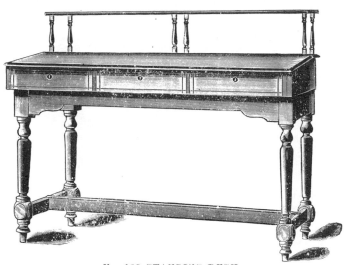

No. 189 STANDING DESK.

Walnut, Cherry or Oak, finished back, solid wood top.

4 foot Desk, in white, $14.00; finished, $16.00
5 " " " 16.00; " 18.00
6 " " " 18.00; " 20.00
8 " " " 22.00; " 24.00

All single Standing Desks are 3 feet wide.

No. 189 Double, 6 feet, in white, $27.00; finished, $31.50
" **189** " 8 " " 33.00; " 37.50

All Double Standing Desks are 4 feet 6 inches wide.

When size is not specified we ship 6-foot Desks.

No. 190 STANDING DESK.

Walnut, Cherry or Oak, finished back, solid wood top.

PRICE.

4 foot Desk, in white.......$19.00; finished.................$23.00
5 " " ....21.00; " 25.00
6 " " ....23.00; " 27.00
8 " " ....27.00; " 31.00

No. 190 DOUBLE.

6 foot Desk, in white.......$32.00; finished.................$37.50
8 " " ....38.00; " 43.50

When size is not specified we ship 6-foot Desks.

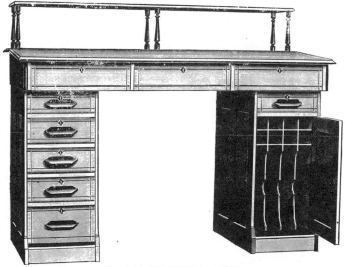

No. 191 STANDING DESK.

Walnut, Cherry or Oak, finished back, solid wood top.

PRICE.

4 foot Desk, in white, $22.00; finished, $29.00
5 " " " 24.00; " 31.00
6 " " " 26.00; " 33.00
8 " " " 30.00; " 37.00

No. 191 DOUBLE.

6 foot Desk, in white, $40.00; finished, $49.00
8 " " " 46.00; " 55.00

When size is not specified we ship 6 foot Desks.

No. 180 DESK.

Size, 52x 31 Inches.

Walnut, Cherry or Oak, bevel top, six drawers in base, book-rack in lower right
hand drawer; top covered with Felt or Enameled Cloth.

Price in white, $24.00; finished, $27.50.

No. **330**—Class C.   60 in. long, 32 in. deep, 51 in. high.   Made only in Antique Finished Oak. Has solid panels and solid quartered Oak Polished Bed.   Three partitioned drawers.

—Class A.   60 in. long, 34 in. deep, 51 in. high.   Made in Walnut, Cherry or Oak. Oak in either Antique or 16th Century finish.   Oak has quartered panels and top.   High polish finish all around.   Has 3-ply framed, figured Oak Writing Bed, and one deep drawer has Leopold's (patent applied for) Adjustable Letter File.   Four partitioned drawers.   Our dust-proof curtain.   Oak pigeon hole, with movable boxes and mirror in centre.   All Oak drawers finished inside.

DERBY ROLL-TOP DESK.

DERBY ROLL-TOP DESK.

No. 15.

33½ inches deep, 51 inches high.

		4 ft. wide.	4 ft. 6 in. wide.	5 ft. wide.	5 ft. 6 in. wide.
Antique Oak, Cherry or Black Walnut,	Price,	$70.00	$75.00	$80.00	$90.00
Mahogany	"		85.00	95.00	110.00

Oak Desks in stock, with Polished Hard-wood writing-bed.
Oak, Cherry and Walnut, with Navy Blue cloth.

Desk No. 15 is our leading and best desk. It gives satisfaction to those who buy it, and in the *five-feet* size is unhesitatingly recommended by us as the best and most satisfactory and economical desk for office use in the market.

No. 15. S. A.
(SWING ARM DESK.)

		4 ft. 6 in. wide.	5 ft. wide.	5 ft. 6 in. wide. To order only.
Antique Oak, Cherry or Walnut,	. . . Price,	$80.00	$85.00	$100.00

Oak Desks in stock, with Polished Hard-wood writing-bed.
Oak, Cherry and Walnut, with Navy Blue cloth.

The Swinging Arm Desk is specially designed and adapted for use in offices where the light is poor, and comes in a slant to either end of the desk. By throwing open the arms the light on the writing-bed is improved.

No. 2 Desk.

42 in. long, 26 in. wide.
Finished on Back Side.

Made of Solid, Kiln Dried Black Walnut, Cherry, or Oak; Enamel or Imitation Leather Top; Smooth, Rubbed-Down Finish. Has five drawers and makes a first-class Office, Library or Study Desk. Covered with Billiard Cloth, 75 cents extra. Can be made to order 48 inches long at an additional cost of $1.00.

No. 11.

LOW ROUND TOP.

33½ inches deep, 44 inches high.

No. 3 Desk.

48 in. long, 27 in. wide. Finished on Back Side.

Made of Solid, Kiln Dried Walnut, Cherry or Oak. Enamel Cloth or Imitation Leather Top. Has one Centre and Seven Side Drawers, one of them double usual depth for books, or can be made with door at same price. This fills the demand for a roomy, practical Office, Library, or Study Desk. Covered with Billiard Cloth at extra cost of $1.00.

No. 13.

LOW OGEE TOP.

The Best Tables on the Market for Offices, Hotels, Reading Rooms, Libraries, Directors' Meetings

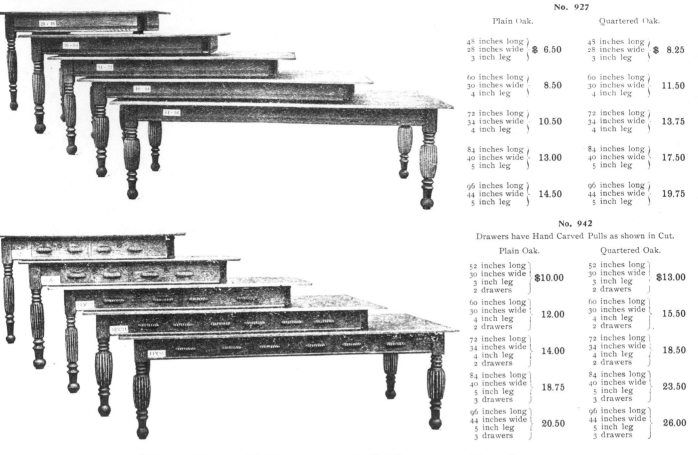

No. 927

Plain Oak.		Quartered Oak.	
48 inches long 28 inches wide 3 inch leg	$ 6.50	48 inches long 28 inches wide 3 inch leg	$ 8.25
60 inches long 30 inches wide 4 inch leg	8.50	60 inches long 30 inches wide 4 inch leg	11.50
72 inches long 34 inches wide 4 inch leg	10.50	72 inches long 34 inches wide 4 inch leg	13.75
84 inches long 40 inches wide 5 inch leg	13.00	84 inches long 40 inches wide 5 inch leg	17.50
96 inches long 44 inches wide 5 inch leg	14.50	96 inches long 44 inches wide 5 inch leg	19.75

No. 942

Drawers have Hand Carved Pulls as shown in Cut.

Plain Oak.		Quartered Oak.	
52 inches long 30 inches wide 3 inch leg 2 drawers	$10.00	52 inches long 30 inches wide 3 inch leg 2 drawers	$13.00
60 inches long 30 inches wide 4 inch leg 2 drawers	12.00	60 inches long 30 inches wide 4 inch leg 2 drawers	15.50
72 inches long 34 inches wide 4 inch leg 2 drawers	14.00	72 inches long 34 inches wide 4 inch leg 2 drawers	18.50
84 inches long 40 inches wide 5 inch leg 3 drawers	18.75	84 inches long 40 inches wide 5 inch leg 3 drawers	23.50
96 inches long 44 inches wide 5 inch leg 3 drawers	20.50	96 inches long 44 inches wide 5 inch leg 3 drawers	26.00

Flat Top Office and Library Desks

No. 910. Solid Golden Oak, 46 inches long, 29 inches deep, well made and well finished............................ $13.00

No. 918 1-2. Same as 910, but with one tier of drawers (see No. 7-42), 42 inches long, Solid Golden Oak, drawer under knee space $11.00

No. 7—50

DESCRIPTION. Solid Golden Oak, piano polish, beveled and cross paneled, double base, drawer in knee space with separate lock. Combination locks like No. 7-42. Book drawer in lower right hand tier. (See No. 7-42.)

50 inches long, 32 inches deep $16.25
55 inches long, 32 inches deep................. 18.75
60 inches long, 32 inches deep................. 19.50

No. 7—42. Solid Golden Oak, piano polish, beveled and cross panels, double base. Drawer in knee space (which has a separate lock). Combination lock. Top drawer being locked with key, locks all the rest. Two bottom drawers make one large book drawer. 42 inches long, 32 inches deep.................... $14.00

No. 12. This is a double desk, having the same arrangement of drawers on each side. A great lawyer's desk. Piano polish, beveled cross panels, combination locks, large drawer in center. Golden Quartered Oak or Solid Mahogany.

60 inches long, 48 inches deep, Oak	$46.75	Mahogany	$ 67.00
66 inches long, 54 inches deep, Oak	60.00	Mahogany	96.00
72 inches long, 60 inches deep, Oak	78.00	Mahogany	120.00

No. 14. Same as No. 12. In Golden plain Oak only.

55 inches long, 48 inches deep.............................. $32.00
60 inches long, 48 inches deep.............................. 36.50

No. 6—50

DESCRIPTION. Golden Quartered Oak or Solid Mahogany, both woods carefully selected. Hand-carved drawer pulls, double base. Combination locks, book drawer in right hand tier. Beveled and cross paneled, 5-ply writing bed.

OAK.

42 inches long, 32 inches wide...... ... . $17.25
50 inches long, 32 inches wide................. 20.25
55 inches long, 32 inches wide................. 23.00
60 inches long, 32 inches wide 26.00

MAHOGANY.

42 inches long, 32 inches wide...... ... . $28.00
50 inches long, 32 inches wide......... .... 31.50
55 inches long, 32 inches wide................. 36.00
60 inches long, 32 inches wide................. 39.00

Send For Our Special Desk Catalogue

We Are Headquarters in Office Furniture

We issue a Special Desk Catalog which we would be pleased to send you.

No. 914. Roll Top Desk. Interior has the regular pigeon hole construction, Solid Golden Oak. 30 inches long. Large drawer under writing bed.

Price...$8 75

Also a good typewriter desk.

No. 25. High roll top. Beveled cross panels, large deep drawer in the middle, with separate lock. Combination locks. Adjustable partitions on the inside of the drawers. Double base. All sizes are 32 in. deep and 50 in. high.

Length, 42 in.	Price, Oak....................	$21 00
Length, 50 in.	Price, Oak....................	22 00
Length, 55 in.	Price, Oak....................	27 00
Length, 60 in.	Price, Oak....................	30 50

No. 1. Same as No. 25, but with beautiful figured Golden Quartered Oak. The drawer-pulls are hand-carved, the same as on No. 8. The drawers are finished on the inside, while the depth is 34 inches. The Mahogany is of the best quality.

Length, 42 in.	Oak.........$26 75	Mahogany..........$44 00
Length, 50 in.	Oak.......... 29 50	Mahogany.......... 50 00
Length, 55 in.	Oak.......... 35 50	Mahogany.......... 56 00
Length, 60 in.	Oak.......... 39 00	Mahogany.......... 62 00
Length, 66 in.	Oak.......... 44 50	Mahogany.......... 74 00

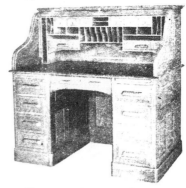

No. 13. High top roll. Double base. Beveled cross panels. Large, deep drawer in center. Combination locks. Enclosed pigeon-hole cases. Each size is 34 in. deep and 50 in. high. Fine polished Golden Oak.

Length, 50 in.	Price....................	$32 00
Length, 55 in.	Price....................	35 25
Length, 60 in.	Price....................	39 75

No. 912. Roll top. Solid Golden Oak. 42 in. long, 45 in. high. Combination locks. Extension slide. Interior is like No. 911.

Price...$12 75

No. 125. High roll top. Beveled cross panels. Double base. Combination locks. Large drawer in center with separate lock. Enclosed pigeon-holes. Letter file on inside left hand drawer. All sizes are 32 in. deep and 50 in. high. Golden Oak, piano polish.

Length, 50 in.	Price....................	$28 00
Length, 55 in.	Price....................	32 25
Length, 60 in.	Price....................	35 50

No. 11. High top roll. Beveled cross panels. Golden Quartered Oak or Solid Mahogany. Piano polish. Hand-carved drawer pulls. Large, deep drawer in center. Letter file on left hand inside drawer. Enclosed pigeon-hole cases. All sizes are 35 in. deep and 50 in. high.

Length, 50 in.	Oak.......$35 00	Mahogany..............$55 00
Length, 55 in.	Oak....... 37 00	Mahogany.............. 60 00
Length, 60 in.	Oak....... 45 00	Mahogany.............. 66 00

No. 911. Roll top. Solid Golden Oak. 46 in. long, 46 in. high. Combination locks. Extension slides.

Price...$17 00

No. 20. High roll top. Beveled cross panels. Double base. Enclosed pigeon-hole cases and rounded filing drawers. Vertical letter file in left end. Eight handy small drawers. Large deep drawer in center. Golden Oak, polish finish. All sizes are 35 in. deep and 50 in. high.

Length, 50 in.	Price....................	$36 50
Length, 55 in.	Price....................	39 75
Length, 60 in.	Price....................	44 50

No. 4. Same as No. 20, but in elegant Golden Quartered Oak and Solid Mahogany and with hand-carved drawer-pulls. Also four long letter file drawers down left side.

Length, 50 in.	Oak. $39 00	Mahogany..........$63 00
Length, 55 in.	Oak.......... 45 00	Mahogany.......... 70 00
Length, 60 in.	Oak.......... 48 00	Mahogany.......... 76 00

No. 8. High roll top. Beveled cross panels. Four long letter files down left side. Full of convenient drawers. Pan tray and ink wells. Large center drawer. Elegant Golden Quartered Oak or Solid Mahogany, piano polish. All sizes are 36 in. deep and 50 in. high.

Length, 50 in.	Oak..........$55 00	Mahogany..........$ 75 00
Length, 55 in.	Oak.......... 63 00	Mahogany.......... 85 00
Length, 60 in.	Oak.......... 70 00	Mahogany.......... 93 00
Length, 66 in.	Oak.......... 80 00	Mahogany.......... 105 00

No. 16. Has the same material and the same interior as No. 8, but is 38 inches deep, all arms pilasters, base and top are of thicker material.

Length, 60 in.	Oak..........$ 75 00	Mahogany..........$108 00
Length, 66 in.	Oak.......... 92 50	Mahogany.......... 130 00
Length, 72 in.	Oak.......... 110 00	Mahogany.. .... 152 00

DANNER'S PATENT REVOLVING BOOK CASES.

LEGAL CASE.

A very popular case—all black walnut, finished in oil. This case stands 46 inches high from floor to top of case, and is 24 inches diameter. On the left hand side, as shown in the cut, are 6 drawers 2 inches high, 9 by 15 inches; also 6 drawers 2 inches high, 9 by 6 inches. The two bottom drawers are 5 inches high and 9 by 10½ inches. All these drawers but one are locked in one operation and with one lock, making the drawers secure from interference. Above the 14 drawers described is one shelf for books 23 inches long, 9 inches wide and 11 inches high. On the back or opposite side from the drawers are 3 shelves for books, each 23 inches long, 9 inches wide and 10 inches high, but as these shelves are *adjustable*, they can be changed to suit any class of books. On either of the other two sides of case are 7 pigeon holes, making *in all* 14. These are 9 inches deep, 4⅓ wide and 4 inches high. All are secured by doors and locks, so as to keep letters and papers safe. Weight when packed, 165 pounds.

For a well furnished law office these cases will be found almost indispensable when once introduced. Revolving principle the same as all my other popular Cases. Every case on my entire list warranted to be as represented or no sale.

Price on Cars at Factory, $30.

CABINET CASE.

46 inches high, 24 inches diameter, holds 125 average law books. On one side is a legal blank department. 12 inches high, 23 inches long, 9 inches deep, with 6 spaces for legal cap and 3 for note paper, with door and lock. Above this department are two shelves, 23 inches long and 9 inches wide, the ordinary height of both is 10 inches, but as the intermediate shelf is *adjustable* by a ratchet, changes can be made as wanted.

The opposite side has three similar shelves, 23 inches long, the lower one 12 inches high, and the upper ones 10 inches, but as they are also *adjustable*, changes can be made to suit. On the other two sides are 14 pigeon holes, 4⅓ inches wide, 4⅓ inches high, and 9 inches deep.

This case, ALL WALNUT or ASH, is very handsome; holds many books, and is exceedingly convenient because of the pigeon holes and cabinet for papers and blanks. Weight when packed, 165 lbs.

Price on Cars at Factory, $25.

—10—

No. 4 STANDARD CASE

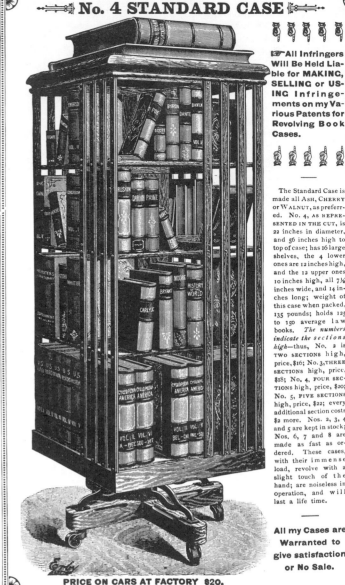

☞ All Infringers Will Be Held Liable for MAKING, SELLING or USING Infringements on my Various Patents for Revolving Book Cases.

The Standard Case is made all ASH, CHERRY or WALNUT, as preferred. No. 4, AS REPRESENTED IN THE CUT, is 22 inches in diameter, and 56 inches high to top of case; has 16 large shelves, the 4 lower ones are 12 inches high, and the 12 upper ones 10 inches high, all 7½ inches wide, and 14 inches long; weight of this case when packed, 135 pounds; holds 125 to 150 average law books. *The numbers indicate the sections high*—thus, No. 2 is TWO SECTIONS high, price, $16; No. 3, THREE SECTIONS high, price, $18; No. 4, FOUR SECTIONS high, price, $20; No. 5, FIVE SECTIONS high, price, $22; every additional section costs $2 more. Nos. 2, 3, 4 and 5 are kept in stock; Nos. 6, 7 and 8 are made as fast as ordered. These cases, with their immense load, revolve with a slight touch of the hand; are noiseless in operation, and will last a life time.

All my Cases are Warranted to give satisfaction or No Sale.

PRICE ON CARS AT FACTORY $20.

13

STUDENT'S CASE

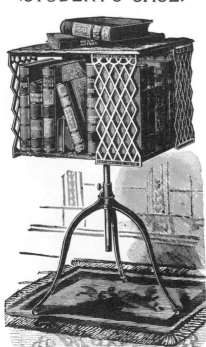

BOOK REST---Price $2.

PATENTED DEC. 4, 1883.

All Walnut or imitation Ebony, as preferred; 10 inches wide, 18 inches long. This Book Rest was first made to be used on my popular Revolving Book Cases, for the purpose of holding the Unabridged Dictionary or other heavy books at any desired angle, enabling said book to be consulted without lifting, and while it fills the desired want it has since been found to be adapted for use on any table, stand or desk, and to be laid on the lap while reading heavy volumes; it is, therefore, of general adaptation in reading or consulting heavy volumes. The construction of the Book Rest is so simple it can not get out of order, and yet so strong as to support the heaviest book that may be laid upon it. Lawyers, Ministers, Doctors and Students generally, who have tried this novel little article, find it a great relief in handling large and heavy books, and it is also quite evident that large volumes are better preserved by laying on this Rest while in use than to be held by hand or laid on the knees as is often done; and the relief to the student is very great. The article is as easily handled as a smooth board of the same size, easily carried from place to place and ready in a moment to be used as BOOK REST, WRITING DESK, or SPEAKERS' INCLINED PULPIT TOP.

DANNER'S NO. 1 CHAMPION TABLE CASE.

Price on Cars at Factory, $10.

THIS Case is made all ash, cherry or walnut, as preferred; is 18 inches diameter and 20 inches high; has 4 shelves 7 inches wide, 10½ inches long and 12 inches high; will hold 20 volumes American Cyclopædia, and afford a nice place on top for Atlas, Unabridged Dictionary, or similar works. Weight, when packed, 40 lbs.

—5—

DANNER'S HANGING SHELF, No. 4.

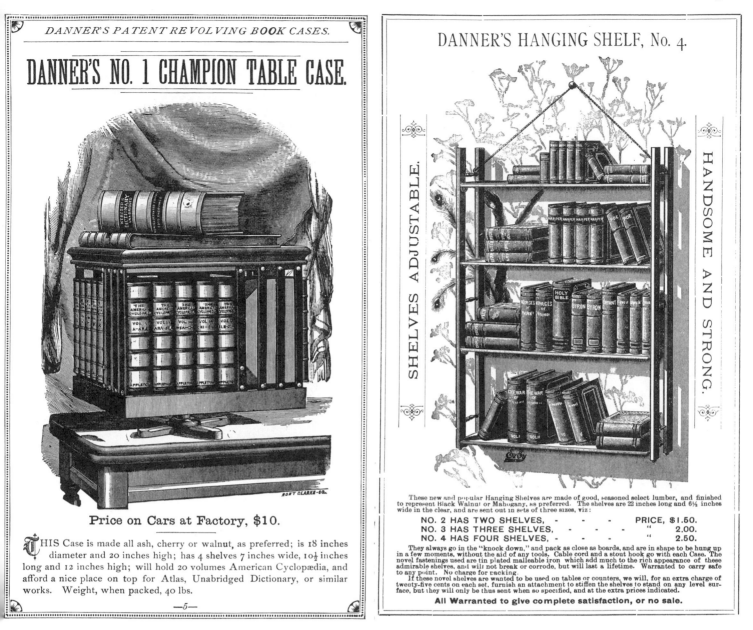

SHELVES ADJUSTABLE.

HANDSOME AND STRONG.

These new and popular Hanging Shelves are made of good, seasoned select lumber, and finished to represent Black Walnut or Mahogany, as preferred. The shelves are 22 inches long and 6½ inches wide in the clear, and are sent out in sets of three sizes, viz:

NO. 2 HAS TWO SHELVES,	PRICE, $1.50.
NO. 3 HAS THREE SHELVES,	" 2.00.
NO. 4 HAS FOUR SHELVES,	" 2.50.

They always go in the "knock down," and pack as close as boards, and are in shape to be hung up in a few moments, without the aid of any tools. Cable cord and a stout hook go with each Case. The novel fastenings used are tin plated malleable iron which add much to the rich appearance of these admirable shelves, and will not break or corrode, but will last a lifetime. Warranted to carry safe to any point. No charge for packing.

If these novel shelves are wanted to be used on tables or counters, we will, for an extra charge of twenty-five cents on each set, furnish an attachment to stiffen the shelves to stand on any level surface, but they will only be thus sent when so specified, and at the extra prices indicated.

All Warranted to give complete satisfaction, or no sale.

"STAR" REVOLVING CASE.

This is one of the most popular Book Cases ever introduced by me. As will be seen, the price is very low—only $12. Another great advantage is that this Case always goes in the "knock down." The box containing one of these Cases is only 8 inches high, 2 feet wide and 4 feet long, and will carry safe to any part of the world, at reduced freight, weighs but 100 lbs. packed. It can be set up in a few minutes, no tools required but a screw driver. When set up as represented by the cut the Case is 56 inches high and 22 inches square, the lower shelves 12½ inches high, the middle ones 11⅜ inches, and the upper ones 10⅛ inches; and all 21 inches long and 9 inches wide. By putting books on the *top* as well as the three shelves below, the Case will hold fully 100 large octavo books, revolves on the same principle of my other Cases, and will turn with a slight touch of the hand. All supported by four strong casters, so as to enable the Case to be moved about. The Cases are made of ash, all finished in good style and warranted to give complete satisfaction or no sale.

Price, $12.

COTTAGE CASE.

44 inches high, 22 inches diameter; has 6 shelves 22 inches long, and 6 shelves 6 inches long, all 7½ inches wide. The lower tier is 12 inches high, the middle tier 10½ inches, and top tier 10 inches high. Holds 150 average octavo books. Weight, when packed, 100 pounds. Made of BUTTERNUT finished BLACK WALNUT, in good style. This case has very large capacity for the price; is strong, handsome and much liked. Stands the same distance from the floor as the Standard Case, and revolves in the same graceful and substantial manner. But one size of this style is made.

Price on Cars at Factory, $15.

BUCKEYE CASE.

A very handsome and convenient little Case, combining book shelves and pigeon holes, 36 inches high, 18 inches diameter. The shelves will hold 20 volumes size of Chamber's or Appleton's Cyclopedia. There are 24 pigeon holes, each 4 inches wide, 3¾ inches high and 9 inches deep, giving room to arrange a large quantity of filed documents. Made all ash or walnut, as preferred. Weight, packed, 75 lbs.

UPON ITS MERITS.—A young friend of ours who recently returned from a trip through Colorado, Wyoming, Nebraska and other Western States, said to us that he had seen more frequent reminders of home in the shape of John Danner's Revolving Book Cases than by any other item or incident. Everywhere he found that the more elegant the appointments, the more important the business, the more certain you are to find this condensed compendium of convenience.—*Stark Co. (O.) Democrat.*

Price on Cars at Factory, $14.

MUSIC CASE.

This Case is found very popular where a large amount of music is kept. The Case will hold 16 to 20 bound volumes and accommodate a large lot of sheet music. The Case is made of Black Walnut, 18 inches diameter, 33 inches high, 4 spaces for bound volumes 6½ inches wide, 16 high and 11 deep. The cabinet department in top of Case for sheet music is secured by door and lock. While this Case holds so much music in safety and compact form, it at the same time serves the purpose of stand or centre table. Weight, when packed, 85 pounds.

Price on Cars at Factory, $18.

No. 2 DAISY CASE.

THIS handsome and strong case is made by the best mechanics, of WALNUT or CHERRY, supported on a finely polished STEEL SHAFT, mounted on casters. The general construction of this case is the same as the larger cases, and revolves with a slight touch of the hand without a particle of noise. The No. 2 Daisy Case as shown in the cut is 16½ inches in diameter and 33 inches high, holds 32 volumes of American Cyclopedia, besides affording room on top for several larger volumes; adapted to all kinds of books, will last a life time, only weighs 50 lbs. when packed. No other case in the world so light and yet so strong as this case. No charge for packing. But two sizes of this case are made viz: No. 2 and No. 3. No. 2, two tiers, full height 33 inches, weight 30 lbs. packed 50 lbs. price on cars at factory, $9.00. No. 3, three tiers, full height 43 inches, weight 40 lbs. packed 65 lbs. price on cars at factory, $11.00. Every case warranted as represented, or no sale.

Price on Cars at Factory, $9

All my Cases are warranted to give Complete Satisfaction or No Sale.

EUREKA REVOLVING BOOK CASE.

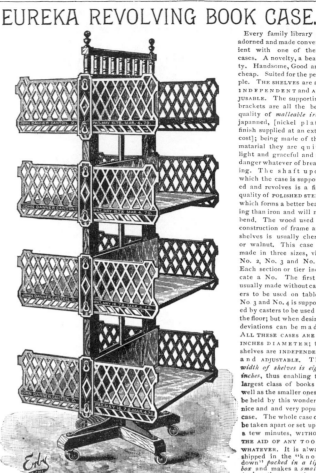

Every family library is adorned and made convenient with one of these cases. A novelty, a beauty. Handsome, Good and cheap. Suited for the people. THE SHELVES are all INDEPENDENT and ADJUSABLE. The supporting brackets are all the best quality of *malleable iron* japanned, [nickel plate finish supplied at an extra cost]; being made of this matarial they are quite light and graceful and no danger whatever of breaking. The shaft upon which the case is supported and revolves is a fine quality of POLISHED STEEL which forms a better bearing than iron and will not bend. The wood used in construction of frame and shelves is usually cherry or walnut. This case is made in three sizes, viz.: No. 2, No. 3 and No. 4. Each section or tier indicate a No. The first is usually made without casters to be used on tables; No. 3 and No. 4 is supported by casters to be used on the floor; but when desired deviations can be made. ALL THESE CASES ARE 18 INCHES DIAMETER; the shelves are INDEPENDENT and ADJUSTABLE. The *width of shelves is eight inches*, thus enabling the largest class of books as well as the smaller ones to be held by this wonderful nice and and very popular case. The whole case can be taken apart or set up in a few minutes, WITHOUT THE AID OF ANY TOOLS WHATEVER. It is always shipped in the "knock down" *packed in a tight box* and makes a *smaller package* than any other revolving book case in the world.

No. 4 Eureka Case.

No. 2 Case—Box 4½ in. high, 19 in. wide, 26in. long. | No. 3 Case—Box 5 in. high, 19in. wide, 36 in. long.
No. 4 Case—Box 5 in. high, 19 inches wide, 46 inches long.

The following weights will show that while the Eureka is ONE OF THE STRONGEST CASES ever made it is also one of the LIGHTEST, being easy to handle and graceful.
No. 2 Case weighs 25 pounds, packed 40 pounds | No. 3 Case weighs 35 pounds, packed 55 pounds.
NO. 4 Case weighs 45 pounds, packed 70 pounds.

And last, though not the least, the following prices will convince every one of the CHEAPNESS of the Eureka Case *above all others ever introduced:*
No. 2 Case, japanned, $9.00, nickle plate, $11.00. | No. 3 Case, japanned, $11.00, nickle-plate $13.00.
No. 4 Case, japanned, $13.00, nickle-plate, $15.00.

This case is warranted in every particular to be as represented and to GIVE COMPLETE SATISFACTION or no sale. In ordering be sure to say *cherry* or *walnut* as preferred; also *japanned* or *nickle-plate.*

◁REVOLVING PRINT SHELF▷

DANNER'S REVOLVING BOOK CASES,

[181]

Patented Oct. 21, 1873; April 6, 1875,; May 16, 1876; May 30, 1876; June 5, 1877; Dec. 11, 1877
March 4, 1879; May 23, 1882; March 13, 1883; Re-issued Feb. 20, 1877;
and January 6, 1880. Patented in Canada July 31, 1876.

THE BEST IN THE WORLD.

USEFUL, ♦ DURABLE ♦ GRACEFUL ♦ AND ♦ NEAT.

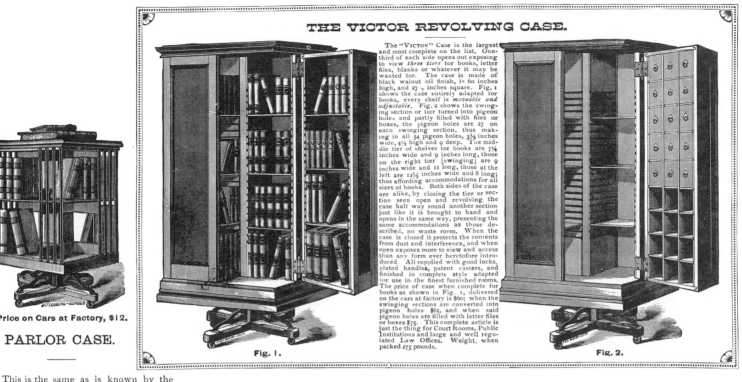

THE VICTOR REVOLVING CASE.

The "VICTOR" Case is the largest and most complete on the list. One-third of each side opens out exposing to view *three tiers* for books, letter files, blanks or whatever it may be wanted for. The case is made of black walnut oil finish, is 60 inches high, and 27 , inches square. Fig. 1 shows the case entirely adapted for books, every shelf is *moveable and adjustable.* Fig. 2 shows the swinging section or tier turned into pigeon holes and partly filled with files or boxes, the pigeon holes are 27 on each swinging section, thus making in all 54 pigeon holes, 3½ inches wide, 4½ high and 9 deep. The middle tier of shelves for books are 7½ inches wide and 9 inches long, those on the right tier [swinging] are 9 inches wide and 11 long, those at the left are 12½ inches wide and 8 long; thus affording accommodations for all sizes of books. Both sides of the case are alike, by closing the tier or section seen open and revolving the case half way round another section just like it is brought to hand and opens in the same way, presenting the same accommodations as those described, no waste room. When the case is closed it protects the contents from dust and interference, and when open exposes more to view and access than any form ever heretofore introduced. All supplied with good locks, plated handles, patent casters, and finished in complete style adapted for use in the finest furnished rooms. The price of case when complete for books as shown in Fig. 1, delivered on the cars at factory is $60; when the swinging sections are converted into pigeon holes $65, and when said pigeon holes are filled with letter files or boxes $75. This complete article is just the thing for Court Rooms, Public Institutions and large and well regulated Law Offices. Weight, when packed 275 pounds.

Fig. 1.

Fig. 2.

Price on Cars at Factory, $12.

PARLOR CASE.

This is the same as is known by the name "No. 2 Champion," a very popular style; 36 inches high, 18 inches in diameter, has 8 shelves, all 10½ inches long; the four lower ones 12 inches high, and the four upper ones 10 inches high, all 7 inches wide. Weight, when packed, 65 pounds. Made of ASH, CHERRY, OR WALNUT, as preferred. A beautiful case for Parlor or Private rooms; answers for a stand as well as book case.

TYLER'S NEW REVOLVING BOOK CASES.

GUARANTEED TO BE THE BEST MADE.

WITH BOOK HOLDER OPEN.

| No. 101 A. | Weight, 50 lbs. | Price, F. O. B....$18 00 | No. 102 B. | Weight, 75 lbs. | Price, F. O. B....$20 00 | No. 103 C. | Weight, 100 lbs. | Price, F. O. B....$24 00 |

We submit this, our new specialty, which far surpasses everything of the kind ever presented. It is entirely distinct in its construction, style and finish from every other. They are constructed of the very best seasoned wood, and are finely oil finished, in walnut, antique oak, or cherry with mahogany finish. The guards at the ends of the shelves are of ly polished brass, of novel and modern design, and are of such a form as to admit of the easy insertion of books and so as not to occupy any shelf space. Bases very heavy and absolutely ble. Have never seen one loose or even shaky.

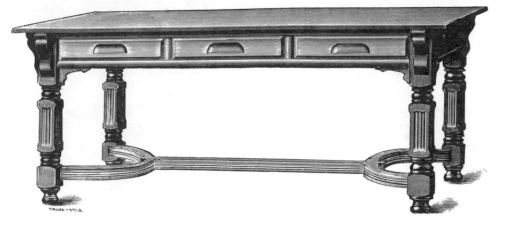

No. **112**—Class A. 72 in. long, 36 in. wide. Two drawers on one side, one on the other.
No. **113**—Class A. 96 in. long, 36 in. wide. Two drawers each side. All drawers go through.
Made in Walnut, Oak or Cherry. Has 3-ply framed, figured Oak top. Yale locks on drawers. Shipped K. D. Built on the truss plan, and will not sag in the middle. High polish finish.

F. E. STUART.

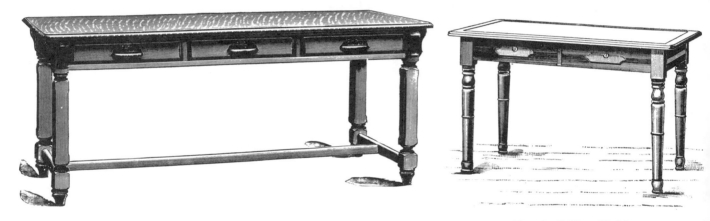

No. 1 Office Table.

No. **114**—Class C. 48 in. long, 32 in. wide. Two drawers, all on one side and go through to back.
No. **115**—Class C. 60 in. long, 32 in. wide. Two drawers, all on one side and go through to back.
No. **116**—Class C. 72 in. long, 34 in. wide. Three drawers, all on one side and go through to back.
No. **117**—Class C. 96 in. long, 34 in. wide. Four drawers, all on one side and go through to back.
Made in Antique finished Oak only, with solid quartered Oak polished top. Shipped K. D. Built on truss plan, and will not sag in centre.

CENTRAL MANUFACTURING CO.

No. 281 DIRECTOR'S TABLE.

Size, 72x34 inches.

Top covered with Billiard Cloth or Imitation Leather.

Price—In Walnut, Cherry or Oak, in white, $32.00; finished, $40.00.

The same with Leather top, $46.00.

No. 280 DIRECTOR'S TABLE.

Size, 72x42 inches.

Top covered with Billiard Cloth or Imitation Leather.

Price—In Walnut, Cherry or Oak, in white, $36.00; finished, $45.00.

The same with Leather top, $51.00.

We guarantee our Tables to be the best made.—Tyler Desk Co., St. Louis, Mo.

[183]

No. 2 & 7. Fine Office Tables. Walnut, Antique Oak, Cherry.

5-Ply Built-up Tops, Covered with Billiard Cloth, Best Locks, Portable, Shipped K. D., Boxed, Casters Fitted.

No. 2. Size, 5 ft. by 32 in. Weight, 90 lbs. Price, F. O. B.........$14 50
No. 7. Size, 6 ft. by 34 in. Weight, 100 lbs. Price, F. O. B.......... 17 00

Nos. 1 & 3. Tyler's Fine Office Tables. Walnut, Antique Oak or Cherry.

5-Ply Built-up Tops, Covered with Billiard Cloth, Best Locks, Portable, Shipped K. D., Boxed, Casters Fitted.

No. 1. Size, 52 in. by 32 in.
Price, F. O. B. (Weight, 60 lbs.)...........$13 00
No. 3. Size, 42 in. by 28 in.
Price, F. O. B. (Weight, 50 lbs.)........... 12 00
Brass Corners Fitted, if desired, at $2.50 extra per set net.

No. 6. Tyler's Fancy Table. Walnut, Antique Oak or Cherry.

24 inches wide and 36 inches long, One Drawer, Covered with Cloth or Polished Wood Top.

Price, F. O. B. $8 50

We know of no Tables Equal to those made by Tyler Desk Co. of St. Louis, Mo.

Nos. 14 & 15—Tyler's Fine Directory Tables.

5-Ply Built-up Top and 5 Legs. Walnut, Antique Oak or Cherry. Covered with Billiard Cloth; A 1 Locks; Portable; Shipped K. D., Boxed; Casters fitted.

No. 14. Size, 84 x 34 in., weight, 100 lbs., Price, F. O. B..........$20 00
No. 15. Size, 96 x 34 in., weight, 120 lbs., Price, F. O. B........... 22 50
Brass Corners, extra, $2.50 net.

Nos. 18, 19 & 20. Tyler's Extra Fine Office or Directory Tables.

5 Ply Built-up Top; 5 Large Carved Legs; Crescent Base; Solid Brass Corners. Walnut, Antique Oak or Cherry. Covered with Billiard Cloth; A 1 Locks; Casters fitted; Shipped K. D., Boxed.

No. 18. Size, 6 ft. long by 34 in. wide, weight, 110 lbs., Price, F. O. B., $27 00
No. 19. Size, 7 ft. long by 34 in. wide, weight, 130 lbs., Price, F. O. B. 30 50
No. 20. Size, 8 ft. long by 34 in. wide, weight, 150 lbs., Price, F. O. B. 34 00

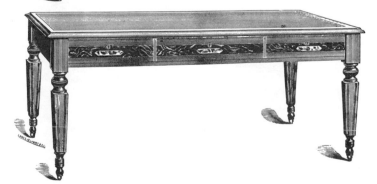

Tyler's Square Leg R. R. or Office Table. Solid Walnut or Cherry.

Covered with Heavy Rubber Duck, Paneled Top, Veneered Fronts. Three Sizes carried in Stock.

No. 24. 4 ft. long by 32 in. wide. Price, F. O. B ....$ 9 00
No. 25. 5 ft. long by 32 in. wide. Price, F. O. B................... 10 50
No. 26. 6 ft. long by 32 in. wide. Price, F. O. B................... 12 00
Extra Lengths to Order at $1.50 per foot.

Nos. 8 & 9—Tyler's Extra Fine Library Tables.

5-Ply Built-up and Solid Cast Brass Corners. Walnut, Antique Oak or Cherry. Covered with Billiard Cloth; A 1 Locks; Casters fitted; Portable; Shipped K. D., Boxed.

No. 8. Size, 32x60 in., weight, 75 lbs., Price, F. O. B.................$22 00
No. 9. Size, 34x72 in., weight, 90 lbs., Price, F. O. B................. 24 00

Nos. 16 & 17 –Tyler's Extra Fine Office or Directory Tables.

5-Ply Built-up Top and Solid Brass Corners. Walnut, Antique Oak or
  Cherry. Covered with Billiard Cloth; A 1 Locks; 5 Large Legs;
  Casters fitted; Shipped K. D., Boxed.

No. 16. Size, 7 ft. long by 34 in. wide; weight, 130 lbs., Price, F. O. B. **$28 00**
No. 17. Size, 8 ft. long by 34 in wide; weight, 150 lbs., Price, F. O. B. **30 00**

Nos. 4 & 5. Tyler's Extra Fine Library Tables.
Walnut, Antique Oak or Cherry.

5-Ply Built-up Tops and Square Legs, Covered
with Billiard Cloth, A 1 Locks, Casters Fitted, Shipped
K. D., Boxed, Weight, 70 lbs.

No. 5. Size, 3 ft. 6 in. by 2 ft. 4 in.
Price, F. O. B............................**$14 00**
No. 4. Size, 4 ft. 4 in. by 2 ft. 8 in.
Price, F. O. B........................ **16 00**
Brass Corners Fitted, if desired, at $2.50 extra per set
net.

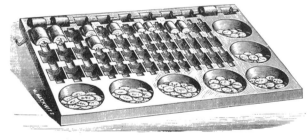

Coin Trays for Gold and Silver.

No. 2. Size, 12½x18½; capacity, $312. Price **$10 00**
No. 6. " 12½x13½; " $216. " **9 00**
No. 5. " 8½x12½; " $150. " **7 00**
  Made of Solid Walnut, and fully endorsed by hundreds of Bankers and others who handle
specie.

Caught by the Bell.

  Shortly after 7 o'clock last evening three unknown
men entered S. D. Rossi's soloon in the rear of his
grocery, 214 North Twelfth street. While they were
drinking some beer which they had ordered and paid
for, Rossi was called into the grocery to wait on a
customer. As soon as he stepped out of the saloon
one of the men reached over the counter and tried to
open the money drawer. The alarm-bell attached to
it rang, and the storekeeper rushed back and de-
manded an explanation. No satisfactory one was
given by the men, and he sent out for a police officer.
They did not wait, however, until he came.

Tucker's Bell Alarm Money Till.

This Drawer will save its cost twenty times every year. It is made of hard wood, strongly
  dovetailed together; has six round cups for coin; is always set; is as easily opened
  as a common drawer; will sound the alarm promptly if tampered with; combination
  changed in a SECOND; needs no key, no repairs; easily fitted to counter or desk.
  Price, F. O. B...**$3 50**

No. 2.—Open.—16 x 8—2 inches deep.   **No. 2.—Closed.**—8 x 7.

The No. 2 box has the same number of compartments and capacity as the No. 3, with
  double ends, which gives it strength, and will not twist open when locked. It
  contains one tray of two bowls for smaller denominations of coins, and one
  cylinder tray for Dollars, Halves and Quarters—both holding about $150.00,
  besides two compartments for currency, checks, etc. Price........... **$3 00**

No. 3.—Open.   **No. 3.—Closed.**

The No. 3 improved with a new folding lock attached to the box that cannot be lost or
  get out of order.
When unfolded, it can be used in any ordinary table, desk or cash drawer, and folded
  with the contents in a space of 3¼ x 8 inches, and locked ready for deposit in the
  safe or vault. Price **$4 00**

No. 4.—Open.   **No. 4.—Closed.**

This box is twice the size of the No. 2, and contains two sets of trays with capacity for
  holding $300.00 in silver, and 4 compartments for bills, checks, etc. Price **$6 00**

Towel Rollers.

No. 1. Cherry or Walnut Roller and Back......................... **$1 00**
  Polished Roller and Varnished Back.

No. XX. Water Bowls.

Finished in Black and Bronze.

Price, Bowl....................**$0 50**
  " Brush............**50c to 1 00**
  " 500-page Letter Book, 10x12, **2 00**

Commercial Presses.

Finished in Black and Bronze.

                                        PRICE.
No. 3 A, Size of Follower, 9x11 in. **$5 50**
No. 4 A, " " 10x12½ " **6 00**
No. 5 A, " " 10x15 " **7 25**

Tyler Desk Co.'s Heavy Railroad and Express Waybill Presses.

[185]

Large Size Business Press.

Finished in Black and Bronze.

No. 6 N. Size of follower, 15x20 in., weight 210 lbs.

Price...................$19 50

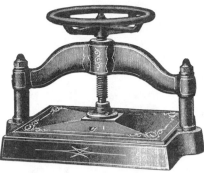

Express Waybill Press.

Finished in Black and Bronze.

No. 4 U. Size of follower, 15x20 in., weight 210 lbs.
Price.....................$20 00
No. 5 U. Size of follower, 16x20 in., weight 220 lbs.
Price.....................$21 00
No. 6 U. Size of follower, 18x22 in., weight 240 lbs.
Price.....................$25 00

Railroad Waybill Press, Steel Arch.

Finished in Black and Bronze.

No. 4 T. Size of follower, 21x26 in., weight 410 lbs.
Price.....................$57 50
No. 5 T. Size of follower, 25x27 in., weight 670 lbs.
Price......... ....$80 00

TYLER'S CABINET PRESS STANDS.

HARD WOOD AND FINE HAND FINISH.

No. 1. Tyler's Walnut, Antique Oak or Cherry Letter Press Stand.

8 in. wide; 28 in. long; 30 in. high; our Built-up Panels and Top; Combination Lock; Extension Leaf in Front pulls out 16 in; Finished all around. Weight, 65 lbs.

rice, F. O. B...........................$13 00

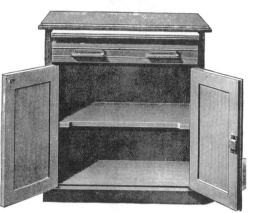

No. 3. Tyler's Letter Press Stand.

18 in. wide; 28 in. long; 30 in. high. Same as No. 1. Weight, 65 lbs.

Price, F. O. B...................$12 50

No. 2. Tyler's Letter Press Stand.

18 in. wide; 28 in. long; 30 in. high. Same as No. 1. Weight 65 lbs.

Price, F. O. B.................$13 50

Business Presses.

Finished in Black and Bronze.

		PRICE.
No. 4 B, Size of Follower, 10x12½ in.		$5 75
No. 7 C, " " 11½x17 "		11 00

Standard Presses.

Finished in Black and Bronze.

With Polished Brass Nut.

		PRICE.
No. 4 D, Size of Follower, 9½x13,		$7 00
No. 5 D, " " 10½x15,		8 50

Copy Press Stand.

Inside Measurement of Drawers, 12½x19x2¼ inches.

o. 5. Walnut, Cherry or Oak........Price, $18 00

Copy Press Stand.

Inside Measurement of Drawers, 12½x19x2¼ inches.

No. 4. Walnut, Cherry or Oak........Price, $10 00

Copy Press Stand.

Inside Measurement of Drawers, 12½x17½x2¼ inches.

No. 6. Walnut, Cherry or Oak.........Price, $18 00

We have dropped the Cup Holders on Right Hand Side of these Stands.

TYLER'S SPECIAL CABINETS.

USEFUL TO ANY MAN WHO HAS PAPERS WORTHY OF PROTECTION.

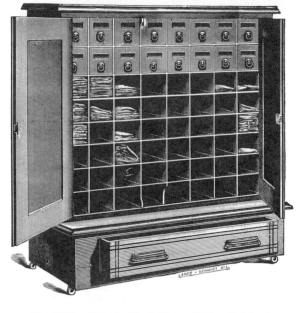

No. 701. Tyler's First Class Office Cabinet.

SOLID WALNUT, OAK OR CHERRY.

Size, 38 in. wide, 42 in. high; with 64 Pigeon Holes 11 inches deep, 16 of which has Heavy Card Board Filing Boxes. Weight, 90 lbs.

Price, F. O. B................$18 00

MADE TO ORDER.

Inside Pigeon Hole work changed to suit customers without extra charge. Extra Filing Cases 16 cents each.

The Seth Thomas Calendar No. 10.

Made in Oak, Walnut or Cherry. 8 Day Weight Time; 10 in. dial; 49 inches high; Perpetual Calendar. Time and Calendar Guaranteed.

Price, F. O. B., Boxed,...$40 00

No. 09. Tyler's Heavy Cardboard File Boxes.

Muslin Bound.

Made to order, any sizes wanted. Patent Fronts for inserting names. In ordering, make sketch of front of Pigeon Hole, giving the exact width, height and length.

Prices, according to size ....8c to 20c

No. 604. Tyler's File Cabinet.

Poplar; Handsome; Walnut or Cherry Finish. Has 50 Heavy Cardboard Files; Muslin Bound, Size, 4½x4, 10½ in. long. Patent Front for inserting names. Cheapest File Case Made.

Price, F. O. B. $16 00
" without File Cases 10 00

No. 700 A. Tyler's Express Case or Office Cabinet.

CHEAPEST CASE FOR THE MONEY EVER MADE.

Size, 31½ in. high, 24½ in. wide and 11 in. deep. Made of Poplar; Stained Walnut or Cherry; good Lock; Cabinet Work Grooved and Fitted Perfectly. Endorsed and used by every Express Company in the country. Weight, 40 lb.

Price, F. O. B..........$4 50

The Seth Thomas Queen Anne.

Made in Oak, Walnut or Cherry.

Eight-Day Spring; Time Warranted; 8½ in. Dial; Cathedral Bell Strike; Strikes slow and graceful. Height, 36 inches.

Price, F. O. B., boxed $20 00
Same Clock without Strike·· 19 00

Any Seth Thomas Clock furnished by the Tyler Desk

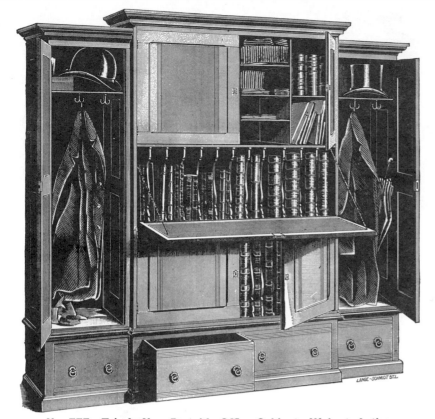

No. 777. Tyler's New Portable Office Cabinet. Walnut, Antique Oak or Cherry.

THE MOST CONVENIENT OFFICE CABINET EVER MADE.

Size, 7 feet high, 7 feet wide, by 16 inches deep. Made to order in 4 Sections; has 2 Wardrobes 16x20 in., Fall Leaf Rest for handling books and papers. Easily handled or set up. Size and style of Pigeon Hole Work changed to suit customers, or made larger or smaller as may be required. Weight, 350 lbs.

Price, F. O. B. $80 00

24-File Cabinet.

6-File Cabinet with Curtain.

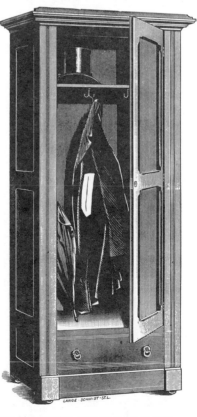

No. 778. Tyler's Office Wardrobe. Walnut or Cherry.

Size, 6 ft. 10 in. high, 32 in. wide by 18 in. deep; 1 Drawer in Base. Weight 125 lbs.

Price, F. O. B. $18 00

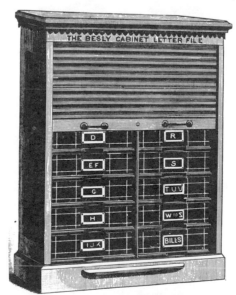

16-File Cabinet with Roll Curtain.

No. 605. Tyler's File Cabinet.

Poplar; Handsome; Walnut or Cherry Finish. Has 25 Heavy Cardboard Files; Muslin Bound; Size, 4½x4, 10 in. long. Patent Front.

Price, F. O. B. $9 00
" without File Cases 6 00

TYLER DESK COMPANY,
ST. LOUIS, MO.

12-File Cabinet.

No. 115. VERTICAL FILE SECTION

Contains three drawers, with an aggregate filing capacity of 15,000 papers and the necessary complement of folders. Dimensions of drawers 11½ x 10¹⁄₁₀. The drawers are fitted with countersunk rods for holding guide cards in place and our regular compressor block. Notice the extension slide under drawer. The No. 20 large size Vertical Filing Section will file 24,000 papers. The drawers are 24 inches in the clear from front to back.

BUILDING A SECTIONAL STACK

The illustration shows the operation of building a stack of sections and indicates the practical results of "Expansion."

No. 155. DOCUMENT FILE SECTION

Same as No. 156, with 7 files, each 5 inches wide, 10½ inches high and 14 inches long. Papers 4⅝ inches wide and 10 inches high may be filed in them.

EXPANSION—A COMPLETE EXAMPLE

Beginning with a single Letter File Section and ending with a combination, three stacks wide and five sections high, ALL DIFFERENT, exhibits the inexhaustive scope of the Sectional System. The possibilities of "Expansion" in Business Systems provoke no popular division of opinion. They are practical and present economies of space, of time and of money that the progressive business man will not overlook.

A complete catalog containing price list furnished on request.

No. 156. DOCUMENT FILE SECTION

Contains six Document Files, 6 inches wide by 10½ inches high, and 14 inches in length, inside measurement. Each file is provided with an automatic locking device that is operated with the utmost ease and celerity.

Our Business Expansion System

Is the most complete system ever put on the market. We show you a few pieces from the line, and ask you to send for our complete catalog, explaining the system and quoting prices.

Our Card Index System is a great labor saver. It can be applied to any business or profession and when once introduced will never be discarded.

Twelve Single Drawer Card Index Cabinet
BOX STYLE

Single Drawer—Folding Rod
The metal plate set in bottom of file is what carries the friction clutch operating the guide block.

Three Double Drawer Card Index Cabinet
CABINET STYLE.   EXTENSION SLIDES

Be sure and send for *Our Catalog* containing *Price List* and *Full Descriptions*.

We are Sole Agents for the Famous "Y and E" *SECTIONAL BOOK CASES*

We show here a few cuts of our Sectional Book Case System. Send for special catalog containing price list and full description.

Showing a single section with top and base.

Showing a large case of sections in process of construction

Showing three rows of sections partially built up.

Tyler's Store or Lunch Counter Metal Stools.—Tyler Desk Co., St. Louis, Mo.

[189]

The Earl Lock and Pivot Stools.

Guaranteed to be the Best Stools Made.

Revolves Perfectly.   Children Cannot Remove the Seats.

No. 10 A. 30 inches High.
Hardwood Seat...... ....$3 25
Hardwood Seat, Nickel Rim, 4 00
Plush or Leather Seat....... 4 00

No. 10 C. 21 inches High.
Hardwood Seat..............$2 00
Hardwood Seat, Nickel Rim, 3 00
Plush or Leather Seat........ 3 50

No. 10 B. 26 inches High.
Hardwood Seat..............$2 75
Hardwood Seat, Nickel Rim, 3 50
Plush or Leather Seat....... 3 75

No. 3. 20¼ inches High.
Hardward Seat $1 50
Hardwood Seat, Nickel Rim, 2 25
Plush or Leather Seat........ 2 75

No. 14. 21 inches High.
Hardward Seat $2 75
Hardwood Seat, Nickel Rim, 3 75
Plush or Leather Seat........ 4 00

THE TAYLOR CHAIR CO.

No. 177. Reception Chair, Metal Trimmed.

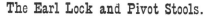

No. 175. Club House Rocker, Metal Trimmed.

No. 141. Reception Chair.

[190]

Tyler's High Desk or Counter Stools.—Tyler Desk Co., St. Louis, Mo.

No. 548. Vienna Rotary Screw Desk Chair.

No. 25l. Bent Stock.

High Adjustable Back Stool; Cane Seat and Back. Price, F. O. B **$5 50**

No. 58. Desk Stool.

Walnut or Cherry Finish. Cane Seat. Price, F. O. B..... ....**$1 50**

No. 52.

Same, Wood Seat.................... 1 25

No. 33. High Screw Stool.

Bent Wood; Rock Elm; Walnut or Mahogany Finish; Perforated Seat. Price, **$3 75**

No. 250. Rock Elm, Bent Stock.

Walnut or Cherry Finish; Adjustable Back; Legs are bolted together through center piece; Patent Back Rest. Price,

No. 60. Desk Stool.

Walnut or Cherry Finish. Cane Seat–Screw Revolving. Price, F. O. B................ ....**$3 00**

No. 544. Vienna Stool.

Walnut or Cherry Finish; Thirty-six inches high. Price, F. O. B. **$2 75**

No. 547. Vienna Rotary Screw Desk Stool.

Walnut or Cherry Finish; Outside Foot Rest; Finest Stool made. Price, F. O. B. **$4 50**

No. 8. Tyler's Square Seat Chair Cushion.

Made of Rubber Duck; wears almost equal to Leather; Stuffed with Moss. Price.............. .$2 00

No. 8 A. Same, in Leather, Stuffed with Hair. Price. 6 00

No. 9. Tyler's Round Back Chair Cushion.

Made for any chair; made of Rubber Duck and Stuffed with Moss. Price..................... ......$2 00

No. 9 A. Same, in Leather, Stuffed with Hair. Price.......................... .... 6 00

If a special size Cushion is wanted, send proper pattern of seat.

No. 134. Walnut or Mahogany Finish.

Double Box Seat; Bolt through Arm, Pillar and Seat; Strong, Handsome and Graceful. Price, F. O. B.............. ......$7 50

No. 401. Tyler's New Senate Chair.

Screw and Springs; Government Standard; Walnut or Mahogany Finish; Upholstered in Embossed Leather; Stuffed with Best Curled Hair; Guaranteed to satisfy any gentleman who may order it, as there is nothing better made. Price, F. O. B.....**$28 00**

No. 579 A. Vienna Rotary Screw and Spring Chair.

Walnut or Mahogany Finish; Full Bent Wood Stock; absolutely perfect in all respects. Price, F. O. B........... **$8 50**

No. 261. Tyler's Walnut Adjustable Back Chair.

Suitable for Photographers' Sitting Chair, Type Writers, Jewelers, Pianos, Organs or Desks. Height, 19 to 23 inches. Weight, 20 lbs. Price, F. O. B........................$ 7 00

No. 261 A. Same, Full Leather............................. 10 00

No. 134 L L. Walnut or Mahogany Finish.

Donble Box Seat; Bolt through Arm, Pillar and Seat, making this a very Strong and Handsome Chair. Price, F. O. B...$12 50

No. 135 A. Same, in Cane................................... 8 00

The Tyler Chair Irons absolutely have no equal on Earth.

No. 143.   Cherry or Walnut Finish.

Cane or Perforated Seat; Full Bent Wood Stock;
Same Size, and Arms secured to base by
Iron Bolt, same as No. 55. Price, F. O. B..**$5 00**

No. 235.   Library Chair.

Walnut or Mahoganized Cherry.   Price, Cane
Seat and Back.........................**$6 00**
No. 235 A.
Same, Full Leather........................ **9 50**

No. 236.   Tyler's Revolving and Tilting.

Upholstered in Embossed Leather; Walnut or Ma-
hoganized Cherry.   Weight, 50 lbs.   Price,
F. O. B...... ....**$15 0**
No. 236 A.
Same, Cane Seat and Back..................... **9 0**
If Tyler Iron and Base, add **$3 00**

No. 61.   Tyler's New Antique Chair.
Oak, Walnut and Imitation Mahogany; High
Back Office—Double Frame; Plain or
Embossed Leather Seat and Top.   No man
ever sat in an easier chair. Price, F. O. B. **$15 00**
No. 61 A.
Same, Perforated Leather over cane......... **12 50**
No. 61 B.
Same, Cane Seat.......................... **10 50**

No. 555. Continental Revolving and Tilting.
Extra Broad Arm; Cane on Perforated Seat; Oak,
Imitation Walnut or Imitation Mahogany.
Weight, 30 lbs   Price, F. O. B....... ....**$6 00**
If with Tyler Iron and Base, add **$3 00**

No. 55. Continental Revolving and Tilting.
Cane or Perforated Seat; Oak, Imitation Walnut
or Imitation Mahogany. Weight, 30 lbs. Price
F. O. B................. ....**$5 50**
If with Tyler Iron and Base, add **$3 00**

Tyler Desk Co., St. Louis, Mo.

Every First-Class Chair should be mounted on the Tyler Iron.

The Tyler Chair Iron, Invented by C. H. Tyler, July 1887, is

the Only Strictly Reliable Iron made.

No. 308. Tyler's Revolving and Tilting.

Walnut or Mahoganized Cherry. Weight, 40 lbs
   Price, Cane Seat.....................$ 8 50
No. 308 A.
Same, Leather Seat............... .... 10 50

No. 8. Tyler's Full Box Frame Office.

With Tyler's New Screw and Spring attached. Walnut,
  Antique Oak or Cherry. Cane Seat and Back. Price,
  F. O. B................. ....$12 00
  Full Leather Seat and Back. Price, F. O. B...... 16 00

   The Tyler Iron has no machinery; it is constructed with one
large 2⅜ inch Hollow Screw, Coil Spring and Arm. Absolutely
indestructible; Noiseless; Easy and Graceful motion; Guaranteed
for twenty years.

   The Tyler Screw and Spring will be attached to any of our
Chairs for $3 00 extra.

No. 309. Tyler's Revolving and Tilting.

Walnut or Mahoganized Cherry. Weight, 35 lbs
   Price, in Cane only.....................$6 50
If Tyler Iron and Base, add **$3 00** (See page 83.)

No. 392. Tyler's New Congress.

Screw and Spring; Upholstered in Embossed or Plain
Leather; Government Standard; Walnut or Mahogany Finish; Stuffed with Best Curled Hair; Bent
Wood Stock; Highly Finished, and guaranteed to
give entire satisfaction. Price, F. O. B............$22 50

No. 241. Tyler's Revolving and Tilting.

High Back; Walnut or Mahoganized Cherry.
  Weight, 40 lbs. Price, Cane, F. O. B......$ 8 50
No. 241 A.
Same, Full Leather......................... 12 50
  If Tyler Iron and Base, add **$3 00** (See page 83.)

No. 280. Tyler's Revolving and Tilting.

Upholstered in Embossed Leather. Walnut or
  Mahoganized Cherry. Weight, 50 lbs. Price,
  F. O. B................................$16 00
280 A.
Same, in Cane Seat and Back................. 10 50
  If Tyler Iron and Base, add **$3 00** (See page 83).

Our Royal Styles

No. 228. Tyler's Library Chair Leon.

No. 227. Tyler's Sir Knight.

No. 229 A. Tyler's Prince Albert.

No. 306. Tyler's Revolving and Tilting.

Upholstered in Embossed or Plain Leather; Very Handsome; Walnut or Mahoganized Cherry; Extra Heavy and Strong Chair.
Weight, 60 lbs. Price, F. O. B..........................$24 00

If with Tyler Iron and Base, add $3.00.

No. 25. Tyler's New Composer.

The Easiest and Finest Chair Made; Solid Walnut or Cherry; Full Leather
Covered; Hair Stuffed; Spring Seat; Screw and Tilt; Very Massive; Portable Base. Weight, 60 lbs. Price, F. O. B..........................$48 0

Our Work is First-Class, and will give Perfect Satisfaction.—Tyler Desk Co., St. Louis, Mo.

[195]

No. 24.   The Tyler New Harmony.

Full Leather Overstuffed; Full Springs; Hair Stuffed; Extra Large; Walnut
or Mahogany Finish. To match No. 25. Weight, 50 lbs. Price, F. O. B. **$36 00**

No. 28. Tyler's New Magnet.

No. 29. Tyler's New Degree.

No. 26. Tyler's Old Comfort.

Mahoganized Cherry or Walnut; Iron Frame; Hair Stuffed; Full
Spring; Full Leather Cover and Trimmings; Easy and Graceful. Weight, 60 lbs. Price, F. O. B...................... **$58 00**

No. 778

A handsome Chair for office or library. Rounded back, shaped arm, French leg, Quartered Golden Oak. Saddle wood seat. Elegant piano polish.

Each.................... $ 7.00
Per dozen............... 80.00

No. 778 R

An elegant piano polished Golden Quartered Oak Office Chair, revolving, with adjustable spring back.

Each...................$8.75

No. 0615 R

A handsome Revolving Office Chair, Bank of England pattern. Saddle wood seat, Golden Quartered Oak with piano polish, adjustable spring back.
Each. .... $ 9.50
Solid Mahogany. Each.. 15.75
Chair to match, not revolving, Golden Quartered Oak.
Each. .... $ 7.90
Solid Mahogany. Each... 14.00

No. 0614 R

Elegant piano polish, Golden Quartered Oak, very closely woven cane seat and back, adjustable spring back revolving chair.
Each................. $8.75
Same in Solid Mahogany.
Each $15.50
Genuine leather seat and back, Golden Quartered Oak.
Each................. $10.75
Same in Solid Mahogany.
Each................... $17.50

No. 0544 R

Revolving Office Chair. Golden Quartered Oak, piano polish. Genuine leather seat and back. Adjustable spring back.

Each......................$9.50

No. 547

Vienna Bent Chair. Suitable for offices, clubs or cafés. Very strong and light. Golden Oak, cane seat.

Each................. $ 1.75
Per dozen 19.50

No. 0719

An elegant Arm Office Chair, also a fine chair for library, hall or assembly room. Golden Quartered Oak, cane or saddle wood seat, gloss finish.
Each. .... $ 4.65
Per dozen 51.75
Piano Polish, 40c. extra each.

No. 0719 R

An elegant Golden Quartered Oak Office Chair. Adjustable spring back. In handsome gloss finish. In cane or wood seat, saddle pattern.
Each................... $5.75

No. 928 C

No. 928 R

Office Chairs. Golden Quartered Oak, piano polish, saddle seat. Revolving chair has adjustable spring back.

Each.................. $ 5.50   Each.................... $7.00
Per dozen............... 62.50

No. 0614

Elegant piano polish, Golden Quartered Oak, very closely woven cane seat and back, French legs.
Each................. $7.00
Solid Mahogany, piano polish.
Each.. .... $13.50
Genuine leather seat and back, Golden Quartered Oak.
Each.... .... $9.00
Solid Mahogany, piano polish.
Each................. $15.50

No. 7675 C   **No. 7675 R**

Bank of England Office Chairs. Golden Quartered Oak, piano polish. Revolving chair has adjustable spring back. Saddle seat.

Each .... $ 8.75   Each...............$10.75
Per dozen 98.00

No. 926 C   **No. 926 R**

Office Chairs. Golden Quartered Oak, piano polish. Revolving chair has adjustable spring back. Saddle seats.

Each. .... $ 5.75   Each $7.75
Per dozen 65.00

No. 4019

OFFICE STOOLS

Wood Seat		Cane Seat	
18 inches high, each...	$ .72	18 inches high, each..	$ 1.25
Per dozen.............	8.50	Per dozen.............	13.25
24 inches high, each...	.83	24 inches high, each...	1.40
Per dozen.............	9.75	Per dozen.............	14.25
30 inches high, each ...	1.00	30 inches high, each...	1.65
Per dozen.............	10.45	Per dozen.............	16.50
36 inches high, each...	1.25	36 inches high, each...	1.75
Per dozen.............	12.75	Per dozen.............	17.25

No. 4045 R

Revolving office stool, 32 inches high when screwed down.

Wood seat, each....................$2.95

Cane seat, each........................ 3.25

With bent wood back and cane seat,
each................................. 4.95

No. 654 R

Revolving office chair. Golden Elm. Elegantly carved back. Rod under arms.

Wood seat, each.....................$4.97

No. 7654 C

Arm office chair. Golden Elm. Elegantly carved back. Rod under arm.

Wood seat, each........ .... $2.50

Per dozen......... .... 26.00

No. 0701 R

Revolving office chair. Solid Golden Oak. Adjustable spring back. Castered. Cane or wood seat.

Each.................... ....$4.25

TYPEWRITER CHAIRS

These Revolving Typewriter Chairs are the greatest inventions ever offered in this line. The back of the chair has an adjustable spring which can be regulated to the work lightly or as stiffly as desired Thus the back forms a constant support to the operator in any position of the body. The back pad also moves up and down and can be adjusted to support any part of the operator's back.

No. 980	No. 978	No. 970	No. 960
Solid Oak, cane seat.	Solid oak, cane seat, genuine leather back pad.	Quartered Oak, polish finish, genuine leather back.	Genuine leather seat and back.
Price.....................$5.75	Price.......................$6.00	Price.......................$7.00	Price.......................$8.75

No. 0701

Stationary office chair. The same as the cut, but not revolving. Cane or wood seat.

Each. .... $ 2.25

Per Dozen... 24.00

No. 886

Solid Golden Oak. Rod running through the arm and seat, making the chair very strong. Cane seat or solid wood seat.

Each..... ....$ 1.95

Per Dozen....................... 20.00

No. 415

Office or Library Chair. Especially adapted to Sunday school rooms, assembly halls, etc. Solid Golden Oak Very strongly built and of neat design. Cane or wood seat.

Each.............................$ 2.20

Per Dozen....................... 24.00

No. 415 R

Revolving Office Chair. Solid Golden Oak. Adjustable spring back. Castered. Cane or wood seat. Wood seat has saddle pattern.

Each................................$4.75

No. 4385

Arm office chair. An excellent chair for hall, hotel or assembly room. The bent wood arm is very strong and fastened with a bolt. Solid Golden Oak. Cane seat or wood seat, saddle pattern.

Each........ ....$ 3.75

Per Dozen.................... 39.75

Genuine Black Walnut, piano polish............................ 5.00

No. 4385 R

Revolving arm office chair. Very comfortable. Adjustable spring back. Cane seat or wood seat, with saddle pattern. Solid Golden Oak.

Each....................... .... $6.00

Genuine Black Walnut, piano polish.............. .... 8.00

No. 147.

FLORENCE DESK CHAIR.

No. 34.
BOOKKEEPER CHAIR.

No. 36.
NEW DOUGLASS OFFICE.

No. 143.
HIGH WOOD STOOL PIVOT.

No. 140.
HIGH CANE STOOL SCREW.

No. 1776.
CENTENNIAL OFFICE.

No. 28.
CONTINENTAL OFFICE.

No. 30.
DOUGLASS OFFICE.
(Chestnut Seat.)

No. 14.
DOUGLASS OFFICE.

No. 37.
NEW DOUGLASS OFFICE.
(Chestnut Seat.)

No. 106

Low Base Book-Keeper.

No. 170

Antique Dining.

Screw and Spring.

No. 171

Piano Chair.

Screw.

No. 111

Book-Keeper.

No. 110½

High Desk Chair.

No. 144

American Office.

Screw and Spring.

No. 145

American Office — Cane Back.

Spring and Screw.

No. 141

American Dining.

Screw and Spring.

No. 107

New Douglass Office.
Screw and Spring.

No. 132

Howe Office.
Spring and Screw.

No. 200

Windsor Office.
Screw and Spring.

No. 143

No. 142

No. 49

Continental Office.
Screw and Spring.

No. 133

Howe Office.

No. 108

New Douglass Office.
Screw.

THE HALE & KILBURN MANUFACTURING COMPANY, 48 & 50 NORTH SIXTH ST., PHILADELPHIA, PA. 15

THE "CABLE" SPRING CHAIR

Still stands superior to any other Spring Chair in the market in point of durability, appearance and comfort. Many experiments have resulted in producing the best Spring Chair ever made, and it is very much improved in every particular since it was first offered to the public.

STRENGTH,   APPEARANCE,   COMFORT.

The Spring warranted never to break or creak.

"CABLE" SPRING ATTACHMENT.

The above cut shows the make-up of the Spring; it is made of the very best quality of tempered steel wire rope; the wire is tightly clasped by irons made for the purpose, and these irons are fastened to the seat of the chair; and the rocking motion is obtained by the twist and return of the rope.

$8.00

$12.00

"CABLE" CHAIR.—CONTINENTAL TOP.

"CABLE" CHAIR.—WEBSTER TOP.

BRANCH STORES, NEW YORK AND BOSTON. SPECIAL AGENTS IN CHICAGO, ST. LOUIS, CLEVELAND, PITTSBURGH, BALTIMORE, BROOKLYN AND ALBANY.

No. 73.
DOUGLASS OFFICE.
(Screw and Spring.)

No. 228.
WEBSTER ARM OFFICE.

No. 39.
FLORENCE DESK CHAIR.

No. 19.
CONTINENTAL OFFICE.
(Screw and Spring.)

E. F. PEIRCE, 162 NORTH ST. BOSTON.

16   THE HALE & KILBURN MANUFACTURING COMPANY, 48 & 50 NORTH SIXTH ST., PHILADELPHIA, PA.

THE "CABLE" SPRING PATENT ROCKER.

Fitted with the "Cable Spring," and the Seat and Back fitted with the Combination Canvas-Back Cane Seating.

Everything about this Chair is calculated to attract and interest any desiring to purchase a first-class article. The design is of the prevailing style; work and finish done by the very best workmen; and the form of the Chair constructed to give all possible comfort.

The seat and back are fitted with our "Combination Canvas-Back Cane Seating," the strongest, neatest, and most comfortable ever made.

For prices see accompanying price-list.

NO. 1. LADY'S.

NO. 2. GENT'S.

BRANCH STORES, NEW YORK AND BOSTON. SPECIAL AGENTS IN CHICAGO, ST. LOUIS, CLEVELAND, PITTSBURGH, BALTIMORE, BROOKLYN AND ALBANY.

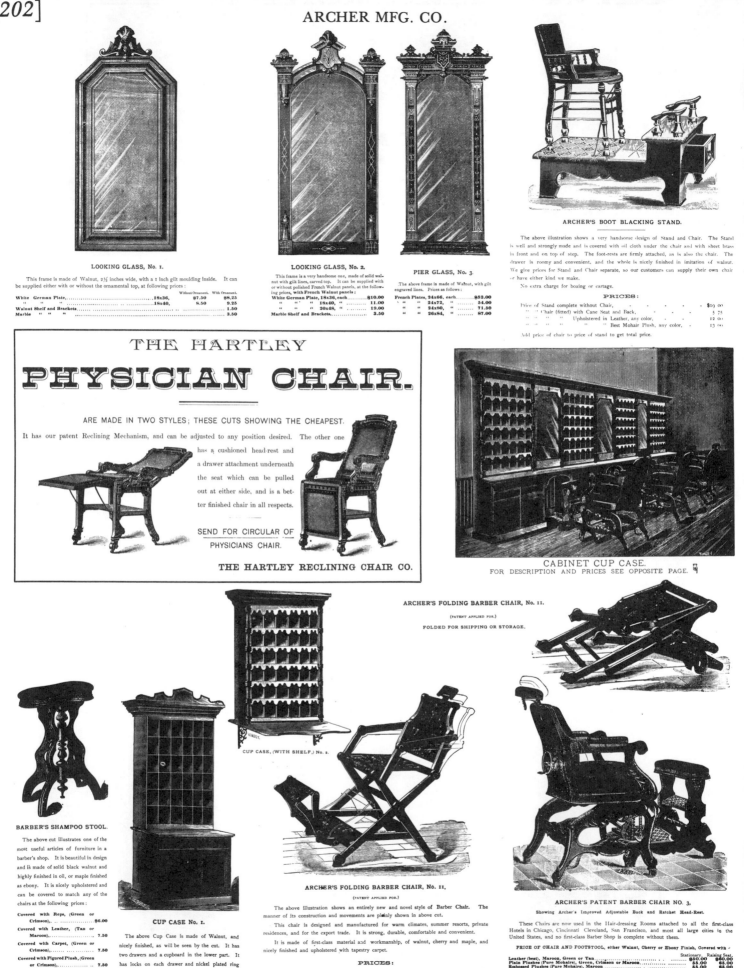

LOOKING GLASS, No. 1.

This frame is made of Walnut, 2½ inches wide, with a 1 inch gilt moulding inside. It can be supplied either with or without the ornamental top, at following prices:

	Without Ornament.	With Ornament.
White German Plate,..........................18x36,	$7.50	$8.25
" " " " 18x40,	8.50	9.25
Walnut Shelf and Brackets......................		1.50
Marble " " "		3.50

LOOKING GLASS, No. 2.

This frame is a very handsome one, made of solid walnut with gilt lines, carved top. It can be supplied with or without polished French Walnut panels, at the following prices, with French Walnut panels.

White German Plate, 18x36, each..........$10.00
"   "   "   18x40, " 11.00
"   "   "   20x48, " 19.00
Marble Shelf and Brackets.................. 3.50

PIER GLASS, No. 3.

The above frame is made of Walnut, with gilt engraved lines. Prices as follows:

French Plates, 24x66, each..........$52.00
"   "   24x72, " 54.00
"   "   24x80, " 71.50
"   "   26x84, " 87.00

ARCHER'S BOOT BLACKING STAND.

The above illustration shows a very handsome design of Stand and Chair. The Stand is well and strongly made and is covered with oil cloth under the chair and with sheet brass in front and on top of step. The foot-rests are firmly attached, as is also the chair. The drawer is roomy and convenient, and the whole is nicely finished in imitation of walnut. We give prices for Stand and Chair separate, so our customers can supply their own chair or have either kind we make.

No extra charge for boxing or cartage.

PRICES:

Price of Stand complete without Chair, - - - - - $19 00
"   Chair (fitted) with Cane Seat and Back, - - - 5 75
"   "   "   "   Upholstered in Leather, any color, - - 12 00
"   "   "   "   Best Mohair Plush, any color, - - 13 00

Add price of chair to price of stand to get total price.

THE HARTLEY
PHYSICIAN CHAIR.

ARE MADE IN TWO STYLES; THESE CUTS SHOWING THE CHEAPEST.

It has our patent Reclining Mechanism, and can be adjusted to any position desired. The other one has a cushioned head-rest and a drawer attachment underneath the seat which can be pulled out at either side, and is a better finished chair in all respects.

SEND FOR CIRCULAR OF PHYSICIANS CHAIR.

THE HARTLEY RECLINING CHAIR CO.

CABINET CUP CASE.
FOR DESCRIPTION AND PRICES SEE OPPOSITE PAGE.

BARBER'S SHAMPOO STOOL.

The above cut illustrates one of the most useful articles of furniture in a barber's shop. It is beautiful in design and is made of solid black walnut and highly finished in oil, or maple finished as ebony. It is nicely upholstered and can be covered to match any of the chairs at the following prices:

Covered with Reps, (Green or Crimson),.................. $6.00
Covered with Leather, (Tan or Maroon),...................... 7.50
Covered with Carpet, (Green or Crimson),...................... 7.50
Covered with Figured Plush, (Green or Crimson),...................... 7.50
Covered with Plain Plush, (Green, Crimson or Maroon, or Moquette),...................... 8.00

CUP CASE No. 1.

The above Cup Case is made of Walnut, and nicely finished, as will be seen by the cut. It has two drawers and a cupboard in the lower part. It has locks on each drawer and nickel plated ring drawer pulls.

Price of Cup Case No. 1,......................$27.00

CUP CASE, (WITH SHELF,) No. 2.

ARCHER'S FOLDING BARBER CHAIR, No. 11.

(PATENT APPLIED FOR.)

FOLDED FOR SHIPPING OR STORAGE.

ARCHER'S FOLDING BARBER CHAIR, No. 11,

(PATENT APPLIED FOR.)

The above illustration shows an entirely new and novel style of Barber Chair. The manner of its construction and movements are plainly shown in above cut.

This chair is designed and manufactured for warm climates, summer resorts, private residences, and for the export trade. It is strong, durable, comfortable and convenient.

It is made of first-class material and workmanship, of walnut, cherry and maple, and nicely finished and upholstered with tapestry carpet.

PRICES:

Walnut or Cherry, Green or Crimson carpet,.......................................$18.00
Maple, Green or Crimson carpet,... 16.00

See cut of chair folded up for shipping.

ARCHER'S PATENT BARBER CHAIR NO. 3,

Showing Archer's Improved Adjustable Back and Ratchet Head-Rest.

These Chairs are now used in the Hair-dressing Rooms attached to all the first-class Hotels in Chicago, Cincinnati Cleveland, San Francisco, and most all large cities in the United States, and no first-class Barber Shop is complete without them.

PRICE OF CHAIR AND FOOTSTOOL, either Walnut, Cherry or Ebony Finish, Covered with

	Stationary.	Raising Seat.
Leather (best), Maroon, Green or Tan............................	$50.00	$60.00
Plain Plushes (Pure Mohairs), Green, Crimson or Maroon..........	55.00	65.00
Embossed Plushes (Pure Mohairs), Maroon........................	55.00	65.00
Moquette, (a very handsome and durable Cover,)..................	55.00	65.00
For improved Ratchet Headpiece, add to above prices............	$5.00	
For improved Adjustable Back,...................................	10.00	
For Chairs made of Mahogany,..................................	5.00	
For Extra Perforated or Cane Seat,.............................	2 00	

ARCHER'S PATENT ADJUSTABLE BARBER CHAIR, No. 1.

PRICE OF CHAIR AND FOOTSTOOL, either Walnut or Ebony Finish, Covered with

Cane Seating	$28.00
Union Terries, Green or Crimson	31.00
Best Tapestry Brussels Carpet, Green or Crimson	32.00
Figured Plushes, Green or Crimson	32.00
Leather (best), Maroon, Green or Tan	33.00
Plain Plushes (Worsted), Green, Maroon or Clouded	33.00
Plain Plushes (Pure Mohair), Green, Crimson or Maroon	35.00
Moquette, (a very handsome and durable cover)	35.00

Above Chairs fitted with an *Extra* Cane Seat and Back, which, by taking off the Upholstered Seat and Back, will fit in same place for summer use. Add to above prices for same, $5.00.

ARCHER'S PATENT ADJUSTABLE BARBER CHAIR, No. 2,
(WITH CLOSED ARMS.)

PRICE OF CHAIR AND FOOTSTOOL, either Walnut or Ebony Finish, Covered with

	Stationary Seat.	Raising Seat.
Union Terries, Green or Crimson	$39.00	$49.00
Figured Plushes, Green or Crimson	40.00	50.00
Leather (best), Maroon, Green or Tan	42.00	52.00
Plain Plushes (Pure Mohair), Green, Crimson or Maroon	45.00	55.00
Moquette, (a very handsome cover)	45.00	55.00
An Extra Patent Perforated or Cane Seat for Summer use		3.00

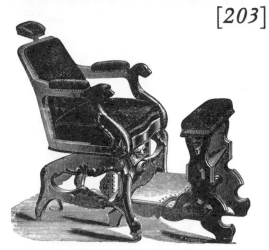

ARCHER'S PATENT ADJUSTABLE BARBER CHAIR, No. 3.

The above is the most elegant and convenient Barber's Chair made. It is gotten up regardless of expense, the workmanship and material used being the very best of their kind. It is solid black Walnut, Cherry or Maple finished as Ebony, elegantly carved, and is upholstered and finished in superb style. It is covered with the best Leather, Fine Mohair Plush, (green, crimson or maroon), or with Moquette, and the gimp is put on with fire gilt nails. The upper part of Footstool is trimmed the same as the Chair, and the Step and Platform are covered with polished sheet brass put on with fire gilt nails.

We call particular attention to the back view of the No. 3 Chair, showing our Improved Adjustable Back, as per dotted lines; also the Improved Ratchet Head Rest. The twenty-eight (28) Chairs furnished to W. S. Eden, for Palmer House barber shop, have this movement, and they are conceded by all to be the handsomest and most perfect Barber Chair ever made. For prices see opposite page.

ARCHER'S PATENT ADJUSTABLE BARBER CHAIR, NO. 4.
Patented May 21, 1878.

The above illustrates our new style of Barber Chair. The Chair is made of Walnut or Maple finished as Ebony, finished in first-class style. The arms, back and seat are connected and securely fastened together by the tasty iron side arm, which is double Japanned and ornamented with gilt lines. The Footstool, as will be seen, is constructed in a similar manner, by tasty iron platform and step. The above connections are protected by Patent, issued May 21st, 1878. The above Chair is the most handsome and durable Chair for its price ever offered to the trade, the iron platform never wearing out and always looking clean and neat. This Chair is upholstered in a good and substantial manner. We can also supply it with Cane Seat and Back, making a very handsome and cool chair for warm climates.

PRICES, EITHER WALNUT OR EBONY FINISH.

Seat and Back finished in Cane $22.00

UPHOLSTERED AND COVERED WITH

Union Terries, Green or Crimson	$26.00	Plain Worsted Plushes, Green or Maroon	28.00
Best Tapestry Brussels Carpet, Green or Crimson	27.00	Clouded Worsted Plushes, Gr'n or Crim'n	28.00
		Pl'n Mohair Pl'shs, Gr'n, Cr'son or M'roon	30.00
Figured Plushes, Green or Crimson	27.00	Embossed Mohair Plushes, Maroon	30.00
Leather (best), Maroon, Green or any col'r	28.00	Moquette	30.00

Above Chair fitted with an *Extra* Cane Seat and Back, which, by taking off the upholstered seat and back, will fit in same place for summer use. Add to above price for same, $7.00.

ARCHER'S PATENT ADJUSTABLE BARBER CHAIR, NO. 5.
(Patented May 21, 1878.)

The above style Barber Chair is made of Iron, of beautiful design and tastily ornamented with gilding. It is adjusted to the position necessary for shaving by placing the foot on the treadle at the rear, which releases the segment and allows the seat and back to be tilted to any desired angle. As will be seen, the Chair and Foot-rest are combined, thereby making it a firm and strong chair. It has rollers under the front legs, to facilitate the moving of the chair about the room. It is the most handsome design, and withal the lowest priced Adjustable Barber Chair ever offered to the trade. It is well upholstered, with Steel Springs in the seat, and the best of materials, and covered with Plushes, Leather, &c., or the Seat and Back are made of cane seating, which makes it a very comfortable and cool chair for warm climates.

ARCHER'S PATENT ADJUSTABLE BARBER CHAIR, No. 6,
(with Open Arms.)

PRICE OF CHAIR AND FOOTSTOOL, either Walnut, Cherry or Ebony Finish, Covered with

	Stationary Seat.	Raising Seat.
Union Terries, Green or Crimson	$37.00	$47.00
Figured Plushes or Carpet, Green or Crimson	38.00	48.00
Leather (best), Maroon, Green or Tan	40.00	50.00
Plain Plushes (Worsted), Green or Maroon	40.00	50.00
Plain Plushes (Pure Mohair), Green, Crimson or Maroon	42.00	52.00
Moquette, (a very handsome and durable cover)	42.00	52.00
An Extra Patent Perforated or Cane Seat for Summer use		3.00

Above Chairs fitted with an *Extra* Cane Seat and Back, which, by taking off the upholstered Seat and back, will fit in same place for summer use. Add to above prices for same, $8.00.

ARCHER'S NEW ADJUSTABLE BARBER CHAIR, No. 7.
(PATENT APPLIED FOR.)

The above illustration shows our latest design, and is a very handsome and durable Chair. It is well and strongly made.

PRICE FOR EITHER WALNUT OR MAPLE, EBONY FINISH, Upholstered with

Cane Seating	$27.00
Best Tapestry Brussels Carpet, Green or Crimson	30.00
Figured Plushes, Green or Crimson	30.00
Best Leather, Maroon, Green, or any color	31.00
Plain Worsted Plushes, Green or Maroon	31.00
Clouded Worsted Plushes, Green and Black or Red and Black	31.00
Plain Mohair Plushes, Green, Crimson or Maroon	33.00
Embossed Mohair Plushes, Maroon	33.00
Moquette	33.00

Above Chairs fitted with an *Extra* Cane Seat and Back, which by taking off the upholstered seat and back, will fit in same place for summer use. Add to above prices for same, $7.00.

ARCHER'S PATENT ADJUSTABLE BARBER CHAIR, No. 8.
(PATENT APPLIED FOR.)

The above Chair is another of our late designs, and is an elegant Chair in every way. It is well made of Walnut or Maple, finished as Ebony or of any kind of wood desired.

PRICES OF EITHER WALNUT OR MAPLE, EBONY FINISH, Upholstered with

Cane Seating	$29.00
Best Tapestry Brussels Carpet	32.00
Figured Plushes, Green or Crimson	32.00
Best Leather, Maroon, or any color	33.00
Plain Worsted Plushes, Green or Maroon	33.00
Clouded Worsted Plushes, Green and Black or Red and Black	33.00
Plain Mohair Plushes, Green or Crimson	35.00
Embossed Mohair Plushes, Maroon	35.00
Moquette	35.00

Above Chairs fitted with an *Extra* Cane Seat and Back, which by taking off the upholstered seat and back will fit in same place for summer use. Add to above prices for same, $7.00.

ARCHER'S PATENT ADJUSTABLE BARBER CHAIR, NO. 9.
(Patented.)

The above chair is the most elegant and convenient chair ever produced. The base and footstool are made of iron. The chair proper can be raised or lowered to any height by raising the post in base. The foot pedal acts as a lever in tipping chair backwards. Also the upright part of foot-rest is adjustable as per dotted lines and is operated by the occupant of the chair at will. For further particulars see description on last page.

PRICE OF No. 9 CHAIR With Top in Walnut, Cherry or Ash, Covered with

Leather (best), Maroon, Green or Crimson	$60.00
Plain Plushes (Pure Mohair), Maroon, Green or Crimson	65.00
Embossed Plushes (Pure Mohair), Maroon	65.00
Moquette, (a very handsome and durable Cover)	65.00
For Improved Ratchet Headpiece, add to above prices	5.00
For Improved Adjustable Back	10.00
For Chairs made of Mahogany	3.00
For Extra Perforated or Cane Seat	2.00

The base and foot-rest of this chair can be attached to any style of top and will be sold separate or prices quoted with the top of any of our styles.

Price of Base and Footstool Complete, finished ready to attach top $32.00

The Wooton Desk Co.,

Indianapolis, Ind., U. S. A.

Ordinary Grade, (Three Sizes.)

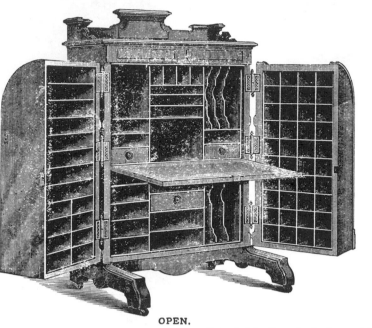

OPEN.

Patented in the principal countries of the World.

CLOSED.

WOOTON'S PATENT

Cabinet Secretaries

AND

Rotary Office Desks,

18 76

Standard Grade, (Three Sizes.)

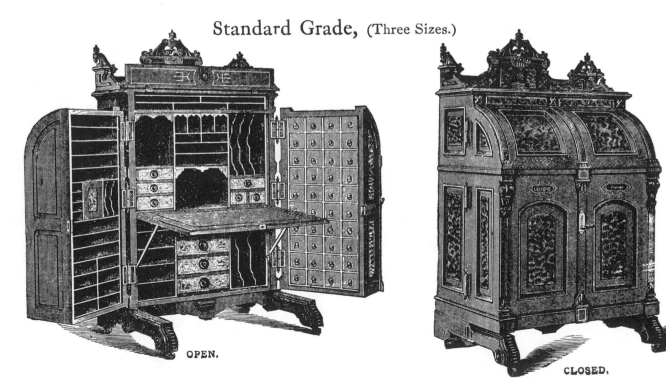

OPEN.

CLOSED.

Patented in the Principal Countries of the World.

Extra Grade, (Three Sizes.)

OPEN.   **CLOSED**

Patented in the Principal Countries of the World.

Superior Grade, (Three Sizes.)

OPEN.   **CLOSED.**

Patented in the Principal Countries of the World.

Ladies' Secretary.

CLOSED.

Patented in the Principal Countries of the World.

Ladies' Secretary.

OPEN.

Patented in the Principal Countries of the World.

No. 5 Rotary Desk.

SINGLE PIER—OFFICE—STANDARD GRADE.

CLOSED

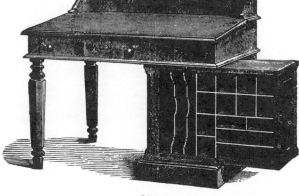

OPEN.

Patented in the Principal Countries of the World.

No. 5 Rotary Desk.

SINGLE PIER—OFFICE—EXTRA GRADE.

CLOSED.

OPEN.

Patented in the Principal Countries of the World.

No. 6 Rotary Desk.

DOUBLE PIER—OFFICE—STANDARD GRADE.

CLOSED.

OPEN.

Patented in the Principal Countries of the World.

No. 6 Rotary Desk.

DOUBLE PIER—OFFICE—EXTRA GRADE.

CLOSED.

OPEN.

Patented in the Principal Countries of the World.

No. 7 Rotary Desk.

DOUBLE PIER—CASHIER'S—STANDARD GRADE.

CLOSED.

OPEN.

Patented in the Principal Countries of the World.

No. 7 Rotary Desk.

DOUBLE PIER—CASHIER'S—EXTRA GRADE.

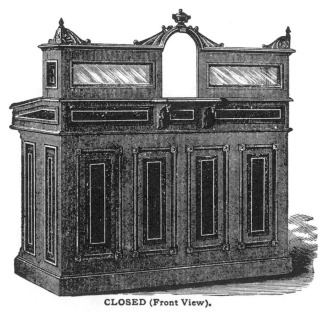

CLOSED (Front View).

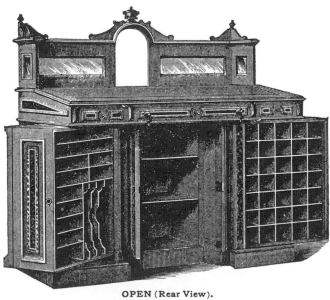

OPEN (Rear View).

Patented in the Principal Countries of the World.

No. 8 Rotary Desk.

DOUBLE PIER—COUNTING-HOUSE—STANDARD GRADE.

CLOSED.

OPEN.

Patented in the Principal Countries of the World.

No. 8 Rotary Desk.

DOUBLE PIER—COUNTING HOUSE—EXTRA GRADE.

CLOSED.

OPEN.

Patented in the Principal Countries of the World.

No. 9 Rotary Desk.

SINGLE PIER—CYLINDER—STANDARD GRADE.

CLOSED.

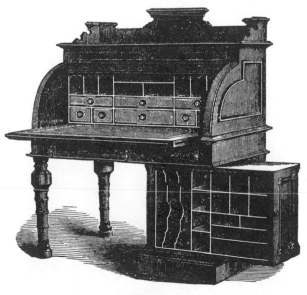

OPEN.

Patented in the Principal Countries of the World.

No. 9 Rotary Desk.

CLOSED.   SINGLE PIER—CYLINDER—EXTRA GRADE.   OPEN.

Patented in the Principal Countries of the World.

No. 10 Rotary Desk.

DOUBLE PIER—CYLINDER—STANDARD GRADE.

CLOSED.   OPEN.

Patented in the Principal Countries of the World.

No. 10 Rotary Desk, Extra Grade.

CLOSED.   OPEN.

Patented in the Principal Countries of the World.

Child's Furniture

Children's Carriages, Toy Wagons, Etc

196 & 198 TWENTY-SECOND ST., CHICAGO, ILL.

The American Furniture Gazette, March 15, 1883, page 20.

THE HALE & KILBURN MANUFACTURING COMPANY, 48 & 50 NORTH SIXTH ST., PHILAD'A., PA. 17

THE CHILD'S CHARIOT CHAIR.
(MADE UNDER THREE PATENTS.)

Fitted with either our Flexible Wood Seat, made of Walnut and Ash Strips cemented to Canvas, or Combination Canvas-Back Cane Seat.

The most perfect, durable and useful article of furniture for use in the care of children; they are intended for service and amusement, and are thoroughly indispensable where the best and most appropriate thing is needed.

To change from High Chair to Chariot, simply lift the latchet on each side of the Chair, lower to the floor and the Chariot will adjust itself. To reverse, lift the Chair by the arms into an upright position, see that the latchets fall into their proper place, and the Chair is then a Table-Chair again.

AS A PARLOR CHARIOT.　　　　**AS A TABLE CHAIR.**

THE CHILD'S "CHARIOT" CHAIR,
(MADE UNDER THREE PATENTS.)
Fitted with ROCKING CHAIR ATTACHMENTS,
(Also with HOBBY HORSE when desired.)

Adding very much to its value as an article of utility and pleasure. Tired with being rolled across the floor, or perched up at the table, the fretful child can be placed in the rocking chair and rocked to quietness and good humor, by a gentle motion of the attendant's foot, or, with whip and lines in hand, can drive his pair and amuse himself for hours.

Nothing surpasses this article in value for the purposes for which it was invented.

For prices see accompanying price-list.

AS ROCKING CHAIR, WITH "HOBBY" ATTACHMENT.　　　**AS "CHARIOT," WITH PROPELLING HANDLES.**

THE CHILD'S "CHARIOT" CHAIR,
(MADE UNDER THREE PATENTS.)
Fitted with ROCKING CHAIR ATTACHMENTS,

With the rockers used as propelling handles for High Chair on wheels, and also for shafts for pulling the Chariot. The general uses of this wonderful combination are clearly shown on this and the foregoing pages, and nothing remains but actual sight of the working of the Chair to convince the most skeptical that it will prove just what is claimed, viz:

A High Chair on Wheels,
A Low Chair on Wheels,
A Rocking-Chair,
A Parlor Chariot,
A Chariot with Propellers,
A Chariot with Shafts.

AS HIGH CHAIR WITH PROPELLERS.　　　**AS PARLOR CHARIOT WITH SHAFTS.**

BRANCH STORES, NEW YORK AND BOSTON. SPECIAL AGENTS IN CHICAGO, ST. LOUIS, CLEVELAND, PITTSBURGH, BALTIMORE, BROOKLYN AND ALBANY.

No. 40.
YOUTHS' DINING.

No. 92.
DOUBLE TOP ROCKING.

No. 295.
GEM FOLDING CHAIR.
(As Rocker.)

No. 295.
GEM FOLDING CHAIR.
(As Table Chair.)

No. 296.
JEWELL FOLDING CHAIR.
(As Table Chair.)

No. 38.
COMET HIGH.

No. 80.
NIGHT CABINET.

No. 193.
QUEEN ANNE HIGH.

No. 296.
JEWELL FOLDING CHAIR.
(As Carriage.)

No. 92 W.
DOUBLE TOP WOOD ROCKING.

No. 88.
CONTINENTAL HIGH.

No. 98.
EASTLAKE HIGH.

No. 91.
DOUBLE TOP HIGH.

No. 99.
CHILDS' EASTLAKE ROCKER.

No. 91 W.
DOUBLE TOP HIGH.
(Wood Seat.)

No. 97.
MISSES' BENT WOOD ROCKER.

No. 24.
MISSES' FLAT ARM WOOD ROCKER.

No. 23.
CHILD'S FLAT ARM WOOD ROCKER.

CLARK & RANNEY.   19

NO. 7 1-2, CHILD'S FOLDING ROCKER.

Price,   – $6.50 per Doz.

NO. 8 1-2, CHILD'S FOLDING ROCKER.

Price,   – $8.00 per Doz.

(See terms for ten per cent discount.)

CHILD'S EASTLAKE.

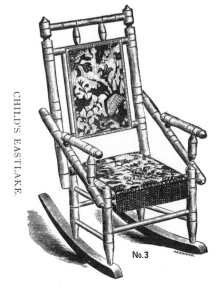

No. 3.

No. 3.   .CHILD'S SQUARE ARM.
(Weight 6 lbs.)   PER DOZ.

Tapestry Brussels......................$ 9 00
Ebony or imitation Mahogany...........,.. 12 00

No. 0449
High Chair. Wood seat, Golden Oak finish.
Each.............. $ .97

No. 0481
High Chair. Golden Oak finish, wood seat.
Each.............. $1.25
Cane Seat, each...... 1.45

No. 957
High Chair. Solid Golden Oak, cane seat.
Each.............. $1.75

No. 955
High Chair. Solid Golden Oak, cane seat.
Each.............. $2.30

No. 362
High Chair. Solid Golden Oak, cane seat.
Each.............. $2.75

No. 932
High Chair. Golden Quartered Oak, box seat.
Cane Seat, Each.....$3.50

Reclining Go-Carts

Both the back and front of these Carts recline to any angle desired, and independent of each other. Our patent adjustment is the best on the market. You don't have to get down and crawl under the cart. You don't have to push a lever with your foot. You merely touch a knob near the handle and the adjustment is made.

The parasol moves with the back so that no matter at what position the back may be the position of the parasol is always the same.

All gears have bicycle wheels and rubber tires, and an automatic brake. The wheels go on automatically and are tipped with rubber hubs to save your doors.

Parasols

We quote the Carts without the Parasols. We can furnish Parasols complete from 75c. up each.

No. 372. Reclining Go-Cart.
(Without Parasol.)
Each.............. $7.40

No. 383. Reclining Go-Cart.
(Without Parasol.)
Each.............. $10.73

No. 398. Reclining Go-Cart.
(Without Parasol.)
Each.............. $12.58

No. 401. Reclining Go-Cart.
(Without Parasol.)
Each.............. $12.96

No. 405. Reclining Go-Cart.
(Without Parasol.)
Each.............. $15.20

No. 410. Reclining Go-Cart.
(Without Parasol.)
Each.............. $17.00

No. 416. Reclining Go-Cart.
(Without Parasol.)
Each.............. $24.00

No. 440. Reclining Go-Cart.
(Without Parasol.)
Each.............. $30.35

Send for Our Catalog of Carriages and Go-Carts

[216]　HALL & STEPHEN, 200, 202 & 204 CANAL ST., AND 185 SIXTH AVE., N.Y.

HALL & STEPHEN, 200, 202 & 204 CANAL ST., AND 185 SIXTH AVE., N.Y. 51

ENGLISH IRON CRIBS.
IRON AND BRASS CRIBS.

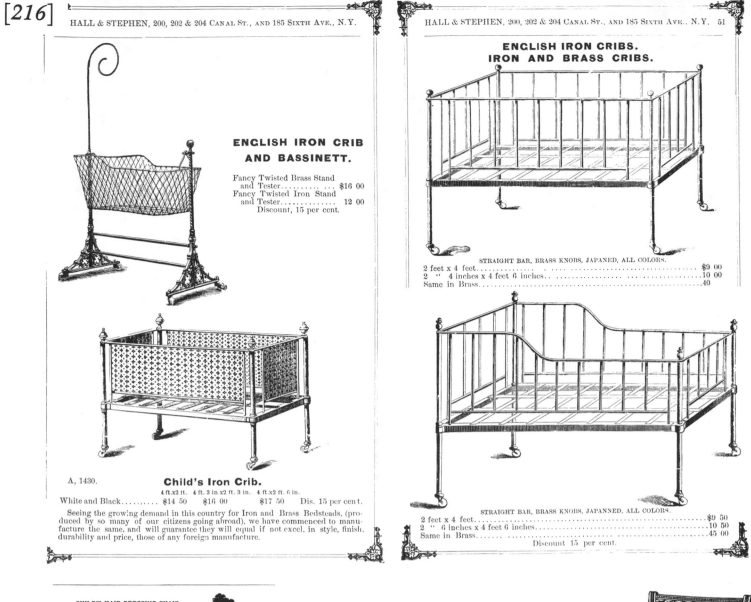

ENGLISH IRON CRIB AND BASSINETT.

Fancy Twisted Brass Stand
and Tester......... ... $16 00
Fancy Twisted Iron Stand
and Tester.............. 12 00
Discount, 15 per cent.

STRAIGHT BAR, BRASS KNOBS, JAPANED, ALL COLORS.

2 feet x 4 feet..	$9 00
2 " 4 inches x 4 feet 6 inches..	10 00
Same in Brass..	40

A, 1430.　**Child's Iron Crib.**

4 ft.x2 ft.　4 ft. 3 in.x2 ft. 3 in.　4 ft.x2 ft. 6 in.
White and Black.......... $14 50　　$16 00　　$17 50　 Dis. 15 per cent.

Seeing the growing demand in this country for Iron and Brass Bedsteads, (produced by so many of our citizens going abroad), we have commenced to manufacture the same, and will guarantee they will equal if not excel, in style, finish, durability and price, those of any foreign manufacture.

STRAIGHT BAR, BRASS KNOBS, JAPANED, ALL COLORS.

2 feet x 4 feet..	$9 50
2 " 6 inches x 4 feet 6 inches...........................	10 50
Same in Brass..	45 00

Discount 15 per cent.

CHILD'S HAIR DRESSING CHAIR.

The accompanying cut represents the handsomest and most durable Chair of the kind ever offered to the trade. The seat being attached with a screw, can be lowered or raised to any required height.

As will be seen by the cut, we have attached an Adjustable Step or Platform to this Chair, which now makes it very convenient and complete.

The Chair is made of Walnut, handsomely finished, and is either upholstered with Leather, Plushes, &c., or finished with cane seat and back, at the following prices :

Chair, with Cane Seat and Back.... .... $ 9.00
Chair, upholstered with Leather, (any color)............. 11.00
Chair, upholstered with Figured Plushes, (any color) 11.00
Chair, upholstered with Plain Plushes or Moquette............. 12.00

F. E. STUART.

No. 91

Bent Cradle.

No. 41

Child's High Dining.

M. KEATING,

SOLE MANUFACTURER OF

KEATING'S PATENT COMBINATION CRIB,

AND WHOLESALE DEALER IN

CHESTNUT AND PAINTED CHAMBER FURNITURE,

141, 143, 145 and 147 North Street, Boston.

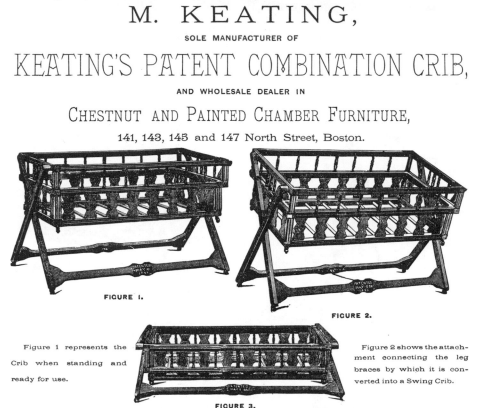

FIGURE 1.

FIGURE 2.

FIGURE 3.

Figure 1 represents the Crib when standing and ready for use.

Figure 2 shows the attachment connecting the leg braces by which it is converted into a Swing Crib.

Figure 3 represents the Crib when folded, without removing bedding, and as rolled under bed for convenience when not in use.

Since the low French beds have come into common use, a Crib that would take the place of the old-fashioned Trundle Bed, and could be pushed under the bed with the mattress, pillows, etc., all in, has become a necessity. But, until the present time, nothing has been found to supply the want. For simplicity of construction, strength and neatness of design, this Crib surpasses anything that has ever been put on the market. By this ingenious combination housekeepers get an article of great convenience, for they get a stationary Crib which, by a simple contrivance, can be made into a Swing Crib. Then, again, this Combination Crib, when not in use, can be by one movement, folded with the bed ready for use, and rolled beneath a common bed which stands not less than eight inches from the floor. When wanted for use it can be, with one movement, placed in position, as shown in Figure 1. The Crib with swing attachment will require a mattress 3 feet long by 1 1-2 feet wide, and will be the only size that will act as a rocker. The 4 and 5 feet long by 2 feet wide will not have this attachment. This Crib, or Trundle Bed, being not over 2 feet 5 inches wide, outside measurement, can be easily moved from room to room, and thus to many families save expense ; and, when not in use, it will be no obstruction as it can be rolled under the bed. It is undoubtedly the most convenient invention of the present age.

Send for Price List.   Correspondence Solicited.

Chamber Suits in Chestnut and Pine, at wholesale, of new and desirable patterns, at the most reasonable prices.

Trusting to receive your valued orders, I am,

Yours very truly,

M. KEATING,

141, 143, 145 and 147 North St., Boston.

CLARK & RANNEY.

ON CASTERS.

24 X 42 INCHES.

(Weight 23 lbs.)   PER DOZ.

Finished on wood imitation Mahogany, Walnut or Ebony.........$36 00

No. 1.—SWING.

No. 6.—SWING, BLACK WALNUT.

No. 79.

No. 31.—TRUNDLE BEDSTEAD.

5 feet long X 3½ feet wide.

No. 82.—BLACK WALNUT.

This Cut represents FOLDING CRIB closed.

Nos. 79, 80, 81, and 82 fold as above.

IRON CRADLE.

WITH CANOPY ROD.   PAINTED ANY COLOR.

We also make cradles in Brass, of any style desired.

Address all Communications to

THE NATIONAL WIRE MATTRESS CO.,

NEW BRITAIN, CONN.

Warerooms at 722 Broadway, New York,

WHERE A FULL STOCK CAN BE SEEN.

No. 25.

IRON CRIB.

WITH BRASS KNOBS.

And Iron Sacking.

WELL CASTERED.   PAINTED ANY COLOR.

2 feet	x 4 feet	- -	$11.00
2 feet 6 inches x 4 feet 6 inches		- -	12.00

No. 400.

YOUTHS' BRASS BED,

With National Wire Mattress.

METAL CASTERS, NICKEL PLATED.

Weight of Bed complete, 160 lbs.

3 feet	x 6 feet 6 inches	
3 feet 6 inches x 6 feet 6 inches		Prices given on application.
4 feet	x 6 feet 6 inches	

No. 26.

IRON CRIB.

WITH BRASS KNOBS.

And Iron Sacking.

WELL CASTERED.   PAINTED ANY COLOR.

2 feet	x 4 feet	- - - -	$13.00
2 feet 6 inches x 4 feet 6 inches		- - - -	14.00

THE HALE & KILBURN MANUFACTURING COMPANY, 48 & 50 NORTH SIXTH ST., PHILADELPHIA, PA.

THE "CHAMPION" AUTOMATIC FOLDING CRIB.

Made upon exactly the same principle as the Bedsteads, and just as complete in all the details of manufacture; perfect in design; durable and well finished.
The side rack folds in upon the mattress when the Crib is to be folded.

Double Cribs, (for two children), inside measure,   in. x   in., made to order of either of the below patterns.

STYLE No. 11.	STYLE No. 23.
Plain, Solid Walnut.	**Veneered, Solid Walnut.**

Inside measure, ... 50 in. x 26 in.
Outside measure, when closed, ... 72 in. x 36 in.

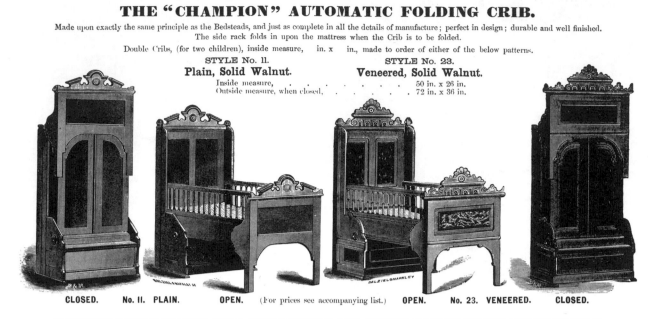

CLOSED.   No. 11. PLAIN.   OPEN.   (For prices see accompanying list.)   OPEN.   No. 23. VENEERED.   CLOSED.

BRANCH STORES, NEW YORK AND BOSTON. SPECIAL AGENTS IN CHICAGO, ST. LOUIS, CLEVELAND, PITTSBURGH, BALTIMORE, BROOKLYN AND ALBANY.

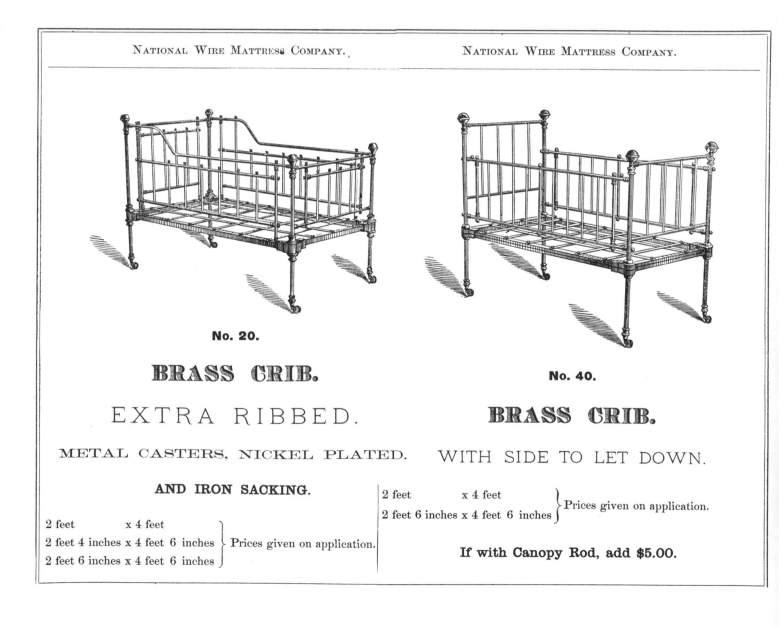

NATIONAL WIRE MATTRESS COMPANY.   NATIONAL WIRE MATTRESS COMPANY.

No. 20.

BRASS CRIB.

EXTRA RIBBED.

METAL CASTERS, NICKEL PLATED.

AND IRON SACKING.

2 feet   x 4 feet
2 feet 4 inches x 4 feet 6 inches } Prices given on application.
2 feet 6 inches x 4 feet 6 inches

No. 40.

BRASS CRIB.

WITH SIDE TO LET DOWN.

2 feet   x 4 feet
2 feet 6 inches x 4 feet 6 inches } Prices given on application.

If with Canopy Rod, add $5.00.

CLARK & RANNEY.

TOY COMBINED CRADLE AND CRIB.

(Weight 4 lbs.) PER DOZ.

12 x 21 Inches..$9 00

(See page 4.)

No. 2. CHILD'S STRAIGHT ARM.
(Weight 5 lbs.) PER DOZ.
Tapestry Brussels..$8 75

NEW HAVEN FOLDING CHAIR CO.

No. 6.
CHILD'S CHAIR.
Designed for Children from 4 to 8 years of age.
Pattern Body Brussels Seat. 12 inches
between Arms.
Oak,................$18.00 per dozen.
Imitation Rosewood,___ 18.00 "

No. 63.—*Secured by Patent.*
CHILD'S CHAIR.
Pattern Body Brussels Seat.
Imitation Rosewood, ___$15.00 per dozen.

THE LEOMINSTER FURNITURE MFG. CO.,
ORDWAY SWING ROCKER CRADLE.

E. W. VAILL, WORCESTER, MASS.

5B

CHILD'S CHAIR.

Patented.

ROSEWOOD OR WALNUT FINISH.

Per Dozen
Pattern Brussels,   -   - - $20 00

102

CHILD'S CHAIR.

ROSEWOOD OR WALNUT FINISH.

Patented.   Per Dozen
Brussels Seat,   ,   - - $17 00
Pattern Brussels Seat,   -   18 00

The new Ordway Swing Rocker Cradle, as represented above, consists of a base resting firmly on the floor, with the rocker suspended on a sagging strap, made expressly for this purpose, which gives it a gentle swinging motion when rocking.

It is noiseless in motion, and has no springs nor iron work to get out of order.

Though but lately introduced into the market, it is selling rapidly, as its merits have only to be seen to secure a demand.

They are made in Maple, finished light or dark, and packed tightly together when shipping.

Price Lists furnished to all dealers upon application.

Manufactured only by H. J. KIMBALL, So. GARDNER, MASS., who has appointed us Selling Agents.

We cordially invite you to send to us for a sample order.

Yours, respectfully,

PLATFORM CRADLES.

No. 19.—Large Size. 20x40 inches.
Oak.

.·. PLATFORM CRADLES .·.

No. 17. LARGE SIZE. 20 x 40 Inches.
+ OAK. +

CRIB BED

No. 6.—Child's Crib Bed. Oak and Walnut.
Size 28x48 inches. One Side Hinged. Fine Antique Trimmings.
These small Beds are very desirable and sell readily.
54 inch Rails if desired.

CRIB BED.

No. 5.—Child's Crib Bed. Oak only.
28x48 inches. One Side Hinged. Fine Antique Trimmings.
These small Beds are very desirable, and sell readily.
54 inch Rails if desired.

THE SAFETY VELOCIPEDE.

STEEL WIRE WHEELS.

No. 31	20 inch front wheel	$3 75
" 32	24 " "	4 13
" 33	28 " "	4 50

THE UNION VELOCIPEDE.

STEEL WIRE WHEELS.

No. 40	16 inch front wheel, iron pedal	$3 37
" 41	20 " " " "	3 75
" 42	24 " " " "	4 13
" 43	28 " " " "	4 50

RUBBER TIRE WHEELS.

No. 45	16 inch front wheel, iron pedal	$5 25
" 46	20 " " " "	6 38
" 47	24 " " " "	7 50
" 48	28 " " " "	9 00

TRICYCLE.

All working parts Wrought Iron and Steel.

No. 3	22 inch driving wheel, 3 to 5 years	$9 60
" 4	26 " " 5 to 9 "	10 60
" 5	30 " " 9 to 13 "	12 60
" 5½	34 " " 13 to 16 "	18 00

RUBBER TIRE STEEL WHEELS.

No. 6	22 inch driving wheel	$15 80
" 7	26 " "	17 80
" 8	30 " "	20 80
" 9	34 " "	30 00

GALLOPING HORSE.

PATENTED.

No. 19.

No. 13.	5 inch block, crooked legs	$2 80
" 14.	6 " "	4 20
" 15.	6 " " full saddle	4 75
" 16.	6 " carved legs, better upholstered	5 65
" 17.	7 " "	7 85
" 18.	8 " "	9 60
" 19.	10 " "	11 25

HAIR-COVERED GALLOPING HORSE.

No. 16½.	6 inch block, carved legs, stitched saddles	$10 00
" 17½.	7 " " "	14 00
" 18½.	8 " " "	16 00
" 19½.	10 " " "	18 00

CHICAGO HOME COMFORT.

A PARLOR SOFA BED.

No. 600. POLISHED ARMS.

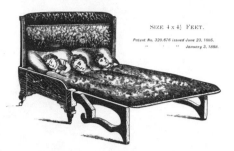

SIZE 4 x 4½ FEET.

Patent No. 320.676 issued June 23, 1885.
"   "   " January 3, 1888.

COMFORT FOR OUR DARLINGS.

No. 601. UPHOLSTERED ARMS.

NEW HAVEN FOLDING CHAIR CO.

CHILD'S ROLLING CHAIR.

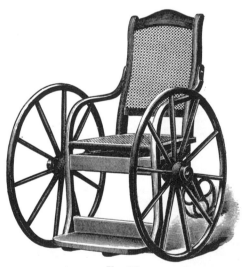

No. 52.

DESIGNED FOR CHILDREN UNDER 13 YEARS OF AGE.

Height of Back from Seat, ___ 19 inches.   Height of Seat from floor, ___ 16 inches.
Width of Seat, ___ 14½ "   "   "   " foot board, 13   "
Weight of Chair, ___ about 30 lbs.   Height of Wheels from floor, __ 24   "

Will pass through a doorway not less than 25 inches wide.

This Rolling Chair is not reclining; has same axle and wheels as the more expensive ones. No outside rim on wheels.

Oak, ___ $16.00 each.
Black Walnut, ___ 18.00 "

With Outside Hand Rim, $2.00 additional.

This Chair can be placed on Springs, same as No. 73, raising seat 3 inches higher from floor, at an additional cost of $3.00.

With Springs and Handle for pushing, $6.00 additional.

Invalid's Chairs and Supplies

INVALID RECLINING ROLLING CHAIR.

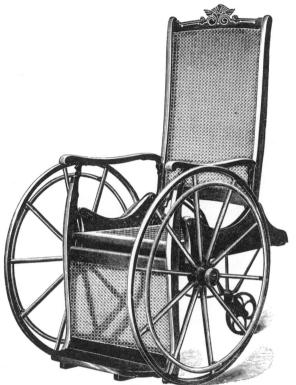

No. 24.

Height of Back from Seat,.... 34 inches.   Height of Seat from floor,.... 20 inches.
Width of Seat,.............. 19 "   "   "   "   foot board, 17 "
Weight of Chair,.......about 60 lbs.   Height of Wheels,........... 30 "

Will pass through a doorway not less than 28 inches wide.

For fuller description, and cuts showing different positions in which it can be used, see next page.

	EACH.
Oak, Caned,	$34.00
Black Walnut, Caned,	37.00
Oak, Upholst'd with all wool Terry, Hair Cloth, or Raw Silk, Spring Back and Seat,	42.00
Black Walnut, " " " " " "	45.00

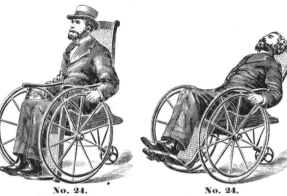

No. 24.
UPRIGHT POSITION.

No. 24.
RECLINING POSITION.

No. 24.
RECUMBENT POSITION.

Nos. 24, 70, 71, 72 and 76 may be used in this position, or intermediate between it and upright.

Since the introduction of this Reclining Rolling Chair in 1865, we have made great improvements in its construction, and it is now one of the best for those unable to walk. By its use the invalid is enabled to sit upright, recline, lie down, and propel himself from place to place at pleasure. It requires no exertion by the occupant to assume any position desired, intermediate from upright to recumbent, the chair being so balanced that, when unfastened, a slight backward motion of the body will cause the back of the chair to move backward, and vice versa. When adjusted to the desired position, it can be securely fastened; thus this Invalid Reclining Rolling Chair perfectly accomplishes all that can be desired for the comfort of the occupant. The wheels have an outside hand rim, for street use, to save hand from contact with dirt; also an *oval* iron tire, which runs with less noise and will not cut carpets. If desired, *flat* iron can be put on. The hubs have nickel plated bands. The axles are ¾ inch square iron, with heavy boxes and right and left hand nuts, which are capped. The back or caster wheel is iron, 10 inches in diameter.

FOR PRICES, SEE PREVIOUS PAGE.

INVALID ROLLING CHAIR.

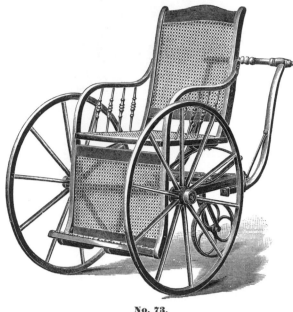

No. 73.

Height of Back from Seat,	23 inches.	Height of Wheels,	30 inches.
Height of Seat from floor,	23 "	Width of Seat,	19 "
	Height of Seat from foot board,	17 inches.	

Will pass through a doorway not less than 28 inches wide.

This is our No. 50 Chair placed on *Springs* and with *Handle* for pushing. The handle can be easily removed when desired.

For invalids or persons too weak for walking long distances, this will be found a very comfortable and desirable chair, allowing them to take out-door exercises by having an attendant to push them.

Wheels have no Hand Rim.

Oak, Caned, ...$29.00 each.

INVALID RECLINING ROLLING CHAIR.

This Chair is the same as our No. 24, described on pages 2 and 3, but with the addition of *Steel Elliptic Springs* placed between the seat and gear, thus preventing the jar caused by rolling over uneven ground and making it very desirable for use out of doors.

Dimensions are the same as No. 24, except seat is 3 inches higher from floor.

Will pass through a doorway not less than 28 inches wide.

	EACH.
Oak, Caned,	$37.00
Black Walnut, Caned,	40.00
Oak, upholstered with all wool Terry, Hair Cloth, or Raw Silk, Springs in Back and Seat, Leg Rest Caned,	45.00
Black Walnut, upholstered with all wool Terry, Hair Cloth, or Raw Silk, Springs in Back and Seat, Leg Rest Caned,	48.00

For general description, see page 3.

No. 70.

INVALID RECLINING ROLLING CHAIR.

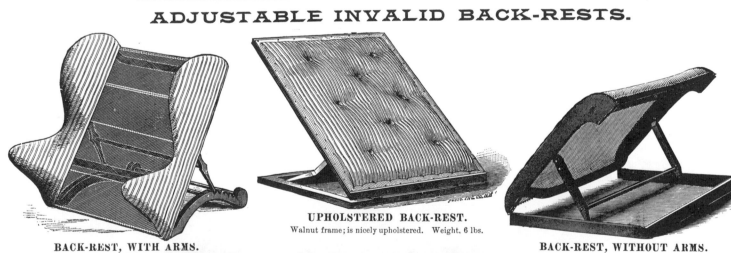

This is the same as our No. 24, but has a recently invented attachment for raising the Leg Rest independently of any motion of the back. The attachment is made of Iron, is very strong and simple in its working; by pushing on the handle the Rest is raised to any desired angle and is at the same time lengthened, thus giving ample room for the limbs. The chair can also be used the same as No. 24, that is, Back and Leg Rest working together.

Dimensions same as No. 24.

Will pass through a doorway not less than 28 inches wide.

For general description, see page 3.

No. 71.

	EACH.
Oak, Caned,	$38.00
Black Walnut, Caned,	41.00
Oak, upholstered with all wool Terry, Hair Cloth, or Raw Silk, Spring Back and Seat, Leg Rest Caned,	46.00
Black Walnut, upholstered with all wool Terry, Hair Cloth, or Raw Silk, Spring Back and Seat, Leg Rest Caned,	49.00

GEORGE HEYMAN, 103 & 105 MOTT STREET, NEW YORK.

ADJUSTABLE INVALID BACK-RESTS.

BACK-REST, WITH ARMS.

Has a woven wire back and upholstered arms, so arranged as to conform to the shape of the body, giving perfect ease and comfort. Weight, 13 lbs.

UPHOLSTERED BACK-REST.

Walnut frame; is nicely upholstered. Weight, 6 lbs.

BACK-REST, WITHOUT ARMS.

The frame of hardwood, with a woven wire back, and not liable to retain the germs of anything infectious. Weight, 7 lbs.

☞ Any of the above can be adjusted at whatever angle may be desired.

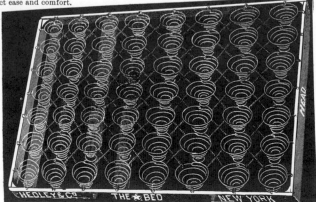

STAR BED.

Weight of 4 ft. 4 in. size, 40 lbs.

INVALID ROLLING CHAIR.

No. 84.

Height of Back from Seat,____ 28 inches.   Height of Seat from floor,____ 20 inches.
Height of Wheels from floor,__ 26 "   Width of Seat,_____ 18 "
Weight of Chair,_____ about 40 lbs.

Will pass through a doorway not less than 28 inches wide.

RATTAN BODY WITH CANED SEAT.

Price, with Hand Rim on Wheels, _____ $27.00 each.
"   with no Hand Rim on Wheels,_____ 25.00 "

INVALID RECLINING CHAIR.

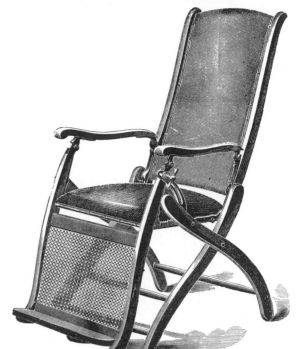

No. 8.

Height of Back from Seat,____ 34 inches.   Height of Seat from floor, ____ 20 inches.
Height of Seat from foot board, 17 "   Width of Seat,_____ 20 "

This Chair is already favorably known to invalids, and is *easily adjusted to either an upright, reclining or recumbent position,* by our new improved fastening. It can also be folded readily for packing away or shipment. Upholstered with all wool plain Terry, Hair Cloth, or Raw Silk, with Springs in Back and Seat. Caned Front.

Oak,_____$21.00 each.
Solid Black Walnut,_____ 22.00 "

INVALID RECLINING ROLLING CHAIR.

No. 79.

Height of Back from Seat,____ 34 inches.   Height of Wheels, _____ 30 inches.
Height of Seat from floor, ____ 20 "   Width of Seat,_____ 19 "

Will pass through a doorway not less than 28 inches wide.

In order to meet the demand for a cheap Reclining Rolling Chair, we have introduced our No. 79, which, though not as desirable as our more expensive ones, is a strong and comfortable chair, and will answer a good purpose where a higher priced one cannot be afforded. It can be used and fastened in any position. from upright to recumbent. Axles and wheels are the same as on No. 24, except that it has no outside hand rim.

Oak, Caned, _____$25.00.

Outside Hand Rim added at an additional cost of $2.00.

INVALID ROLLING CHAIR.

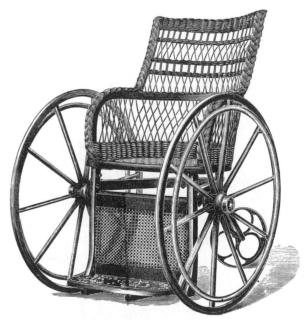

No. 81.

Height of Back from Seat,____ 21 inches.   Height of Seat from floor, ____ 20 inches.
Height of Wheels from floor,__ 30 "   Width of Seat,_____ 18 "
Weight of Chair,_____about 40 lbs.

Will pass through a doorway not less than 28 inches wide.

RATTAN BODY WITH WOVEN CANE SEAT.

Price, with Hand Rim on Wheels,_____$22.00 each.
"   with no Hand Rim on Wheels,_____ 20.00 "

INVALID ROLLING CHAIR.

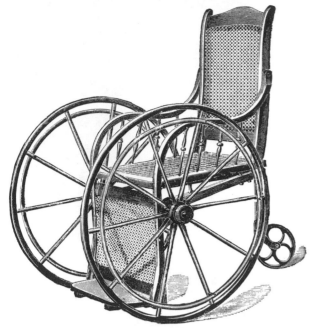

NO. 50.

Height of Back from Seat,.... 23 inches.	Height of Seat from floor,.... 20 inches.
Width of Seat,.............. 19 "	" " " foot board, 17 "
Weight of Chair,...... about 40 lbs.	Height of Wheels from floor,.. 30 "

Will pass through a doorway not less than 28 inches wide.

This Rolling Chair is *not* reclining, but has the same running parts, viz: wheels and axles, as the more expensive No. 24 Reclining Chair, the difference in the construction being in the style of chair used, and which, in this particular, is made of the most approved *fixed* shape for affording rest to the occupant. This Chair has an outside hand rim on wheels for street use, to save hand from contact with mud.

Oak, ... $26.00 each.
Black Walnut,...... .... 29.00 "

INVALID ROLLING CHAIR.

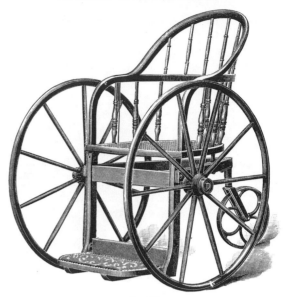

NO. 51.

Height of Back from Seat,.... 21 inches.	Height of Seat from floor,.... 20 inches.
Width of Seat,.............. 18 "	" " " foot board, 17 "
Weight of Chair,...... about 40 lbs.	Height of Wheels from floor,.. 30 "

Will pass through a doorway not less than 28 inches wide.

This Rolling Chair is *not* reclining, but has the same running parts, viz: wheels and axles, as the more expensive No. 24 Reclining Chair, the difference in the construction being in the style of Chair used. This chair has *no* outside hand rim on wheels as in Nos. 24 and 50, and back is, as shown in cut, *not* caned.

Oak, ...$16.00 each.

Outside Hand Rim added at an additional cost of $2.00.

This Chair can be placed on Springs, same as used on No. 73; they will raise the seat 3 inches higher from the floor, and will cost $3.00 additional.

INVALID ROLLING CHAIR.

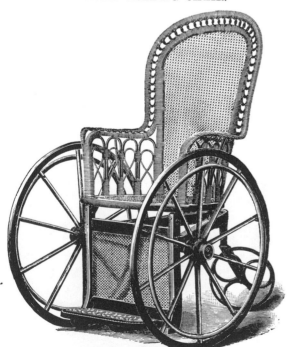

NO. 74.

Height of Back from seat,.... 28 inches.	Height of Wheels,.......... 26 inches.
Height of Seat from floor,.... 20 "	Width of Seat............... 18 "
" " " foot board, 17 "	Weight of Chair,......about 40 lbs.

Will pass through a doorway not less than 28 inches wide.

This is a very light, roomy. comfortable and strong Rolling Chair. The frame of the chair is rattan, with cane seat, back and front, and wide arm rest. The axles and wheels are the same as used on our other Rolling Chairs. Outside hand rim on wheels.

Price, ... $30.00.

BATH ROLLING CHAIR.

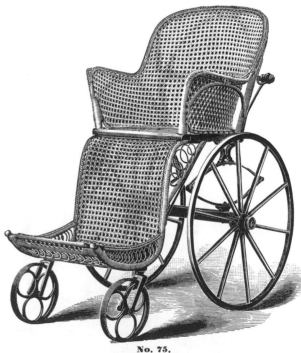

NO. 75.

Height of Back from Seat,.... 23 inches.	Height of Wheels,.......... 30 inches.
Height of Seat from foot board, 20 "	Width of Seat,.............. 20 "

Will pass through a doorway not less than 28 inches wide.

This Rolling Chair is intended for an attendant to propel, for which purpose a handle is strongly attached to the back. It is placed on springs, thus making it easy riding, and very desirable for use out of doors. The chair is made in the most approved shape for securing the comfort of the occupant, having back and sides caned and arm rests. The wheels do not have the outside hand rim, otherwise are the same as those used on No. 24. Axle is iron. The front wheels are iron, 10 inches in diameter, and working on a pivot, allow the chair to be easily turned.

Price, ... $40.00.

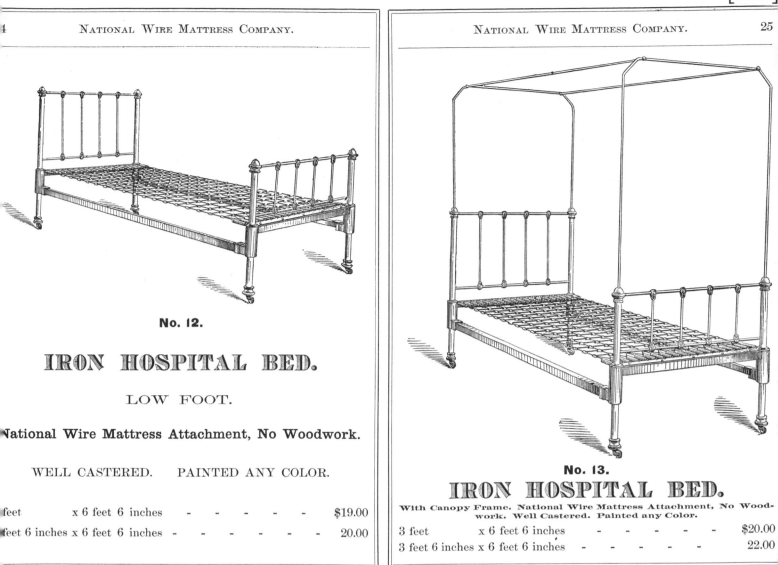

No. 12.

IRON HOSPITAL BED.

LOW FOOT.

National Wire Mattress Attachment, No Woodwork.

WELL CASTERED.   PAINTED ANY COLOR.

feet x 6 feet 6 inches	- - - - -	$19.00
feet 6 inches x 6 feet 6 inches	- - - - -	20.00

No. 13.

IRON HOSPITAL BED.

With Canopy Frame. National Wire Mattress Attachment, No Woodwork. Well Castered. Painted any Color.

3 feet x 6 feet 6 inches	- - - - -	$20.00
3 feet 6 inches x 6 feet 6 inches	- - - - -	22.00

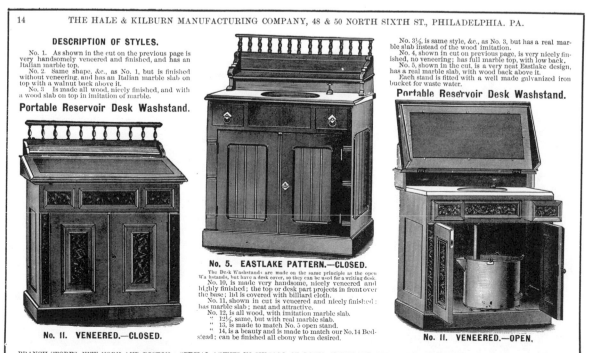

14   THE HALE & KILBURN MANUFACTURING COMPANY, 48 & 50 NORTH SIXTH ST., PHILADELPHIA. PA.

DESCRIPTION OF STYLES.

No. 1. As shown in the cut on the previous page is very handsomely veneered and finished, and has an Italian marble top.

No. 2. Same shape, &c., as No. 1, but is finished without veneering, and has an Italian marble slab on top with a walnut back above it.

No. 3 Is made all wood, nicely finished, and with a wood slab on top in imitation of marble.

Portable Reservoir Desk Washstand.

No. 3½, is same style, &c., as No. 3, but has a real marble slab instead of the wood imitation.

No. 4, shown in cut on previous page, is very nicely finished, no veneering; has full marble top, with low back.

No. 5, shown in the cut, is a very neat Eastlake design, has a real marble slab, with wood back above it.

Each stand is fitted with a well made galvanized iron bucket for waste water.

Portable Reservoir Desk Washstand.

No. 5. EASTLAKE PATTERN.—CLOSED.

The Desk Washstands are made on the same principle as the open Washstands, but have a desk cover, so they can be used for a writing desk

No. 10, is made very handsome, nicely veneered and highly finished; the top or desk part projects in front over the base; lid is covered with billiard cloth.

No. 11, shown in cut is veneered and nicely finished; has marble slab; neat and attractive.

No. 12, is all wood, with imitation marble slab.
" 12½, same, but with real marble slab.
" 13, is made to match No. 5 open stand.
" 14, is a beauty and is made to match our No. 14 Bedstead; can be finished all ebony when desired.

No. 11. VENEERED.—CLOSED.

No. 11. VENEERED.—OPEN.

BRANCH STORES, NEW YORK AND BOSTON.   SPECIAL AGENTS IN CHICAGO, ST. LOUIS, CLEVELAND, PITTSBURGH, BALTIMORE, BROOKLYN AND ALBANY.

QUEEN ANNE RECLINING CHAIR, WITH DESK ATTACHMENT.

MEDIUM RECLINING CHAIR.

No. 3 WHEEL CHAIR.

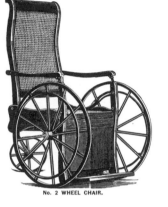

No. 2 WHEEL CHAIR.

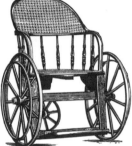

No. I WHEEL CHAIR.

Cortland * Furniture * Company

Cortland N. Y.

No. 4.

Rocking Chairs

G. M. LEAVENS & SON 34 Canal St.,

No. 840 Large Rocker. Silk Plush and Taps.; Oak and Mahog.

No. 850 Large Rocker. Silk Plush and Taps.; Oak and Mahog. finish.

No. 826 Lady's Rocker. Silk Plush and Taps.; Oak and Mahog. finish.

No. 822 Lady's Rocker. 16th Century finish; Plush and Taps.

No. 192.
Boston Wood Seat Rock.

No. 190.
Boston Wood Seat Nurse.

F. E. STUART.

No. 24

Boston Rocker.

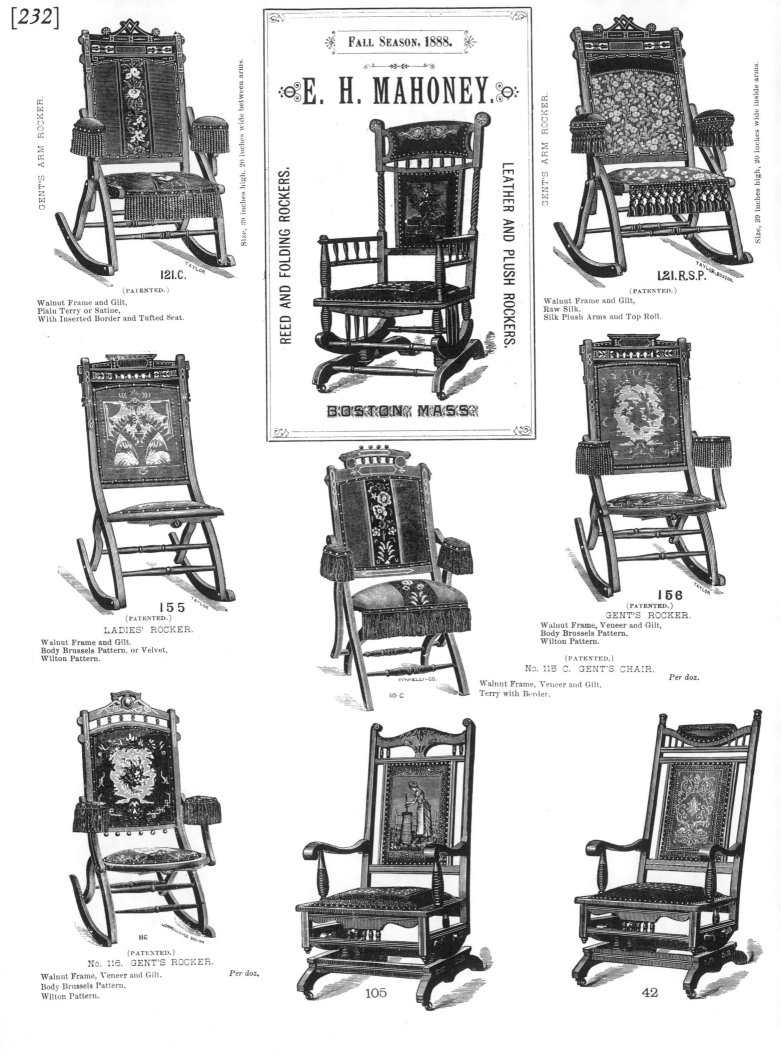

GENT'S ARM ROCKER.

Size, 39 inches high. 20 inches wide between arms.

121.C.
(PATENTED.)
Walnut Frame and Gilt,
Plain Terry or Satine,
With Inserted Border and Tufted Seat.

TAYLOR

FALL SEASON, 1888.

E. H. MAHONEY.

REED AND FOLDING ROCKERS.

LEATHER AND PLUSH ROCKERS.

BOSTON MASS.

GENT'S ARM ROCKER.

Size, 39 inches high, 20 inches wide inside arms.

121.R.S.P.
(PATENTED.)
Walnut Frame and Gilt,
Raw Silk,
Silk Plush Arms and Top Roll.

TAYLOR, BOSTON.

155
(PATENTED.)
LADIES' ROCKER.
Walnut Frame and Gilt,
Body Brussels Pattern, or Velvet,
Wilton Pattern.

TAYLOR

156
(PATENTED.)
GENT'S ROCKER.
Walnut Frame, Veneer and Gilt,
Body Brussels Pattern,
Wilton Pattern.

TAYLOR

(PATENTED.)
No. 115 C. GENT'S CHAIR.   Per doz.
Walnut Frame, Veneer and Gilt.
Terry with Border.

CONNELLY-CO.
115-C

(PATENTED.)
No. 116. GENT'S ROCKER.   Per doz.
Walnut Frame, Veneer and Gilt.
Body Brussels Pattern,
Wilton Pattern.

CONNELLY-CO BOSTON
116

105

42

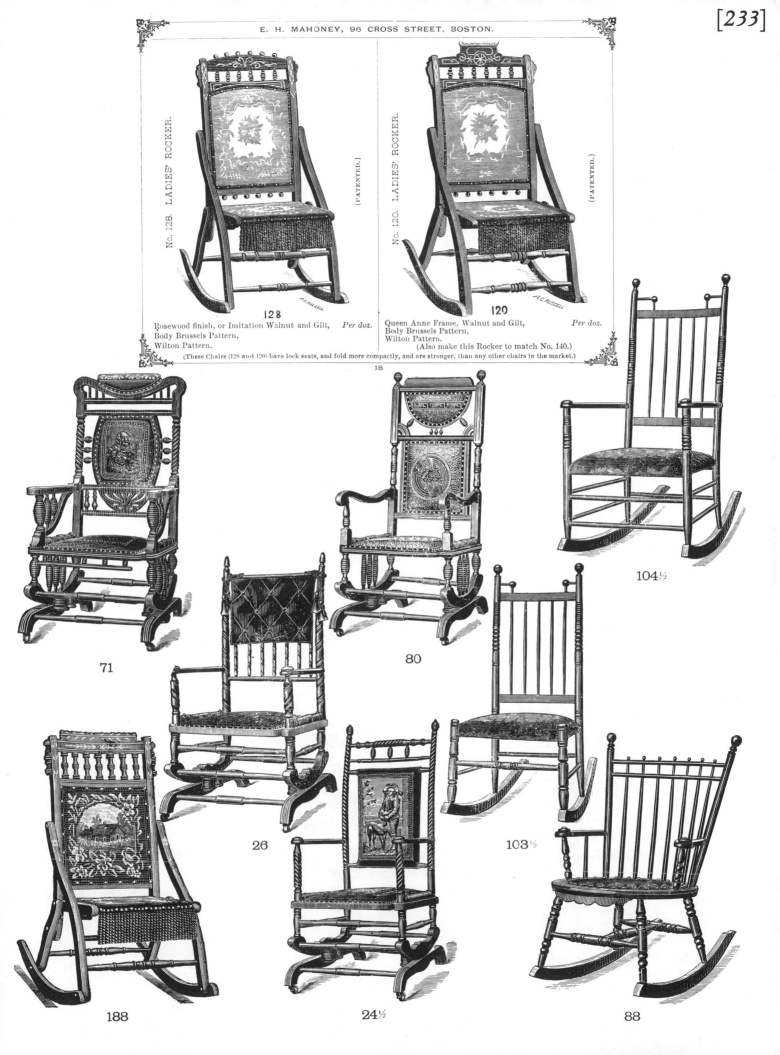

NO. 128. LADIES' ROCKER.

(PATENTED.)

128

Rosewood finish, or Imitation Walnut and Gilt,   *Per doz.*
Body Brussels Pattern,
Wilton Pattern.

NO. 120. LADIES' ROCKER.

(PATENTED.)

120

Queen Anne Frame, Walnut and Gilt,   *Per doz.*
Body Brussels Pattern,
Wilton Pattern.
(Also make this Rocker to match No. 140.)

(These Chairs (128 and 120) have lock seats, and fold more compactly, and are stronger, than any other chairs in the market.)

18

71

80

104½

26

103½

188

24½

88

108

45

52½

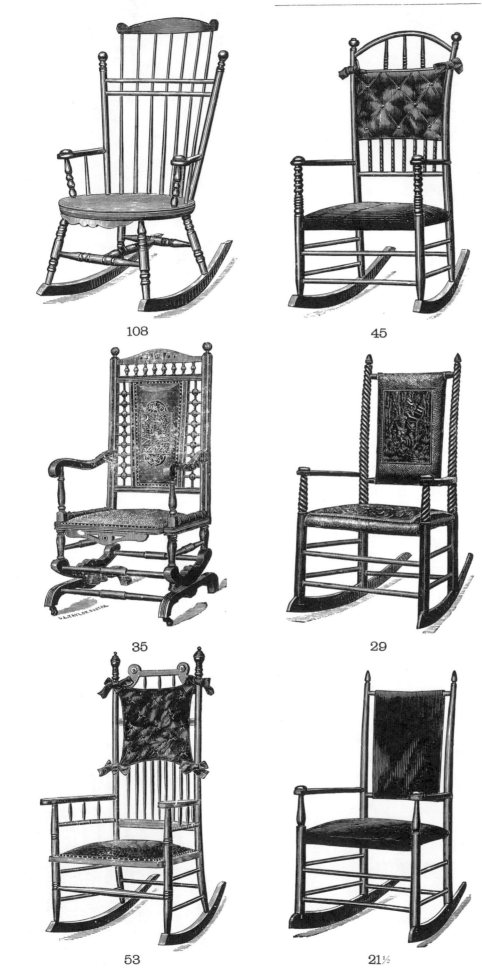

35

29

47

53

21½

No. 208.

No. 46, B.

No. 40, B.

No. 115.

No. 122.

No. 4.

No. 265.

No. 128.

No. 250.

No. 72.

No. 8.

No. 19 1-2.

No. 136.

No. 25.

PLATFORM ROCKER, PLAIN.

PER DOZ.
Same as No. 20, except plain turning..........................$39 00

It has been our design with Nos. 20, 25, 30 and 35, to furnish beautiful, roomy, easy, light, and at the same time strong rockers, suitable for lady or gentleman, parlor or sitting-room. The arms have triple fastenings making them twice as strong as the usual way.

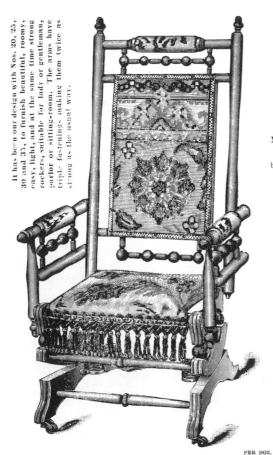

No. 35.   PLATFORM ROCKER, PLAIN.

PER DOZ.
$42 00

Same as No. 30 except plain turning.

No. 20.   PLATFORM ROCKER, FANCY.

PER DOZ.
$42 00

Padded seat. Silk Gimp. Best Wilton Carpet. Weight 22 lbs. Width between arms, 18 inches. Height of back, 27 inches.
Finish on wood, imitation Mahogany, Walnut or Ebony.

PER DOZ.
Same as No. 40 except carpet running over the top...............$40 00
Finish on wood, imitation Mahogany, Walnut or Ebony.

No.45

No.50

HEAVY CANE ROCKER.

PER DOZ.
$45 00

Same size as No. 40. Seat and back of double cane. Top and arms wound with cane.
Finish on wood or imitation Mahogany.

HARWOOD, SYRACUSE.

No. 168. Large Rocker, Metal Trimmed

No. 142. Ladies' Rocker.

Cortland * Furniture * Company,
Cortland, N. Y.

No. 300 and 301.

CLARK & RANNEY.

CLARK & RANNEY.

No. 8

EASTLAKE.

(Weight 12 lbs.)   PER DOZ.

Tapestry Brussels..............................$16 50
Ebony, Walnut or imitation Mahogany..... .... 19 50

Hayes * Chair * Company,
Cortland, N. Y.

No. 9.

No. 8.

HIGH BACK, FANCY SQUARE ARM.

(Weight 13 lbs.)   PER DOZ.

Tapestry Brussels...............................$16 50
Ebony, Walnut or imitation Mahogany...............19 50

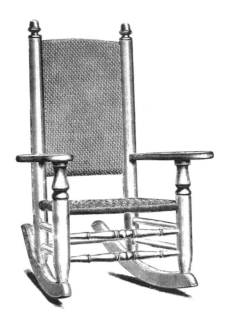

No. 173. Ladies' Rocker, Metal Trimmed.　　　No. 10. Mammoth Rocker, Double Cane.　　　No. 164. Large Rocker, Double Cane.

No 183 A.　Large Rocker　　　No. 155.　Large Rocker, Metal Trimmed.　　　No. 184 B.　Ladies' Rocker

No. 33.
WASHBURN NURSE.
(Chestnut Seat.)

No. 89.
MISSES' HARVARD ROCKER.

No. 43.
QUAKER NURSE.
(Chestnut Seat.)

No. 44.
DOUBLE CANE SEWING.

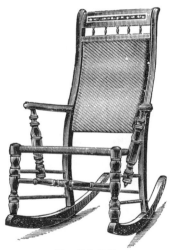

No. 34 1-2.
DOUBLE CANE SEWING.

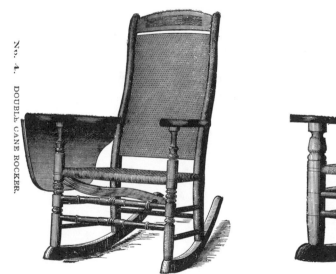

No. 4. DOUBLE CANE ROCKER.

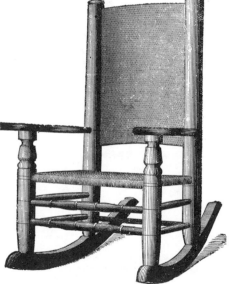

No. 111.
BENT WOOD NURSE.
(Chestnut Seat.)

No. 110.
BENT WOOD ROCKER.
(Chestnut Seat.)

No. 6.   DOUBLE CANE ROCKER.

No. 80.
BAMBOO ROCKER.

No. 725. Fancy Rocker. Golden Quartered Oak or Mahogany finish. Piano polish.
Each...$2.97

No. 723. Fancy Rocker. Golden Quartered Oak or Mahogany finish. Piano polish.
Each...$3.25

No. 789. Fancy Rocker. Golden Quartered Oak or Mahogany finisn. Piano polish.
Each...$3.25

No. 784. Fancy Rocker. Golden Quartered Oak or Mahogany finish. Piano polish.
Each...$3.50

No. 752. Fancy Rocker. Golden Quartered Oak or Mahogany finish. Piano polish.
Each...$5.20

No. 791. Fancy Rocker. Golden Quartered Oak or Mahogany finish. Piano polish.
Each...$5.90

No. 727. Fancy Rocker. Golden Quartered Oak or Mahogany finish. Piano polish.
Each...$6.30

No. 727 1-2. Fancy Chair. Golden Quartered Oak or Mahogany finish. Piano polish.
Each...$6.30

No. 753. Fancy Rocker. Golden Quartered Oak or Mahogany finish. Piano polish.
Each...$7.00

No. 797. Fancy Rocker. Golden Quartered Oak or Mahogany finish. Piano polish.
Each...$7.75

No. 788. Fancy Rocker. Golden Quartered Oak or Mahogany finish. Piano polish.
Each...$8.15

No. 809. Fancy Rocker. Mahogany only. Piano polish.
Each...$8.15

We make an arm chair to match each of the above rockers at the same price. (See 727½).

No. 789 C .... $3.50   No. 437 .... $4.50   No. 435 .... $4.50   No. 459 .... $4.50

These Rockers are all made in Golden Quartered Oak or Mahogany finish, and are upholstered in best quality fancy figured velour or tapestry.

No. 454 .... $5.20   No. 278 .... $6.65   No. 390 .... $7.00   No. 391 .... $7.40

These Rockers are all made in Golden Quartered Oak or Mahogany finish, piano polish.   They are upholstered in best grade fancy figured velour or tapestries.

No. 725 1-2 .... $3.25   No. 723 1-2 .... $3.50   No. 752 .... $5.20   No. 797 1-2 .... $7.75

Four elegant Library, Den or Office Chairs.   Golden Quartered Oak or Mahogany finish, piano polish, saddle seats.

No. 0174

Large Easy Arm Rocker. Wide and comfortable seat, carved top, finished light color.
Price $1.45

No. 7562

Fancy Rocker. Golden Elm, shaped wood seat, carved back and spiral spindles.
Each $1.50

No. 7562 A

Fancy Rocker. Golden Elm, shaped wood seat, carved back and spiral spindles.
Each $1.75

No. 7724

Fancy Rocker. Golden Elm, shaped wood seat, carved back and spiral spindles.
Each $1.95

No. 7432

Fancy Rocker. Golden Elm, shaped wood seat, carved back and spiral spindles.
Each $1.97

No. 7429

Fancy Rocker. Wood seat, handsomely carved back and shaped arms, fancy posts, large and roomy, Golden Elm.
Each $2.20

No. 0755

Fancy Rocker. With cobbler seat, Solid Golden Oak, handsomely carved back.
Each $2.40

No. 0756

Fancy Rocker. Solid Golden Oak, cobbler seat, handsomely carved back.
Each $2.50

No. 890

Fancy Rocker. Solid Golden Oak or Mahogany finish, elegantly carved top and back slat, very large and easy, in saddle wood seat or cobbler seat.
Each $2.65

No. 891

Fancy Rocker. Solid Golden Oak or Mahogany finish, elegantly carved top and back slat, very large and easy, in saddle wood seat or cobbler seat.
Each $2.65

No. 889

Fancy Rocker. Solid Golden Oak or Mahogany finish, elegantly carved top and back slat, saddle wood seat or cobbler seat, very large and comfortable.
Each $2.75

No. 7464

Fancy Rocker. Solid Golden Oak or Mahogany finish, handsomely carved back, fancy posts and spindles, in cobbler seat or saddle wood seat.
Each $2.85

No. 7566

Fancy Rocker. Solid Golden Oak or Mahogany finish, elegantly carved top and back slat, saddle wood seat.
Each $2.97

No. 7398

Fancy Rocker. Solid Golden Oak or Mahogany finish, cobbler seat, elegantly carved top and back slat, fancy posts and spindles.
Each $3.75

No. 7611

Fancy Rocker. Solid Golden Oak or Mahogany finish, elegantly carved top and back slat, shaped wood seat.
Each $4.50

SUPPLEMENTARY SHEET, ISSUED BY
G. M. LEAVENS & SON,
WHOLESALE DEALERS IN
Cane and Wood Seat Chairs, Pine Furniture, Etc.
34 Canal Street, BOSTON, MASS.

No. 871 Large Base Rocker. Velvet Carpet; Wal. and Mahog. finish.

No. 873 Large Base Rocker. Velvet Carpet; Mahog., Wal. and Oak finish.

No. 875 Large Base Rocker. Silk Plush; Mahog. and Oak finish.

No. 881 Large Base Rocker. Silk Plush; Mahog. and Oak finish.

No. 883 Large Base Rocker. Silk Plush; Oak and Mahog. finish.

No. 863 Child's Base Rocker. Body Carpet; Mahog. and Wal. finish.

No. 865 Child's Base Rocker. Body Carpet; Mahog. and Wal. finish.

No. 802 Lady's Rocker. Silk Plush and Taps.; Mahog. and Oak finish.

No. 834 Lady's Rocker. Silk Plush; Mahog. and Oak finish.

No. 838 Lady's Rocker. Silk Plush or Taps.; Mahog. and Oak finish.

No. 846 Lady's Rocker. Silk Plush or Taps.; Mahog. and Oak finish.

No. 894 Lady's Rocker. Silk Plush; Mahog. and Oak finish.

MANUFACTURERS FOR THE TRADE.   NO GOODS SOLD AT RETAIL.

No. 23.   No. 14.   No. 22.

PATENT STUDENT ROCKERS AND ADJUSTABLE CHAIRS COMBINED.

No. 28.   No. 27.   No 24.

The above Student Rockers are made with Spring Seats, or Spring Seats, Backs and Arms, as desired. When made with Spring Seats,
Backs and Arms, are highly recommended for ease and comfort, being only equaled by expensive Turkish Rockers.

MANUFACTURERS.   PARLOR FURNITURE

60   20

E   G   81   82

WALNUT OR EBONIZED.

Above Chairs are made with or without Rockers, with Grape or Leaf Top.

61   24

R   N   70   71

WALNUT OR EBONIZED.

Above Chairs are made with or without Rockers, with Grape or Leaf Top.

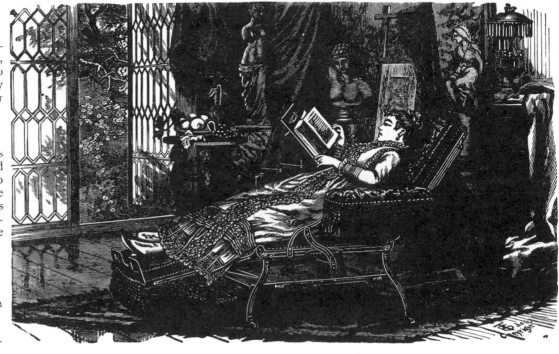
The American Furniture Gazette,
August 1, 1887, page 3.

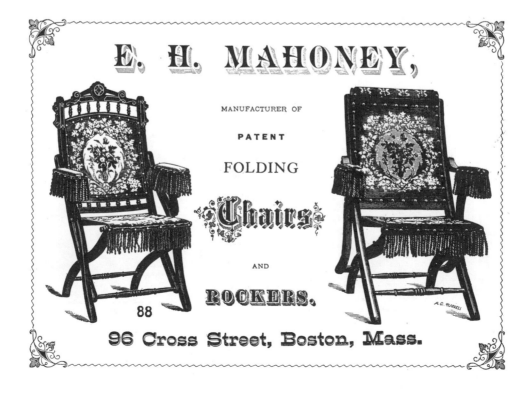

Folding Chairs

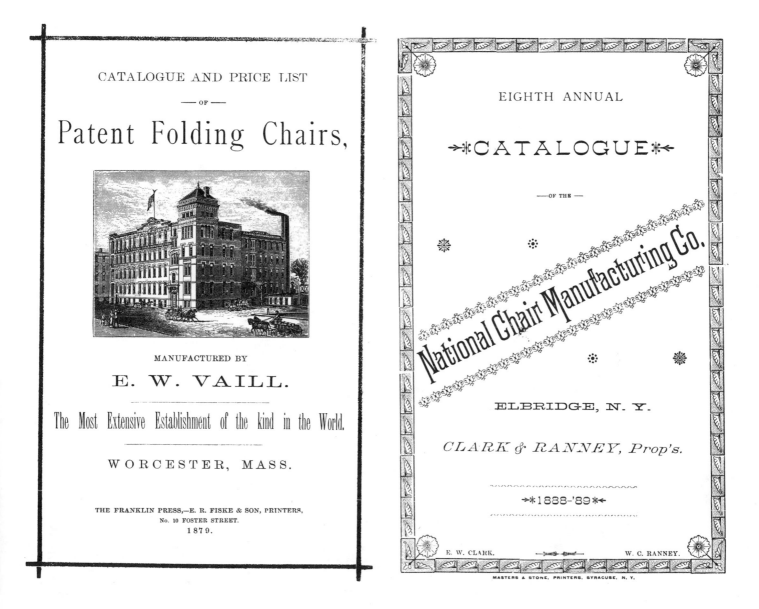

CATALOGUE AND PRICE LIST

— OF —

Patent Folding Chairs,

MANUFACTURED BY

E. W. VAILL.

The Most Extensive Establishment of the kind in the World.

WORCESTER, MASS.

THE FRANKLIN PRESS,—E. R. FISKE & SON, PRINTERS,
No. 10 FOSTER STREET.
1879.

EIGHTH ANNUAL

CATALOGUE

— OF THE —

National Chair Manufacturing Co.

ELBRIDGE, N. Y.

CLARK & RANNEY, Prop's.

1888-'89

E. W. CLARK.   W. C. RANNEY.

MASTERS & STONE, PRINTERS, SYRACUSE, N. Y.

No. 131.

Secured by Patent.

78 C

IMPROVED.

Patented.   Per Dozen

BLACK WALNUT FRAME.

Pattern Brussels,   -   -   -   - $70 00
Pattern Wilton,   -   -   -   -   84 00

BLACK WALNUT FRAME.

This is a new and handsome design in the Norman style. Pillars and Arms veneered, beaded, engraved and gilded. Back, 30 inches high. Width between Arms, 19 inches.

Price per dozen.

Body Brussels Carpet Back and Seat,..............$120.00
Wilton Carpet Back and Seat, ... 138.00

Cortland ⁕ Furniture ⁕ Company,
Cortland, N. Y.

No. 300 and 301.

No. 9.

No. 300 and 301.

No. 250.

W. Heywood Chair Co.

FITCHBURG, MASS }
BOSTON, MASS. }

442 Pearl Street,

New York, May, 1883.

Gents:

We beg to call your attention to a New Folding Chair, which we are now introducing and which you will find fully illustrated in this circular.

It has the great merit of simplicity and strength and can be packed in very small compass, one dozen measuring only eighteen inches in height when packed for shipment.

They are specially adapted to the "Undertaking Trade," for use on Boats, Halls, Verandahs, and wherever economy in space needs to be considered.

We should be pleased to receive a sample order from you.

Yours Truly,

OPEN. FOLDED.

DECKER FOLDING.

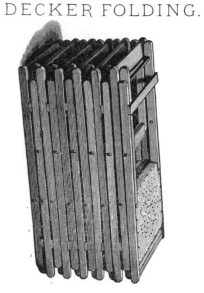

PRICE PER DOZEN.

Varnished on Wood,	-	$8 00
Imitation Walnut,	-	8 00
" Cherry,	-	9 00
Ebonized,	-	10 00

ONE DOZEN

PACKED FOR SHIPMENT.

E. H. MAHONEY, 96 CROSS STREET, BOSTON.

(PATENTED.)

No. 142. LADIES' CHAIR.

Walnut Frame and Gilt,
Body Brussels Pattern,
Wilton Pattern.

Per doz.

110

(PATENTED.)

No. 110. GENT'S CHAIR.

Per doz.

Rosewood finish, Body Brussels Pattern,
" " Wilton Pattern.

(PATENTED.)

No. 43. GENT'S CHAIR.

Rosewood finish, Body Brussels Pattern,
" " Wilton Pattern.

Per doz.

88

(PATENTED.)

No. 88. GENT'S ARM CHAIR.

Walnut Frame, Veneer and Gilt,
Body Brussels Pattern,
Wilton Pattern.

Per doz.

85 C

(PATENTED.)

No. 85 C. GENT'S ARM CHAIR.

Walnut Frame and Gilt,
Extra Stripe Terry.

Per doz.

(PATENTED.)

No. 140. GENT'S CHAIR.

Walnut Frame and Gilt,
Body Brussels Pattern,
Wilton Pattern.

Per doz.

85

(PATENTED.)

No. 85 B. GENT'S ARM CHAIR.
Per doz.

Walnut Frame and Gilt,
Body Brussels Pattern,
Wilton Pattern.

(PATENTED.)

No. 86 B. GENT'S ARM CHAIR.
Per doz.

Rosewood finish, Body Brussels Pattern,
"   "   Wilton Pattern.

61

1½

1

60

CLARK & RANNEY.

No. 17.

CAMP STOOL.

(Weight 4 lbs.)   PER DOZ.

Carpet...$5 50
Canvas...4 50

No. 15.

CHILD'S SPINDLE BACK FOLDING CHAIR.

(Weight 4 lbs.)

Per dozen................................$6 00

No. 16.

CHILD'S CARPET BACK FOLDING CHAIR.

(Weight 4 lbs.)

Per dozen................................$7 50

LADIES' ARM ROCKING CHAIR.

Black Walnut Frame.   Queen Anne Top.   Top Slat carved,
veneered, engraved and gilded.   Pillars engraved and gilded.   Arms
padded and with fringe.   Back 24 inches high.   Width between
Arms, 16 inches.

	Price per dozen.
Body Brussels Carpet, Back and Seat,	$66.00
Velvet Carpet, Back and Seat,	66.00
Wilton Carpet, Back and Seat,	80.00

No. 125.

Secured by Patent.

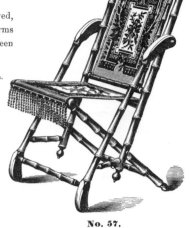

No. 57.

Secured by Patent.

LADIES' CHAIR.

Made in Black Walnut and White Maple, turned in imitation of
Bamboo and polished, creases gilded or striped in colors to match
Carpet.   Upholstered with handsome designs of Brussels and Wilton
Carpet, with 5 inch fringe.   A showy and salable chair.   Height of
Back, 24 inches.   Width of Seat, 16 inches.

	Price per dozen.
Solid Black Walnut Frame, Body Brussels Back and Seat,	$66.00
White Maple Frame, Body Brussels Back and Seat,	66.00
White Maple Frame, Wilton Back and Seat,	81.00
Solid Black Walnut Frame, Wilton Back and Seat,	81.00

10

QUEEN ANNE STYLE.

Heavy turned Frame, large and roomy.   Height of Back, 28
inches.   20 inches between Arms.   Upholstered in Spun Silk, with
Knotted Fringe.   Spring Seat.

	Each.
Black Walnut Frame, Spun Silk Covering,	$14.00
Black Walnut Frame, Spun Silk and Plush Puffs,	16.00

No. 58.

Secured by Patent.

No. 167.

Secured by Patent.

RECEPTION CHAIR.

Very unique in design, with nondescript top ornament and Egyptian foliage.   Crane centre panel, raised carving.   Arms carved Swan's
Neck.   Frame Ebonized and finely finished.

	Each.
Upholstered with stuffed Plush Seat,	$15.00
Frame finished,	10.00

No. 134.

No. 124.

LADIES' ARM CHAIR.

Black Walnut Frame.   Queen Anne Top.   Top Slat carved,
veneered, engraved and gilded.   Pillars engraved and gilded.   Arms
padded and with fringe.   Back 23 inches high.   Width between
Arms, 16 inches.

	Price per dozen.
Body Brussels Carpet, Back and Seat,	$61.00
Velvet Carpet, Back and Seat,	61.00
Wilton Carpet, Back and Seat,	75.00

CARVED ROCKER.

Ebonized Frame, neat in design, very elaborately carved, Egyptian top and raised carved Crane centre. Finely finished throughout.

	Each.
Upholstered with stuffed Plush Seat,	$15.00
Frame finished,	10.00

No. 166.

Secured by Patent.

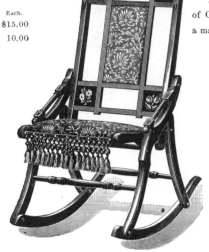

No. 136.

Secured by Patent.

IMITATION EBONY FRAME.

Top Slat, Pillars and Arms creased and gilded. Corner Panels of Back ornamented in colors. Centre Panel of Back, and Seat Upholstered in Spun Silk.

Price per dozen, ... $90.00

LADIES' CHAIR.

Carpet Seat. Slat Back. Low bent Arms, a companion chair for No. 4, taking the same size and pattern of Carpet Seat.

This Chair, as well as No. 4, is particularly adapted for the use of Churches, Public Halls, Undertakers, &c., folding so closely that a man can carry at once a dozen from the room easily.

Price per dozen.

Oak, varnished on the wood, Pattern Seats, ... $25.00

No. 5.

MISSES' ROCKER.

No. 144.

Secured by Patent.

MISSES' ROCKER.

Top Slat and Pillars creased and gilded. Back, 19 inches high. Width between Arms, 13 inches.

Pattern Brussels Back and Seat.

	Per doz.
Imitation Rosewood,	$28.00
Black Walnut,	30.00

Fringe. $1.00 per doz. extra.

No. 4.

PREMIUM CHAIR.

This Chair is 17 inches between Arms. Carpet Seat. Slat Back. Bent Arms. Thoroughly riveted together and unsurpassed for strength and portability.

Price per dozen.

Oak, varnished on wood, Pattern Seats, ... $26.00

PATENT ROCKER.

Black Walnut Frame. Pillars and Arms beaded. Top Slat carved, veneered and gilded. Rockers and Base engraved and gilded. Back, 30 inches high. Width between Arms, 19 inches.

	Each.
Pattern Wilton Back and Seat,	$11.00
Spun Silk Back and Seat,	12.00

37

No. 147.

No. 143.

MISSES' CHAIR.

Top Slat and Pillars creased and gilded.
Back, 19 inches high. Width between
Arms, 13 inches.

Pattern Brussels Back and Seat.

	Per doz.
Imitation Rosewood,	$25.00
Black Walnut,	27.00

Fringe, $1.00 per doz. extra.

116

LARGE CHAIR.
BLACK WALNUT FRAME.

	Patented.				Per Dozen
Pattern Brussels,	-	-	-	-	$ 68 00
Pattern Wilton,	-	-	-	-	80 00
Raw Silk,	-	-	-	-	85 00
Raw Silk and Plush Border,	-	-	-	100 00
Spun Silk,	-	-	-	-	100 00
Spun Silk and Plush Border,	-	-	-	115 00

116A

BLACK WALNUT FRAME.

	Patented.		Per Dozen
Pattern Brussels,	-	-	$78 00
Pattern Wilton,	-	-	92 00

10

105

105A

116A

BLACK WALNUT FRAME.
Patented.

117

BLACK WALNUT FRAME.
Patented.

104A

128

FOLDING DINING CHAIR.

129

91

BLACK WALNUT FRAME.
Patented.

		Each
White,	- - - -	$ 5 50
Finished,	- - - -	6 00
Raw Silk,	- - - -	12 25
Raw Silk and Plush Border,	- - -	14 25
Spun Silk,	- - -	14 25
Spun Silk and Plush Border,	- -	16 25

94

FOLDING ROCKER.
ROSEWOOD OR WALNUT FINISH.
Patented.

	Per Dozen
Pattern Brussels Seat,	$30 00
Brussels, or Pattern Tapestry,	28 00

CATALOGUE OF FOLDING CHAIRS.

107 A

IMPROVED.
QUEEN ANNE TOP. ENGRAVED AND GILDED.
Patented.

		Per Dozen
Pattern Tapestry,	- - - -	$29 00
Pattern Velvet or Pattern Brussels,	-	35 00
Pattern Wilton,	- - - -	45 00

78

IMPROVED.
Patented.
BLACK WALNUT FRAME.

		Per Dozen
Pattern Brussels,	- - -	$60 00
Pattern Wilton,	- - -	72 00

130

Patented.

Ebony Finish, Pattern Brussels, - - $30 00

Per Dozen

105

MISSES' CHAIR.

ROSEWOOD, OR WALNUT FINISH.

Patented.

Pattern Brussels, - - - - $26 00

Per Dozen

1

2

33

Patented.

ROSEWOOD OR WALNUT FINISH

	Per Dozen
Pattern Brussels, - -	$21 00
Pattern Tapestry,	18 00

Without Fringe, $1 per dozen less.

32

3

ROSEWOOD OR WALNUT FINISH.

Pattern Brussels, - - - $38 00

Per Dozen

	Per Dozen
Duck Seat, - -	$6 00
Brussels or Pattern Tapestry Seat,	9 00

OB

126A

	Per Dozen
Duck Seat, - - - - -	$11 00
Brussels, or Pattern Tapestry Seat, - -	13 00

Patented.		Per Dozen
Light Finish, - - - -		$12 00
Vermilion " - - - -		13 00

131

126

Patented.		Per Dozen
Ebony Finish, Pattern Brussels, - -		$35 00

Patented.		Per Dozen
Light Finish, - - - -		$11 00
Vermilion " - " - -		12 00

Hall Trees, Mirrors and Mantles

—Top | In XVI. Century Finish.
—Base |

It will pay you to examine our line of WOOD MANTELS. We manufacture Wood Mantels EXCLUSIVELY. Have ever
ty for turning out FIRST-CLASS WORK, and our goods in STYLE, WORKMANSHIP and FINISH compare very favorably wit
made. Goods furnished in any finish desired.

STERN BUYERS:—A. J. McINTOSH, 66 West 23rd Street, New York City,
is our Eastern agent, and carries a line of samples. Call and see him.

ROCKFORD CABINET CO., 307 Tile Street

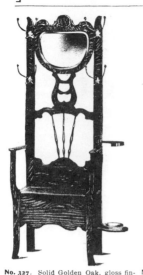

No. 327. Solid Golden Oak, gloss finish, pattern French bevel mirror 12x16, 73 inches high, 34 inches wide, 15 inches deep, umbrella rack attached................... **$10.75**

No. 314. Quartered Golden Oak, piano polish, pattern French bevel mirror 16x20, 80 inches high, 39 inches wide, 17 inches deep, umbrella rack attached........... **$15.75**

No. 809. Quartered Golden Oak, piano polish, pattern French bevel mirror 20x 28, 82 inches high, 43 inches wide, 17 inches deep, umbrella rack attached................... **$26.50**

No. 333. Quartered Golden Oak, piano polish, pattern French bevel mirror 20x30, 78 inches high, 28 inches wide, 18 inches deep, umbrella rack attached................... **$27.00**

Hall Furniture

No. 325. Solid Golden Oak, gloss finish, oval French bevel mirror 12x18, 75 inches high 31 inches wide, 19 inches deep, umbrella rack attached............. **$8.95**

No. 376. Hanging Hall Rack. Quartered Golden Oak, piano polish, pattern French bevel mirror 20x16 inches, frame 24x40 inches....................... **$9.50**

No. 420

Hall Rack. Golden Quartered Oak. Piano polish. 6 feet 6 inches high, 2 feet 6 inches wide. Oval French bevel mirror 12x12 inches. Umbrella rack attached.

Each.... ....**$8.75**

No. 334. Solid Golden Oak, gloss finish, French bevel mirror 12x18, 62 inches high, 23 inches wide, 14 inches deep.................... **$5.75**

No. 330. Quartered Golden Oak, piano polish, pattern French bevel mirror 16x22, 82 inches high, 37 inches wide, 17 inches deep, umbrella rack attached............. **$16.50**

No. 324. Hanging Hall Rack. Golden Quartered Oak, piano polish, French bevel mirror 14x18, frame 19x35................... **$6.75**

No. 373. Hanging Hall Rack. Golden Quartered Oak, piano polish, pattern French bevel mirror 16x16 inches, frame 30x24 inches........................... **$7.50**

No. 318. Hall Seat. Quartered Golden Oak or Mahogany Finish, piano polish, swell front, 38 inches high, 39 inches wide, 18 inches deep.................... **$15.00**

No. 312. Quartered Golden Oak, piano polish, pattern French bevel mirror 18x24, 81 inches high, 42 inches wide, 18 inches deep, umbrella rack attached................... **$23.00**

No. 309. Hall Seat. Quartered Golden Oak, or Solid Mahogany. Piano polish, roll front, 38 inches high, 52 inches wide, 21 inches deep—Oak.................. **$24.50**
Mahogany............................. **29.00**

No. 494

Hall Rack. Golden Quartered Oak. Piano polish. 6 feet 5 inches high, 2 feet 9 inches wide. Pattern French bevel mirror 14x14. Umbrella rack attached.

Each.... ....**$12.00**

No. 817. Hall Seat. Golden Quartered Oak, piano polish, 37 inches high, 53 inches wide, 19 inches deep. **$11.95**

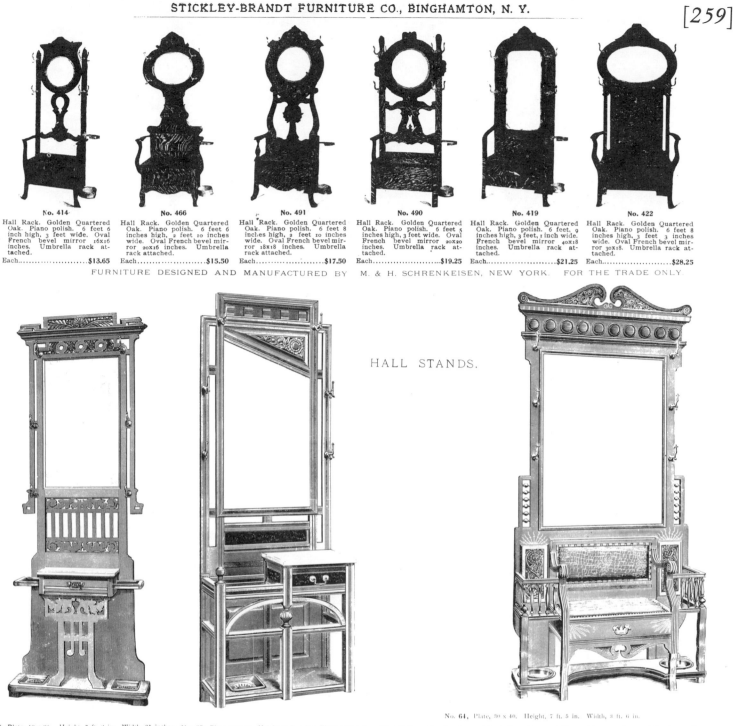

No. 414

Hall Rack. Golden Quartered Oak. Piano polish. 6 feet 6 inch high, 3 feet wide. Oval French bevel mirror 16x16 inches. Umbrella rack attached.

Each........................$13.65

No. 466

Hall Rack. Golden Quartered Oak. Piano polish. 6 feet 6 inches high, 2 feet 10 inches wide. Oval French bevel mirror 20x16 inches. Umbrella rack attached.

Each........................$15.50

No. 491

Hall Rack. Golden Quartered Oak. Piano polish. 6 feet 8 inches high, 2 feet 10 inches wide. Oval French bevel mirror 18x18 inches. Umbrella rack attached.

Each........................$17.50

No. 490

Hall Rack. Golden Quartered Oak. Piano polish. 6 feet 5 inches high, 3 feet wide. Oval French bevel mirror 20x20 inches. Umbrella rack attached.

Each........................$19.25

No. 419

Hall Rack. Golden Quartered Oak. Piano polish. 6 feet 9 inches high, 3 feet, 1 inch wide. French bevel mirror 40x18 inches. Umbrella rack attached.

Each........................$21.25

No. 422

Hall Rack. Golden Quartered Oak. Piano polish. 6 feet 8 inches high, 3 feet 3 inches wide. Oval French bevel mirror 30x18 inches. Umbrella rack attached.

Each........................$28.25

FURNITURE DESIGNED AND MANUFACTURED BY   M. & H. SCHRENKEISEN, NEW YORK.   FOR THE TRADE ONLY.

HALL STANDS.

No. 7, Plate, 18 x 30. Height, 7 ft. 2 in. Width, 31 inches.

Walnut or Imitation Mahogany.

No. 60, Plate, 20 x 36. Height, 7 ft. 1 in. Width, 2 ft. 5 in.

Walnut or Imitation Mahogany.

No. 64, Plate, 30 x 40. Height, 7 ft. 5 in. Width, 3 ft. 6 in.

With Embossed Leather Seat and Back, Brass Pans and Pins, and handsomely carved Panels and Top.

Mahogany only.

No 201

KELLER, STURM & EHMAN, CHICAGO, ILL.

HALL STANDS.

No. 3, Plate, 10 x 14. Height, 6 ft. 9 in. Width, 26 inches.

Walnut only.

No. 5, Plate, 13 x 22. Height, 6 ft. 8 in. Width, 30 inches.

Walnut or Imitation Mahogany.

No. 67, Plate, 24 x 42. Height, 6 ft. 10 in. Width, 2 ft. 6 in.

With burnished Brass Umbrella Holders, Pan, and Pins. Top is richly carved, and Back of Seat engraved.

Walnut or Imitation Mahogany.

No. 1, Plate, 10½ x 17. Height, 6 ft. 8 in. Width, 30 inches.

Walnut only.

No. 2, Plate, 12 x 18. Height, 6 ft. 10 in. Width, 31 inches.

Walnut only.

No. 6, Plate, 14 x 24. Height, 7 ft. Width, 30 inches.

Walnut or Imitation Mahogany.

No. 27

No. 25

No. 26

No. 160

Cloth Stand.

154

No. 171

No. 401

142

No. 163

300

No. 169

151

No. 162   No. 170   152

No. 3

✳1883.✳

KELLER, STURM & CO.,

✦MANUFACTURERS OF✦

Pier and Mantel Frames,

HAT TREES,

CORNER ELIZABETH AND FULTON STREETS,

(Take Lake or Randolph St. Cars to Elizabeth St.),

CHICAGO, ILL.

J. J. Spalding & Co., Printers, 158 Clark Street, Chicago.

No. 167

No. 165

No. 206

201

153

51

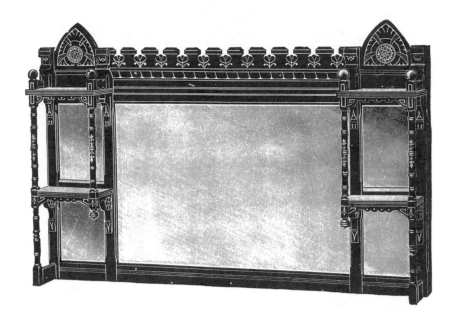

160

No. 155

No. 262

Mantel Top No. 7

156

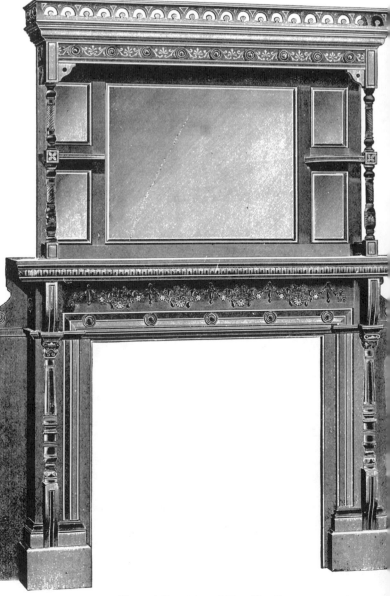

Mantel No. 11 and Top No. 7

No. 263

No. 106   301   302   303

No. 210

308

311

309

312

No. 255.

313

314

No. 168

No. 266

FRANK W. WHITE, 269 CANAL ST., N.Y.

No. 10

No. 1.
Imitation Rose and Gilt Arch Top.

No. 12

10.

FINE CORNICES.

No. 10	$7 00	No. 30	$5 00
" 20 (Gilt)	6 00	" 40	3 00

20.

40.

30.

A large assortment of cheaper Cornices made to order at short notice.

CATALOGUE.

FRANK W. WHITE

Formerly, 82 BOWERY,

269 CANAL STREET

NEW-YORK,

LOOKING GLASSES

PICTURE FRAMES, MOULDINGS,

CORNICES, &c.

10   13   13.   14.

51

MANUFACTURER OF

LOOKING GLASSES &

PICTURE FRAMES

FRANK W. WHITE
269

*39
MANTLE*

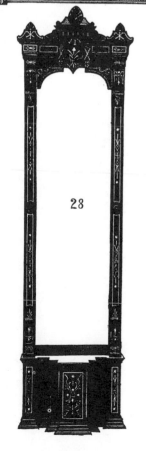

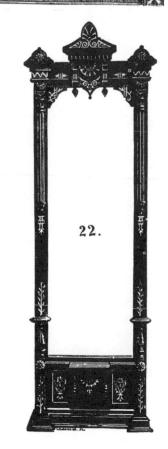

40

Nº 52BB

28

22.

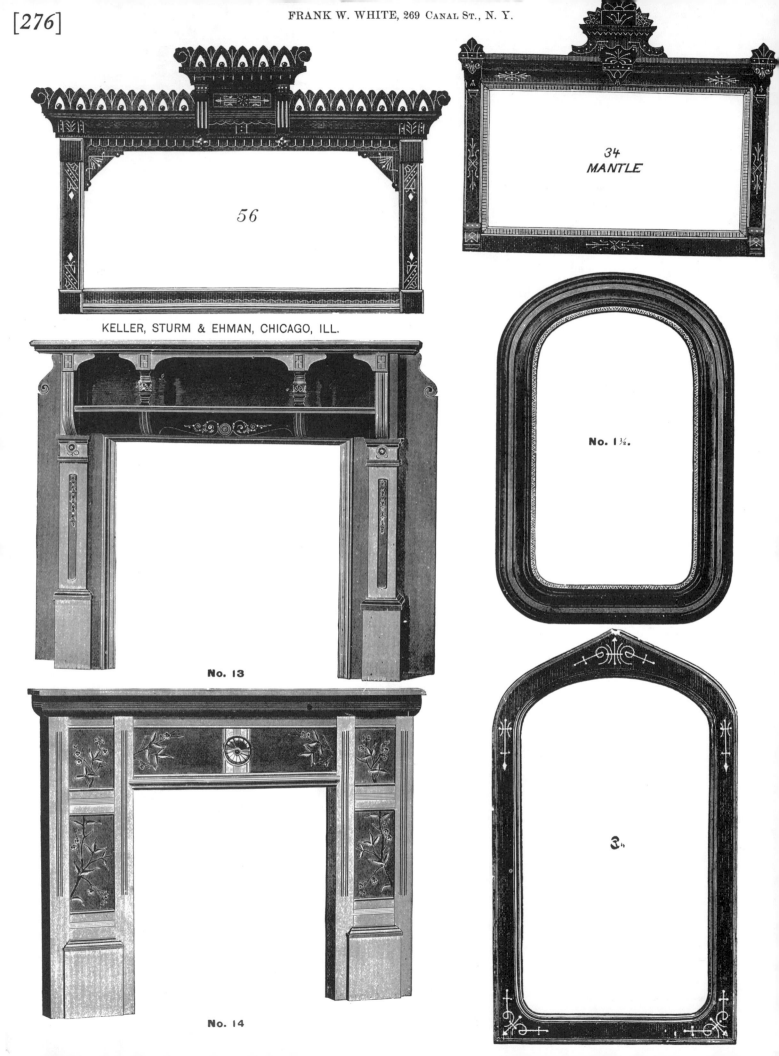

56

34
MANTLE

KELLER, STURM & EHMAN, CHICAGO, ILL.

No. 1½.

No. 13

No. 14

3⁴

Rattan and Outdoor Furniture

Rattan is a tough, flexible wood of the climbing palm tree. It is more a vine than a tree.

STICKLEY-BRANDT FURNITURE CO., BINGHAMTON, N. Y.

WIRE GRASS FURNITURE
From the Prairies of the West to the Homes of the World

This Furniture is made of woven prairie grass. It is of a rich dark green color and of beautiful design. Very strong and durable. Admirably suited to dens, parlors, libraries and piazzas. We issue a catalog showing not only chairs and rockers, but tables, stools, go-carts, work baskets, tabourettes and settees.

These four cuts are only suggestions. Send for Special Catalog containing 150 cuts. We have these goods

From $1.35 to $50.00 Each

No. 311. Large Arm Chair. Each..........................$12.25

No. 251. Large Arm Chair. Each $18.35

No. 300. Large Arm Chair. Each...... ....$22.25

No. 253. Large Arm Chair. Each.........................$16.66

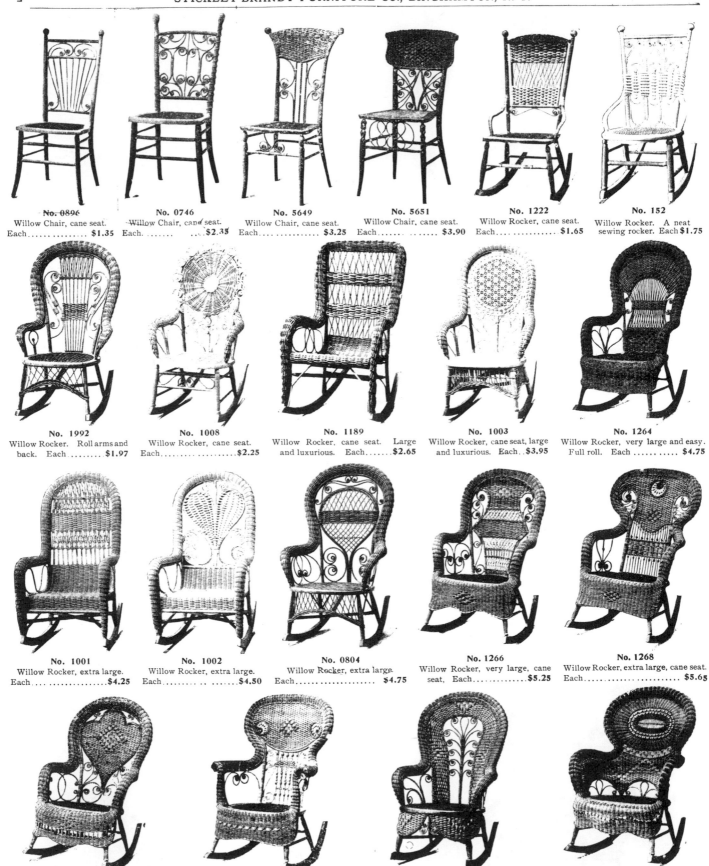

No. 0896
Willow Chair, cane seat.
Each $1.35

No. 0746
Willow Chair, cane seat.
Each $2.35

No. 5649
Willow Chair, cane seat.
Each $3.25

No. 5651
Willow Chair, cane seat.
Each $3.90

No. 1222
Willow Rocker, cane seat.
Each $1.65

No. 152
Willow Rocker. A neat
sewing rocker. Each $1.75

No. 1992
Willow Rocker. Roll arms and
back. Each $1.97

No. 1008
Willow Rocker, cane seat.
Each $2.25

No. 1189
Willow Rocker, cane seat. Large
and luxurious. Each $2.65

No. 1003
Willow Rocker, cane seat, large
and luxurious. Each . . $3.95

No. 1264
Willow Rocker, very large and easy.
Full roll. Each $4.75

No. 1001
Willow Rocker, extra large.
Each $4.25

No. 1002
Willow Rocker, extra large.
Each $4.50

No. 0804
Willow Rocker, extra large.
Each $4.75

No. 1266
Willow Rocker, very large, cane
seat, Each $5.25

No. 1268
Willow Rocker, extra large, cane seat.
Each $5.65

No. 1271
Willow Rocker, extra large. Each $6.50

No. 1275
Willow Rocker, extra large. Each $7.75

No. 0836
Willow Rocker, extra large. Each $7.95

No. 1277
Willow Rocker, large, cane seat $8.50

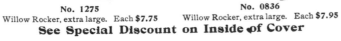

See Special Discount on Inside of Cover

NOVELTY RATTAN CO. Chas. G. Pease & Co. Prop's.

SAMPLE AGENCY,
203 & 205 Wabash Av.
CHICAGO, Ill.

[279]

Plate No. 1.

140

142

404

402

146

240

242

338

256

352

150

450

86

360

380

400

68

70

88

348

368

388

46

72

382

248

266

250

270

487

NOVELTY RATTAN CO. Chas. G. Pease & Co. Prop's.

Plate No. 2.

SAMPLE AGENCY,
203 & 205 Wabash Av.
CHICAGO, Ill.

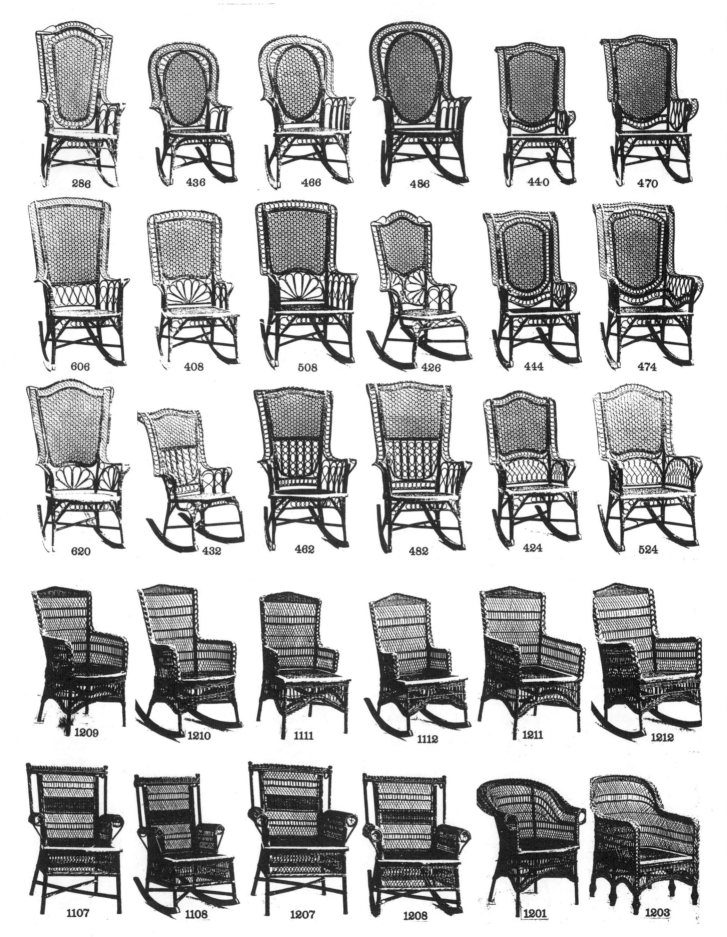

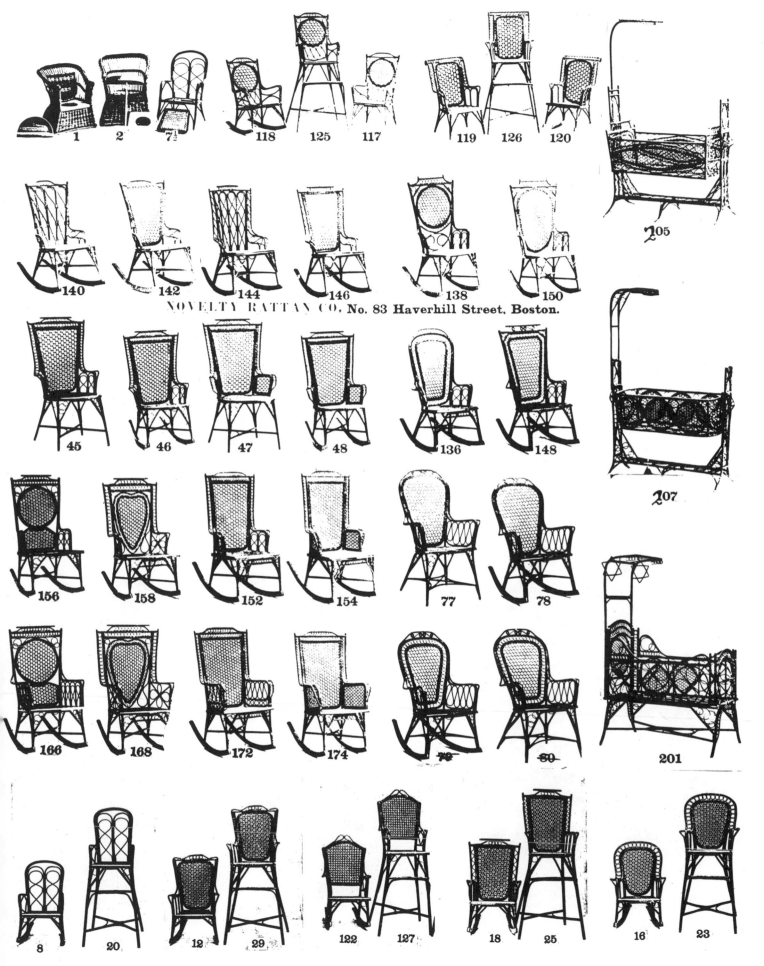

1   2   7   118   125   117   119   126   120

140   142   144   146   138   150

205

NOVELTY RATTAN CO. No. 83 Haverhill Street. Boston.

45   46   47   48   136   148

207

156   158   152   154   77   78

166   168   172   174   79   80   201

8   20   12   29   122   127   18   25   16   23

238   256   242   248   250   270

NOVELTY RATTAN CO.

252   254   202   265   266

No. 83 Haverhill Street. Boston.

271   272   281   282   273   274

NEW HAVEN FOLDING CHAIR CO.

STICKLEY-BRANDT FURNITURE CO., BINGHAMTON, N. Y.

No. 53.—Rattan.

Patent Pending.

Rattan Frame, Star Back.   Wilton Carpet Seat.   Folds compactly.
Back 25 inches high.   19 inches between Arms.

$10.00 each.

No. 5045. Willow Chair.
Each **$7.75**

No. 5207. Willow Chair. Large and luxurious.
Each $11.65

No. 1270. Willow Chair.   Large and easy.
Each **$6.50**

No. 5215. Willow Chair.   Extra large.
Each $12.75

No. 86.

Reed body. Upholstered in cretonne. No. 0 parasol. Price......$8 25

No. 87.

Body same as above. Upholstered in ramies. No. 1 parasol. Price..$9 75

No. 88.

Body same as above. Upholstered in silk plush. No. 1 parasol. Price..$12 00

These are full sized carriages. Body 39 inches. Wheels 20 and 22 inches.

No. 84.

Reed body. Upholstered in sides, back and seat with cretonne, carpet bottom. No. 0 parasol. Price...............................7 50

No. 85.

Body same as above. Upholstered in ramies. No. 0 parasol Price...$8 25

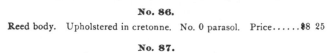

No. 217.

Reed wound body, varnished. Upholstered in combination of fine silk plush and heavy brocade satin damask. No. 5 brocade satin damask parasol, silk lace edge. Nickel plated springs and axles. Shave spoke or steel wheels. Price...$40 50

No. 161.

Rattan, cane wound body, upholstered in satin, silk plush roll, pointed. No. 3 satin parasol, silk lace edge. Nickel rod and hub caps, flat shaved spoke wheels. Price...............................$31 50

No. 162.

Upholstered in combination of fine silk plush and heavy brocade satin damask. No. 5 brocade silk parasol, silk lace edge. Nickel plated springs and axles. Price.....................................$40 50

No. 156.

Reed wound body, with hood top, varnished. Upholstered in combination of satin and plush, rolled and pointed. Price............$27 00

No. 227.

Reed wound body, varnished. Upholstered in combination of fine silk plush and heavy brocade satin damask. No. 3 parasol. Shave **spoke** or steel wheels. Price.............................. ....$30 00

No. 155.

Reed wound body, upholstered in combination of satin and silk plush, rolled and pointed. No. 2 satin parasol. Price...............$24 00

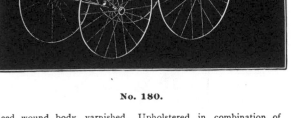

No. 180.

Reed wound body, varnished. Upholstered in combination of satin and plush, rolled and pointed. No. 3 satin parasol, silk lace edge. Price................... ....$27 00

No. 116.

Finely woven reed body, rolls on back, varnished. Upholstered in silk plush. No. 2 satin parasol. Price..............................$16 50

N. B.—Only one parasol is furnished with this carriage. For price extra parasol, see page 2.

No. 200.

Square rattan reed body. Upholstered in spun silk ; silk plush roll. No. 2 satin parasol. Price.............. ....$24 75

No. 201.

Square reed body. Upholstered in imported silk goods ; silk plush roll ; shave spoke wheels. No. 3 silk parasol. Price.................$30 00

No. 203.

Twin carriage. Reed body. Upholstered in ramies. No. 1 satin parasols. Price... . ...$18 00

No. 58.

Wood frame, reed body Upholstered in ramies, with plush roll. No. 1 satin parasol Price......................................$12 00

No. 59.

Body same as above. Upholstered in silk plush. No. 1 satin parasol. Price....................................$14 25

No. 65.

Reed body. Upholstered in ramies. No. 1 satin parasol. Wheel guard. Price $12 00

No. 66.

Reed body. Upholstered in silk plush. No. 1 satin parasol. Wheel guard. Price $14 25

No. 93.

Rattan reed body, adjustable hood top. Upholstered with spun silk in sides, back and seat. Price $12

No. 94.

Body same as above. Upholstered in silk plush. Price $15

No. 55.

Wood frame, reed body. Upholstered in ramies, with plush roll. No. 1 satin parasol. Price $10 50

No. 56.

Body same as above. Upholstered in silk plush. No. 1 satin parasol. Price $12 75

No. 89.

Square reed rattan body. Upholstered with ramies, plush roll. No. 1 parasol. Price $11 25

No. 250.

Highly carved solid mahogany body, upholstered in combination of fine silk plush and heavy brocade satin damask. No. 5 brocade satin damask parasol, fine silk lace edge. Nickel plated springs and axles. Price...$45 00

No. 70.

Reed body, wound ring border. Upholstered in silk plush. No. 2 satin parasol. Price..$13 75

STEEL WHEELS.

With or Without Rubber Tires.

We put Steel Wheels on all Carriages without extra charge.

RUBBER TIRE STEEL WHEELS.

We furnish rubber tire steel wheels at net extra. $2 50

NEW ROD AND FIXTURE.

We introduce this season a new adjustable Rod and Fixture, which by a simple movement places the Parasol in any position required. We shall use this on all our Carriages.

EXCEPT Nos. 84, 85 AND 86.

FOLDING LAWN SETTEES.

Light or Vermilion.

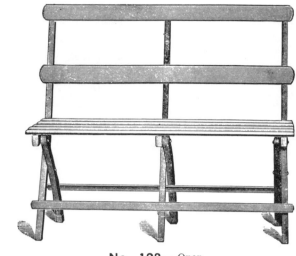

No. 124 — Open.

Closed.

No. 123 — Open.

No. 148. Park Settee.

Very Strong Iron Frame.

SHOE SETTEE.

No. 248 — Ash Frame.   **No. 249** — Walnut Frame.

17 inches wide.

DOUBLE SETTEE.

No. 240 — Ash Frame.   **No. 241** — Walnut Frame.

Height 36 inches.   Width 39 inches.

Tyler's Court-House or Lawn Settees.—Tyler Desk Co., St. Louis.

[289]

No. 1. Star Settee.—Without Arms.

Malleable Iron Frames and Ash Seats. Made to Order any Length.
Shipped K. D. Price, per foot, F. O. B........................$1 25

No. 3. Star Settee—With Division Arms.

Malleable Iron Frames and Ash Seats. Made to Order any Length.
Shipped K. D. Price, per running foot, F. O. B...................$1 40

No. 39. Settee.—Single.

Made to Order any Length. Shipped Set Up. Price, per foot..... ....$3 50

No. 13. Settee.

Made to Order any Length. Shipped Set Up. Price, per running foot..$3 00

No. 247. Full Bent Lawn Rocker.

Red Color. Price, F. O. B........ ....$5 00
No. 246.
Without Rockers................................ 4 00

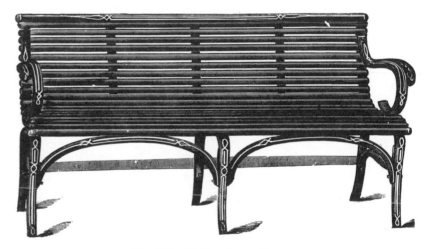

No. 160. Hall or Lawn Settee.

Red Color. 4, 5 and 6 feet long; over 6 feet long made to order only.
Price of 4 ft...$4 00
Price of 5 ft... 4 50
Price of 6 ft... 5 00

White Mountain
Hammock Chair Stands

(OAKS' PATENT)

READY FOR USE.

CLOSED.

THE WHITE MOUNTAIN.

THE above cut represents "Patent Hammock Chair Stand," which fills a long-felt want, as it is so light and strong that by its use our Hammock Chairs can be readily moved from one place to another without trouble, and the occupant always remains in the shade. For porches or in the house the use of this Stand is almost indispensable. It can be quickly and easily taken apart and folded into a compact portable package 3 inches square. Directions for use accompany each stand.

PRICE PER DOZEN: { OILED $9 00
{ PAINTED (RED) 12 00

Burk & McFetridge, Printers, Philadelphia, Pa.

Miscellaneous

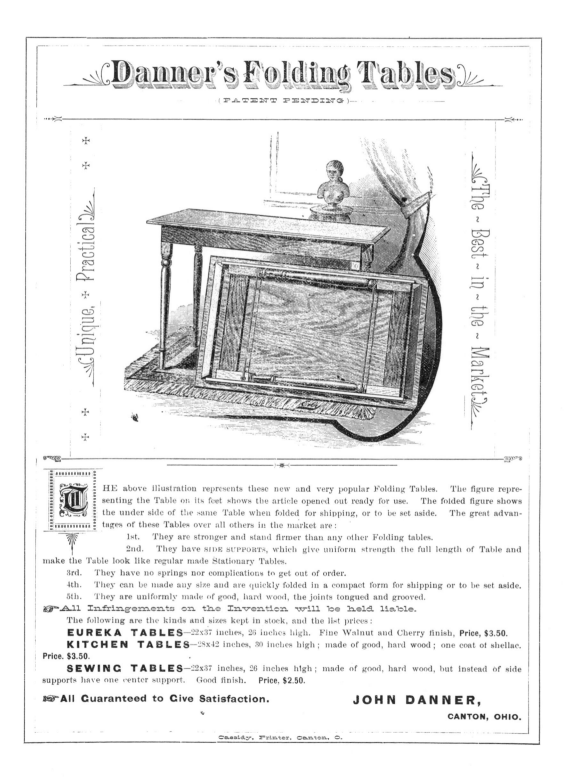

Danner's Folding Tables
(PATENT PENDING)

Unique · Practical

The · Best · in · the · Market

HE above illustration represents these new and very popular Folding Tables. The figure representing the Table on its feet shows the article opened out ready for use. The folded figure shows the under side of the same Table when folded for shipping, or to be set aside. The great advantages of these Tables over all others in the market are:

1st.   They are stronger and stand firmer than any other Folding tables.

2nd.   They have SIDE SUPPORTS, which give uniform strength the full length of Table and make the Table look like regular made Stationary Tables.

3rd.   They have no springs nor complications to get out of order.

4th.   They can be made any size and are quickly folded in a compact form for shipping or to be set aside.

5th.   They are uniformly made of good, hard wood, the joints tongued and grooved.

☞ All Infringements on the Invention will be held liable.

The following are the kinds and sizes kept in stock, and the list prices:

EUREKA TABLES—22x37 inches, 26 inches high. Fine Walnut and Cherry finish, Price, $3.50.

KITCHEN TABLES—28x42 inches, 30 inches high ; made of good, hard wood ; one coat of shellac. Price. $3.50.

SEWING TABLES—22x37 inches, 26 inches high ; made of good, hard wood, but instead of side supports have one center support. Good finish. Price, $2.50.

☞ All Guaranteed to Give Satisfaction.   **JOHN DANNER,**
CANTON, OHIO.

Danner's Household Specialties.

Combined Shelf and Coat Rack.

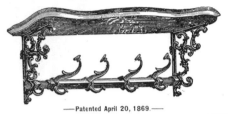

—Patented April 20, 1869.—

A very popular and useful article, adapted for residences offices, hotels, etc. Can be used for clocks, lamps, books, etc., and at the same time afford a nice Coat Rack; very convenient in bed rooms. Each shelf is 6 inches wide and 2 feet long, good hard wood, oil finish. In shipping they go in the "knock down," one dozen occupying a space only 2 feet long and 1 foot square, are soon put together with the aid of a screw driver. **Price, $6 per dozen.**

HALL RACK.

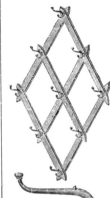

Hook Pat'd March 10, 1873.

These Hall Racks have the same capacity and convenience of many racks that cost $5 or more. The rods are all hard wood, FINELY FINISHED with GOTHIC ENDS, as represented, each rod being 1¼ in. wide and 2 feet long, thus making a good sized diamond rack. The hooks are nicely japanned and will hold a garment or hat much better than wooden pins and are twice as strong. They were patented several years ago. The racks are taken apart when shipped, and pack so compactly that one dozen will go in a box two feet long and one foot square. Warranted to carry safe. They are rapidly put together, requiring no tools. **Price per dozen, $6.**

EXTENSION RACK.

These Racks are made of good, hard wood, in the usual Standard form, oiled, the rods being a little HEAVIER and LONGER than the ordinary wooden pin rack. The patent hooks are invariably used, ten of these hooks will hold more articles than 20 wooden pins, and at the same time be much handsomer in appearance. Many of the best dealers say that my ten-hook Racks at $3 a dozen are CHEAPER than the ten wooden pin racks would be at $1.50 per dozen. They pack nicely, being nested four in a bunch.

Price per dozen, 7 Hooks,	$2 25
" " 10 "	3 00
" " 13 "	3 75

—STRAIGHT—
HAT AND COAT RACK.

These Standard Racks are got up in good style, good, hard wood, oiled, japanned hooks and hangers. The hooks are six inches apart, thus making No. 4 Racks 24 inches long; No. 5, 30 inches, and No. 6, 36 inches long.

Price of No. 4—4 Hooks,	$2 25 per dozen.
" " No. 5—5 "	3 00 "
" " No. 6—6 "	3 75 "

—DANNER'S—
CLOTHES RACK.

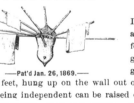

—Pat'd Jan. 26, 1869.—

These popular Dryers have nine arms, each three feet long, thus giving an aggregate of twenty-seven feet, hung up on the wall out of the way; each arm being independent can be raised or lowered without interfering with the others. Thousands in use throughout the country. First Premium awarded at the State Fairs in New York, Ohio, Indiana, Illinois and Michigan. Go in the "knock down." One dozen will go in a box three feet long and one foot square. **Price per dozen, $6.**

All my goods are packed in the best possible manner, so as to carry safe anywhere, and delivered to the railroad or express free of charge. **ALWAYS GIVE SHIPPING DIRECTIONS.**

DANNER'S

BOOK REST---Price $2.
PATENTED DEC. 4, 1883.

All Walnut or imitation Ebony, as preferred; 10 inches wide, 18 inches long. This Book Rest was first made to be used on my popular Revolving Book Cases, for the purpose of holding the Unabridged Dictionary or other heavy books at any desired angle, enabling said book to be consulted without lifting, and while it fills the desired want it has since been found to be adapted for use on any table, stand or desk, and to be laid on the lap while reading heavy books; it is, therefore, of general adaptation in reading or consulting heavy volumes. The construction of the Book Rest is so simple it can not get out of order, and yet so strong as to support the heaviest book that may be laid upon it. Lawyers, Ministers, Doctors and Students generally, who have tried this novel little article, find it a great relief in handling large and heavy books, and it is also quite evident that large volumes are better preserved by laying on this Rest while in use than to be held by hand or laid on the knees as is often done; and the relief to the student is very great. The article is as easily handled as a smooth board of the same size, easily carried from place to place and ready in a moment to be used as BOOK REST, WRITING DESK, or SPEAKERS' INCLINED PULPIT TOP.

CLARKE BROS.

DISCOUNT SHEET. ALL GOODS IN BLACK WALNUT UNLESS OTHERWISE

188 Flower Stand finished in Ebony with Gilt lines. Chain, 31 in. high. Price $1.50 each.
187 Same Design in Walnut and Gilt. Price $1.50 each.

361 Fancy Flower stand. Gilt. 31 in. high. Top 12x11 in. Price $1.50 each.

17 Flower Stand. K. D. 30 in. high, 12 in. top. 3 lower shelves. Price $1.50 each.

261 Parlor or Flower Stand, all Ebony finish with gilt lines. Polished. Heavy Gilt Chain. K. D. 30 in. high. 13 in. Top. Price $3.20 each.

111 Flower Stand. K. D. Ebony and Gilt Striping. Chain. 12 in. sunk top, 31 in. high. Price $1.50 each.

306 Ebonised Parlor Stand. Chain and Pendants. 30 in. high. 18 in. Top. K. D. Polished. Price $3.00 each.

350 Side or Corner Wall Cabinet, in Ebony and Gold. Polished. 30 in. high; 15½ in. broad; 8½ in. deep; 6x8 in. glass panel. Price, $13.00 each.

79 Swiss Match Safe. Rabbit & Game Bag. Elegantly carved from solid Walnut. 4½x7 in. Price $1.50 each.

133 Swiss Match Safe. Oriole & nest. Exquisitely carved from solid Walnut. Bird and nest in relief. Size 4xx in. Price $1.50 each.

101 Checker Stand, with Drawer, and Checkers. Tyrolese Marquetrie Top Walnut. K. D. Size of top 15¼ inch. square, with raised rim. Height, 30 in. Price $1.50 each.

47 Flower Stand, finished in Ebony, Gilt Stripings, 31 in. high. 13 in. top. K. D. Chain. Price $1.50 each.

308 Black and Gold Flower Stand. 30 in. high. K. D. Heavy gilt Chain. Price $4.00 each.

800 Jardinere Stand. Handsome Bronze Figure. Elegantly Engraved and Gilt, 32 in. high. superior workmanship, fine French polish. $12.00 each.

114 Vatican Stand. K. D. Gilt. 15 in. top 31 in. high. Price $4.00 each. A few dozen only on hand.

824 New Parlor Stand. Marbleized Slate Top, in Venetian, Egyptian or Plymouth Black. Finished Edges. Top surface, 12x12 in. Height 33½ in. Price $4.00 each.

115 Top 12x12 in. Height 33½ in. K. D. Gilt Stripings. Chain and Pendants. Price $1.50 each.

362 Toilet Case. In Black and Gold. Polished. 12x25 in. 6 in. Cylinder Box. German Plate Mirror, 6x9 in. Price $3.00 each.

66 Match Safe. Carved from solid Walnut. Elegant and Substantial. Size 3x3x4½ inch. Price $1.50 each.

809 Corner Pedestal. Ebony finish. Polished. 34½ in. Top. 13 in. wide. Price $8.00 each.

808 Corner Pedestal. Ebony finish. Polished. 72 in. high. Top, 12 in. wide. Price $5.50 each.

349 Pedestal in Black and Gold. Polished. 4 Marquetry Ornaments. 35 in. high. Top 12x12 in. Price $6.00 each.

348 Pedestal in Black and Gold. Polished. The only K. D. Pedestal in the market. Easily put together. Marquetry Ornament. 35 inch high. Top 12x12 inch. Price $6.00 each.

355 Music Cabinet in Black and Gold. Polished 36 in. high. Top 18½x12¾ in. Price $14.00 each.

208 Star. Standard Size, 13 Pins. $7.50 per doz.

238 Elegant Match Safe. Carved from solid Walnut. Butterfly & leaves. Size 5½x8 in. Price $1.50

337 Eastlake Hall and Hat Rack. Mirror, 6x9 inch. 10 pins. Adjustable. 28x26 inches. List. $2.00 each.

821 Masonic Hat Rack. K. D. 29x32 inches. Mirror 5x9 inches. Price $1.50 each.
PAT. DEC. 19, 1882.

205 Cheap Extension Hat Rack, 7 Pins, $2.00 per doz.
206 Cheap Extension Hat Rack, 10 Pins, $3.00 per doz.
207 Cheap Extension Hat Rack, 13 Pins, $4.30 per doz.

268 Anchor Hat Rack, with Mirror. Size 20x29 inches. Price $1.50 each.

28 Comb Case and Wall Pocket. Carved and Chromo. 18x21. Gilt. $1.70 each.

817 Pedestal in Black and Gold. Polished. 32 in. high. Top of Marbleized Slate. Square Edged. Polished Egyptian, Venetian, or Plymouth Black. 12x16 in. Price $11.00 each.

332 Fine Pedestal in Black and Gold. Polished. Extra make. Framed and Doweled. Deep rustic Carving. 35 inch high. Top 13x13, inch. Price $14.00 each.

814 Music Easel in Black and Gold. Marquetry Ornaments. Polished. 38 in. high. 16 in. wide. Price $7.50 each.

868 Enlarged Music Cabinet. Walnut with Ebony and gilt stripings. Veneered Panels. New Dimensions. 30x20x14 inch. Price $26.00 each.
283 Same Design. Polished Ebony. Gilt stripes. Price $26.00 each.

315 Slipper Back. Walnut and Gilt. 23x14 in. Price $1.25 each. N. B.— This is a Back only, for embroidered or worsted work front, &c.

173 Unique Wall Pocket. Marquetrie Drop Front. Chain. Length 21 in. Price $1.76 each.

812 Rustic Pocket, in Black and Gold. Polished. Deeply Carved 11x23 in. Price $2.70 each.

119 Slipper Pocket, Ebony and Gilt striping. Chromo front. Size 11½x21 inch. Price $1.50 each.

818 Combination Wall Pocket, Comb Box, and Towel Rack. In Black and Gold. Polished. German Plate Mirror 6x9 in. Carved. 11x21 in. $3.00 each.

4 Carved Wall Pocket. 14x19 in. Gilt, with Chromo. $1.50 each.

819 Book Shelf. Gilt. 27½x21x8½ K. D. Price $1.50 each.

230 Gothic Bookshelf. K. D. Ebony and Gilt striping. Size 31x25 in. Price $3.00 each.

813 Black and Gold Book Shelf. K. D. Polished. 28x21x8½ in. Price $3.00 each.

338 Umbrella Stand. Walnut back and rail; stained base. Painted pan. 34 inch. high, 18 inch. broad. List, $2.00 each.

26 Improved Comb Box, with Shelf, Rod and Glass. 6x9 in. Carved. Size, 13x23 in. Price, $1.70 each.

267 New Match Safe. Carved from solid Walnut. Squirrel and Corn. Attractive pattern. Size 6x6x3½ in. Price $1.50 each.

327 Swiss Match Safe, carved from solid walnut. 3x4x7 inch. Price, $1.50 each.

107 Swiss Match Safe. Carved from solid Walnut, attractive design. Size 3x4x5 in. Price $1.50 each.

252 Fine New Towel Rack, with German Plate Mirror. All Ebony finish, striped with Gilt. Polished. K. D. Handsome Rustic Carving. Size 15x22 in. Price $2.70 each.

289 Towel Rack. Black and Gold. Polished. Landscape Panels. German Plate Mirror. Finely finished. Size 14x28 inches. Price $4.00 each.

363 Comb Case and Towel Rack. Gilt. 9x14 in. Price $1.00 each.

216 Quinby Towel Rack. Two Rods. Folding Arms. Rabited. Ebony and Gilt Striping. Size 12½x22 in. Price $1.50 each.

292 Towel Rack. Polished. Gilt and Ebony Stripings. 26x14 in. Rustic Deep carving. List, $4.00 each.

23 Towel Rack and Comb Case, with Stag Head. Carved. Size, 12x22. Price, $1.70 each.

83 Egyptian Comb Case, with Shelf. Ebony and Gilt. Size 16x19. Price $1.60 each. A few dozen left.

340 Elegant Side or Corner Cabinet, finished in Polished Ebony. Gilt. Beveled Plate Glass Panel 6x8 in. Extra make and finish. 37 in. high; 17¾ in. broad; 10½ in. deep. Price, $25.00 each.

339 Fine Wall Cabinet, in Black and Gold. Polished. Beveled Plate Glass Panel 8x10 in. 29 in. high; 22 in. broad; 7¾ in. deep. Price, $21.00 each. Extra make and finish.

379 Walnut Side Bracket. Carved. 5½x9 in. Price, 60 cts. each.

140 Side Bracket. Size 6½x11 in. Price 31 cents each.

169 New Music Rack, striped with Ebony and Gilt. Size 34x18x13 inch. Price $5.70 each.

77 Lambrequin Side Bracket. Carved and Hinged. Size 9x13¾ inch. Price 75 cents.

41 Side Bracket, Walnut. 6½x11. Price 34 cts. each.

219 New Music Easel. Marquetrie ornaments. Ebony and Gilt striping. Height 39 in., width, 14½ in. Price $5.50 each.

256 New Side Bracket. All Ebony finish. Gilt lines. Marquetrie Ornament. Size 13x14 in. Depth of Shelf, 7 in. Price $1.60 each.

391 Walnut Side Bracket. Carved. 7½x7½ in. Price, 50 cts. each.

300 Easel, Walnut, with Gilt & Ebony Stripes. 30 inches high. Price $1.50 each.
301 Same.—All Ebony finish, with Gilt Striping. Price, $2.00 each.

312 Foot Rest, with Box. Polished Walnut. No Gilt. Veneered Panels. 13½ in. high, 19 in. long, 10½ in. wide. Price, $7.00 each.

298 Easel, with Pocket. Walnut, with Gilt and Ebony Stripings. 6 feet high. Price, $24.00 each.
299 Same.—All Ebony finish with Gilt Stripings. Price, $25.00 each.

341 Fine Wall Cabinet in Black and Gold. Polished. Beveled plate glass panel. 8x10 in. Extra make and finish. 28 in. high, 12 in. broad, 8½ in. deep. Price $15.00 each.

85 National Side Bracket. 7 in. Round Shelf. Bird in Green and Bronze. Size, 8½x16 in. Price, $1.70 each.

98 Egyptian Side Bracket. 8 in. Round Shelf. Carved. Ebony and Gilt Stripes. Hinged. Size, 9x18 in. Price, $1.25 each.

78 Side Bracket. Carved. Size, 11x15 in. Price, $1.25 each.

45 Lamp Bracket. Ebony and Gilt Stripings. Size, 7x12¼ in. Price, 75 cts. each.

2 Swinging Lamp Bracket. Carved. 13x11 in., 6 in. Shelf. Price, $1.50 each.

296 Easel with Pocket. Walnut, with Gilt and Ebony Stripings. Polished. 6 feet high. Price, $21.00 each.
297 Same.—All Ebony finish, with Gilt Stripings. Price, $36.00 each.

128 Shaving and Toilet Case. Extra deep box to admit Shaving Cup. Mirror, 6x9. Carved. Ebony and Gilt Stripes. Size, 13x21 in. Price, $1.50 each.

359 Music Stand. In Black and Gold. Polished. 32 in. high. Top 18x15 in. Price $10.00 each.

343 Fine Pedestal in Black and Gold. Polished. Extra make. Framed and Doweled 4 Plate Glass Panels 7x9 in. Door Panel Beveled. 33 in. high. Top 13x17 in. Price $21.00 each.

280 Very fine Music Easel. Queen Anne Style. Finished in Ebony with Gilt lines. Polished. Size45x24x8 inch. Price $15.00 each.

131 Wall Pocket. Veneered Panel Front. Chain. Ebony and Gilt Striping. Size 14x22 inch. Price $1.50 each.

177 Building Blocks. 74 Pieces. Box 8½x6½x3 in. Price $10.00 per doz.
178 Building Blocks. 92 Pieces. Box 10½x7½x3 in. " $15.00 per doz.
179 Building Blocks. 116 Pieces. Box 10½x4x4½ in. " $20.00 per doz.
180 Building Blocks. 116 Pieces. Box 13x10x1½ in. " $30.00 per doz.
One of the most entertaining amusements ever invented for children. Over 22,000 sets sold last Fall.

152 Side Bracket. Size 4½x9 in. Price 26 cts. each.

104 Egyptian Side Bracket. 5 in. Shelf. Ebony and Gilt Striping. Size 12x5½ inch. Price 75 cts. each.

223 New Parlor or Bed-room Stand. Ebony and Gilt Striping. K. D. 30x20x20 in. Price $4.00 each.

140 Side Bracket. Size 6½x11 in. Price 34 cents each.

138 Side Bracket. Size 7½x8½ in. Price 34 cents each.

58 Improved Side Bracket. Ebony and Gilt Striping. K. D. Hinged. Size 11x20 in. Price $1.50 each.

156 Corner Bracket. Size 4x6½ in. Price 26 cts. each.

271 New Match Safe. Size 8x5½ in. Price 26 cts. each.

151 Round Shelf. Side Bracket. 4 in. shelf. Size 4x8½in. Price 26 cts. each.

103 Side Bracket. Striped with Ebony and Gilt. Size 8x11 inch. Price 75 cts. each.

314 Foot Rest with Box. Yellow Birch, finished in natural color. Walnut Panels. Gilt. Size 16 in. high, 19 in. long, 10 in. wide. Price $3.00 each.

84 National Clock Shelf. Ebony and Gilt. Bronze Eagle. Size 12x5½ in. Price $1.50 each.

317 Slipper Back. Walnut and Gilt. 24x11½ in. Price $1.50 each. N. B.—This is a Back only, for embroidered or worsted work front, &c.
318 Same Design. All Ebony finish, with Gilt Lines. Back only. Price $1.70 each.

221 Ladies' Work Stand. Entirely new pattern. Ebony and Gilt Striping. Knocks down, packs close and is easily put together. Very low in price and certain to sell. Size of closed box, 11x15 in. Size of open box, 6x12 in. Total dimensions 15x29 in. Price $6.50 each.

129 Round Shelf Side Bracket with Deer Head. K. D. Ebony and Gilt striping. Size 9x19 in.; 5 in. shelf. Price $1.50 each.

98 Egyptian Side Bracket. 8 in. Round Shelf. Hinged. Striped with Ebony & Gilt. For vase, lamp, statuette, &c. Size 9x18. Price $1.25 each.

806 Music Cabinet. Veneered Panels. Etruscan Mountings. Elegant Finish. Can be rolled under Piano. Size 13x18x22 inch. Price $17.50 each.

172 Unique Wall Pocket. Gilt. Finished in Ebony with enamel drop front. Chain. Total length 21 in., width 13 in. $1.50 each.

235 Toy Side Board. Ash with Walnut Trimmings. Ebony and Gilt Striping. Glass. Size 13x22 inch. Price $1.50 each.

10 Slipper Case, carved. Walnut with Ebony and Gilt Striping. Chromo. Size 14x24 in. Price $1.25 each.

315 Slipper Back. Walnut and Gilt. 24x14 in. Price, $1.25 each. N. B.—This is a Back only, for embroidered or worsted-work front, &c.

16 Corner, with Stag Head. Carved. Size, 16x16 inch. Price $1.50 each.

302 Easel. Walnut, with Gilt & Ebony Stripings. 24 inch. high. Price, $1.40 each.
303 Same.—All Ebony finish, with Gilt Stripings. Price, $1.80 each.

94 Egyptian Corner. Hinged. Ebony and Gilt Striping. Size 9½x19 in. Price $1.50 each.

New Idea in Corner Brackets. Queen Anne Style. Turned Supports. This looks very stylish and handsome when hung up. Gilt lines. Size 10x14 inch. Price 80 cents each.

96 Toy Bedstead. Veneered Panels. Hinged. Ash with Walnut Trimmings. Ebony and Gilt Stripings. Size 12x18x25 inch. Price $1.50 each.
245 Toy Cradle. Same as above, with Rockers. Price $1.50 each.

192 Pinafore Music Rack, to roll under the Piano. Castors. Ebony and Gilt Striping. Veneered Panels. Elegantly Carved. Size 18x21 inch. Price $5.50.

290 Music Rack, to roll under the Piano. Black and Gold. Size, 17x21 inches. Price, $3.50 each.

168 Music Rack. Veneered Panels. Ebony and Gilt Striping. Extremely Ornamental and Salable. Size 34x18x13 inch. Price $6.00 each.

123 Cleopatra Toilet Bracket. 2 Round Shelves. Elegant ornament. Ebony & Gilt Striping. Hinged. Size 9x29 in. Price $1.50 each.

216 New Quinby Towel Rack. Two Rods. Folding Arms, Rabbitted. Ebony and Gilt Striping. Size 13½x22. Price, $1.50 each.

294 Book Case. Five Shelves. Walnut, with Gilt Stripings. Turned Sides. K. D. 48 in. high, 37 in. wide, 10 in. deep. Price, $18.00 each.

304 Queen Anne Easel. All Ebony finish. 6 feet high. Price, $7.00 each.

324 Book Case. Walnut. Veneered Panels. K. D. Well finished. 75 in. high, 36 in. wide, 13 in. deep. Price, $25.00 each.

325 Book Case. Walnut. Veneered Drawers and Panels. K. D. Well finished. 75 in. high, 56 in. wide, 12 in. deep. Price, $35.00 each.

263 New Blacking Box with large and deep Drawer for Shoes, etc. Ebony and Gilt Striping. Carpet Top. Size 15x15x18 in. Price $5.00 each.

311 Queen Anne Foot Rest. Walnut, with Gilt Stripings. Veneered Box. 17 in. high, 18 in. long, 13 in. wide. Price, $12.00 each.

322 Black and Gold Foot Rest, with Box. Size, 15½x19x9½ in. Price, $5.50 each.

323 Black and Gold Foot Rest, with Box. Metal Ornament. Size, 15x19x10 in. Price, $6.

313 Black and Gold Foot Rest, with Box. Landscape Panels. 15½ in. high, 19 in. long, 10 in. wide. Price, $6.00 each.

234 Toy Bureau. Ash with Walnut Trimmings. Ebony Stripings. Glass. Size 13x21 inch. Price $1.50 each.

376 Side Bracket. Carved 7x7 in. Price, 36 cts. each.

839 Side Bracket. Carved. Size, 5x7½ in. List, 36 cts. each.

807 Foot Rest. Queen Anne Style. Veneered Panels. Ebony and Gilt Striping. Rounding ends. Very handsome. 10x17x19 in. $8.00 each.

352 Side Cabinet, in Black and Gold. Polished. 8x10 in. Beveled Plate Glass Panel. 23 in. high; 11 in. broad; 8 in. deep. Price, $10.50 each.

321 Foot Rest. Black and Gold. Rustic. Deep Carving. Box. 16 in. high, 19 in. long, 10 in. wide. Price, $8.00 each.

604 Blacking Case, Carpet Top, Iron Foot Piece. Size 15x15x16½x½ inches. Price $4.00 each.

295 Book Case. 4 Shelves. Finished in Ebony with Gilt Stripings. Turned Sides. K. D. 36 in. high, 30 in. wide, 10 in. deep. Price $15.50 each.

184 Tripod Stand, Bamboo supports, Butterfly ornament. 13 in. top, 31 in. high, chain and pendants. Ebony and Gilt Striping. $2.00 each.

264 Nightingale Music Pocket. Entirely new and novel. Swinging Box. 8 inch shelf. Ebony and Gilt striping. Size 35x16 in. Price $7.00 each.

55 Chromo Clock Shelf. Ebony and Gilt Striping. Size 13x15 in. Price $1.50 each.

272 New Pattern Chromo Side Bracket. Gilt Striping. Size 10x12x7 in. Price 50 cents each.

141 Towel Rack, with Deer Head, Ebony and Gilt Striping. Folding Arms. Rabbitted space for Glass, Embroidery, &c. Size 11x25 in. Price $1.50 each.

278 Floor Cabinet, for Music, Bric-a-brac, &c. Walnut, with Gilt Stripings and Ebony Ornamentation. Veneered Door, Drawers, Sides and Panels. 52 in. high, 44 in. wide, 15 in. deep.

CLARKE BROS. & CO.

DISCOUNT SHEET. ALL GOODS IN BLACK WALNUT UNLESS OTHERWISE SPECIFIED. { K. D. Means Knock Down. Take Apart for Shipping }

275 Music Cabinet. Walnut, with Gilt Striping. Veneered Panels. Polished. Adjustable Box Pocket. 49 in. high, 20 in. wide, 14 in. deep. Price $30.00 each.

220 Music Stand. Handsome Marquetrie Decorations. Ebony and Gilt Striping Castors. Knocks down and packs very close. In all respects a desirable article, and very low in price. Height 39 in.; width 18 in. Price $13.00 each.

170 Very fine Music Easel. Queen Anne Style. Ebony and Gilt Striping. Finished with exceptional care. Polished. With Veneered Panels. Size 45x24x8 inch. Price $15.00 each.
280 Same Design. Finished in Ebony with Gilt Stripings. Price $17.00 each.

333 Music Cabinet in Black and Gold. Polished. 44 in. high, 21 in. broad, 13½ in. deep. Gilt Key. Price $30.00 each.

266 New Pattern Music Cabinet. The most sensible and practical Cabinet in the market, and very handsome. Veneered Panels. 5 shelves; 6 spaces. Walnut with Ebony and Gilt Striping. Size 14x18x36 inches. Price $19.00 each.
283 Same Design. Finished in Ebony with Gilt Stripings. Price $21.00 each.

277 Combined Music Cabinet, Writing Desk, and Bric-a-brac Shelves, with Cylinder Front. 62 in. high, 22 in. wide, 18 in. deep. Walnut, with Gilt Stripings and Ebony Ornamentation. Polished. Veneered Doors, Sides, Front and Panels. Exact and careful workmanship in all respects. Price, $45.00 each.

171 Music Cabinet. Queen Anne Style. Superior Finish. Polished. Ebony and Gilt Striping. Veneered Panels. Size 41½x19¾x14½ in. Price $27.00 each.
281 Same Design. Finished in Ebony with Gilt Stripes. Price $30.00 each.

276 Floor Cabinet for Music, &c., with bric-a-brac Shelves. Black and Gold. Polished. 52 in. high, 21 in. wide, 15 in. deep. Price $37.00 each.

265 Enlarged Music Cabinet. Walnut with Ebony and Gilt Stripings. Veneered doors. New dimensions, 39x20x13½. Price $24.00 each.
282 Same Design. Polished Ebony. Gilt Stripes. Price $24.00 each.

266 Enlarged Music Cabinet. Walnut with Ebony and Gilt Stripings. Veneered Panels. New dimensions. 39x20x14 in. Price $26.00 each.
283 Same Design. Polished Ebony. Gilt Stripes. Price $26.00 each.

ARCHER MFG. CO.

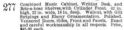

286 Entirely new Music Easel. Walnut with Ebony and Gilt Striping. Size 40x1x inch. Price $11.50 each.
273 Same Design. All Ebony Finish with Gilt Lines. Price $12.50 each.

265 New Pattern Music Cabinet. Veneered Panels. Walnut with Ebony and Gilt Striping. Handsome, and listed very low. Size 13½x17½x37 in. Price $18.00 each.
282 Same Design. Finished in Ebony with Gilt Stripings. Price $21.00 each.

CANTERBURY No. 1.

This Canterbury or Music Stand is an elegant piece of furniture. It is tastily carved and engraved, and handsomely gilded, with blacked edges, and polished in oil. It is calculated as a match piece of furniture with Ottoman No. 2.

PRICE, $15.00.

We can also furnish the same design without the engraving, gilding and carving, at $12.00.

CANTERBURY No. 2.

The above Canterbury is in design similar to the No. 1. The whole difference being in its width. The dimensions are as follows: The extreme height from the floor is 37 inches; width in full, 29 inches. The height of lower department for books is 15 inches, and the size of the upper compartments for sheet music, are 9x12½x9 inches.

The sizes of No. 1 are the same, with the exception of the width, which is 17 inches.

All the material and workmanship on these Canterburys are of the very best.

PRICE, $17.00.

WE HOPE THAT YOU ENJOY THIS BOOK . . . and that it will occupy a proud place in your library. We would like to keep you informed about other publications from Schiffer Publishing Ltd.

TITLE OF BOOK: _____

☐ Bought at: _____

☐ Received as gift

☐ hardcover

☐ paperback

COMMENTS: _____

☐ *Please send me a free Schiffer Arts, Antiques & Collectibles catalog.*

☐ *Please send me a free Schiffer Woodcarving, Woodworking & Crafts catalog*

☐ *Please send me a free Schiffer Military /Aviation History catalog*

☐ *Please send me a free Whitford Press Mind, Body & Spirit and Donning Pictorials & Cookbooks catalog.*

Name _____

Address _____

City _____ State _____ Zip _____

Schiffer Publishing Ltd.
77 Lower Valley Road
Atglen, PA 19310

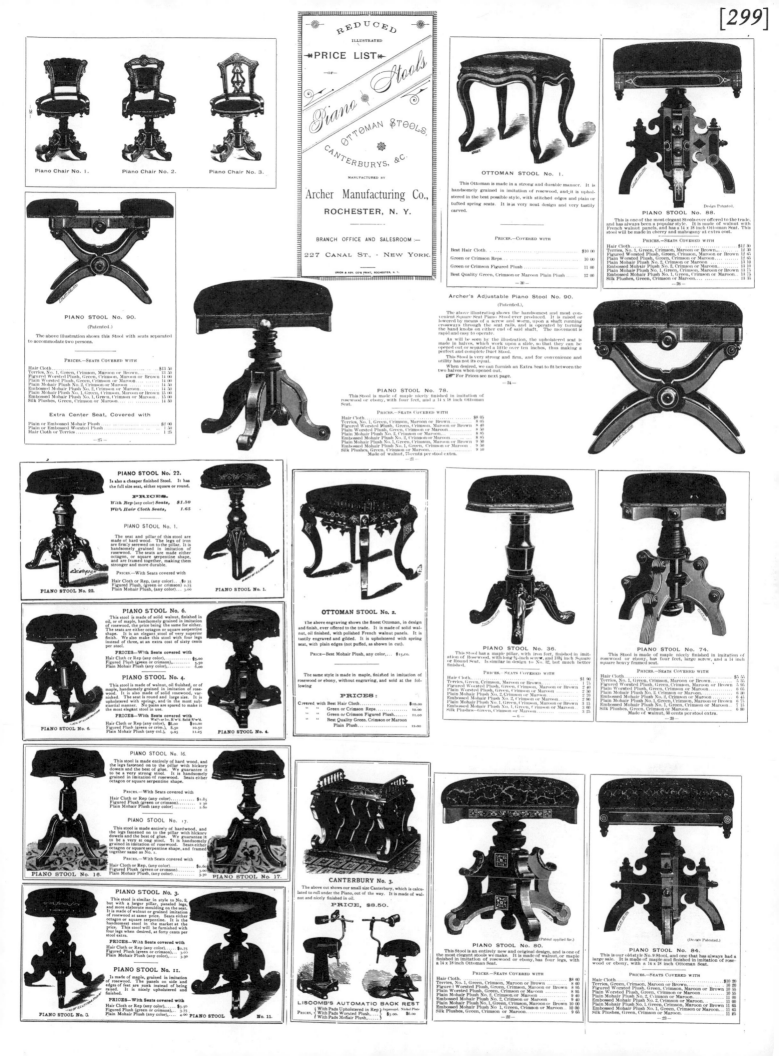

Piano Chair No. 1.

Piano Chair No. 2.

Piano Chair No. 3.

REDUCED

ILLUSTRATED

PRICE LIST

OF

Piano Stools

OTTOMAN STOOLS,

CANTERBURYS, &C.

MANUFACTURED BY

Archer Manufacturing Co.,

ROCHESTER, N. Y.

BRANCH OFFICE AND SALESROOM :—

227 CANAL ST., - NEW YORK.

UNION & ADV. CO'S PRINT, ROCHESTER, N. Y.

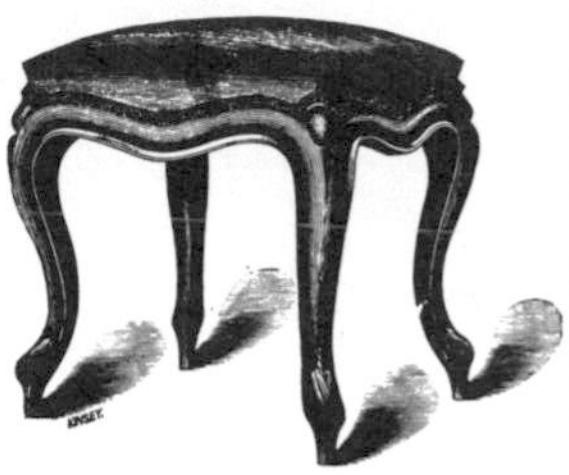

OTTOMAN STOOL No. 1.

This Ottoman is made in a strong and durable manner. It is handsomely grained in imitation of rosewood, and it is upholstered in the best possible style, with stitched edges and plain or tufted spring seats. It is a very neat design and very tastily carved.

PRICES.—COVERED WITH

Best Hair Cloth	$10 00
Green or Crimson Reps	10 00
Green or Crimson Figured Plush	11 00
Best Quality Green, Crimson or Maroon Plain Plush	12 00

— 30 —

Design Patented.

PIANO STOOL No. 88.

This is one of the most elegant Stools ever offered to the trade, and has always been a popular style. It is made of walnut with French walnut panels, and has a 14 x 18 inch Ottoman Seat. This stool will be made in cherry and mahogany at extra cost.

PRICES.—SEATS COVERED WITH

Hair Cloth	$12 30
Terries, No. 1, Green, Crimson, Maroon or Brown	12 30
Figured Worsted Plush, Green, Crimson, Maroon or Brown	12 65
Plain Worsted Plush, Green, Crimson or Maroon	12 65
Plain Mohair Plush No. 2, Crimson or Maroon	13 10
Embossed Mohair Plush No. 2, Crimson or Maroon	13 10
Plain Mohair Plush No. 1, Green, Crimson, Maroon or Brown	13 75
Embossed Mohair Plush No. 1, Green, Crimson or Maroon	13 75
Silk Plushes, Green, Crimson or Maroon	13 35

— 26 —

PIANO STOOL No. 90.

(Patented.)

The above illustration shows this Stool with seats separated to accommodate two persons.

PRICES.—SEATS COVERED WITH

Hair Cloth	$13 50
Terries, No. 1, Green, Crimson, Maroon or Brown	13 50
Figured Worsted Plush, Green, Crimson, Maroon or Brown	14 00
Plain Worsted Plush, Green, Crimson or Maroon	14 00
Plain Mohair Plush No. 2, Crimson or Maroon	14 50
Embossed Mohair Plush No. 2, Crimson or Maroon	14 50
Plain Mohair Plush No. 1, Green, Crimson, Maroon or Brown	15 00
Embossed Mohair Plush No. 1, Green, Crimson or Maroon	15 00
Silk Plushes, Green, Crimson or Maroon	14 50

Extra Center Seat, Covered with

Plain or Embossed Mohair Plush	$2 00
Plain or Embossed Worsted Plush	1 50
Hair Cloth or Terries	1 25

— 25 —

Archer's Adjustable Piano Stool No. 90.

(Patented.),

The above illustration shows the handsomest and most convenient Square Seat Piano Stool ever produced. It is raised or lowered by means of a screw and worm, upon a shaft running crossways through the seat rails, and is operated by turning the hand knobs on either end of said shaft. The movement is rapid and easy to operate.

As will be seen by the illustration, the upholstered seat is made in halves, which work upon a slide, so that they can be opened out or separated a little over ten inches, thus making a perfect and complete Duet Stool.

This Stool is very strong and firm, and for convenience and utility has not its equal.

When desired, we can furnish an Extra Seat to fit between the two halves when opened out.

☞ For Prices see next page.

— 24 —

PIANO STOOL No. 78.

This Stool is made of maple nicely finished in imitation of rosewood or ebony, with four feet, and a 14 x 18 inch Ottoman Seat.

PRICES.—SEATS COVERED WITH

Hair Cloth	$8 05
Terries, No. 1, Green, Crimson, Maroon or Brown	8 05
Figured Worsted Plush, Green, Crimson, Maroon or Brown	8 40
Plain Worsted Plush, Green, Crimson or Maroon	8 50
Plain Mohair Plush No. 2, Crimson or Maroon	8 85
Embossed Mohair Plush No. 2, Crimson or Maroon	8 85
Plain Mohair Plush No. 1, Green, Crimson, Maroon or Brown	9 50
Embossed Mohair Plush No. 1, Green, Crimson or Maroon	9 50
Silk Plushes, Green, Crimson or Maroon	9 10

Made of walnut, 75 cents per stool extra.

— 21 —

PIANO STOOL No. 22.

PIANO STOOL No. 22.

Is also a cheaper finished Stool. It has the full size seat, either square or round.

PRICES.

With Rep (any color) *Seats,*	*$1.50*
With Hair Cloth Seats,	*1.65*

PIANO STOOL No. 1.

The seat and pillar of this stool are made of hard wood. The legs of iron are firmly screwed on to the pillar. It is handsomely grained in imitation of rosewood. The seats are made either octagon, or square serpentine shape, and are framed together, making them stronger and more durable.

PRICES.—With Seats covered with

Hair Cloth or Rep, (any color)	$2 35
Figured Plush, (green or crimson)	2.75
Plain Mohair Plush, (any color)	3.00

PIANO STOOL No. 1.

OTTOMAN STOOL No. 2.

The above engraving shows the finest Ottoman, in design and finish, ever offered to the trade. It is made of solid walnut, oil finished, with polished French walnut panels. It is tastily engraved and gilded. It is upholstered with spring seat, with plain edges (not puffed, as shown in cut).

PRICE—Best Mohair Plush, any color,... $15.co.

The same style is made in maple, finished in imitation of rosewood or ebony, without engraving, and sold at the following

PRICES:

Covered with Best Hair Cloth	$10.00
" " Green or Crimson Reps	10.00
" " Green or Crimson Figured Plush	11.00
" " Best Quality Green, Crimson or Maroon Plain Plush	12.00

PIANO STOOL No. 36.

This Stool has a maple pillar, with iron feet, finished in imitation of Rosewood, with long ¾-inch screw, and 13¾ inch Square or Round Seat. Is similar in design to No. 32, but much better finished.

PRICES.—SEATS COVERED WITH

Hair Cloth	$1 90
Terries, Green, Crimson, Maroon or Brown	1 75
Figured Worsted Plush, Green, Crimson, Maroon or Brown	2 40
Plain Worsted Plush, Green, Crimson or Maroon	2 50
Plain Mohair Plush No. 2, Crimson or Maroon	2 70
Embossed Mohair Plush No. 2, Crimson or Maroon	2 90
Plain Mohair Plush No. 1, Green, Crimson, Maroon or Brown	3 15
Embossed Mohair Plush No. 1, Green, Crimson or Maroon	3 60
Silk Plushes—Green, Crimson or Maroon	3 25

— 6 —

PIANO STOOL No. 74.

This Stool is made of maple nicely finished in imitation of rosewood or ebony, has four feet, large screw, and a 14 inch square heavy framed seat.

PRICES.—SEATS COVERED WITH

Hair Cloth	$5 55
Terries, No. 1, Green, Crimson, Maroon or Brown	5 35
Figured Worsted Plush, Green, Crimson, Maroon or Brown	5 95
Plain Worsted Plush, Green, Crimson or Maroon	6 05
Plain Mohair Plush No. 2, Crimson or Maroon	6 30
Embossed Mohair Plush No. 2, Crimson or Maroon	6 45
Plain Mohair Plush No. 1, Green, Crimson, Maroon or Brown	6 75
Embossed Mohair Plush No. 1, Green, Crimson or Maroon	7 15
Silk Plushes, Green, Crimson or Maroon	6 80

Made of walnut, 50 cents per stool extra.

— 20 —

PIANO STOOL No. 6.

PIANO STOOL No. 6.

This stool is made of solid walnut, finished in oil, or of maple, handsomely grained in imitation of rosewood, the price being the same for either. The seats are either octagon or square serpentine shape. It is an elegant stool of very superior finish. We also make this stool with four legs instead of three, at an extra cost of sixty cents per stool.

PRICES—With Seats covered with

Hair Cloth or Rep (any color),	$5.00
Figured Plush (green or crimson),	5.50
Plain Mohair Plush (any color),	6.00

PIANO STOOL No. 4.

This stool is made of walnut, oil finished, or of maple, handsomely grained in imitation of rosewood. It is also made of solid rosewood, varnished. The seat is round and large size. It is upholstered with springs, and in the most substantial manner. No pains are spared to make it the most elegant stool in use.

PRICES—With Seats covered with

	Wal't or Im. R'w'd.	Solid R'w'd.
Hair Cloth or Rep (any color),	$8.00	$10.00
Figured Plush (green or crim.),	8.50	10.50
Plain Mohair Plush (any col.),	9.25	11.25

PIANO STOOL No. 4.

PIANO STOOL No. 16.

PIANO STOOL No. 16.

This stool is made entirely of hard wood, and the legs fastened on to the pillar with hickory dowels and the best of glue. We guarantee it to be a very strong stool. It is handsomely grained in imitation of rosewood. Seats either octagon or square serpentine shape.

PRICES.—With Seats covered with

Hair Cloth or Rep (any color)	$1.85
Figured Plush (green or crimson)	2 30
Plain Mohair Plush (any color)	2.60

PIANO STOOL No. 17.

This stool is made entirely of hardwood, and the legs fastened on to the pillar with hickory dowels and the best of glue. We guarantee it to be a very st ong stool. It is handsomely grained in imitation of rosewood. Seats either octagon or square serpentine shape, and framed together same as No. 1.

PRICES.—With Seats covered with

Hair Cloth or Rep, (any color)	$2.60
Figured Plush (green or crimson)	3.00
Plain Mohair Plush, (any color)	3.30

PIANO STOOL No. 17.

CANTERBURY No. 3.

The above cut shows our small size Canterbury, which is calculated to roll under the Piano, out of the way. It is made of walnut and nicely finished in oil.

PRICE, $8.50.

LISCOMB'S AUTOMATIC BACK REST

PRICES,		Japanned.	Nickel Plate
	With Pads Upholstered in Rep		
	With Pads Worsted Plush,	$3.00.	$6.00
	With Pads Mohair Plush,		

(Patent applied for.)

PIANO STOOL No. 80.

This Stool is an entirely new and original design, and is one of the most elegant stools we make. It is made of walnut, or maple finished in imitation of rosewood or ebony, has four legs, with a 14 x 18 inch Ottoman Seat.

PRICES.—SEATS COVERED WITH

Hair Cloth	$8 60
Terries, No. 1, Green, Crimson, Maroon or Brown	8 60
Figured Worsted Plush, Green, Crimson, Maroon or Brown	8 95
Plain Worsted Plush, Green, Crimson or Maroon	8 95
Plain Mohair Plush No. 2, Crimson or Maroon	9 40
Embossed Mohair Plush No. 2, Crimson or Maroon	9 40
Plain Mohair Plush No. 1, Green, Crimson, Maroon or Brown	10 00
Embossed Mohair Plush No 1, Green, Crimson or Maroon	10 00
Silk Plushes, Green, Crimson or Maroon	9 65

— 22 —

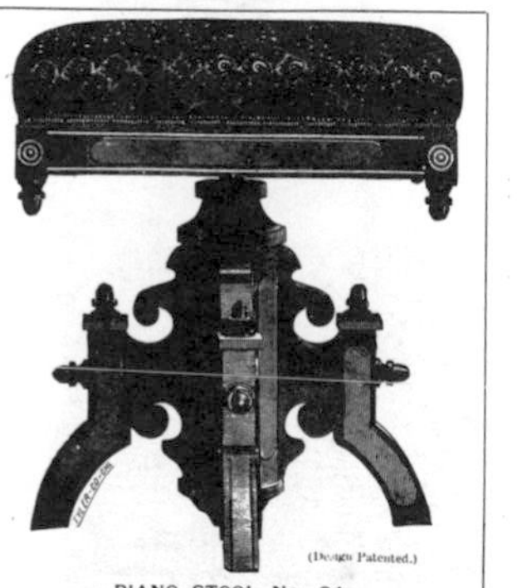

(Design Patented.)

PIANO STOOL No. 84.

This is our old style No. 9 Stool, and one that has always had a large sale. It is made of maple and finished in imitation of rosewood or ebony, with a 14 x 18 inch Ottoman Seat.

PRICES.—SEATS COVERED WITH

Hair Cloth	$10 20
Terries, Green, Crimson, Maroon or Brown	10 20
Figured Worsted Plush, Green, Crimson, Maroon or Brown	10 55
Plain Worsted Plush, Green, Crimson or Maroon	10 55
Plain Mohair Plush No. 2, Crimson or Maroon	11 00
Embossed Mohair Plush No. 2, Crimson or Maroon	11 00
Plain Mohair Plush No. 1, Green, Crimson, Maroon or Brown	11 65
Embossed Mohair Plush No. 1, Green, Crimson or Maroon	11 65
Silk Plushes, Green, Crimson or Maroon	11 25

— 23 —

PIANO STOOL No. 3.

PIANO STOOL No. 3.

This stool is similar in style to No. 2, but with a larger pillar, paneled legs, and more elaborate moulding on the seat. It is made of walnut or grained imitation of rosewood at same price. Seats either octagon or square serpentine. It is the handsomest stool in the market at the price. This stool will be furnished with four legs when desired, at forty cents per stool extra.

PRICES—With Seats covered with

Hair Cloth or Rep (any color)	$2.75
Figured Plush (green or crimson),	3.00
Plain Mohair Plush (any color),	3.30

PIANO STOOL No. 11.

Is made of maple, grained in imitation of rosewood. The panels on side and edges of feet are sunk instead of being raised. It is nicely upholstered and finished.

PRICES—With Seats covered with

Hair Cloth or Rep (any color),	$3.50
Figured Plush (green or crimson),	3.75
Plain Mohair Plush (any color),	4.00

PIANO STOOL No. 11.

COMMON HASSOCK.

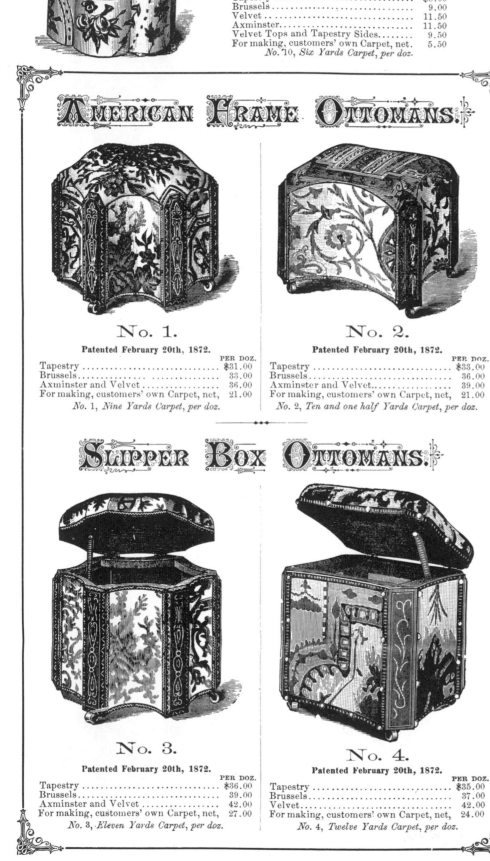

No. 10.

	PER DOZ.
Tapestry	$8.00
Brussels	9.00
Velvet	11.50
Axminster	11.50
Velvet Tops and Tapestry Sides	9.50
For making, customers' own Carpet, net.	5.50

No. 10, Six Yards Carpet, per doz.

𝔸merican 𝔽rame 𝕆ttomans.

No. 1.

Patented February 20th, 1872.

	PER DOZ.
Tapestry	$31.00
Brussels	33.00
Axminster and Velvet	36.00
For making, customers' own Carpet, net,	21.00

No. 1, Nine Yards Carpet, per doz.

No. 2.

Patented February 20th, 1872.

	PER DOZ.
Tapestry	$33.00
Brussels	36.00
Axminster and Velvet	39.00
For making, customers' own Carpet, net,	21.00

No. 2, Ten and one half Yards Carpet, per doz.

𝕊lipper 𝔹ox 𝕆ttomans.

No. 3.

Patented February 20th, 1872.

	PER DOZ.
Tapestry	$36.00
Brussels	39.00
Axminster and Velvet	42.00
For making, customers' own Carpet, net,	27.00

No. 3, Eleven Yards Carpet, per doz.

No. 4.

Patented February 20th, 1872.

	PER DOZ.
Tapestry	$35.00
Brussels	37.00
Velvet	42.00
For making, customers' own Carpet, net,	24.00

No. 4, Twelve Yards Carpet, per doz.

DIAMOND OTTOMAN.

No. 50.

Patent applied for.

	PER DOZ.
Tapestry	$18.00
Brussels	21.00
Axminster and Velvet	24.00
For making, customers' own Carpet, net,	12.00

No. 50, Eight and one half Yards, per doz.

TURKISH OTTOMAN.

No. 9.

	PER DOZ.
Tapestry	$13.00
Brussels	14.50
Axminster and Velvet	22.50
For making, customers' own Carpet, net,	10.50

No. 9, Eight and one half Yards Carpet, per doz.

DIAMOND HASSOCK.

No. 13.

Patent applied for.

	PER DOZ.
Tapestry	$11.50
Brussels	13.00
Velvet	15.00
Axminster	15.00
For making, customers' own Carpet, net,	7.20

No. 13, Seven and one half Yards, per doz.

CHURCH HASSOCK.

No. 11.

	PER DOZ.
Ingrain	$10.50
Tapestry	12.00
Brussels	13.00
Velvet	15.00
For making, customers' own Carpet, net,	5.50

No. 11, Four and one half Yards Ingrain,
Six Yards Brussels, per doz.

SCOLLOP HASSOCK.

No. 14.

	PER DOZ.
Tapestry	$9.50
Brussels	11.00
Axminster and Velvet	13.00
For making, customers' own Carpet, net,	5.50

No. 14, Six Yards Carpet, per doz.

CHILD'S HASSOCK.

No. 12.

	PER DOZ.
	$2.40

ORIENTAL FRAME HASSOCK.

No. 15.

Patent applied for.

	PER DOZ.
Tapestry	$10.50
Brussels	11.00
Velvet	13.50
For making, customers' own Carpet, net,	7.80

No. 15, Five Yards Carpet, per doz.

Slipper Box Ottomans.

No. 5.

	PER DOZ.
Tapestry	$31.50
Brussels	34.00
Axminster and Velvet	37.50
For making, customers' own Carpet, net,	21.00

No. 5, Twelve Yards Carpet, per doz.

No. 6.

Patented February 20th, 1872.

	PER DOZ.
Tapestry	$36.00
Brussels	39.00
Axminster and Velvet	42.00
For making, customers' own Carpet, net,	27.00

No. 6, Eleven Yards Carpet, per doz.

BLACKING CASE.

No. 38.

WALNUT CASE OPEN.

Price, per dozen $19.00

BLACKING CASE.

No. 7.

Patented February 20th, 1872.

	PER DOZ.
Tapestry	$35.00
Brussels	38.00
Axminster and Velvet	42.00
For making, customers' own Carpet, net,	27.00

No. 7, Ten Yards Carpet, per doz.

No. 8.

	PER DOZ.
Tapestry	$34.50
Brussels	37.00
Axminster and Velvet	39.00
For making, customers' own Carpet, net,	27.00

No. 8, Twelve Yards Carpet, per doz.

No. 8½, same as No. 8, except being without walnut moulding around the bottom. Price, same as No. 5 Ottoman.

No. 36.

WALNUT CASE OPEN.

Price, per dozen $16.50

Music Stands.

No. 3.
3 ft. 4 in. high.
2 ft. 2 in. wide.
1 ft. 1 in. deep.

No. 0, No Drawer.
23 in. high.   23 in. wide.
13 in. deep.

No. 0, With Drawer.
3 ft. 2 in. high.   1 ft. 11 in. wide.
13 in. deep.

No. 1.
3 ft. 2 in. high.
1 ft. 8 in. wide.
1 ft. 1 in. deep.

Music Cabinet. Music Portfolio. Screen.

No. 4.
4 ft. 4 in. high.   1 ft. 8 in. wide.
1 ft. 4 in. deep.

3 ft. 4 in. high.   1 ft. 6 in. wide.
1 ft. 1 in. deep.

4 ft. high.   1 ft. 10 in. wide.

Full size, 43x30.
Frame size, 18x21.

Book Racks.

No. 2
3 ft. 1 in. high.
2 ft. 2 in. wide.
1 ft. 2 in. deep.

No. 1.
5 ft. high.

No. 2.
5 ft. 5 in. high.

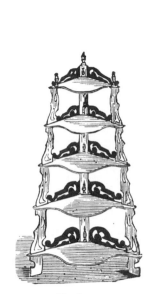

No. 3.
5 ft. 7 in. high.

No. 4.
5 ft. 7 in. high.

No. 5.
5 ft. 6 in. high.

No. 6.
5 ft. 4 in. high.

Corner Stands.

No. 7.
5 ft. high.

No. 9.
5 ft. 10 in. high.

No. 1.
3 ft. high.
2 ft. 1 in. wide.
8 in. deep.

Side Cabinets.

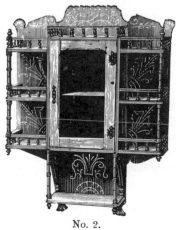

No. 2.
Same Size as No. 1.

Hanging Towel Racks and Brackets.

No. 1. No 3. No. 5. No. 7.

No. 2. No. 4. No. 6. No. 8. No. 9.

LAMBREQUIN BRACKETS. CORNER CABINET. CORNER RACKS.

Side.—No. 1, 20 in. wide.
"   2, 25 "   "
"   3, 30 "   "

Corner.—No. 1, 10 in. wide.
"   2, 11½ "   "
"   3, 14 "   "

1 ft. 9 in. high.
1 ft. 1 in. wide.

No. 2, 19 in. high. No. 1, 32 in. high.

KELLER, STURM & EHMAN, CHICAGO, ILL.

No. 30

No. 31

No. 32

No. 29

No. 28

COOPER & McKEE,

MANUFACTURERS OF

REFRIGERATORS,

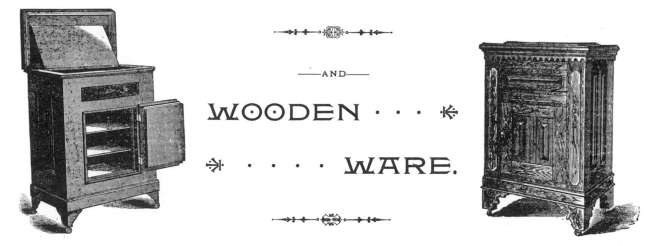

—AND—

WOODEN · · · ⚔

⚔ · · · WARE.

113, 115, 117 and 119 GWINNETT STREET,   BROOKLYN, E. D., NEW YORK.

☞ SEND FOR CATALOGUE AND PRICE LIST TO COOPER & McKEE.

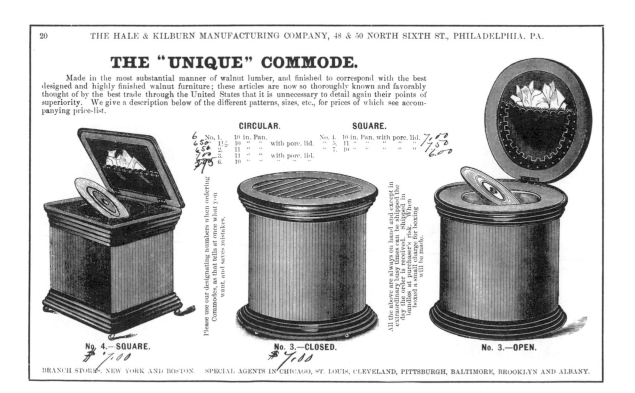

20   THE HALE & KILBURN MANUFACTURING COMPANY, 48 & 50 NORTH SIXTH ST., PHILADELPHIA, PA.

THE "UNIQUE" COMMODE.

Made in the most substantial manner of walnut lumber, and finished to correspond with the best designed and highly finished walnut furniture; these articles are now so thoroughly known and favorably thought of by the best trade through the United States that it is unnecessary to detail again their points of superiority. We give a description below of the different patterns, sizes, etc., for prices of which see accompanying price-list.

CIRCULAR.   SQUARE.

No. 1.   10 in. Pan.   No. 4.   10 in. Pan. with porc. lid.
No. 1½.   10 "   "   with porc. lid.   No. 5.   11   "   "   "   "
No. 2.   11 "   "   No. 7.   10   "   "   "   "
No. 3.   11 "   "   with porc. lid.
No. 6.   10 "   "

Please use our designating numbers when ordering Commodes, as that tells at once what you want, and saves mistakes.

All the above are always on hand and except in extraordinary busy times can be shipped the day the order is received. Shipped in bundles at purchaser's risk. When boxed a small charge for boxing will be made.

No. 4.—SQUARE.   No. 3.—CLOSED.   No. 3.—OPEN.

BRANCH STORES, NEW YORK AND BOSTON.   SPECIAL AGENTS IN CHICAGO, ST. LOUIS, CLEVELAND, PITTSBURGH, BALTIMORE, BROOKLYN AND ALBANY.

C. D. HOLMES'
PATENT AUTOMATIC EARTH CLOSET.

" A Portable Commode, in drawing-room, bedroom, or closet, the care of which is no more disagreeable than that of a stove." — *Prof. A. B. Palmer, Medical Department Michigan University.*

"The mechanism is simple but durable, the action automatic and invariable, the odor from them less than from the water-closets in our city houses." — *Rev. Geo. F. Pentecost, Pastor Warren Aveuue Baptist Church, Boston.*

Figure 2.

This Illustration represents C. D. HOLMES' EARTH CLOSET ventilated at a chimney flue.

Figure 4.

This Engraving represents a sectional view of C. D. HOLMES' EARTH CLOSET, a detailed description of which may be found on the opposite page.

"The Earth Closet is one of the most useful inventions of modern times." — *Mass. Board of Health Report.*

"A convenience for the use of invalids, which greatly facilitates nursing." — *Prof. A. B. Palmer, Medical Department Michigan University.*

Figure 1.

Height, 42 inches ; Width, 20 inches ; Depth, front to rear, 26½ inches.

Figure 3.

This Cut illustrates C. D. HOLMES' EARTH CLOSET ventilated at a window.

"If the Earth Closet should be generally introduced, cholera, dysentery, typhoid fever, &c., would be exterminated." — *Prof. F. L. Cracour, New Orleans School of Medicine.*

Tables.

No. 1, 33 in. high, Top 13x13.

No. 1½, 33 in. high, Top 17x17.

No. 2, 33 in. high, 13 in. diam.

No. 3, 34 in. high, 11 in. diam·

No. 4, 33 in. high, 11 in. diam.

9 or 11 in. Mble top; 33 in. high.

CHESS TABLE.

BLACKING CASE

Carpet Top and Dust Slide.

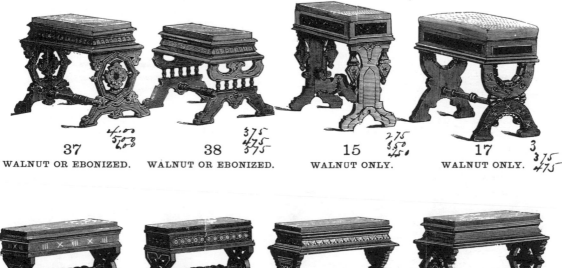

37
WALNUT OR EBONIZED.

38
WALNUT OR EBONIZED.

15
WALNUT ONLY.

17
WALNUT ONLY.

83
EBONIZED ONLY.

82
EBONIZED ONLY.

81

37
WALNUT OR EBONIZED.

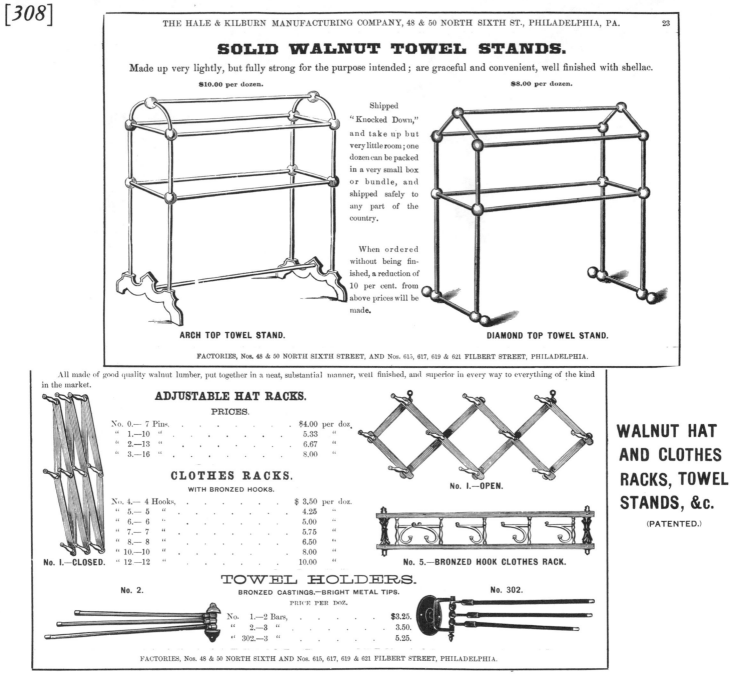

SOLID WALNUT TOWEL STANDS.

Made up very lightly, but fully strong for the purpose intended ; are graceful and convenient, well finished with shellac.

$10.00 per dozen.   **$8.00 per dozen.**

Shipped "Knocked Down," and take up but very little room ; one dozen can be packed in a very small box or bundle, and shipped safely to any part of the country.

When ordered without being finished, a reduction of 10 per cent. from above prices will be made.

ARCH TOP TOWEL STAND.   **DIAMOND TOP TOWEL STAND.**

FACTORIES, Nos. 48 & 50 NORTH SIXTH STREET, AND Nos. 615, 617, 619 & 621 FILBERT STREET, PHILADELPHIA.

All made of good quality walnut lumber, put together in a neat, substantial manner, well finished, and superior in every way to everything of the kind in the market.

ADJUSTABLE HAT RACKS.

PRICES.

No. 0.— 7 Pins	$4.00	per doz.
" 1.—10 "	5.33	"
" 2.—13 "	6.67	"
" 3.—16 "	8.00	"

No. I.—OPEN.

CLOTHES RACKS.

WITH BRONZED HOOKS.

No. 4.— 4 Hooks,	$3.50	per doz.
" 5.— 5 "	4.25	"
" 6.— 6 "	5.00	"
" 7.— 7 "	5.75	"
" 8.— 8 "	6.50	"
" 10.—10 "	8.00	"
" 12.—12 "	10.00	"

No. I.—CLOSED.

No. 5.—BRONZED HOOK CLOTHES RACK.

WALNUT HAT AND CLOTHES RACKS, TOWEL STANDS, &c.

(PATENTED.)

TOWEL HOLDERS.

BRONZED CASTINGS.—BRIGHT METAL TIPS.

PRICE PER DOZ.

No. 2.   **No. 302.**

No. 1.—2 Bars,	$3.25.
" 2.—3 "	3.50.
" 302.—3 "	5.25.

FACTORIES, Nos. 48 & 50 NORTH SIXTH AND Nos. 615, 617, 619 & 621 FILBERT STREET, PHILADELPHIA.

"COMBINATION" CANVAS BACK CANE SEATING.

Patented May 1st, and October 9th, 1877.

Made with woven cane cemented to canvas, making the most durable cane seat in existence. It has every advantage over every cane or woven seat, in that it has a much greater resistance to heavy weight, or wear and tear; it is the *only* cane seat that can be nailed on; it can readily be cut with shears; it is easily applied; will never break through. Examination will convince of its great merit.

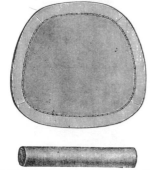

"Combination" Canvas-Back Cane Seating.

THE UNIQUE BLACKING CASE.

Well made, of walnut lumber, nicely finished, and in every way a most satisfactory article of this kind.

Made only in one size, on hand at all times and can be shipped on receipt of order.

BLACKING CASE.

THE "FAVORITE" WATER COOLER.

The Most Durable, Economical of Ice, Scientific in Construction, Elegant in Design.

With polished solid walnut outside; cast-iron porcelain-lined tank; metal rims top and bottom, so that warping or springing is out of the question; has no joints to loosen by moisture, and by every consideration of care in manufacture, best known methods of construction, and first quality of materials used we claim to offer the most perfect Water Cooler in existence.

Patented Dec. 30, 1873. Re-issued Jan. 15, 1878.   Patented Jan. 22, 1878.

THE "FAVORITE."

Manufacturers

Some furniture manufacturers

The Archer Manufacturing Co. of Rochester, N.Y. was the formost concern of its kind in the last quarter of the nineteenth century. They manufactured barber and dentist chairs and piano stools.

The Boyington Folding Bed Co. of Chicago was the successor to L. C. Boyington (spring beds and woodenware). As the folding bed business grew, he dropped his other lines.

The Central Furniture Co. of Rockford, Illinois was formed in 1879 with a capital stock of $25,000. By 1889 their capital stock was $75,000 and they had a factory comprised of several buildings. Some of their great specialties were combination bookcases and cylinder bookcases. The company used water power in their factory. The president was S. A. Johnson and August Peterson was the secretary.

The Chicago Desk Mfg. Co. on Kinzie Street and Peorie Street was originally organized by Skelvig and Peterson on Clinton Street. A Mr. J. H. Minges came to Chicago from the east coast and incorporated the business and it became a most successful firm. Mr. Minges managed the firm.

The Co-operative Furniture Co. was established in Rockford, Illinois in 1880. They employed 100 men. The stock of the company was held by 75 men, most of whom worked in the factory.

The Excelsior Furniture Co. was organized in 1881. John P. Anderson was the organizer. It was the only Rockford, Illinois firm at the time making upholstered furniture. They employed 80 men and sold mostly to the south and west.

The Forest City Furniture Co. was one of the very earliest in Rockford, Illinois. It was founded in 1870 by A. C. Johnson. By 1873 John P. Anderson and L. O. Upson were partners and a large stone factory that used water power had been built. By 1889 the factories (an additional one had been built) employed 300 people. A branch was established at 17 and 19 Elizabeth Street in New York City. This branch was managed by John E. Foster and Co. who were also agents for Berkey and Gay and the Widdicome Furniture Co.

Hale and Kilburn Co. began in 1867 as Hale, Moseley, Goodman & Co.; looking glass and picture manufactory. It went through a succession of name changes and locations until 1873 when it became Hale, Kilburn Co., manufacturers of cabinet-wares, frames and moldings. Kilburn was also in business with a Joel Gates manufacturing cottage furniture from 1857 until 1877. In 1877 he withdrew from his partnership with Gates. Hale and Kilburn exhibited their "Champion Folding Bedstead" at the Philadelphia Centennial. They were also producers of the "Peerless Portable Resovoir Washstand" and the "Unique Odorless Commode" and the "Favorite Water Cooler". All of these pieces were patented pieces.

In the **Hall and Stephens** catalogue of 1882 the folding bed/settee was patented and designed by Joseph Greenlief and assigned to himself and Mr. O. F. Case.

George Henshaw the Cincinnatti chair maker had a branch at 171 Canal Street in New York. The firm was one of the oldest houses in Cincinnati. It was established in 1847. George Sr. retired in 1876 and left the business to his sons, Edward and George. George Sr. died in 1881. They were famous for an elegant lounge they produced.

In 1888 **The Indianapolis Cabinet Works** was able to produce and send out 25 desks a day. The owner, Francis Coffin had patented the improved drawer fitting machine.

S. Karpen and Bros. the parlour furniture manufacturers at 205 E. Lake Street, Chicago were established in 1881. By 1886 only two brothers, Sal and Oscar Karpen were active in the business.

Kent Furniture Co. in February of 1883 completed its new building. It was a 4 story structure 64 x 176 feet in area. This new plant increased its furniture capacity by 40%. In February of 1888 they added a marine boiler to the factory. The boiler was 9 feet high, eighteen feet long and weighed 18 tons. It would run a 400 horse power engine and it cost $5000. It was the largest boiler in Grand Rapids.

Kreimer Bros. Furniture had a six story building in Cincinnati in 1888. They were signed up for exhibition space at the Cincinnati Centennial of 1888 but fair officials did not provide proper space so he and J. H. Wiggers, H. H. Wiggers and the Phoenix Furniture Co. withdrew from showing.

The **Moore Desk Co.** was located at 84 East Market Street in Indianapolis, IN in 1888.

The Oriel Cabinet Co. of Grand Rapids, MI, in the 1880's confined their work to the manufacture of fine cabinets. During this period the firm was managed by C. W. Black. In 1911 Berkey & Gay bought out the Oriel Cabinet Co.

In March of 1888 the **Ott Patent Lounge** Co. moved to 141 Kinzie Street in Chicago.

Phoenix Chair Co. was incorporated in 1875 with T. M. Blackstock, president and James H. Mead as secretary. They were considered a very modern and liberal firm. In February of 1883 they ran 9—9½ hours of work per day (or so long as the men could see by daylight). The men were paid, however, the same wage for 9 or 9½ hours as if they had worked the full 10 hour day. This was not only considered quite generous, but was thought to prevent union organization and strikes.

Phoenix Furniture Co. of Grand Rapids, MI succeeded the Phoenix Manufacturing Co. in 1872. William Berkey former of Berkey & Gay founded it. He retired in 1879. In 1886 J. W. Converse was president, R. W. Merrill was vice president and general manager and F. W. Kleindrenst was secretary. Mr. Merrill had replaced O. L. Howard who had resigned due to ill health. By 1886 the factory was one of the largest and most complete. They had a branch in New York at 177 & 179 Canal Street and a Chicago branch at 307 & 309 Wabash Avenue. The Chicago branch was managed by W. D. Snyder and W. H. Martin

S. K. Pierce the founder of Pierce and Son Chair Mfg. died in South Gardiner, MA on February 28, 1888.

E. F. Sweet was president of **Princess Dressing Case Co.** They absorbed the **American Patent Dressing Case Company's** patents and business in 1890.

The Rockford Chair and Furniture Co. was formed in 1882. They put out a standard grade of goods. They employed 130 men. Andrew Kjellgren was the president of the company.

The factory of the **Rockford Furniture Co-op** was totally destroyed by fire on January 7, 1888. The factory they rebuilt was larger than the original one.

The Rockford Skandia Furniture Co. was composed principally of Swedish

ROCKFORD CHAIR AND FURNITURE COMPANY,
MANUFACTURERS, ROCKFORD. ILL.

No. 309 SIDEBOARD.—XVI. Century Finish.   No. 301 TABLE.

The Rockford Furniture Journal,
April 15, 1890, page 25.

Americans. It was organized in 1889 with a Mr. Knight and a Mr. Rood each donating half of the factory site. Capital stock of $50,000 was subscribed to by the men who were to work in the factory. The main building was 4 stories tall on the river bank in Knightsville. They used the very latest in machinery in the plant. Horace Brown was the president, Charles Bjorsland was vice president and C. H. Woolsey was the secretary-treasurer.

Taylor Chair Co. of Bedford, OH succeedeed the chair firm of William O. Taylor and Son. Charles A. Wear, 24 Van Buren Street, Chicago was their agent in 1888.

The Tyler Desk Co. is listed in the St. Louis City directories from 1884 to 1892. The firms president, Charles H. Tyler was listed as an auctioneer from 1871—83. He is listed from 1893—97 but without an occupation. In addition to Mr. Tyler, L. G. Conant was listed as secretary-treasurer of the firm. Their address was 500—502 North 4th Street in St. Louis, MO.

The Union Furniture Co. was organized in 1876 and was extremely successful. They employed 165 men and had a large water powered factory.

Several of the patent chairs made by **Vail Chair Co.** were designed by one of his employees, a Mr. E. Wakefield and assigned by him to Mr. Vail.

Wakefield Rattan Co. was managed by C. W. H. Frederick. By 1891 they had plants in New York, San Francisco, Boston and Chicago.

J. H. Wiggers was a manufacturer of parlour furniture in Cincinnati in 1888.

H. H. Wiggers was well known as a manufacturer of office desks, china closets, wardrobes and bookcases in the same city.

Jacob © Gottlieb
MANUFACTURER OF
△ FINE △
UPHOLS-
TERED
-:-FURNI-
TURE:

OFFICE AND SAMPLE ROOMS 920 MILWAUKEE AVE., CHICAGO, II

Furniture, June, 1890, page 36.

Materials Consulted

CATALOGS

American Ottoman & Hassock Co.
110 Leonard Street
New York, New York
ca. 1885 price list

American Shade Roller Co.
Boston, Massachusetts
1877 price list

A. H. Andrews & Co.
215—221 Wabash Avenue
Chicago, Illinois
January 1891 price list of folding beds.
February 1891 bed catalog supplement.

Archer Manufacturing Company
5, 7, & 9 North Water Street
Rochester, New York
ca. 1885, gynecological chairs catalog.
1886 Piano stools catalog.
ca. 1890 patent barber chairs and barber's
  furniture.
no date. Piano stools, ottoman stools,
  canterburys catalog.

Bardwell Anderson and Company
19 Charlestown Street
Boston, Massachusetts
1884 catalog. Tables, desks and pedestals.
1889—90 catalog. Tables, desks and
  sideboards
Warerooms: No. 81 Union Street, Boston,
  Massachusetts.

T. M. Beal & Co.
26 Haverhill Street
Boston, Massachusetts
March 1, 1886 Italian marble top centre
  tables price list.

Bragg, Conant & Co.
Nos. 14 and 16 Washington Street
Boston, Massachusetts
ca. 1875 price list for looking glasses.

Brooks Bro's Manufacturers
Rochester, New York
1885 trade cards & price list.

Central Manufacturing Company
37, 39, and 41 Armour Street
Chicago, Illinois
ca. 1880 catalog of office and library
  furniture.
1890 catalog of bookcases and desks with
  price guide.

J. A. Cilley & Co.
Fairfield, Maine
No date, price list of pine furniture.

Colie & Son
112 to 122 Exchange Street
Buffalo, New York
1884 catalog and price list of parlour
  furniture, patent rocking chairs,
  center tables, lounges, mattresses, etc.

The Converse Mfg. Co.
Manufacturers of the Grand Rapids
  Folding Bed Co.'s beds. no date.

Cron, Kills & Co.
Piqua, Ohio
1890 catalog of wardrobes, sideboards,
  cupboards, and chiffoniers.

Daniels, Badger & Co.
25 Sudbury and 130 Friend Streets
Boston, Massachusetts
No date, catalog of chamber furniture and
  sideboards.
April 1, 1876 hand bill of a bedroom suit.
April 6, 1881, letter.

John Danner
Canton, Ohio
ca. 1886, catalog of revolving bookcases.

Derby & Kilmer Desk Co.
93 Causeway Street
Boston, Massachusetts
ca. 1885

Philander Derby & Co.
101 and 104 Cross Street
Boston, Massachusetts
No date. Price list for automatic foot rest.

Elastic Chair Company
Williamsport, Pennsylvania
September 1st. 1882 price list.

P. M. Fogler & Co.
No. 164 North Street
Boston, Massachusetts
ca. 1880, catalog of bedsteads, patent bow
    cradles, folding cribs, etc.

J. T. and L. J. Gilman
No. 9 Granite Block
Bangor, Maine
No date, price list of chamber sets.

Goodell Co.
Antrim, New Hampshire
Ca. 1880 hand bill of White Mountain
    Hammock Chair.

Grand Rapids School Furniture Company
Grand Rapids, Michigan
ca. 1880, catalog of church furniture.

The Hale & Kilburn Manufacturing Co.
No. 48 & 50 North Sixth Street
Philadelphia, Pennsylvania
1880 catalog of patented furniture, includ-
    ing the "Champion Automatic" fold-
    ing bedstead.

Hall & Stephen
200, 202 & 204 Canal Street
New York, New York
1880 catalog of beds
1880 catalog of beds.

The Hartley Reclining Chair Co.
153 and 155 Superior Street
Chicago, Illinois
1885 catalog.

The Hayes Chair Co.
Cortland, New York
March 1, 1889 hand bills and price list.

Lewis S. Hayes
Cortland, New York
March 15, 1882 catalog of patent folding
    chairs.

George Heyman
103 and 105 Mott Street
    and 179 Canal Street
New York, New York
1890 catalog of bedding.

Heywood Bros. & Co.
81 Causeway Street
Boston, Massachusetts
1889 catalog of cane seat chairs.

W. Heywood Chair Co.
442 Pearl Street
New York, New York
May 1883 hand bill of Decker folding
    chair.

M. Keating
141, 143, 145, 147 North Street
Boston, Massachusetts
No date, hand bill for patent combination
    crib.

Peter Kehr
123 to 135 Mangin Street
New York, New York
March 1, 1882 price list for desks.

Keller, Sturm & Co.
Corner Elizabeth & Fulton Streets
Chicago, Illinois
1883 price list and catalog of pier and
    mantle frames and hat trees.

Keller, Sturm & Ehman
Corner Elizabeth and Fulton Streets
Chicago, Illinois
1885 catalog of pier and mantle frames,
    mantles, hat trees, cabinets, etc.

Kent Furniture Manufacturing Co.
Grand Rapids, Michigan
January 1, 1887 price list and hand bills.

Kilborn Whitman & Co.
34 Canal Street
Boston, Massachusetts
May 1, 1880 catalog and price list of
    parlour suites and patent rockers, etc.

C. & A. Kreimer Company
S. E. corner Richmond & Carr Streets
Cincinnati, Ohio
1890—91 catalog and price list for
    bedroom suits.

Leominster Furniture Manufacturing Co.
Leominster, Massachusetts
No date, hand bill of Ordway Swing
    Rocker Cradle.

Leominster Piano Stool Company
Leominster, Massachusetts
July 1, 1882 catalog and price list.

Charles Lersch
Nos. 189, 191 & 193 Stanton Street
New York, New York
ca. 1880 catalog and price list of whatnots,
    towel racks, music stands, fancy
tables, etc.

C. W. Lyman
No. 425 Medford Street
Charlestown, Massachusetts
June 1, 1881 price list for extension tables.

E. H. Mahoney
96 Cross Street
Boston, Massachusetts
1880 catalog of folding chairs.
Fall 1888 catalog of rocking chairs.

McKee & Harrington
173 & 175 Grand Street
New York, New York
January 1, 1890 catalog of baby carriages,
    velocipedes, and reed chairs.

National Chair Manufacturing Company
E. W. Clark and W. C. Ranney,
    proprietors.
Elbridge, New York
1888—1889 catalog and price list.

National Wire Mattress Co.
New Britain, Connecticut
1879 catalog and price list of brass and
    iron beds, cribs, cradles, etc.

New Haven Folding Chair Company
552 State Street
New Haven, Connecticut
July 15, 1881 catalog and price list of
    folding chairs and invalid rolling
    chairs.

Nichols Furniture Company
Portsmouth, Ohio
No date, hand bill of chamber suits.

Northwestern Furniture Company
Burlington, Iowa
January 1890 catalog and price list of office
    desks, tables and bookcases.

Ott Lounge Company
1890 catalog

E. F. Peirce
160 & 162 North Street
Boston, Massachusetts
Ca. 1875 catalog of chairs.
Spring 1882 price list of chairs.

A. Petersen and Co.
15 to 21 Armour Street
Chicago, Illinois
1890 catalog of desks and office furniture.

Phoenix Chair Company
Sheboygan, Wisconsin
January 2, 1923 catalog and price list.

Pond Desk Company
152 Charlestown Street
Boston, Massachusetts
1890 price list and catalog.

Princess Dressing Case Co.
Grand Rapids, Michigan
Ca. 1880 catalog.

Ring, Merrill & Tillotson
Saginaw, Michigan
No date, hand bills of bedroom suits.

Rockford Union Furniture Company
Rockford, Illinois
June 1, 1890 catalog and price list of
walnut and oak furniture.

A. Roda
Rochester, New York
Ca. 1879 catalog and price list of solid
wood furniture carvings, carved
heads, carved drawer handles, mirror
and frame carvings.

M. Samuels & Co.
164 Mott Street
New York, New York
Fall, 1890 catalog & price list of folding
beds.

L. H. Sawin & Co.
West Gardner, Massachusetts
1886 catalog of chairs.

M. & H. Schrenkeisen
23 to 29 Elizabeth Street
New York, New York
March, 1885 catalog and price list of
parlour furniture.

A. B. & E. L. Shaw
27 Sudbury Street
Boston, Massachusetts
Ca. 1880 catalog of church furniture
Ca. 1890 catalog of lodge furniture.

Shaw, Applin & Co.
(successors to Braman, Shaw & Co.)
27 Sudbury Street and 69 Portland Street
Boston, Massachusetts
Ca. 1880 catalog of church furniture.
1879—80 catalog of parlour, church, and
lodge furniture.
1881—82 catalog and price list for
parlour, church, and lodge furniture.

Sidney Squires & Co.
329 & 331 Tremont Street
Boston, Massachusetts
Ca. 1890 catalog of automatic sofa and
cabinet beds.

S. C. Small & Co.
71 & 73 Portland Street
Boston, Massachusetts
No date, catalog of church furniture.
1886—87 catalog of church furniture.
1887—88 catalog of church furniture.
1887—88 catalog of lodge furniture.

Steinman & Meyer Furniture Co.
560, 562, 564 & 566 West Sixth Street
Cincinnati, Ohio
No date, price list for sideboards, cradles,
and child's beds.
Ca. 1880 catalog of sideboards.

Stickley—Brandt Furniture Co.
Binghamton, New York
Ca. 1902 catalog

F. E. Stuart
93 to 101 Fulton Street
Boston, Massachusetts
Ca. 1880 catalog of chairs and settees.

The Taylor Chair Company
Bedford, Ohio
Spring 1890 catalog and price list.

E. M. Tibbetts
Dexter, Maine
Trade card listing coffins, caskets and
robes, children's carriages.

Tyler Desk Company
St. Louis, Missouri
Ca. 1889 catalog.

E. W. Vaill
Worcester, Massachusetts
October 29, 1879 catalog and price list of
patent folding chairs.
1881 catalog and price list of patent
folding chairs.

Frank W. White
269 Canal Street
New York, New York
Ca. 1870 catalog of looking glasses, picture
frames, mouldings, cornices, etc.

R. T. White
Boston, Massachusetts
January 23, 1884 letter. Garfield adjust-
    able cot bed and stretcher.

Kilborn Whitman & Co.
34 Canal Street
Boston, Massachusetts
May 1, 1880 catalog and price list of
    parlour suits and patent rockers, etc.

O. Whitney & Co.
Winchenden, Massachusetts
Ca. 1880 catalog and price list of chairs.

W. F. Whitney
South Ashburnham, Massachusetts
Spring 1883 price list of cane seat chairs.

Charles P. Whittle
35 Fulton Street
Boston, Massachusetts
No date, trade card for chamber furniture.

The Wooten Desk Company
Indianapolis, Indiana
1876 catalog.

Magazines

The American Furniture Gazette,
    1882—1888.
Furniture, June, 1890.
The Furniture Trade Review, April, 1890.
The Furniture Tradesman, January, 1886
    to June 1887.
The Furniture Worker, May 25, 1887 to
    February 25, 1891.
Michigan Artisan, February, 1883 to
    February, 1891.
Ohio Valley Furniture Journal, June 1,
    1888 to April 1, 1889.
The Rockford Furniture Journal, October
    15, 1888 to February 15, 1891.
The Saw-mill Gazette, October 15, 1885.
The Shroud, October 15, 1888.

The Authors

Eileen Dubrow was born and grew up in New York City. She graduated from Parsons College in Fairfield, Iowa and completed her graduate work at New York University after which she worked as a textiles converter.

Richard C. Dubrow also comes from New York City and went to City College of New York. He has served as a lieutenant in the U.S. Army and Military Infantry, and had his own very successful prime-meat business for 25 years serving the leading restaurants and hotels in the U.S. and Europe.

The Dubrows now live in New York with their four children. Together, they started as dealers in American folk art and gradually have specialized in mid-19th century cabinetmakers' furniture. They now handle primarily cabinetmaker furniture. Their investigative research into the origins and manufacture of Wooton desks and furniture by John Henry Belter has enabled them to identify many previously unknown forms by each of these makers. They are actively seeking both pictures and information about furniture with makers' labels, and the original catalogs which document the forms. Questions from the readers may be addressed to the publisher.

Newly Revised
PRICE GUIDE

to
Eileen & Richard Dubrow's

FURNITURE
Made In
America
1875 ~ 1905

Compiled by
Mary M. Whitford

77 Lower Valley Road, Atglen, PA 19310

Published by Schiffer Publishing, Ltd.
77 Lower Valley Road
Atglen, PA 19310
Please write for a free catalog.
This book may be purchased from the publisher.
Please include $2.95 postage.
Try your bookstore first.

We are interested in hearing from authors
with book ideas on related subjects.

Newly revised price guide included.

Printed in the United States of America.
ISBN: 0-88740-695-5

TABLE OF CONTENTS

Introduction

This price reference is just that, a guide. The prices have been gathered in the middle Atlantic states. Value will vary tremendously because of location and condition. These prices are based on a country setting at fair market value, in relatively good condition for age and use. Values keep changing so an accurate price today will be slightly different the following day. I hope this will be of some help.

In each column,

—The number at the left is the page number.
—The R1, R2, R3 etc. refers to the row of illustrations on that page.
—The numbers preceded by the mark "#" indicate the catalog numbers on the illustrations.

For example:

page	row	cat. no.	price
200	**R2**	**#143 -**	**$70.00**

Parlour and Library Furniture

22 R1 #836-$1700.00; #398-$2300.00; #846-$950.00.

22 R2 #395-$1250.00; #348-$1350.00; #396-$950.00.

23 R1 #1A-$950.00; #2B-$750.00.

23 R2 #410-$700.00; #412-$675.00.

24 R1 #612-$2300.00; #603-$2100.00; #604-$2200.00.

24 R2 #605-$2000.00; #608-$1950.00; #609-$1900.00.

25 R1 #26-$1200.00; #25-$1300.00.

25 R2 Bookcases-$1150.00; $1100.00.

26 R1 #288-$1000.00; #'s 258 & 259-$1000.00

26 R2 #278-$1700.00; #277-$1600.00.

27 R1 #207-$1650.00; #205-$1300.00; #208-$1050.00.

27 R2 # 105-$750.00; #512-$750.00.

28 R1 #275-$1250.00; #274-$1300.00.

28 R2 #270-$1100.00; #273-$1100.00.

29 R1 #252-$2000.00; #216-$1400.00.

29 R2 #206-$950.00; #276-$1500.00.

30 R1 #16-$1500.00; #3-$550.00; #9-$1300.00; #4-$800.00.

30 R2 #15-$800.00; #18-$900.00; #19-$1200.00.

30 R3 #2-$325.00; #6-$550.00; #7-$300.00; #5-$275.00.

31 R1 #668-$295.00; #656-$240.00; #659-$275.00.

31 R2 #985 1/2-$200.00; #996-$225.00; #988-$220.00; #982-$200.00.

31 R3 #893 1/2-$550.00; #446-$425.00; #530-$250.00; #527-$300.00.

32 R1 #394-$600.00; #403-$725.00; #392-$675.00; #400-$850.00; #684-$350.00.

32 R2 #'s 393 & 391-$725.00; #'s 396 &796-$800.00.

32 R3 #928-$250.00; #650-$500.00;#651 -$400.00.

33 R1 #'s 204 & 600-$235.00; #678-$200.00.

33 R2 #602-$250.00; #599-$300.00;#535-$275.00.

33 R3 #'s 783 & 784-$700.00; #786-$600.00;#782-$700.00.

34 R1 #4562-$190.00; #4577-$210.00.

34 R2 #4562-$125.00; $100.00; #4577-$140.00;$95.00.

34 R3 #4562-$175.00; $95.00; #4577-$145.00;$90.00.

35 R1 #70-$160.00; #82-$195.00.

35 R2 Morris chair-$200.00.

36 R1 #352-$80.00; #351-$95.00; #353-$95.00.

36 R2 #307-$80.00; 305-$95.00; #306-$70

36 R3 #362-$65; #361-$85; #363-$105.

37 R1 #4512-$145; #4514-$175.00.

37 R2 #4512-$125.00; $95.00; #4514-$125.00;$95.00.

37 R3 #4512-$95.00; $95.00; #4514-$110.00; $90.00.

38 R1 #832-$75.00; #831-$90.00; #525-$65.00; #802-$80.00.

38 R2 #586-$175.00; #588-$145.00; #589-$295.00.

38 R3 #532-$195.00; #660-$145.00; #698-$120.00; #815 1/2-$90.00.

39 R1 #4501-$110.00; $75.00; $175.00.

39 R2 #4569-$125.00; $95.00; $175.00.

30 R3 #4555-$135.00; $80.00; $200.00.

40 R1 #954-$95.00; #953-$145.00; #930-$160.00; #894-$125.00.

40 R2 #7674-$145.00; #999-$220.00; #971-$230.00; #970-$245.00.

40 R3 #969-$145.00; #972-$155.00; #998-$225.00; #990-$265.00.

41 R1 #4329-$95.00; #3758-$85.00; #4733-$95.00.

41 R2 #2358-$165.00; #3341-$175.00; #4025-$120.00.

41 R3 #1767-$120.00; #4572-$120.00; #4075-$150.00.

42 R1 #4641-$175.00; #4723-$135.00.

42 R2 #4741-$200.00; #4683-$300.00.

42 R3 #4288-$300.00; #3390-$90.00.

43 R1 #3-$200.00.

43 R2 #4-$200.00; #5-$165.00; $170.00.

43 R3 #1-$275.00.

43 R4 #1-$200.00; #4-$160.00.

44 R1 #93-$200.00; #500-$160.00.

44 R2 #10-$175.00; #506-$200.00.

44 R3 #98-$300.00.

44 R4 #16-$350.00; #8-$210.00.

45 R1 #1-$320.00; #3-$330.00.

45 R2 #207-$350.00; #202-$325.00.

45 R3 #99-$375.00; #208-$375.00.

46 R1 #5-$325.00; #53-$335.00.

46 R2 #2-$325.00; #4-$300.00.

46 R3 #57-$325.00; #54-$295.00.

47 R1 #123-$300.00; #200-$325.00.

47 R2 #199-$275.00.

47 R3 #214-$325.00; #201-$375.00.

48 R1 #4-$335.00; #5-$250.00.

48 R2 #24-$285.00; #15-$260.00.

48 R3 #13-$85.00; #37-$400.00; chair-$110.00.

48 R4 $135.00; $250.00; $115.00.

49 R1 #506-$220.00; #888-$245.00.

49 R2 #746-$220.00; #747-$245.00.

49 R3 #897-$165.00; #794-$150.00.

50 R1 #4885-$240.00.

50 R2 #4875-$220.00.

50 R3 #4874-$240.00.

51 R1 #400 suit-$900.00.

51 R2 #190-$190.00; #128-$185.00; #200-$220.00; #109 1/2-$225.00; #140-$245.00.

51 R3 #95 suit-$500.00.

52 R1 $400.00; $200.00; $210.00.
52 R2 $350.00; $140.00; $140.00.
52 R3 #14-$65.00; #17-$65.00; Sofa-$250.00.
52 R4 #11-$150.00; #13-$160.00; #21-$135.00; #23-$155.00.
53 R1 #10-$400.00; "Lincoln" lounge-$375.00; #21 -$300.00.
53 R2 #54-$90.00; #5-$150.00; #6-$95.00.
53 R3 #55-$100.00; #3-$100.00; #29-$135.00.
54 R1 #169-$300.00; #102-$275.00.
54 R2 $55.00; $65.00; $55.00; $65.00.
54 R3 $60.00; $55.00; $60.00; $60.00.
54 R4 #84-$300.00; #56-$145.00; #49-$190.00.
55 R1 #66-$150.00; #63 1/2-$130.00.
55 R2 #67-$145.00; #68 1/2-$165.00; #68-$145.00. 55 R3 #9-$110.00; #2-$95.00; #3-$110.00.
56 R1 #153-$70.00; #164-$70.00; #46-$65.00; #71-$95.00; #153-$75.00.
56 R2 $120.00; #61-$140.00; #164-$110.00.
56 R3 #167-$195.00; #143-$200.00; #146A-$110.00; #146-$185.00.
56 R4 #167-$150.00; #143-$130.00; #152-$160.00.
56 R5 #167-$110.00; #151-$165.00; #143A-$165.00.
56 R6 #62-$195.00; #1, S-$225.00; #148-$170.00.
57 R1 #90-$165.00; #9-$155.00; #68-$160.00; #69-$170.00.
57 R2 #185-$165.00; #194-$165.00; #20-$160.00; #91 -$160.00.
57 R3 #87-$250.00; #67-$175.00; #191-$190.00.
57 R4 #8-$460.00; #1-$400.00; G-$135.00; E-$155.00.
58 R1 #45-$140.00; #44-$210.00; #42-$185.00; #38-$220.00.
58 R2 #34-$220.00; T-$120.00; #46-$185.00; K-$110.00; #33-$220.00.
58 R3 #'s 1, 89, 15, 38, & 81-$90.00; #'s 84, 87, & 88-$90.00; I-$120.00; #6-$75.00; #3-$75.00; #4-$50.00.
58 R4 #'s 4, 3, & 1-$60.00; #2-$55.00; #9-$90.00. 58 R5 O-$75.00; R-$120.00; M-$75.00; #5-$65.00; #8-$55.00; #'s 7 & 81-$50.00; #1776-$65.00.
59 R1 #70 1/2-$1600.00; #70-$1800.00.
59 R2 #96 left-$350.00; #96 right-$250.00.
60 R1 #112-$300.00; #98-$300.00; #97-$310.00.
60 R2 #75-$300.00; #76-$300.00; #78-$320.00.
60 R3 #114-$235.00; #96-$220.00.
61 R1 #95-$230.00.
61 R2 #78-$350.00; #81-$395.00.
61 R3 #90-$330.00; #79-$320.00.
61 R4 #93-$330.00; #94-$350.00.
62 R1 #67 1/2 Top set-$1600.00.
62 R2 #67 Bottom set-$2000.00.
63 R1 #533-$400.00.
63 R2 #49-$300.00.

63 R3 #347 1/2-$950.00; #218-$300.00.
64 R1 #83-$400.00; #84-$450.00.
64 R2 #85-$410.00; #86-$475.00.
64 R3 #88-$450.00; #89-$475.00.
64 R4 #87-$475.00; Right-$450.00.
65 R1 #51-$100.00; #86-$125.00.
65 R2 #50-$110.00; #55-$125.00; #4-$110.00.
65 R3 #57-$135.00; #47-$110.00; Chair-$75.00.
65 R4 #39-$200.00; #23 1/2-$110.00; #62-$85.00.
65 R5 #59-$45.00; #64-$60.00; #25-$65.00; #51 -$75.00.
65 R6 #'s 1 & 2-$65.00; #3-$75.00; #46-$80.00.
66 R1 #50 1/2-$125.00; #95-$1200.00.
66 R2 #47-$125.00; #26-$125.00; #80-$900.00.
66 R3 #106-$1000.00; #43-$250.00.
66 R4 #91-$2000.00; #48-$350.00.
67 R1 #954-$95.00; #953-$110.00; #930-$110.00; #894-$110.00.
67 R2 #7674-$135.00; #999-$200.00; #971-$145.00; #970-$175.00.
67 R3 #969-$110.00; #972-$120.00; #998-$125.00; #990-$145.00.
68 R1 #887-$200.00; #836-$100.00; #700-$100.00; #702-$120.00.
68 R2 #810-$175.00; #831-$225.00; #714-$35.00; #708-$35.00; #704-$30.00.
68 R3 #755-$400.00; #706-$65.00; #835-$80.00; #814 1/2-$55.00.
69 R1 #147-$250.00; #117-$250.00; #146-$145.00. 69 R2 #48-$240.00; #62-$260.00.
69 R3 #143-$175.00; #114-$310.00; #15-$110.00.
70 R1 #109-$200.00; #116-$125.00.
70 R2 # 113-$145.00; #102-$120.00; #110-$95.00; Table on right-$85.00.
70 R3 #18-$220.00; #9-$180.00; #8-$210.00; #5-$230.00; #7-$230.00.
71 R1 #22 1/2-$310.00; #65-$145.00.
71 R2 #144 1/2-$175.00; #56-$250.00; #42-$145.00. 71 R3 #95 1/2-$160.00; #162-$175.00; #111-$65.00. 72 R1 #41-$65.00; #112-$95.00; #24-$65.00; #21-$65.00; #139-$135.00.
72 R2 #172-$140.00; #25-$165.00; #144-$135.00.
72 R3 #133-$230.00; #150-$225.00.
73 R1 #26-$195.00; #85 1/2-$950.00; #166-$135.00. 73 R2 #39-$150.00; #30-$90.00; #27-$95.00.
73 R3 #91-$500.00; #85 1/2-$1250.00; #86-$1000.00.
74 R1 #46-$95.00; #142-$120.00; #54-$95.00.
74 R2 #15-$120.00; #75-$90.00; #100-$120.00.
74 R3 #140-$110.00; #151-$110.00; #14-$95.00.
75 R1 #62-$250.00; #43-$110.00; #48-$120.00.
74 R2 #57-$120.00; #139-$100.00; #153-$90.00.
75 R3 #59-$95.00; #28-$90.00; #152-$80.00.
76 R1 #102-$310.00; #61-$310.00; #70-$290.00.

76 R2 #82-$335.00; #33-$320.00; #31-$340.00.
76 R3 #101-$220.00; #106-$300.00; #113-$300.00.
77 R1 #289-$60.00; #'s 288, 287, & 286-$60.00; #285-$55.00; #284-$50.00; #283-$50.00.
77 R2 #'s 282, 281, & 280-$48.00; #229-$55.00; #228-$50.00; #227-$65.00.
77 R3 #226-$60.00; #225-$50.00; #239 1/2-$50.00; #238-$50.00; #237-$50.00; #236-$65.00.
77 R4 #235-$75.00; #'s 219 & 218-$60.00; #'s 217 & 216-$55.00; #215-$60.00.
77 R5 #'s 209 & 208-$60.00; #207-$70.00; #206-$90.00; #205-$80.00; #'s 169 & 168-$80.00; #167-$80.00.
77 R6 #166-$85.00; #165-$95.00; #179-$85.00; #178-$80.00; #177-$90.00; #176-$95.00; #175-$95.00.
78 R1 #104-$335.00; #'s108-$365.00.
78 R2 #110-$300.00; #111-$295.00.
78 R3 #20-$125.00; #61-$145.00; #62-$155.00; #64-$135.00.
79 R1 #102-$55.00; #104-$65.00; #113-$55.00.
79 R2 #114-$55.00; #117-$55.00; #115-$55.00.
79 R3 #109-$55.00; #110-$65.00; #112-$65.00.
79 R4 #80-$95.00; #82-$95.00.
80 R1 #55-$100.00; #48-$165.00.
80 R2 Armchair-$125.00; Chair-$95.00.
80 R3 #162-$250.00; Side chair-$95.00; Fancy chair-$90.00.
81 R1 #9-$250.00; #8-$225.00.
81 R2 #5-$295.00; #7-$295.00.
81 R3 #1-$90.00; #2-$100.00; 3rd table-$120.00; Last table-$80.00.

Bedroom Furniture and Sets

83 R1 #117 1/2-$2000.00.
84 R1 #1-$150.00; #2-$300.00; #3-$550.00.
84 R2 #1-$150.00; #4-$900.00.
85 R1 #'s 54, 55, & 60-$245.00; #'s 54, 55, & 60-$375.00; #'s 67 & 68-$285.00.
85 R2 #73-$750.00; #74-$850.00.
86 R1 #58-$1200.00; #50-$1250.00; #59-$1150.00.
86 R2 #66-$1100.00; #53-$1100.00; #52-$1200.00.
87 R2 #104 Closed and open-$260.00.
88 R1 #16-$800.00.
88 R2 #11 Closed and open-$350.00.
88 R3 #16-$850.00.
89 R1 #14 Closed and open-$875.00.
89 R2 #7 Closed and open-$350.00.
90 R1 #102-$460.00; #17-$360.00
90 R2 #9 Closed and open-$350.00.
91 R1 #211-$250.00; #460-$350.00; #499 1/2-$250.00; #496-$265.00.

91 R2 #459-$350.00; #487 1/2-$320.00; #447 1/2-$300.00; #116-$270.00.
91 R3 #24-$410.00; #489-$310.00; #486-$300.00; #446 1/2-$365.00.
92 R1 #999-$400.00; #996-$360.00; #968-$400.00; #980-$325.00; #969-$400.00.
92 R2 #972-$475.00; #964-$460.00; #973-$430.00; #197-$220.00; #196-$230.00.
92 R3 #236-$1000.00; #255-$12000.00.
93 R1 #238-$900.00; #238 1/2-$850.00.
93 R2 #248-$900.00; #165-$500.00.
94 R1 #76-$850.00.
94 R2 #73-$950.00.
94 R3 #69-$1050.00.
95 R1 #104-$325.00; #105-$375.00; #103-$300.00.
95 R2 #45-$400.00; #50-$400.00.
96 R1 #73-$750.00; #30-$600.00.
96 R2 #70-$700.00; #74-$750.00.
97 R1 #72-$675.00.
97 R2 #122-$850.00; #164-$400.00.
98 R1 #932-$250.00; #932 & 900-$550.00; #900-$2500.; #899 Left-$400; Right-$260.00.
98 R2 #898 Left-$275.00; Right-$320.00; #898 1/2 Left-$310.00; Right-$400.00.
98 R3 #897 Left-$300.00; Right-$350.00; #376 Left-$325.00; Right-$295.00.
99 R1 Left to right-$900.00; $950.00; $950.00.
99 R2 #56-$900.00; #61-$900.00; #63-$875.00.
100 R1 #52 1/2-Bed and dresser-$1400.00.
100 R2 #52 1/2-Bottom pair-$1800.00.
101 R1 #53 1/2-Bed and dresser-$1400.00.
101 R2 #53 1/2-Bottom pair-$1800.00.
102 R1 #56 1/2-Bed and dresser-$2000.00.
102 R2 #56 1/2-Bottom pair-$1800.00.
103 R1 #66 Bed and dresser-$1400.00.
103 R2 #59 Bed and dresser-$1500.00.
104 R1 #67 Bed and dresser-$1300.00.
104 R2 #68 Bed and dresser-$1100.00.
105 R1 #550-$500.00; #550-$425.00; #549-$400.00; #547-$425.00; #550-$300.00.
105 R2 #520-$400.00; #520-$375.00; #519-$350.00; #546-$365.00; #520-$295.00.
105 R3 #545 Left-$525.00; Right-$600.00; #500 Left-$500.00; Right-$465.00; #500-$325.00.
106 R1 #815-$500.00; #822-$450.00; #714-$375.00; #86-$475.00.
106 R2 #788-$325.00; #789 1/2-$280.00; #794-$240.00; #794 1/2-$240.00.
106 R3 #700-$300.00; #800-$320.00; #793-$300.00; #793 1/2-$300.00; #791 1/2-$310.00.
107 R1 #38-$55.00; #49-$75.00; #65-$65.00.
107 R2 #65-$90.00; #37-$110.00.
107 R3 #65-$65.00; #84-$55.00.

Brass, Iron and Folding Beds

111 R1 #4003-$1700.00.
111 R2 #4032-$950.00.
111 R3 #4102-$1100.00.
111 R4 #4100-$1075.00.
112 R1 #4054-$400.00; #4038-$420.00.
112 R2 #4066-$350.00.
112 R3 #4064-$350.00; #4034-$340.00.
112 R4 #4114-$350.00.
113 R1 Left bed-$575.00; #100-$575.00.
113 R2 Left bed-$250.00; #103-$325.00.
113 R3 Left bed-$550.00; Right bed-$600.00.
114 R1 Left bed-$500.00; Right bed-$700.00.
114 R2 #100-$1100.00; Top bed-$850.00; Bottom bed-$650.00.
115 R1 #407-$700.00; #409-$800.00.
115 R2 #10-$300.00; #5-$280.00.
116 R1 #62 Closed and open-$250.00.
116 R2 #63 Closed and open-$225.00.
116 R3 #14-$650.00; #15-$300.00.
117 R1 A-$110.00; #3 1/2-$145.00.
117 R2 #2-$300.00; C-$225.00.
117 R3 #111-$250.00; #109 1/2-$420.00.
117 R4 #429-$420.00; #123-$500.00.
118 R1 #217-$400.00; #253-$325.00; #121 - $500.00.
118 R2 #58-$500.00; #481-$325.00; #80- $450.00.
118 R3 #143-$500.00; #483-$300.00; #71- $500.00.
119 R1 #18 Closed and open-$600.00.
119 R2 #23 Closed and open-$550.00.
119 R3 #24 Open and closed-$500.00.
120 R1 #20 Open and closed-$700.00.
120 R2 #14 Closed and open-$800.00.
120 R3 #12 Open and closed-$900.00.
121 R1 #7-$400.00.
121 R2 #15-$600.00; #25-$575.00; #26-$475.00.
121 R3 #20-$500.00; #30-$500.00; #13-$475.00.
122 R1 A Closed and open-$400.00; B Closed and open-$300.00.
122 R2 Mantel bed, closed and open-$195.00; Children's folding beds, closed and open- $155.00.
122 R3 The Fulton, closed and open-$145.00; Manhattan, closed and open-$175.00.
123 R1 #5 Closed and open-$220.00; New York, Closed and open-$170.00.
123 R2 #2 Closed and open-$700.00; Portier, closed and open-$165.00; Excelsior, closed and open-$145.00.
124 R1 Wire cot-$45.00; Canvas cot-$55.00.
124 R2 Self adjustable-$60.00; Common square- $60.00; Flexible hoop-$50.00; Turn over- $55.00.

125 R1 Left top-$45.00; Bottom-$60.00; Right top-$40.00; Center-$50.00; Bottom-$60.00.
125 R2 #1-$50.00; #2-$50.00; Right, woven wire cot-$45.00; #9-$45.00.
126 R1 Left, Ladd cot-$40.00; #2-$40.00; Old fashioned cot-$42.00; Right, #6-$40.00; Canvas cot-$40.00; Oriental cots-$40.00.
126 R2 Right, wire mattress-$40.00; Steel spring-$35.00.
127 R1 #1-$40.00.
127 R2 #2-$45.00.
127 R3 United States cot-$40.00.
127 R4 Braided wire cot-$38.00.
128 R1 $45.00.
128 R2 $60.00.
128 R3 $45.00.
129 R1 $30.00.
129 R2 $30.00.
129 R3 #84-$30.00.
129 R4 $20.00.
130 R1 #304-$500.00; #311-$600.00.

Diningroom Furniture

131 R1 #51 -$600.00; #49-$675.00.
132 R1 $1000.00.
133 R1 #174-$800.00; #170-$700.00.
133 R2 #160-$1000.00; #175-$950.00.
133 R3 #187-$650.00; #141-$575.00.
134 R1 #12-$950.00; #4-$1350.00.
134 R2 #3 1/2-$1100.00; #11-$1050.00.
135 R1 #14-$1000.00; #9-$1000.00.
135 R2 #7-$1100.00; #13-$1050.00.
136 R1 #162-$900.00; #158-$900.00.
136 R2 #161-$900.00; #157-$850.00.
137 R1 #1-$900.00; #6-$800.00.
137 R2 Left-$1100.00; Right-$1050.00.
138 R1 #12-$1200.00; #4-$1650.00.
138 R2 Left-$1100.00; Right-$1100.00.
139 R1 #10-$550.00; #12-$560.00.
139 R2 #23-$400.00; #25-$525.00.
140 R1 #345-$500.00; #597-$475.00; #600- $500.00; #526-$545.00; #599-$400.00.
140 R2 #323-$475.00; #318-$500.00; #325- $340.00; #296-$190.00.
140 R3 #295-$300.00; #989-$400.00; #992- $350.00.
141 R1 #843-$425.00; #840-$550.00; #830- $410.00; #811 -$450.00; #832-$395.00.
141 R2 #829-$510.00; #846-$500.00; #835- $575.00; #850-$535.00; #827-$525.00.
141 R3 #822-$560.00; #598-$500.00; #837- $575.00; #347-$500.00; #828-$500.00.
142 R1 128 1/2-$475.00.
142 R2 #34-$600.00; #107-$500.00.
142 R3 #125-$350.00; #131-$375.00.
143 R1 #36-$425.00; #124-$350.00.

143 R2 #109-$225.00; #16-$165.00.
143 R3 #201-$310.00; #200-$320.00.
144 R1 #202-$365.00; #203-$365.00.
144 R2 #7-$345.00; #105-$215.00.
144 R3 #157-$85.00; #70-$250.00.
145 R1 #117-$550.00; #114-$400.00.
145 R2 #134-$450.00; #102-$500.00.
145 R3 #113-$500.00; #135-$525.00.
146 R1 #993-$390.00; #985-$475.00.
146 R2 #977-$450.00; #975-$560.00.
146 R3 #956-$450.00; #947-$500.00.
147 R1 #665-$350.00; #667-$250.00.
147 R2 #672-$275.00; #699 1/2-$320.00.
147 R3 #721-$250.00; #721 1/2-$235.00.
148 R1 #660-$500.00; #659 1/2-$435.00.
148 R2 #658-$400.00; #652 1/2-$450.00.
148 R3 #730 1/2-$400.00; #655 1/2-$450.00.
149 R1 #9 1/2-$50.00; #4-$50.00; #4 1/2-
$50.00.
149 R2 #1-$45.00; #8-$45.00; #9-$45.00.
150 R1 #167-$70.00; #152-$80.00; #166-$90.00.
150 R2 #159-$75.00; #165-$105.00; #153-
$110.00.
150 R3 #124-$70.00; #125-$75.00; #128-$75.00;
#99-$80.00.
151 R1 #16-$45.00; #32-$50.00; #42-$65.00.
151 R2 #57-$70.00; #65-$45.00; #66-$55.00.
151 R3 #112-$65.00; #123-$65.00; #162-$55.00;
#164-$55.00.
152 R1 #21-$90.00; #23-$85.00; #22-$100.00;
#59-$80.00.
152 R2 #233-$90.00; #191-$85.00; #189-$85.00;
#275-$85.00.
152 R3 #7-$80.00; #71-$70.00; $60.00; $60.00.
153 R1 Left to right-$55.00; $55.00; $65.00;
$55.00; $70.00; $70.00.
153 R2 Left to right-$70.00; $65.00; $65.00;
$55.00; $65.00; $55.00.
153 R3 Left to right-$50.00; $55.00; $50.00;
$65.00; $60.00; $70.00.
154 R1 #13-$40.00; #13A-$55.00; #15-$70.00;
#15A-$75.00.
154 R2 #17-$55.00; #17A-$90.00; #18-$100.00;
#18A-$110.00.
154 R3 #19-$55.00; #19A-$100.00; #10-
$115.00; #10A-$175.00.

Desks and Office Furniture

158 R1 #2251-$6000.00; #2205-$300.00.
158 R2 #2245-$5000.00.
158 R3 #2241-$4500.00; #2207-$200.00.
159 R1 #1008-$1200.00; Rostrum A-$1000.00.
159 R2 #2244-$1500.00.
159 R3 #2242-$3000.00.
160 R1 #70 Open and closed-$1100.00.

160 R2 #83-$600.00; #81-$800.00.
161 R1 #852 Closed and open-$1200.00.
161 R2 #4446-$600.00.
161 R3 #872 Open and closed-$2500.00.
162 R1 #870 Open and closed-$1550.00.
162 R2 #871 Closed and open-$1750.00.
162 R3 #835 Open and closed-$2600.00.
163 R1 #734-$600.00; #737-$600.00.
163 R2 #735-$500.00; #99-$480.00.
163 R3 #40-$475.00; #738-$500.00.
164 R1 #730-$450.00; #731-$475.00.
164 R2 #733-$500.00; #861-$1050.00.
164 R3 #818-$825.00; #732-$675.00.
165 R1 #834-$2600.00; #606A-$2600.00. 165
R2 #600A Open and closed-$2200.00. 166 R1
#4-$1600.00.
166 R2 Left-$1800.00; Right, #'s 1, 2, & 2 1/2-
$1800.
167 R1 #124-$400.00; #128-$400.00.
167 R2 #125-$500.00; #127-$600.00.
167 R3 #221-$1100.00; #222-$1250.00. 168 R1
#154-$450.00; #198-$1300.00.
168 R2 #217-$220.00.
168 R3 #201-$1200.00; #218-$350.00; #142-
$410.00.
169 R1 Left-$1100.00; #226-$1100.00.
169 R2 #155-$1250.00; #225-$900.00.
169 R3 #156-$400.00; #158-$375.00.
170 R1 #194-$600.00; #121-$400.00.
170 R2 #120-$250.00; #123-$375.00.
170 R3 #122-$325.00; #192-$600.00.
171 R1 #175-$725.00; #168-$600.00.
171 R2 #162-$575.00; #196-$1100.00.
171 R3 #164-$575.00; #197-$1100.00.
172 R1 #170-$550.00; #172-$800.00.
172 R2 #176-$650.00; #178-$1100.00.
173 R1 #189-$300.00; #190-$500.00.
173 R2 #191-$500.00; #180-$625.00.
174 R1 #330—Class C left-$1100.00; Right-
$1600.00.
174 R2 #330—Class C left-$500.00; Right-
$600.00.
174 R3 Class A—left-$2000.00; Right-$600.00.
175 R1 #15-$1600.00; #15 S.A.-$1700.00.
175 R2 #2-$400.00; #11-$700.00.
175 R3 #3-$500.00; #13-$1100.00.
176 R1 $300.00.
176 R2 $300.00.
176 R3 Left to right-$400.00; $400.00; $425.00.
176 R4 $400.00; $400.00.
177 R1 #914-$1000.00; #25-$1800.00; #13-
$1800.00.
177 R2 #912-$1000.00; #125-$2500.00; #11-
$2600.00.
177 R3 #911-$1300.00; #20-$2400.00; #8-
$2800.00.
178 R1 Left—top-$550.00; Bottom-$550.00;
Right—#4-$600.00.

178 R2 Students case-$450.00; Book rest-
$60.00.
179 R1 #1-$145.00; #4-$125.00.
179 R2 Star case-$400.00; Cottage case-
$400.00.
180 R1 Buckeye case-$350.00.
180 R2 Music case-$375.00; #4-$400.00. 180 R3
#2-$400.00; Print shelf-$350.00. 181 R1
Parlor case-$450.00; #1-$550.00; #2-
$500.00.
181 R2 #101A-$250.00; #102B-$300.00; #103C-
$425.00.
182 R1 #112-$400.00.
182 R2 #114-$200.00; #1-$125.00.
182 R3 #281-$400.00; #280-$425.00.
183 R1 #2 & 7-$175.00; #1 & 3-$150.00.
183 R2 #6-$135.00.
183 R3 #14 & 15-$300.00.
183 R4 #18, 19, & 20-$400.00.
183 R5 #24-$275.00; #8 & 9-$250.00.
184 R1 #16 & 17-$400.00; #2 Open and closed-
$35.00.
184 R2 #4 & 5-$275.00; #3 Open and closed-
$35.00; #4 Open and closed-$46.00.
184 R3 #2-$45.00; #1-$30.00.
184 R4 #XX-$30.00.
184 R5 #3A-$85.00.
185 R1 #6N-$200.00; #4U-$300.00; #4T-
$335.00.
185 R2 #1-$200.00; #3-$190.00; #2-$195.00.
185 R3 #4B-$95.00; #4D-$95.00.
185 R4 #5-$200.00; #4-$200.00; #6-$230.00.
186 R1 #701-$400.00; #10-$925.00; #604-
$350.00.
186 R2 #700A-$300.00; Seth Thomas Queen
Anne-$700.00.
187 R1 #777-$800.00; #24-$600.00; #6-$310.00.
187 R2 #605-$200.00; #16-$400.00; #778-
$400.00.
188 R1 #12-$450.00; $450.00; $540.00.
188 R2 #115 -$50.00; #156-$50.00.
188 R3 $50.00; $25.00; $50.00.
188 R4 $85.00 each section; $100.00 each
section.
189 R1 #10A-$55.00; #10B-$50.00; #10C-
$50.00.
189 R2 #3-$45.00; #14-$65.00.
189 R3 #177-$90.00; #175-$145.00; #141-
$70.00.
190 R1 #548-$75.00; #251-$65.00; #58-$55.00;
#33-$55.00.
190 R2 #250-$125.00; #60-$95.00; #544-$90.00;
#547-$110.00.
191 R1 #8-$25.00; #9-$25.00.
191 R2 #134-$200.00; #401-$185.00; #579A-
$90.00.
191 R3 #261-$95.00; #134L-$210.00.
192 R1 #235-$135.00; #143-$75.00; #236-
$180.00.

192 R2 #555-$110.00; #61-$90.00; #55-$140.00.
193 R1 #308-$200.00; #309-$150.00; #8-
$180.00.
193 R2 #241-$200.00; #392-$200.00; #280-
$260.00.
194 R1 #228-$210.00; #227-$245.00; #229A-
$265.00.
194 R2 #306-$265.00; #25-$265.00.
195 R1 #24-$220.00; #28-$250.00.
195 R2 #29-$200.00; #26-$240.00.
196 R1 #778-$90.00; #778R-$110.00; #0615R-
$110.00; #0614R-$110.00; #0544R-$210.00.
196 R2 #547-$50.00; #0719-$80.00; #0719R-
$90.00; #928C-$85.00; #928R-$90.00.
196 R3 #0614-$80.00; #7675C-$100.00;
#7675R-$110.00; #926C-$110.00; #926R-
$135.00.
197 R1 #4019-$50.00; #4045R-$40.00; #654R-
$150.00; #7654C-$150.00.
197 R2 #980-$65.00; #978-$65.00; #970-
$65.00;#960-$60.00; #0701R-$110.00.
197 R3 #886-$90.00; #415-$65.00; #415R-
$120.00; #4385-$110.00; #4385R-$120.00.
198 R1 #147-$95.00; #34-$100.00; #36-$95.00.
198 R2 #143-$45.00; #140-$55.00; #1776-
$110.00; #28-$100.00.
198 R3 #30-$100.00; #14-$110.00; #37-$110.00.
199 R1 #106-$65.00; #170-$70.00; #171-
$80.00. 199 R2 #111-$90.00; #110 1/2-
$80.00.
199 R3 #144-$65.00; #145-$65.00; #141-$60.00.
200 R1 #107-$110.00; #132-$135.00; #200-
$150.00.
200 R2 #143-$70.00; #142-$70.00.
200 R3 #49-$110.00; #133-$100.00; #108-
$140.00. 201 R1 $150.00; $160.00.
201 R2 #73-$95.00; #228-$60.00; #39-$65.00;
#19-$95.00.
201 R3 #1-$160.00; #2-$160.00.
202 R1 #1-$50.00; #2-$75.00; #3-$85.00;
$170.00.
202 R2 $125.00; $125.00; $125.00.
202 R3 #2-$100.00; #11-$225.00.
202 R4 $75.00; #1-$225.00; #11-$225.00; #3-
$245.00.
203 R1 #1-$180.00; #2-$190.00; #3-$200.00.
203 R2 #4-$190.00; #5-$175.00; #6-$175.00.
203 R3 #7-$190.00; #8-$180.00; #9-$170.00.

THE WOOTON DESK CO.

Wooton desks range in price from $5,500 to
$25,000 depending upon size, grade, decorative
elements, and condition.

Each desk is so individual that ones which
look the same could vary as much as $5,000. For
a current expert opinion, please write to the
author in care of the publisher with photos, size,
and self-addressed, stamped envelope. We will
estimate the value at no cost.

Child's Furniture

212 From top to bottom; $400.00 each item.
213 R1 #40-$60.00; #92-$70.00; #295-$400.00; #295-$400.00.
213 R2 #296-$375.00; #38-$160.00; #80-$100.00; #193-$145.00.
213 R3 #296-$400.00; #92W-$65.00; #88-$95.00; #98-$160.00.
214 R1 #91-$135.00; #99-$130.00; #91W-$130.00.
214 R2 #97-$65.00; #24-$65.00; #23-$65.00.
214 R3 #7 1-2-$65.00.
214 R4 #81-2-$60.00; #3-$85.00; #3-$85.00.
215 R1 #0449-$145.00; #0481-$160.00; #957-$155.00; #955-$165.00; #362-$185.00; #932-$185.00.
215 R2 #372-$450.00; #383-$450.00; #398-$490.00; #401-$490.00.
215 R3 #405-$550.00; #410-$550.00; #416-$550.00; #440-$565.00.
216 R1 $145.00; $145.00.
216 R2 $115.00; $115.00.
216 R3 $145.00; #91-$95.00; #41-$145.00.
217 R1 #'s 1,2,&3-$95.00.
217 R2 $95.00.
218 R1 #1-$120.00; #6-$120.00.
218 R2 #79-$120.00; #31-$120.00.
218 R3 #82-$275.00.
219 R1 $175.00; #25-$220.00.
219 R2 #400-$220.00; #26-$190.00.
220 R1 #11-$450.00; #23-$425.00.
220 R2 #20-$250.00; #40-$250.00.
221 R1 $90.00.
221 R2 #6-$45.00; #63-$45.00; #2-$45.00.
221 R3 #5B-$50.00; #102-$50.00; $125.00.
222 R1 #19-$200.00; #17-$210.00.
222 R2 #6-$210.00; #5-$220.00.
223 R1 #31-$500.00; #40-$500.00.
223 R2 #3-$500.00; #19-$650.00.
224 R1 #600-$160.00; #601-$170.00.
224 R2 #52-$175.00.

Invalid's Chairs and Supplies

225 R1 #24-$185.00.
226 R1 #70-$165.00.
226 R2 #73-$165.00; #71-$175.00.
226 R3 $25.00 each item.
227 R1 #84-$220.00; #8-$140.00.
227 R2 #79-$125.00; #81-$145.00.
228 R1 #50-$165.00; #51-$145.00.
228 R2 #74-$210.00; #75-$190.00
229 R1 #12-$85.00; #13-$300.00.

229 R2 #11-$300.00; #5-$350.00; #11-$350.00.
230 R1 $150.00; $150.00; #3-$170.00.
230 R2 #2-$165.00; #1-$145.00.
230 R3 #4-$95.00.

Rocking Chairs

231 R1 #840-$125.00; #850-$135.00; #826-$120.00; #822-$110.00.
231 R2 #192-$200.00; #190-$165.00; #24-$160.00.
232 R1 #121C-$185.00; $160.00; #121R.S.P.-$155.00.
232 R2 #155-$95.00; #115C-$105.00; #156-$110.00.
232 R3 #116-$100.00; #105-$105.00; #42-$100.00.
233 R1 #128-$105.00; #120-$95.00.
233 R2 #71-$150.00; #80-$125.00; #104 1/2-$85.00.
233 R3 #26-$130.00; #103 1/2-$75.00.
233 R4 #188-$100.00; #24 1/2-$120.00; #88-$115.00.
234 R1 #108-$80.00; #45-$80.00; #5 1/2-$95.00.
234 R2 #35-$125.00; #29-$115.00; #47-$100.00.
234 R3 #53-$85.00; #21 1/2-$95.00; #208-$90.00.
235 R1 #46B-$85.00; #40B-$95.00; #115-$90.00; #122-$95.00.
235 R2 #4-$65.00; #265-$65.00; #128-$90.00; #250-$65.00.
235 R3 #72-$110.00; #8-$80.00; #19 1/2-$120.00; #136-$130.00.
236 R1 #25-$190.00; #45-$210.00.
236 R2 #20-$210.00.
236 R3 #35-$220.00; #50-$200.00.
237 R1 #168-$95.00; $85.00; #142-$70.00.
237 R2 #300-$75.00.
237 R3 #8-$145.00; #9-$95.00; #8-$110.00.
238 R1 #173-$140.00; #10-$110.00; #164-$130.00.
238 R2 #183A-$150.00; #155-$160.00; #184B-$135.00.
239 R1 #33-$75.00; #89-$145.00; #43-$85.00; #44-$75.00.
239 R2 #34 1/2-$110.00; #4-$115.00; $110.00.
239 R3 #111-$65.00; #110-$85.00; #6-$115.00; #80-$115.00.
240 R1 725-$175.00; #723-$175.00; #789-$175.00; #784-$170.00.
240 R2 #752-$200.00; #791-$190.00; #727-$210.00; #727 1/2-$200.00.
240 R3 #753-$210.00; #797-$225.00; #788-$245.00; #809-$200.00.
241 R1 #789C-$165.00; #437-$185.00; #435-$220.00; #459-$190.00.
241 R2 #454-$200.00; #278-$165.00; #390-$135.00; #391-$165.00.

241 R3 #725 1/2-$155.00; #723 1/2-$165.00; #752-$175.00; #797 1/2-$200.00.

242 R1 #0174-$165.00; #7562-$140.00; #7562A-$100.00; #7724-$130.00; #7432-$170.00.

242 R2 #7429-$190.00; #0755-$170.00; #0756-$120.00; #890-$155.00; #891-$190.00.

242 R3 #889-$200.00; #7464-$210.00; #7566-$220.00; #7398-$230.00; #7611-$220.00.

243 R1 #871-$150.00; #873-$165.00; #875-$190.00; #881-$210.00.

243 R2 #883-$200.00; #863-$120.00; #865-$120.00; #802-$110.00.

243 R3 #834-$70.00; #838-$95.00; #846-$100.00; #894-$85.00.

244 R1 #23-$230.00; #14-$260.00; #22-$240.00.

244 R2 #28-$275.00; #27-$265.00; #24-$275.00.

245 R1 E-$125.00; G-$115.00; #81-$250.00; #82-$275.00.

245 R2 R-$200.00; N-$180.00; #70-$290.00; #71-$280.00.

246 R2 #88-$85.00; $95.00.

Folding Chairs

248 R1 #78C-$110.00; #131-$120.00.

248 R2 #300 & 301-$75.00; $65.00; $60.00; $25.00.

248 R3 #300 & 301-$65.00; #9-$60.00; #300 & 301-$65.00; #250-$50.00.

249 R1 $25.00 each.

249 R2 #142-$60.00; #110-$70.00; #43-$60.00.

249 R3 #88-$75.00; #85C-$75.00; #140-$75.00.

250 R1 #85-$90.00; #86B-$80.00; #61-$75.00.

250 R2 #1 1/2-$30.00; #1-$20.00; #60-$30.00.

250 R3 #17-$25.00; #15-$35.00; #16-$35.00.

251 R1 #57-$100.00.

251 R2 #125-$145.00; #58-$165.00.

251 R3 #167-$100.00; #134-$95.00; #124-$100.00. 252 R1 #166-$125.00; #136-$135.00; #5-$85.00. 252 R2 #144-$75.00; #4-$60.00; #147-$165.00.

253 R1 #143-$110.00; #116-$130.00; #116A-$145.00.

253 R2 #105-$100.00.

253 R3 #105A-$90.00; #116A-$110.00; #117-$100.00.

254 R1 #91-$130.00; #94-$60.00; #104A-$65.00. 254 R2 #128-$95.00.

254 R3 #107A-$95.00; #78-$100.00; #129-$90.00. 255 R1 #130-$70.00; #1-$25.00.

255 R2 #105-$80.00; #2-$25.00.

255 R3 #33-$45.00; #32-$65.00; #3-$35.00.

256 R1 #0B-$60.00; #126A-$60.00.

256 R2 #131-$95.00; #126-$50.00.

Hall Trees, Mirrors and Mantles

258 R1 #327-$300.00; #314-$260.00; #809-$375.00; #325-$300.00; #333-$350.00.

258 R2 #376-$180.00; #420-$275.00.

258 R3 #334-$275.00; #330-$285.00.

258 R4 #373-$145.00; #318-$135.00.

258 R5 #312-$300.00; #309-$180.00; #494-$255.00; #817-$275.00.

259 R1 #414-$275.00; #466-$300.00; #491-$300.00; #490-$310.00; #419-$290.00; #422-$310.00.

259 R2 #7-$400.00; #60-$295.00; #64-$390.00.

259 R3 #201-$145.00.

260 R1 #3-$350.00; #5-$340.00; #67-$310.00.

260 R2 #1-$255.00; #2-$280.00; #6-$360.00.

261 R1 #27-$110.00; #25-$80.00; #26-$110.00.

261 R2 #160-$575.00; $165.00; #154-$285.00. 262 R1 #171-$550.00.

262 R2 #401-$250.00; #163-$240.00.

262 R3 #142-$85.00.

263 R1 #300-$350.00; $450.00; #151-$350.00.

263 R2 #169-$165.00.

264 R1 #162-$310.00; #170-$450.00; #152-$385.00.

264 R2 #3-$210.00.

265 R1 #167-$390.00; #165-$340.00.

265 R2 #206-$135.00.

266 R1 #201-$145.00.

266 R2 #153-$375.00; #51-$425.00.

266 R3 $475.00.

267 R1 $200.00.

267 R2 #160-$450.00; #155-$400.00.

268 R1 #262-$165.00.

268 R2 #156-$275.00; #'s 11 & 7-$290.00.

269 R1 #263-$165.00.

269 R2 #106-$275.00; #301-$290.00; #302-$295.00; #303-$295.00.

270 R1 #210-$165.00.

270 R2 #308-$250.00; #311-$225.00; #309-$290.00; #312-$240.00.

271 R1 #313-$275.00; #255-$175.00; #314-$260.00.

271 R2 #168-$320.00.

272 R1 $375.00.

272 R2 $350.00.

273 R1 #266-$400.00.

273 R2 #1-$40.00; #10-$120.00.

273 R3 #12-$120.00.

274 R1 #10-$95.00.

274 R2 #20-$105.00.

274 R3 #40-$85.00.

274 R4 #30-$95.00.

274 R5 #10-$75.00; #13-$80.00; #13-$85.00; #14-$90.00.

275 R1 #39-$85.00.
275 R2 #51-$95.00; $75.00.
275 R3 #40-$115.00; #52BB-$85.00; #28-$95.00; #22-$105.00.
276 R1 #56-$95.00; #34-$80.00.
276 R2 #13-$145.00; #1 1/2-$45.00.
276 R3 #14-$100.00; #3-$45.00.

Rattan and Outdoor Furniture

277 R1 #311-$160.00; #251-$190.00.
277 R2 #300-$220.00; #253-$210.00.
278 R1 #0896-$35.00; #0746-$45.00; #5649-$45.00; #5651-$50.00; #1222-$65.00; #152-$90.00.
278 R2 #1992-$210.00; #1008-$170.00; #1189-$220.00; #1003-$220.00; #1264-$190.00.
278 R3 #1001-$180.00; #1002-$275.00; #0804-$250.00; #1266-$300.00; #1268-$350.00.
278 R4 #1271-$395.00; #1275-$365.00; #0836-$350.00; #1277-$400.00.
279 R1 #140-$55.00; #142-$50.00; #404-$50.00; #402-$60.00; #146-$60.00; #240-$75.00.
279 R2 #242-$75.00; #338-$75.00; #256-$75.00; #352-$95.00; #150-$95.00; #450-$90.00.
279 R3 #86-$90.00; #360-$100.00; #380-$95.00; #400-$90-$90-$90.00; #70-$90.00.
279 R4 #88-$100.00; #348-$80.00; #368-$80.00; #388-$90.00; #46-$70.00; #72-$80.00.
279 R5 #382-$90.00; #248-$80.00; #266-$100.00; #250-$85.00; #270-$105.00; #487-$85.00.
280 R1 #286-$140.00; #436-$140.00; #466-$140.00; #486-$165.00; #440-$140.00; #470-$155.00.
280 R2 #606-$160.00; #408-$160.00; #508-$160.00; #426-$150.00; #444-$160.00; #474-$155.00.
280 R3 #620-$170.00; #432-$180.00; 462-$190.00; #482-$200.00; #424-$180.00; #524-$200.00.
280 R4 #1209-$75.00; #1210-$90.00; #1111-$90.00; #1112-$95.00; #1211-$80.00; #1212-$95.00.
280 R5 #1107-$155.00; #1108-$155.00; #1207-$165.00; #1208-$165.00; #1201-$175.00; #1203-$110.00.
281 R1 #1-$75.00; #2-$65.00; #7 1/2-$65.00; #118-$75.00; #125-$75.00; #117-$75.00; #119-$75.00; #126-$75.00; #120-$75.00; #205-$165.00.
281 R2 #140-$70.00; #142-$70.00; #144-$80.00; #146-$80.00; #138-$70.00; #150-$70.00.
281 R3 #45-$70.00; #46-$70.00;# 47-$60.00; #48-$60.00; #136-$60.00; #148-$70.00; #207-$150.00.

281 R4 #156-$100.00; #158-$100.00; #152-$90.00;
#154-$90.00; #77-$90.00; #78-$90.00.
281 R5 #166-$105.00; #168-$110.00; #172-$105.00; #174-$100.00; #70-$110.00; #80-$100.00; #201-$300.00.
281 R6 #8-$50.00; #20-$55.00; #12-$80.00; #29-$80.00; #122-$65.00; #127-$75.00; #18-$75.00; #25-$85.00; #16-$90.00; #23-$100.00.
282 R1 #238-$70.00; #256-$60.00; #242-$60.00; #248-$65.00; #250-$65.00; #270-$65.00.
282 R2 #252-$65.00; #254-$65.00; #202-$85.00; #265-$75.00; #266-$75.00.
282 R3 #271-$95.00; #272-$95.00; #281-$70.00; #282-$90.00; #273-$75.00; #274-$75.00.
282 R4 #5045-$165.00; #5207-$155.00.
282 R5 #53-$155.00; #1270-$155.00; #5215-$155.00.
283 R1 #86-$450.00; #84-$450.00.
283 R2 #217-$500.00; #161-$500.00.
284 R1 #156-$425.00; #227-$525.00.
284 R2 #155-$425.00; #180-$525.00.
285 R1 #116-$400.00; #200-$475.00.
285 R2 #203-$300.00; #58-$310.00.
286 R1 #65-$400.00; #93-$450.00.
286 R2 #55-$350.00; #89-$360.00.
287 R1 #250-$350.00; #70-$320.00.
287 R2 New rod and fixture-$85.00.
288 R1 #124-$70.00; #123-$80.00.
288 R2 #148-$85.00; #'s 248 & 249-$200.00.
288 R3 #'s 240 & 241-$360.00.
289 R1 #1-$90.00; #3-$140.00.
289 R2 #39-$210.00; #13-$235.00.
289 R3 #247-$90.00; #160-$ 150.00.
290 R1 The White Mountain-$55.00.

Miscellaneous

291 R1 Danner's Folding Tables-$65.00.
293 R1 #350-$75.00.
293 R2 #188-$60.00; #361-$80.00; #17-$100.00; #261 -$70.00; #111-$65.00; #306-$65.00; #79-$40.00; #133-$40.00.
293 R3 #101-$70.00; #47-$80.00; #308-$90.00; #800-$90.00; #114-$70.00; #824-$60.00; #362-$65.00.
293 R4 #809-$60.00; #808-$60.00; #349-$60.00; #348-$65.00; #355-$80.00; #66-$30.00; #208-$35.00.
293 R5 #238-$35.00; #337-$60.00; #821-$60.00; #205-$20.00; below-$25.00; #268-$25.00.
294 R1 #28-$65.00; #817-$80.00; #332-$75.00; #814-$65.00; #'s 265 & 283-$70.00.
294 R2 #315-$35.00; #173-$35.00; #812-$45.00; #119-$55.00; #818-$75.00; #4-$65.00.
294 R3 #819-$80.00; #230-$75.00; #813-$60.00; #26-$80.00; #267-$50.00; #327-$50.00.

294 R4 #252-$70.00; #289-$70.00; #338-$70.00; #363-$35.00; #107-$35.00.
294 R5 #216-$75.00; #292-$85.00; #23-$90.00; #83-$65.00.
295 R1 #340-$95.00; #339-$90.00; #379-$40.00; #77-$35.00; #41-$35.00; #219-$50.00; #140-$25.00.
295 R2 #169-$60.00; #256-$60.00; #391-$50.00; #300-$40.00; #312-$65.00; #298-$80.00.
295 R3 #341-$80.00; #85-$60.00; #98-$40.00; #78-$25.00; #45-$45.00; #2-$60.00.
295 R4 #128-$70.00; #359-$80.00; #280-$95.00; #343-$65.00; #296-$95.00.
296 R1 #140-$20.00; #131-$40.00; #138-$20.00; #177-$40.00; #58-$50.00; #'s 156, 152, & 104-$25.00; #223-$55.00.
296 R2 #271-$25.00; #'s 151 & 103-$20.00; #314-$50.00; #84-$45.00; #317-$40.00; #221 -$55.00.
296 R3 #'s 129 & 98-$30.00; #'s 806 & 172-$70.00; #235-$190.00; #10-$80.00.
296 R4 #315-$40.00; #16-$55.00; #302-$40.00; #94-$60.00; Corner bracket-$35.00; #96-$100.00.
296 R5 #'s 192 & 290-$65.00; #'s 168 & 123-$50.00; table-$40.00.
297 R1 #216-$75.00.
297 R2 #294-$150.00; #304-$45.00; #324-$275.00; #325-$285.00.
297 R3 #263-$75.00; #311-$80.00; #'s 322, 323, & 313-$65.00.
297 R4 #234-$125.00; #'s 376 & 839-$50.00; #321-$70.00.
297 R5 #604-$60.00; #295-$75.00; #184-$50.00; #264-$75.00.
297 R6 #'s 55 & 272-$60.00; #141-$85.00; #278-$300.00.
298 R1 #275-$300.00; #220-$225.00; #170-$275.00; #333-$285.00; #266-$240.00.
298 R2 #277-$340.00; #171-$300.00; #276-$300.00; #265-$340.00; #266-$275.00.
298 R3 $175.00; #286-$150.00; #265-$200.00; #1-$70.00; #2-$95.00.
299 R1 #1-$130.00; #2-$150.00; #3-$170.00; #1-$60.00; #88-$60.00.
299 R2 #90-$65.00; #78-$70.00; #90-$60.00.

299 R3 #'s 22 & 1-$75.00; #'s 6 & 4-$70.00; #2-$50.00; #36-$80.00; #74-$70.00.
299 R4 Piano stool #16 and others-$65.00;$65.00; $45.00; $55.00; $60.00; $45.00; $40.00; $60.00; $60.00.
300 R1 #10-$20.00; #50-$30.00.
300 R2 #1-$60.00; #2-$60.00; #9-$30.00.
300 R3 #3-$60.00; #4-$60.00; #'s 13 & 11-$20.00.
301 R1 #14-$20.00; #12-$20.00; #15-$45.00.
301 R2 #5-$65.00; #6-$60.00; #38-$50.00.
301 R3 #7-$40.00; #8-$50.00; #36-$55.00.
302 R1 #3-$120.00; #0, No drawer-$100.00; #0, With drawer-$105.00; #1-$80.00.
302 R2 #4-$90.00; $80.00; $110.00; $100.00.
302 R3 #2-$105.00; $80.00; $80.00; $90.00.
303 R1 #1-$160.00; #2-$230.00; #3-$120.00; #4-$145.00.
303 R2 #'s 5, 6, & 7-$175.00; #9-$120.00.
303 R3 #1-$400.00; #2-$350.00.
304 R1 #1-$65.00; #3-$55.00; #5-$35.00; #7-$20.00.
304 R2 #'s 2 & 4-$30.00; #6-$30.00; #'s 8 & 9-$40.00.
304 R3 Side—#1-$55.00; Corner—#1-$45.00; $55.00; #2-$40.00; #1-$45.00.
304 R4 #31-$85.00; #32-$95.00; #29-$65.00; #28-$85.00.
305 R1 Refrigerators-$350.00-$500.00.
305 R2 #'s 4 & 3-$80.00; #3-$85.00.
306 R1 #'s 2 & 4-$275.00.
306 R2 #1-$250.00; #3-$200.00.
307 R1 #1-$80.00; #1 1/2-$90.00; #2-$100.00; #3-$100.00.
307 R2 #4-$60.00; $60.00; Chess table-$80.00; Blacking case-$45.00.
307 R3 #37-$70.00; #38-$80.00; #'s 15 & 17-$85.00.
307 R4 #83-$45.00; #'s 82 & 81-$50.00; #37-$55.00.
308 R1 Towel stands-$70.00; $60.00.
308 R2 #1 closed-$45.00; #1 open-$45.00; #5$20.00; #2-$10.00; #302-$20.00.
308 R3 Blacking case-$120.00; Water cooler-$110.00.

ISBN: 0-88740-695-5